D1271249

22763899

REVOLT AND PROTEST

For Rocky

REVOLT AND PROTEST
Student Politics and Activism in Sub-Saharan Africa

Leo Zeilig

Tauris Academic Studies
London • New York

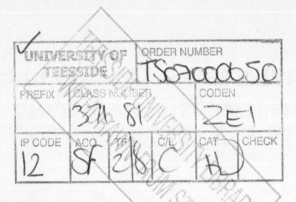
Published in 2007 by Tauris Academic Studies,
an imprint of I.B.Tauris & Co Ltd
6 Salem Road, London W2 4BU
175 Fifth Avenue, New York NY 10010
www.ibtauris.com

In the United States of America and Canada distributed by
Palgrave Macmillan a division of St Martin's Press
175 Fifth Avenue, New York NY 10010

International Library of African Studies 20

ISBN: 978 1 84511 476 3

A full CIP record for this book is available from the British Library
A full CIP record is available from the Library of Congress

Library of Congress catalog card: available

Printed and bound by Thomson Press India Limited
camera-ready copy edited and typeset by
Oxford Publishing Services, Oxford

CONTENTS

MAPS, FIGURES AND TABLES

ACRONYMS AND ABBREVIATIONS

Acronyms and abbreviations

AMEAN	Association Musulmane des Etudiants d'Afrique Noire
ANC	African National Congress
AOF	Afrique-Occidentale française
BAI	Book Aid International
BTTC	Belvedere Teachers' Training College
CAFA	Committee for Academic Freedom in Africa
CED	Coordination des Etudiants
CES	Coordination des Elèves du Sénégal
CFA	West African franc
CGC	Comité de Gestion de la Crise
CIP	Comité d'Initiative et de Pilotage
CIRMES	Collectif d'Initiative pour la Réorganization du Mouvement Etudiant Sénégalais
CJPO	Coordination des Jeunesses Politiques de l'Opposition
CNTS	Confederation Nationale des Travailleurs du Senegal
CODESRIA	Council for the Development of Social Science Research in Africa
COSATU	Congress of South African Trade Unions
COUD	Centre des Oeuvres Universitaires de Dakar
CPDM	Cameroon People's Democratic Movement
CPE	Contrat Première Embauche
CSTS	Coordination des Syndicats des Travailleurs du Supérieur
CUR	*collèges universitaires régionaux*
DRC	Democratic Republic of Congo
ECA	Economic Commission for Africa
EFI	Ecole de Formation des Instituteurs
ENS	Ecole Normale Supérieure
ESAP	economic structural adjustment programme
FASEC	Faculty of Economic Science
FEANF	Fédération des Etudiants d'Afrique Noire en France
FRTE	Front pour la Régularité des Elections

FSM	Free Speech Movement
GARMES	Groupe d'Action pour la Reconstruction du Mouvement Etudiant Sénégalais
GDP	gross domestic product
GMI	Groupement Mobile d'Intervention
HIT	Harare Institute of Technology
HIV	human immunodeficiency virus
ICU	Industrial and Commercial Workers Union
IFAN	Institut Fondamental d'Afrique Noire
IFE	Institut Français pour les Etrangers
IFIs	international financial institutions
IGAs	income generating activities
ILO	International Labour Office
IMF	International Monetary Fund
ISO	International Socialist Organization
IUIU	Islamic University in Uganda
LD	League Démocratique
LD/MPT	Ligue Démocratique–Mouvement pour le Parti du Travail
LONASE	Loterie Nationale Sénégalaise
LURD	Liberians United for Reconciliation and Democracy
MDC	Movement for Democratic Change
MEEJIR	Mouvement des Elèves et Etudiants de la Jamaatou Ibadou Rahmane
MEEL	Mouvement des Elèves et Etudiants Libéraux
MEES	Mouvement des Elèves et Etudiants Socialistes
MFDC	Mouvement des Forces Democratique de la Casamance
MJML	Mouvement des Jeunes Marxiste Léniniste
MMD	Movement for Multi-Party Democracy
NAB	Non-Academic Bachelor
NANS	National Association of Nigerian Students
NCA	National Constitutional Assembly
NDP	National Democratic Party

Acronyms and abbreviations

NEPAD	New Partnership for Africa's Development
NGO	non-governmental organization
NLC	National Liberation Council
NSS	national strategic studies
NUC	National Universities Commission
NURS	National Union of Rhodesian Students
NUST	National University of Science and Technology
NWPC	National Working People's Convention
NYS	National Youth Service
OPEC	Organization of the Petroleum Exporting Countries
PAES	Programme d'Amélioration de l'Enseignement Supérieur
PAI	Parti Africain de l'Indépendence
PCF	Parti Communiste Français
PDEF	Programme Décennal d'Education et de Formation
PDS	Parti Démocratique Sénégalais
PF	Patriotic Front
PIT	Parti de l'Indépendance et du Travail
POSA	Public Order and Security Act
PRA	Parti du Regroupment Africain
PRESBY	President Biya's Youth
PS	Parti Socialiste
SAES	Syndicat Autonome des Enseignants du Supérieur
SAIH	Norwegian Students' and Academics' International Assistance Fund
SANCO	South African National Civic Organization
SAP	Students Against Privatization
SAPES	Southern Africa Political Economy Series
SAPs	structural adjustment programmes
SDF	Social Democratic Front
SECC	Soweto Electricity Crisis Committee
SOAS	School of Oriental and African Studies

SPD	Social Democratic Party of Germany
SRB	strong rural background
SRC	Student Representative Council
SRTUC	Southern Rhodesia Trade Union Congress
SST	Student Solidarity Trust
UBA	University Bachelors Association
UCAD	Université Cheikh Anta Diop
UDED	Union Démocratique des Etudiants de Dakar
UDES	Union Démocratique des Etudiants Sénégalais
UDF	Union pour la Démocratie et le Fédéralisme
UDI	unilateral declaration of independence
UDPM	Union Démocratique du Peuple Malien
UED	Union des Etudiants de Dakar
UGB	Université Gaston Berger
UGEAO	Union Générale des Etudiants d'Afrique de l'Ouest
UGED	Union Générale des Etudiants de Dakar
UMU	Uganda Martyrs University
UNAPES	Union Nationale Patriotique des Etudiants Sénégalais
UNDES	Union Nationale Démocratique des Etudiants du Sénégal
UNDP	United Nations Development Programme
UNISA	University of South Africa
UNTS	Union Nationale des Travailleurs du Sénégal
UNZA	University of Zambia
UPA	Université Populaire Africaine
UPS	Union Progressiste Sénégalaise
URD	Union pour le Renouveau Démocratique
USA	University Spinsters' Association
USSR	Union of Soviet Socialist Republics
UNAPES	Union Nationale Patriotique des Étudiants du Sénégal
UVA	Université Virtuelle d'Afrique
UZ	University of Zimbabwe

Acronyms and abbreviations

WAC	Wade pour l'Alternance avec la Coalition 2000
WASU	West African Student Union
WPC	Working People's Convention
WSSD	World Summit on Sustainable Development
ZANLA	Zimbabwe African National Liberation Army
ZANU	Zimbabwe African National Union
ZANU–PF	Zimbabwe African National Union Patriotic Front
ZAPU	Zimbabwe African People's Union
ZBC	Zimbabwe Broadcasting Corporation
ZCTU	Zimbabwe Congress of Trade Unions
ZGWU	Zimbabwe Graphical Workers Union
ZICSU	Zimbabwe Congress of Student Unions
ZIMPREST	Zimbabwe Policy Reforms for Social and Economic Transformation
ZINASU	Zimbabwe National Students Union
ZIPA	Zimbabwe People's Army
ZIPRA	Zimbabwe People's Revolutionary Army
ZSF	Zimbabwe Social Forum
ZYDT	Zimbabwe Youth Democracy Trust

ACKNOWLEDGEMENTS

I owe a great deal of thanks, but first of all to the Department of Geography at Brunel University for funding most of this study. Their patience with my idiosyncrasies and curiosity with my work have made all that follows possible. My first, greatest debt in the department is to my supervisor Nicola Ansell. She was immensely helpful at every stage of the research pulling it apart, putting it back together, arguing over the themes and always urging me on. Secondly, I would like to thank Alan Patterson and Lorraine van Blerk, for their criticism and close reading of earlier drafts of the book.

I have benefited from other colleagues and friends. Sue Buckingham has always encouraged me. I do not know where I would be without her support. Other friends from the department include Genevieve Dewez, Anna Batchelor, John Baker, Pedro Costa, Paul Szadorski and Phil Teasdale. It is still incomprehensible to me that the university in its deep stupidity has decided to close such an extraordinary department, which combined intellectual rigour with a complete commitment to its students and staff.

Outside university and among my comrades and friends I am fortunate as well. David Renton, for getting me to write in the first place years ago, and telling me to do a Ph.D. and giving me the confidence that I could finish it. Peter Dwyer is another friend whose long emails, telephone calls and wisdom have helped propel me along.

Acknowledgements

Other comrades and friends deserve my thanks. Gavin Capps, Raj Patel, John Lea, Caroline O'Reilly and Lawrence Black have all offered me immensely useful comments at different stages of this study. Hannah Zeilig and Matt Reid have helped me in various ways; the most important has been their patience in putting up with my itinerant lifestyle and flying visits. Pascal Bianchini's friendship has been invaluable. He opened his impressive personal archive on the student movement in Senegal to me. Peter Alexander has always supported me, most recently in ensuring my continued employment in Johannesburg. But most thanks go to Rachel Cohen, who has been my most loyal and loving friend over the last ten years.

I owe my mother a lot. She has been insanely generous, with the house that I sometimes squat in and her love, that I have never doubted. Her own politics – a mixture of anarchism and Leon Rosselson – have helped to shape my own. I am indebted to my stepfather Maurice who manages to be patient, kind and loving despite my extraordinary liberties. My extended life as a student – like the eternal (and faintly despised) student in *The Cherry Orchard* – has lasted now for an eternity and has turned me into the difficult adolescent that I never really was.

My father, Ken, who died in 1990, is probably for better or worse the abiding influence on my life. Ken was a freelance broadcaster and made his precarious way in the world by interviewing people. His constant fascination with other people's lives has infected my sister and me. I was eight years old when I was taken to my first interview with the British stunt man Eddie the Kid (who Ken interviewed on the back of Eddie's motorcycle).

The last two years have been particularly difficult for all the reasons that should have made them joyous. Nadine suffered most from my meltdown. I have seen so much of my angry father in me that I started to despair at my ability to change (a despair I never feel for political change). For what it is worth this book is for her.

Still there is an element of the research that haunts me; that I was essentially parasitical on the hardship, pain and experiences of my interviewees. My sole objective, after all, was to unearth the experiences and history of the student movement, in doing this I would often tread clumsily on the lives of those I met and interviewed. The circumstances I found myself in and the intimacy of the interviews frequently left me feeling exhausted and useless. I could not be a friend to those interviewed, and yet I found the objectivity of the research sometimes impossible to sustain. I was constantly 'running off', stepping in and out of people's lives without always realizing the consequences of doing this. Terkel has written beautifully about this dilemma (and pain) during interviews conducted for his famous collection *Working*:

> It was a Brooklyn fireman who astonished me to shame. After what I had felt was an overwhelming experience – meeting him – he invited me to stay 'for supper. We'll pick something up at the Italian joint on the corner'. I had unplugged my tape recorder ... 'Oh Jesus' I remember the manner in which I mumbled. 'I am supposed to see this hotel clerk on the other side of town.' He said, 'You runnin' off like that? Here we been talkin' all afternoon. It won't sound nice. This guy, Studs, comes to me house, gets my life on tape, and says, 'I gotta go'.' ... Not that it was a revelatory experience for me. Though I had up to that moment succeeded in burying it, this thief-in-the-night feeling, I knew it was there. The fireman stunned me into facing up to it.
>
> (Terkel, *Working*, 1975, pp. xxii-xxiii)

But at least I also benefited from the close friendship of many people in Zimbabwe and Senegal. Hamidou Ba and Jean-Claude Kongo helped immeasurably during my fieldwork in Senegal. In Zimbabwe I benefited from Benson Mutape's intimate knowledge of the University of Zimbabwe, as well as his impressive work on the institution. Most of all the International

Acknowledgements

Socialist Organization in Zimbabwe, which has taught me – among many other things – the one thing I believe absolutely (my immutable law): Struggle makes history and struggle makes us. For this I thank my friends Tafadzwa Choto, John 'Briggs' Bomba, Munyaradzi Gwisai and Ashley Fataar.

Lastly, I owe thanks to Paul Benson and Pete Berman who shamelessly recruited me to the Socialist Workers Party when I was 17 and inspired me with their sociology classes at school (which were little more than excuses to teach us Marxism). The study is also in part dedicated to the memory of Cheikh Tidiane Fall, a 32 year old student at Université Cheikh Anta Diop in Dakar who committed suicide in April 2001. I never knew him but his despair at not being able to find work or see a real alternative in Abdoulaye Wade's *changement politique*, must harden our efforts to build another world that is not dominated by neo-liberalism, austerity and under-development.

FOREWORD
By David Seddon

In 1967–68, I was 25 years old and a graduate student in the anthropology department at the London School of Economics. It was an exciting period, with student leaders like David Adelstein[1] and Daniel Cohn-Bendit[2] haranguing large crowds from the steps at the main entrance of the LSE and calling on them to fulfil their historic destiny, and various forms of 'collective action' – the invasions of the staff common room and restaurant stand out in my memory. But, having recently returned from South Africa, where my arrival in late 1964 had coincided with massive demonstrations in response to the introduction of the 90-day detention laws and my departure in 1967 had followed the shooting of President Vervoerd, I did not find the student protests at the LSE as 'radical', nor the regimes against which they struggled as oppressive, as did many who took part and commented on them at the time.[3]

Nor did the economic and political situation in Britain, or even in France, where the revolts and demonstrations were on a much larger scale, and were more closely linked with workers' strikes and other forms of industrial and street action, seem to me to be ripe for revolution. Even in the USA, where the student movement was both active and widespread, where in California, Herbert Marcuse was lauding the students as an important element of the revolutionary forces,[4] and where, memorably, state troopers fired live rounds killing protestors at Duke

University, the state did not appear ready to be overthrown. Many have written in retrospect of 'May 1968', some with nostalgia, some with bitterness, and some with an acute critical sensibility of the limitations of the student movement. Few have set the student protests in the West in a wider global context – although Fred Halliday tried at the time to look more widely than most.[5]

There is no doubt, however, that these protests and other aspects of social unrest in the late 1960s were linked to a deep political–economic malaise, affecting not only the advanced capitalist countries of 'the West', but also many other parts of the post-colonial world – for a time (*c.*1955–75) identified as a 'Third World' but subsequently more evidently and more deeply integrated into the Western-dominated global capitalist system.[6] Numerous commentators have analysed – from different economic, political and cultural/ideological perspectives – the deepening world crisis (and the crisis of the Third World) of the late 1960s and the even more turbulent decade that followed[7] and saw the beginnings of the painful global restructuring required to restore the dynamics of profitable capital accumulation and the waves of popular protest that accompanied that process.[8]

If student protest was a part of the wider political ferment of the late 1960s and early 1970s in the West, the same could be said of Africa (and elsewhere in what was still referred to then as the 'Third World'). But whereas 1968 was, in retrospect, a 'high-point' of student collective involvement in politics in the West, students have continued to play a significant, if not sometimes crucial, role in the political life of the 50 or so independent states of sub-Saharan Africa. Their role has, however, been ambivalent. Many newly independent states in Africa and Asia inherited from the colonial period a distinctively elitist approach to education – indeed many of those who became the new political elite were themselves university graduates, often having received their further education in France or England, and had a special place in their hearts for the universities and for academia. The new post-colonial regimes were initially committed to maintaining the highest standards in the universities that had already been established during the colonial period and to creating new centres of excellence, to demonstrate their bona fides with respect to investment in human resources for the future.

They were less pleased, however, with the fact that, often, it was from the universities (from both faculty and students) that political opposition was fiercest. Students have always played an ambiguous role in class terms, usually coming from the more privileged sections of society and expecting to take their place among the commercial and social elites, if not among the political elite itself, and yet rebelling against authority and orthodoxy and sometimes setting themselves not only against the government or regime of the day but against the state itself and expressing radical if not revolutionary ideas about the need for social and economic change.

In countries where access to education is more difficult and where, generally school-going starts at a later age, those at school and in colleges of further education should also be regarded as part of this student body. This has contributed to the wider role of students in Africa and Asia than in the West – they have tended to be a larger and more diverse body than simply the university elites. In the West it is relatively rare to find recent examples of collective action by school pupils in furtherance of wider social and political objectives – although their involvement in protests against US and British intervention in Iraq in 2003 might be considered one such example. In Africa it is more common – in South Africa, in particular, action taken by school 'children' has often been more significant than action by university students.

The decades from the 1970s onwards have seen an increasing tendency among university students in the West to political 'moderation' and even quietism, paralleling the similar decline in worker activism, particularly from the early 1980s onwards, as the state and its various branches (including the educational structures) exercised a combination of authoritarianism and repression with an emphasis on individual enterprise and competition. This was associated with reductions in funding for universities and a greater reliance on securing funding from non-state ('public') sources. It meant for students less public funding and fewer scholarships, more investment of private (parents or own) funds and a greater concern with the university as a means to an end – successful (lucrative) employment – than as an end in itself – a place of learning and education and an opportunity to think critically and act in support of critical and rebellious ideas. These were the years of Thatcherism and Reaganomics, with their wider influence across the world, when 'economic reform and liberalization' were the order of the day and when neo-classical economics became the orthodoxy, even for non-economists and particularly for university managers.

If many in Britain look back on the 1960s and early 1970s as the highpoint for universities and on the 1980s and 1990s as 'hard times', the same is also the case for African universities for related reasons. Structural adjustment meant austerity, for public sector institutions, including universities, and for students it also meant that employment in the state sector, the expectation of many students, was less readily available. Universities were hard hit; so were students. But, unlike in the West, students continued to be politically active, providing some of the most principled and radical opposition to regimes increasingly losing their principles and their ideologies in the face of the economic and political pressures of the day.

When a new wave of political protest, responding to the fundamentally undemocratic nature of so many regimes as well as to their economic and social policies – which were generally a continuation of those of the 1980s – broke across Africa and Asia in the 1990s, students were to the forefront. There is a need to understand the nature of student involvement in national politics during this period better than we do. This book is about student politics in Senegal and Zimbabwe in their historical context. It attempts to go beyond providing a detailed account of the evolving role of students in national politics in the two countries and seeks to explain what happened and why. Simplistic notions of cause and effect are avoided in favour of a more nuanced analysis, setting students as a social category and student politics as a distinctive form of political action in its broader social, economic and political context. The students are seen as actors and agents in the making of their own and their country's history, but always within the constraints of existing structures.

Leo Zeilig is very familiar with the empirical contexts of Senegal and Zimbabwe, with student activism and the prevailing social structures there, having worked and studied in both countries. He is also familiar with the different ideological and theoretical approaches to student politics in Africa. His study is based on a mode of analysis that derives from Marxist political economy but is far more aware than most writing in that tradition of the social, cultural and ideological dimensions of politics; the influence of the English historian E. P. Thompson is clearly visible, and indeed explicit.[9] He is concerned primarily to 'rescue' students as social and political activists from relative oblivion, but in so doing also provides a counter to two dominant (and related) 'external' generalizations – an African history of marginalization, failed development, dysfunctional 'patrimonial' states, kleptocratic regimes and underdeveloped social formations and a utopian African future of development through globalization and 'modernization', economic liberalization, social transformation, democracy and 'good governance'. He also, implicitly, provides a critique of the dominant 'indigenous' version of African under-development as a result of simple unalloyed imperialism and neo-imperialism, so often echoed by African intellectuals and politicians as an excuse for 'the African trajectory'.

The struggles of student activists are, for Zeilig, struggles within rapidly changing African social formations, both reflecting and affecting those changes; they are an integral part of the very dynamic of African development – social, economic and political – effectively contributing to the making of African contemporary history. They are also part of the wider movement of popular protest that shook the sub-continent during the 1970s and 1980s, and then again, with greater political force, in the 1990s.[10]

Zeilig's strength is his commitment to investigative research in which the subjects are allowed to speak for themselves and in which crude generalizations are avoided in favour of nuanced analysis. The interplay between the experiences in the two countries concerned, Senegal and Zimbabwe, also allows for revealing comparisons.

The research in Senegal on which this book is based was conducted amongst students at Cheikh Anta Diop Université in Dakar on two main occasions, the first in 2000–1 during 'the transition' and the second in the first half of 2004. Extensive semi-structured interviews with student activists were carried out at the university, and during the student strike in 2001 a prolonged period of participant observation was employed over the duration of the dispute. Similarly, in Zimbabwe there were two research periods: the first during the presidential election in March 2002 and the second between May and September 2003. Again interviews with student activists across the political movement were combined with in-depth research amongst members of the International Socialist Organization (ISO), a radical anti-privatization group at the centre of the protest movement from the mid-1990s that emerged from campus politics at the University of Zimbabwe (UZ) in the early 1990s.

On the basis of these studies, the book explores the dynamics of student activism in Senegal and Zimbabwe in two markedly different and rapidly changing political–economic and ideological contexts and in the light of the available literature on student protest and African politics in particular. The study concludes with a consideration of the two experiences of Senegal and Zimbabwe together. The synthesis of both movements, in Zeilig's own words, 'demonstrates vital differences and similarities in the experience in both countries, and in the evolution of student activism in conditions of increasing poverty and underdevelopment'. It is argued that students (and indeed the intelligentsia more widely) continue to play a privileged political role on the continent, but in very different ways in very different contexts. The conclusions are intentionally preliminary and, as a consequence, demand further careful research. Let us hope that others will take up that challenge and that Zeilig himself will continue to build on this significant contribution to African studies.

David Seddon
Universities of East Anglia and of Bradford

INTRODUCTION

Insurgent architects

The year 1968 was the high point of student unrest and politics for more that one continent. In Paris it was the protests of university students outside Paris, in Nanterre, that sparked a prolonged period of political turmoil. In the United States students at Columbia University in New York launched a wave of student unrest that incorporated public and private universities across the country.[1] The year 1968 became quite widely known as the year of the student. The decade had seen unprecedented numbers of student revolts. In America it was black students in southern universities that inspired the protests in northern universities and the civil rights movement.[2] Book after book during the period described student power, and saw in the campus rebellions across Europe and America the 'arrival of a new social force'.[3] Students were now frequently seen as the sole revolutionary class in society, with the analysis and organizations to break the chains of an affluent society. The revolutionary student movement we were told signalled the rise of a new proletariat,[4] as the old one had been hopelessly co-opted by the 'totalitarian tendencies of the one-dimensional society' that had rendered traditional (namely working class) forms of protest ineffective.[5]

Despite a few honourable exceptions,[6] one of the problems with the huge amount of literature that poured out of the social movements in the late 1960s and 1970s was its extraordinary Eurocentrism. The decade was also, in many ways, as important for student activists in Africa as it was in Europe and North America. Similarly, 1968 was a crucial year for student revolutionaries on the continent. In Senegal, in events that some have claimed predated the upheavals in France, students were central to the worst political crisis the president, Léopold Senghor, had faced since independence eight years previously, forcing him to flee the capital and call in the French army to restore order after only eight years of independence.[7]

Students in sub-Saharan Africa had been involved in a rapid political evolution, from being a pampered elite supporting the state's attempts to develop society they became the first group to criticize the frequent corruption (and disappointment) in post-independent Africa. They were also increasingly among the first victims. The massacres of student demonstrators – and later the execution of student leaders – in 1969 in Zaire represented both the power of student protest on the continent and the enormous risks activists would take.[8] The era of cooperation with the state was over. The significance of these events for the continent and in understanding student activism generally is usually ignored or written out of most accounts of the period.[9]

Students on the continent, hastened by the erosion of promises of graduate employment in the 1970s, quickly evolved into hardened opponents of the independence settlement. By the 1980s, under the impact of both international recession and structural adjustment, the previously privileged conditions of students had been largely reversed. While the picture of the African university today varies across the continent, on the whole there is no doubting the severity of the situation for students. Students face an astonishingly bleak set of circumstances linked to the collapse of jobs traditionally regarded as 'graduate work' as employment in the formal sectors has almost completely fallen away.

Today's students face massively overcrowded classes, in underfunded facilities. The resulting environment can make learning a fairly impossible process. As one Nigerian lecturer observed:

> Physical clashes occasionally occur between students in different classes as lecture timetables are often not

Map 1: Locations of Senegal and Zimbabwe

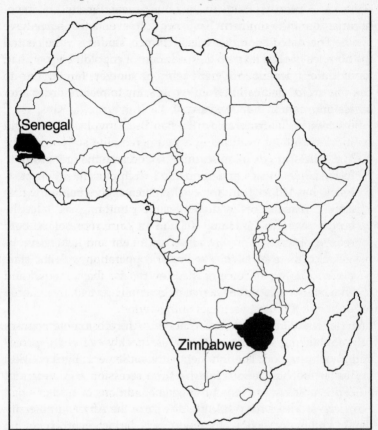

observed – students scramble to outpace their colleagues, in being the first to occupy classrooms in the desperate desire to take some hours of lectures before the examination period. The frustrations encourage some students to stay away from classes, thus leaving room for engagement in anti-social behaviour such as cultism.[10]

Compounding these frustrations are additional problems. Libraries, the symbols of a period of early and hopeful investment, are crumbling; they either lack any books whatsoever or use an old and worn stock that has not been replaced since the 1970s. As a direct consequence of budget cuts, many university libraries on the continent have no access to new journals or books. The Association of African Universities (AAU) has noted the absence of core textbooks, academic journals and basic texts; in addition almost 90 per cent of universities have no computerized databases from which students and staff can access information.[11] In the case of the Université de Kinshasa,[12] toilets have been turned into offices:

> The toilets in corridors leading to auditoriums are trans-formed into offices and rented. ... Such closing down of toilets has led to pollution of the green spaces behind the FASEC [Faculty of Economic Science] building, as it has been converted into Home 40 [student jargon for a place to relieve oneself]. ... [M]aintenance workers ... have assigned themselves to new posts ... [making] students or other visitors pay for access to the toilets. Thus, students who cannot afford the fee make do with Home 40.

The university in many parts of modern Africa is a contemporary ruin, tantalizing students with the old promise of development and transformation. Though their activism still animates political protest it too has been recast by the narrowing parameters of austerity, poverty and structural adjustment.[13]

African students have suffered the same poverty and austerity that has hit every section of society. Some writers even argue that they come from increasingly working-class or rural households, and have been in this respect proletarianized.[14] They are often forced to repeat the same year many times – *cartouchard* in Senegal[15] – a penalty that most students accept as inevitable. The dream of personal advancement for a social group long regarded as in transition – described as a transitory group in some of the literature[16] – to a higher status is a distant prospect for most students. The student in sub-Saharan Africa is today frequently locked into a student life characterized by poverty, failure and unemployment. A bitter caricature of the eternal (and ridiculed) student, Pyotr Sergeyevitch Trofimov, in Chekhov's play *The Cherry Orchard*.[17] Students are forced to commute from extended family members, or if they are fortunate enough to live in university accommodation they must share small rooms with four or five other students.[18]

From the late 1970s, however, the continent was punctuated by protest, politics and resistance, from which the transitions examined in this book, would eventually emerge. It was during these years that state-led policies of development unravelled under the combined pressure of international recession and what is today fashionably termed poor governance.[19] The effect of these dramatic changes was to bring about a period of global readjustment that in many parts of the African continent involved the implementation of World Bank and International Monetary Fund structural adjustment programmes (SAPs).[20] The austerity measures associated with these programmes had a dramatic effect on the continent (including a sustained attack on university education). Some writers have noted how these measures brought about a (first) wave of political protest.[21] Labelled bread riots, they brought together wide coalitions of mostly urban protestors.[22]

The second wave of protests was more explicitly political and organized than the first. Developing in the late 1980s this second wave of protests spread across many countries on the continent.[23] These movements were often organized by powerful opposition parties, or newly created coalitions. University students were vital elements of these movements (see Chapter 2), which were part of a wave of democratic and popular resistance, amounting to, in Celestin Monga's words, the 'collective insubordination' of Africa against structural adjustment and parasitic governments.[24] The movements for change in Senegal and Zimbabwe (both organized around the slogan 'change') were part of this wave of protest, and student activists among the most enthusiastic advocates for political transformation.

In Zimbabwe widespread opposition to the government first emerged at the University of Zimbabwe (UZ). A rising tide of political resistance and protests from 1996 culminated in the formation of the Movement for Democratic Change (MDC) in 1999. Afterwards there followed a period of intense crisis around parliamentary (2000) and presidential (2002) elections leading to the eventual frustration of the movement. The ability of the ruling ZANU regime to recover its momentum after 2000 led to a prolonged period of crisis and repression. Still the mass protests described by one activist as a sort of revolution saw the crucial combination of student unrest and widespread urban protests.[25]

In Senegal the pattern was similar, though ultimately more successful. Although protest punctuated the 1990s, it never reached the scale of the mass mobilizations in Zimbabwe. The Parti Démocratique Sénégalais (PDS), led by the charismatic Abdoulaye Wade, dominated the opposition. In the presidential elections in 2000 he managed to defeat the ruling Parti Socialiste (PS) that had governed since independence. The victory of the opposition coalition – *coalition alternance* – was completed in the legislative elections the following year, when the PS was reduced to a rump of ten seats in a parliament it had dominated for a generation. The role of students in registering the rural population to vote, in organizing caravans during the election campaign and galvanizing the country around the idea of *sopi* (change) was a vital element to the *changement politique* that swept Senegal.

In some ways, however, the experiences of Senegal and Zimbabwe were atypical. Both experienced the political wave of change later than the rest of the continent, after a period of consolidation for those earlier movements that had already undergone political change – most notably Zambia and the experience of the Movement for Multi-Party Democracy (MMD) that had come to power after democratic elections held in 1991. What were the experiences of these movements once they turned from opposition groups into ruling parties? How did the student activists in them respond to these changes?

For many years before the political transitions in Senegal and Zimbabwe students had been important elements in the struggles for democratic change. The processes involved in their activity, in the evolution of their activism and in their contribution to recent democratic transitions is the subject of this study. I examine the experience of both countries, through the period of protest and mobilization. There are several central questions for the study. How have students as a social group been transformed since independence? What role have they played in the waves of political unrest and protest since the 1980s and specifically in the political transitions in the 1990s? How can student activism in sub-Saharan Africa be understood today, and to what extent are students politically privileged actors who are able to exercise political agency? These questions will be examined in a range of contexts that have emerged from the two case studies: their ability to engage other groups in society, the level of participation in student politics, the manipulation of student politics by external forces and the presence of an independent ideology in the student movement.

Three important works have emerged in recent years that directly impinge on the study. First, a collection of essays and studies by Alidou, Caffentzis and Federici[26] that acknowledges African universities and student activism as crucial arenas in the struggles for democratization and political change. Second, Mark Edelman Boren's popular history of student resistance,[27] is important for another reason, it provides a vital general sketch of the history of student activism. The last is CODESRIA's superb two-volume study of practically every aspect of the African university, edited by Paul Tiyambe Zeleza and Adebyo Olukoshi. All three studies have, of course, followed a developed discipline that has seen a body of research on both student resistance and the predicament in Africa universities. They, however, form a vital and important contemporary commentary on the role of students and the university and the peculiarities (and similarities) of student activism in Africa.

But there are serious weaknesses in the research on students. Although university student activism has in recent years been the subject of important research,[28] most of the studies have been descriptive rather than seriously analytical. While they give very good accounts of the role of student action across many sub-Saharan African universities, none provides a satisfactory explanation of the reasons for the peculiarly prominent role students continue to play in national politics, preferring to explain the micro processes of student organization or to see students simply as manipulated by cynical politicians and fighting each other on an ethnic basis.[29] Mills is right to lament the lack of serious research into the recent phases of student activism: 'Given the key role student politics has played in the post-colonial history of the African state, one would like to know more about this new phase of student activism.'[30] Olukoshi and Zeleza also note the absence of research on student activism on the continent: 'African students and staff have a long history of activism, yet the subject has not attracted as much research attention in its own right as it surely deserves.'[31] Some suggest[32] that with the privatization of higher education students have ceased to play their historic role and have become, instead, paralysed by the neo-liberal crisis and motivated only by a desire to 'secure a place in a fragile post-university job market'.[33] The study directly engages with this work and extends and contests some of the conclusions reached in the recent literature.

The book makes a number of important contributions. First, the research brings together the work on student activism and the experience commonly (and controversially) described today as democratization. In addition, it penetrates the dynamics of student protests in two important case studies, and through the words of student activists themselves. The voices of activists are frequently drowned in the literature. Here, however, the democratic struggles in both countries are told not 'through the carefully modulated words of politicians and intellectuals, but in the often rough, earnest cadences' of student activists.[34] And, finally, the study makes an original comparison between seemingly disparate experiences in Senegal and Zimbabwe, helping to reveal the meaning of student action across contemporary sub-Saharan Africa.

The study was conducted among students at Université Cheikh Anta Diop (UCAD) in Dakar on two separate occasions, the first in 2000–1 during the transition and the second in the first half of 2004. Extensive semi-structured interviews with student activists were carried out at the university, and during the student strike in 2001 a prolonged period of participant observation was employed over the duration of the dispute. Similarly, in Zimbabwe there were two extended research periods: the first was during the presidential election in March 2002 and the second was between May and September 2003. In addition, a short trip was made to secure a number of extra interviews in August 2006. Again interviews with student activists across the political movement were combined with in-depth research among members of the International Socialist Organization (ISO), a radical anti-privatization group at the centre of the protest movement from the mid-1990s that emerged from campus politics at UZ in the early 1990s.

Certain ideas in the book, and in this introduction, have been developed in other places. I edited a collection of essays on protest and resistance in Africa[35] and, although they are not directly linked to the phenomenon of student action, they deal with a political and economic context that has informed much of this study. I have described the student strike in Senegal in 2001, a key moment in the evolution of activism after the election of Abdoulaye Wade,[36] and this description is elaborated further in Chapter 5. Similarly, the historical background to Zimbabwe's crisis has already appeared,[37] and has helped in the development of the first part of Chapter 4. Three further journal articles have directly drawn on ideas from this research. The first is an article on the Senegalese student movement since *alternance* (the political transfer of power in 2000) in the French journal of African studies, *Politique Africaine*.[38] The second article was in the *Journal of Asian and African Studies* and explored the evolution of student activism in Zimbabwe during the 'frustrated transition'.[39] The third article, in the *Review of African Political Economy* and co-written with David Seddon, deals more directly with some of the historical issues associated with the use of a Marxist epistemology in understanding protest in Africa.[40]

Approaching students

Although the research recognizes the dangers in making general statements about sub-Saharan Africa, the study argues for a broad – and indeed global – conception of political and economic change. Williams argues that there is a requirement for detailed and inter-disciplinary research in the study of African realities and that researchers must be aware of the danger of dissolving 'regional specificities into comparative propositions' that gather up disparate phenomena into a 'generalizing basket'.[41] Africa is a complex continent, divided by distinct political and economic histories. For example, South Africa is in some respects an exception to many of the political and economic changes discussed in the book. One can anticipate that a study of students in South Africa, in particular, would add a new layer of complexity to the research on sub-Saharan student activism.[42]

The agents of social change considered in this study are university students. But even the term student demands explanation. In this study I discuss the activism of university (and, in the case of Zimbabwe, also polytechnic) students and the literature that has attempted to understand them. This is not an accidental choice. The activism and organization of university students in sub-Saharan Africa is distinct in academic literature[43] and in its political and social significance[44] from that of other students.[45]

Although the study emphasizes the activism of students who participated in the two moments of democratic struggle and change in sub-Saharan Africa, it regards these individual militants and their activism as embedded in a political, economic and social world. This creates a dynamic tension between the inherited structures constantly constraining (and offering opportunities to) collective actors seeking to effect social change.[46] The research makes an explicit appeal to the *subjectivities of resistance* but only in the context of a specific and pre-existing historical and political reality.[47] As a result, the study can be seen as an historical and political consideration of how students bring about social and political change, in 'circumstances directly encountered'.[48] The lives of the students are not considered in isolation, but in the vital social and political context they encountered and sought to change.[49] This vital context has long preoccupied academics who have sought to ground social change in specific historical and political circumstances.[50] Resistance can emerge in certain counter-hegemonic spaces 'which allow challenges to the dominant order'.[51]

Therefore, the concerns of the research are both macro and micro – the motivation of individual activists involved in the democratic transitions, and the broader political and economic worlds they were forced to negotiate. The methods used to uncover these experiences, and to explore this micro world, are various. Extensive use of oral testimony (principally interviews and life histories) was combined in the study with an attention to the historical and political macro world. The study is a fusion of personal experiences of the struggles that gripped Zimbabwe and Senegal and broad political and economic structures.

Social change, then, is at least partly made by students and the popular resistance of which they were increasingly an important element. To some, these may seem obvious observations; however, frequently 'only political, constitutional and administrative history is real history'.[52] Thompson, in his famous study *The making of the English working class*, wrote that he was consciously 'writing against the weight of prevailing orthodoxies'.[53] These orthodoxies derived from various sources, one was the work of 'the empirical economic historians in which working people are seen as a labour force, as migrants, or as the data for statistical series.' Thompson's quarrel with these histories is an important signpost for this research: 'They tend to obscure the agency of working people, the degree to which they contributed by conscious efforts, to the making of history. ... Only the successful ... are remembered. The blind alleys, the lost causes; and the losers themselves are forgotten.'[54]

The tendency to exclude the 'agency of working people' is not limited to the Western academy (or to pre-1960 historical writing). On the contrary, the literature on African student movements is replete with these orthodoxies,[55] where the crucial agents are missing from their own histories. Indignant readers find themselves yelling: 'Where is the protagonist? Where are the students?'[56]

In this book I consequently take Thompson's historical method as a marker: 'I am seeking to redeem the poor stockinger, the Luddite cropper, the "obsolete" hand-loom weaver, the "utopian" artisan … from the enormous condescension of posterity.'[57] The research is a sustained attempt not to forget the anti-privatization campaigns led by student activists in Zimbabwe and the euphoria of those who organized them, or the students who travelled day and night across Senegal before the final round of the presidential elections in 2000 to ensure that their villages and towns were mobilized to vote for the *changement politique*.[58] These are the histories told against a frequently hostile and seemingly unbending social world.

The student's determination to bend this world came from a refusal to believe in the inevitability (or impossibility) of their encountered circumstances, and this is one of the reasons why they were such an intransigent agent of social change in Zimbabwe and Senegal. The ideological tools (organizations, initiative and leadership) that students used in the transitions were one of the ways that their agency was exercised, and they are an important focus of the study. These students who are excluded by the orthodoxies Thompson detested were responsible for making, in part, the history in these case studies. In Hill's words, this is the 'realization that they may have played a greater part in determining the shape of the historical process whether for change or for continuity, than we have thought.'[59]

Researching students

I should admit to a certain opportunism, which I suspect informs all research. I was teaching in Senegal at UCAD during the historic elections in 2000, and witnessed the involvement of students (many of them I taught) first hand. This period marked the start of my research. For entirely different reasons I was in Zimbabwe in 2002. I was there helping to coordinate the Independent Media Centre during the presidential elections. Most of my contacts at the time were students from the UZ in Harare and the National University of Science and Technology (NUST) in Bulawayo.

Social science research in Senegal is a relatively easy process.

There is a rich and developed tradition of research stretching back to independence, from Cheikh Anta Diop's pioneering work at the Institut Fondamental d'Afrique Noire (IFAN) at the University of Dakar in the 1960s and 1970s, to the establishment of the Council for the Development of Social Science Research in Africa (CODESRIA). Dakar now has numerous research institutes and centres. Most of the archival research was conducted at the school of journalism at the university's Centre d'Etudes des Sciences et Techniques de l'Information (CESTI). The library has a full newspaper archive. I conducted 30 interviews in 2001 with a combination of student activists – members of faculty *amicales* (departmental unions) – and ordinary students whose activity would increase and diminish with the pace of mobilization. Despite intense political competition, student activists frequently introduced me to their political foes. In the second period of research, in 2004, 28 further interviews were conducted. Although the interviews followed a semi-structured approach, their depth and length varied widely. The majority of the second set of interviews in 2004 were with leading current and ex-student activists, and these were frequently conducted in the evening and interrupted by prayers, or by *camarades* who would join the discussions, which often transformed them into group interviews (the fashionable focus group I suppose). Further interviews were much shorter and conducted using a notebook with students at both UCAD and at Université Gaston Berger (UGB) in Saint Louis. In contrast to Zimbabwe, the only questioning from the police or security services were enquiries about the nature of my research, which frequently prompted advice and opinions. The majority of interviews were conducted in French, although a number were carried out in English.

It was impossible for me to conduct certain interviews with members of the National Youth Service (NYS) in Chegutu. I was forced to use a research assistant and native Shona speaker, at the time a student journalist on the *Herald* newspaper, Tawanda Kanhema.

It was against a background of the politicization of race that the research was undertaken in Zimbabwe. In these conditions I

13

constructed a substantial façade, denying the real nature of the visit on both fieldtrips and a willingness to undertake considerable risks. There are perhaps two issues here that need to be enunciated more clearly. The first is obvious: I was white in a context in which race is politicized, so clearly no façade was possible here. The second was that my research itself was contentious: I was conducting research in the highly charged political environment of the university, and among a group of political actors who had been the most vociferous in their condemnation of the regime. I had also arrived during a period when the self-confidence of the opposition had been undermined by state violence and the internal decay of the opposition itself. Although the university campus afforded me a certain freedom, I was told repeatedly that students from the ruling party – Zimbabwe African National Union Patriotic Front (ZANU– PF) – who were paid by the state were aware of my presence at the university. What this meant was unclear, but I was advised to leave the campus for several days. I conducted interviews on a very haphazard basis, when student activists were able to find a space to see me. It was also imperative that the majority of interviews at UZ were conducted before the start of June. The date had been fixed for the final push, which involved mass mobilizations across the country, called and organized by the MDC. The potential for continuing the research beyond this date was uncertain. So the entire period of research was in one respect illegal, I was forced to enter the country on false pretences. I lied repeatedly to the authorities, neighbours and even friendly contacts about what I was doing in the country. This raises the question of the ethics of research that have been discussed in the context of global activism.[60]

I conducted 40 interviews in Zimbabwe with a range of activists and non-political students. Four key interviews were also undertaken in South Africa, with recent student leaders from Zimbabwe who were studying in exile in Johannesburg and Durban, and with the doyen of ex-student militants from the 1980s, then working as a banker in Johannesburg. The later part of the fieldwork involved extensive use of a newspaper archive, more or less hidden in the basement of the law library. This provided access to vital material that was difficult to access in the national archives without exposing myself to further questioning. For much of the historical background I made extensive use of the *Herald,* which was, until 1999, the only daily newspaper. The *Herald* has traditionally been the mouthpiece of the government and its validity as an historical source was approached critically throughout the study.

The most obvious point is that the research in Zimbabwe was not conducted in ideal circumstances. Indeed, it was punctuated by arrest, surveillance and the pressure of living in a country in the midst of an economic and political crisis. Access to a number of people was impossible and certain national archives were unreachable: undoubtedly, the research would have benefited from being able to draw on these sources. However, in a certain respects, examining the activism of students in conditions that they have had to confront in the country's polytechnics and universities gave me a rare insight into the nature of their political action.

As the research was informed by Thompson's commitment to rescue those agents of historical change forgotten by the 'enormous condescension of posterity', it was important that those recorded are not just the successful (those remembered in the historical accounts) but also those voices rarely heard, much less remembered. I could have dwelt on the great successes of the student movement; those who had reached the heights of political office from the lowly ranks of student unionism. There were many of these in both case studies. I needed their experiences as well (more on this below) but I made a conscious decision early on in the research to concentrate on grass-root activists, and other students, who fell in and out of activity.

This reasoning is tied directly to an attempt not to provide another vehicle for the 'modulated words of politicians and intellectuals',[61] but to include those who do not have their answers on stand-by or have not already constructed their narrative before you walk into the room. Terkel found himself removing many of those whom he had interviewed for his study, 'there are deliberate omissions ... doctors ... politicians, journalists and writers of any kind. ... I felt that their articulateness and expertise offered them other forums. ... I was interested in other countries not often heard from.'[62] These were problematic objectives among students, particularly those active politically. These activists were used to expressing themselves and reflecting on political choices, still they were not familiar with the probing of an interviewer and in general I did not feel that their answers were ready made.

The approach adopted could not exclude interviewing politicians who had been student activists. The elevation of a layer of student activists to national parliaments during the democratic transitions was a vital element in the recent history of the student movements in both countries. Still, their accounts could not be taken at face value; often I gleaned less from their modulated words than I did from activists who remained at the university. Some of these issues arose during an interview with an MP in Zimbabwe. Job Sakhala, still an MP for a poor township in Harare in 2006, is one of the most colourful ex-leaders of the student movement. After a titanic struggle to arrange an interview with him (which finally took place in his car, then in three Harare bars and finally at his constituency home), he used the opportunity to set the record straight, and gave me an incredibly detailed account of the student movement and the evolution of the opposition MDC that had, in his words, degenerated into a 'scramble and fight for economic riches'.[63] Inevitably he saw the interview as a way of responding to his critics in the party but also as an opportunity to record the extraordinary events in which he had been an actor.

In both countries there were two principal gatekeepers. In Zimbabwe one was an organization, the International Socialist Organization (ISO), with which I had worked in 2002 when I was helping to coordinate the Independent Media Centre. Many of its members were students; some of them had been key activists in the recent transitions. This was a unique opportunity to have access both to the historical actors, and those current ones who maintained a very keen sense of the background and evolution of the movement they now led. Arriving at interviews with ISO accreditation made me immediately credible. This was still the case with interviews conducted in 2006.

In Senegal it helped to have been a temporary lecturer at the Faculté des Lettres et Sciences Humaines before the main period of my fieldwork. My initial gatekeeper, a former student Jean-Claude Kongo, had played a small role in the events described in the book. He put me in touch with Hamidou Bâ, who was also interviewed for the role he had played in 2000. Hamidou became my chief informant and contact. In many ways he was typical of a generation of activists. He knew how to negotiate life at the university, but was less successful with his studies. He was never without accommodation on the university (a scarce resource), having well-established connections with the university administration, the Centre des Oeuvres Universitaires de Dakar (COUD). His activism gave him a formidable contact list, and for those he did not know he had the self-confidence to convince them that he did. Hamidou revealed as much about the student movement from his behaviour as he did through the contacts with whom he was so generous. My abiding memory is of him raging in the dinner hall at the quality of the food being served, hitting his fist against the table so that our trays jumped into the air, exclaiming: 'This food is not fit for intellectuals!' He was symbolic in many ways of the perpetual student of my study who is no longer in transition to a prefixed social world but paralysed within the university circuit. From Hamidou I was able to make contacts of my own, which eventually led me to UGB in Saint Louis.

I am acutely aware of the dangers in revealing the identities of student activists. These were questions that preoccupied me in both Senegal and Zimbabwe. In Senegal a layer of student activists has been co-opted into political parties or received bursaries for foreign studies and in a number of limited cases students have been elected to parliamentary office. In this environment accusation and counter accusation are hurled backwards and forwords by activists, making the interviews hazardous processes, and potentially dangerous for the interviewees. Students would use my research to implicate other activists in contentious events, and also, occasionally, to throw dirt at each other. This was graphically illustrated in the violent attack and hospitalization of Madiop Biteye (one of my inter-viewees) – the leading PDS student militant in Dakar – after a dispute among PDS partisans at the university in Dakar in 2005. The current violence of campus politics illustrates the disinte-gration of the student movement since the election of Wade in 2000.[64] In Zimbabwe the principal source of violence against activists has come from the state, and students have been regularly targeted, arrested and tortured. During both periods of fieldwork I asked interviewees if they agreed to have their identity revealed. In many cases students would pre-empt the question by raising it themselves, insisting that their accounts were recorded and voices heard. Female students in Zimbabwe were, however, far more hesitant and I was asked on a number of occasions to ensure their anonymity. This concern stems from the particular vulnerability of female students to violence, some of it sexual, by other students and the security forces. As a consequence the book is inconsistent in the use of the students' real names, and I have indicated where students have requested the use of a pseudonym.

Summary of chapters

In the first chapter I consider the development of student acti-vism as part of the pre-colonial intelligentsia in the years immediately before independence. I go on to examine how their role as privileged actors evolved in the first two decades of independence, and the general significance and meaning of student activism. I also consider questions of protest, politics and resistance in Africa from the 1970s. It was during these years that state-led policies of development unravelled under the combined pressure of international recession and what is today fashionably termed poor governance. From the late 1970s students were forced to negotiate a world radically different from the one that they had expected to inherit.

Chapter 2 comprises a survey of several bodies of literature that inform the research: one of the principal ones covers the role of students, the nature of their protest and their relationships with civil society in a wave of multi-party elections and democratic struggles in sub-Saharan Africa. Here I focus specifically on the literature that relates to student activism and protest, though it is acknowledged that their activism brings into play many other factors. The context in which students become political actors in contemporary Africa is tied to the transformation of higher education in sub-Saharan Africa, often under the auspices of IMF and World Bank led reform. I also explore the changing nature of higher education in the political economy of sub-Saharan Africa.

Chapter 3 is taken up with the processes of political change and student activism in Zimbabwe, and it forms the first full case study. It situates the rising tide of the student movement in two distinct spaces. The first was the contradictory experience after independence, which almost simultaneously saw both the massive expansion of higher education and at the same time a growing financial crisis that severely affected the new state from the late 1980s. Out of this contradiction emerged a vocal and militant opposition to the regime among student activists at UZ. The chapter is divided into three main parts. The first deals with the political and social history of Zimbabwe, focusing on the recent period of political resistance. The second looks at the evolution of student protest and activism through the 1970s and 1980s. The final part concentrates on the period of transition or the convergence of forces from 1995. In it I examine the dynamics of student action in the context of widening political unrest.

In Chapter 4 I follow a similar structure to examine the trajectory of political and social change in Senegal. In the first part of the chapter I give a brief description of political change since independence in 1960. In the second part I detail the emergence of the student movement and chart its development from a widely perceived heyday of political vanguardism in the 1960s and 1970s to the crisis in higher education since the 1980s. In the final part I cover the recent participation of students in the *changement politique* since 1998; then, focusing on the role of key student activists and groups, I chart the participation of students in Wade's *coalition alternance*. I describe how student activists in the years that followed were co-opted and corrupted by a regime they had laboured to elect.

In Chapter 5 I explain the meaning of student protest in the light of the research, bringing the comparison between Senegal and Zimbabwe together. I also summarize the principal conclusions reached by the study. In the Conclusion I bring the research back to the role of the student intelligentsia examined in the Chapter 1, arguing that they continue to play a privileged political role on the continent but in wildly divergent movements. The ideas in the Conclusion are intentionally preliminary and as a consequence call for further careful research.

Chapter 1

POLITICS, STUDENTS AND PROTEST: THE MAKING OF THE STUDENT INTELLIGENTSIA

In the first years of independence, university students could be characterized as a pampered section of society being educated to run the post-colonial state. But, within a very brief period, they became oppositional, regarded in the literature of the day as 'rival politicians rather than students'.[1] Student militants frequently fuelled the early protest movements that questioned the legitimacy of the new states. Many commentators regarded them as a democratic vanguard, powered by left-wing ideology. In later years the literature despaired at their activism, regarding students in Africa as non-ideological and fighting daily struggles for government handouts.[2]

Between independence in 1960 and the mid-1970s university students were part of a privileged transitory social group waiting to be allotted graduate employment in an expanding civil service and across the state sector. Some described them as members of Africa's intelligentsia or new petit bourgeoisie. The period corresponded to a brief moment of state-led development across much of the continent, with overwhelmingly well funded students living comfortably on government grants and scholarships. By the mid-1970s this picture was beginning to unravel. In tandem with the economic crisis that led to a collapse in the price of primary commodities in the 1970s, university provision began to decline.[3] Students saw the level of grants fall and their privileged conditions crumble. By the mid-1980s under the impact of SAPs, students had to a large extent been proletarianized and, according to some observers, they comprised part of the new popular classes that helped to empower many of the political protests (and democratic transitions) in the 1980s and 1990s.[4] Although this study focuses on the later period of their evolution, and particularly the convergence of forces in the 1990s, student activism is only understandable when viewed historically as a transition from an early post-independent elitism.

There are essentially two arguments at the centre of this chapter. The first is that students were a vital element in pre-independent nationalist struggle in sub-Saharan Africa. They belonged to the intelligentsia, which included university educated graduates, civil servants working for the colonial service and trade union bureaucrats.[5] They were able to play this role because of the relative organizational and political weaknesses of other social groups in society. They were also political modernizers who were going to bring development to the new states. Students were clearly politically privileged actors. They continued to play their privileged role after independence, through the early years of state-led development and, in an adjusted form, through the economic crisis in the 1970s. In the first section of this chapter I consider the development of student activism as part of the pre-colonial intelligentsia in the years preceding independence. I go on to examine how their privileged role evolved in the first two decades of independence and the general significance and meaning of student activism.

The second broad theme of the study centres on protest, politics and resistance in Africa from the 1970s. It was during these years that state-led development policies unravelled under the combined pressures of international recession and what is today termed poor governance.[6] The effect of these dramatic changes was to bring about a period of global readjustment, which in many parts of Africa involved implementing World Bank and International Monetary Fund SAPs. The austerity measures associated with these programmes had a dramatic effect on the continent (including a sustained attack on university education). Some writers have noted how these measures brought about waves of political protest.[7] Labelled bread riots, the action brought together wide coalitions of mostly urban protestors. In the final section of the chapter I look at these changes, at the effect of the economic crisis in Africa from the 1970s and at the corresponding increase in popular resistance. How these changes impacted on higher education and student activism is taken up in Chapter 2.

Class suicide and the intelligentsia

How far can students be considered part of an intelligentsia? On this question there is a tension in the literature, for intelligentsia and student are frequently used interchangeably. Even in Cliff's otherwise precise text[8] there is a confusion between the two terms; in fact, contemporary student activists in Senegal and Zimbabwe often employ the term intellectual to describe their social role. The conflation of terms continues in a recent study on the African intellectual[9] that addresses the historical role and future trajectory of intellectuals on the continent, but makes no serious conceptual distinction between the terms.[10]

There was a serious exploration of these questions during the student revolts in the 1960s. Flacks, for example, reflecting many of the contradictions in the literature and debates at the time, defines the intelligentsia as 'those engaged vocationally in the production, distribution, interpretation, criticism and inculcation of cultural values'.[11] This group has grown from 'small pockets of isolated, independent intellectuals' to become, in the course of several decades, a significant 'stratum of the population, including many in new white collar vocations'. Although Flacks argued that New Left students aspired to become members of the intelligentsia, he argued that the expansion of the intelligentsia has been largely due to the growth of university education, 'The newest and largest generation of this stratum was thronging the nation's [United States] colleges.'[12] The same debates took place among scholars in Africa. In a public debate on 'The role of the

African intellectual in the African revolution' in Uganda in 1969 with the head of the country's intelligence service, the scholar Ali Mazrui defined an intellectual as a 'person who has the capacity to be fascinated by ideas and has acquired the skill to handle many of them effectively'.[13]

It is argued that the main reason for the conflation of student and intelligentsia in much of the African literature is because students – particularly in the period immediately before and after independence – were engaged, as Flacks describes, 'in the production, distribution, interpretation, criticism and inculcation of cultural values'.[14] However, it is important to situate these arguments in the political changes that were taking place across much of sub-Saharan Africa.

There are three vital and related aspects to the immediate pre-independence period in much of Africa. First, contrary to many ideological and political beliefs at the time, it was not usually a working-class or trade-union leadership that led the struggles for independence. Although labour mobilizations after the war were often crucial sparks to nationalist movements, generally speaking another social group took up the leading positions in the movements that were to oust the colonial powers (see below). Second, the group that assumed responsibility for leading nationalist struggles was called the intelligentsia. It was made up largely of colonial staff, trade union bureaucrats, university students and graduates who had often been educated abroad on colonial scholarships and who had been immersed in a left-wing (frequently communist) milieu in American, British and French universities in the 1930s, 1940s and 1950s.[15] Third, this student intelligentsia was attracted to the Soviet model of development.[16] The Soviet Union was regarded as offering the intelligentsia of the Third World the option of raising their countries to a level of technological development equal to the advanced West. This was often seen in terms of a radical project of socialist transformation, where the levers of state control could be wielded in the interests of the newly independent nation.

Future leaders developed their politics in student groups.[17] Two organizations stand out: the West African Student Union

(WASU), formed in 1925 in London, was regarded as the 'training ground for Nigerian nationalists'.[18] WASU welcomed students from West Africa who found themselves in London, however briefly, often providing them with accommodation and support. However, WASU was not principally a welfare service but a political and campaigning union: it denounced colonial racism, forced labour, the expropriation of land and the unequal relationship linking the colonial metropoles with their African dependencies. Far from limiting its agenda to student issues, WASU sought to 'agitate for and emphasize the needs of the future "United West Africa"'.[19]

Similar, and similarly radical, political organizations of Francophone African students were active in Paris: the Association des Etudiants Sénégalais (AES) and the Fédération des Etudiants d'Afrique Noire en France (FEANF) were seen as crucial to the emergence of students as a distinct social group.[20] Marcel-Eloi Chambrier Rahandi, a former activist and leading member of FEANF, explained that the organization assured the political formation of a generation of soon to be African leaders, and crucially the union gave an ideological coherence to the disparate communities of African students studying in France.[21] As Chambrier Rahandi put it: 'one learnt to live, to think and to act together, FEANF was a school where we took our first political lessons. It was within FEANF that African students formed a concept of African nationalism. ... Through the practice and theory of the union they forged an idea of freedom.'[22]

The list of those transformed by the metropolitan university and by their *luttes syndicales* in these countries testifies to the importance of the student/intelligentsia: Amilcar Cabral in Portugal, Léopold Senghor in France and Kwame Nkrumah in the USA and Britain. These students were forced, partly, to study overseas for the simple reason that there were very few universities on the continent. The reluctance of the colonial powers to build universities came out of a fear of educating the 'native'. Olukoshi and Zeleza make clear the consequences of this fear, for 'it was this attitude that set the stage for the historic confrontation that was to fire the nationalist movement.'[23] Nobody ever underestimated the role students would play. Léopold Senghor, Senegal's first president, addressed students in 1956, 'you are the elite of the elite, the best elements of our people'[24] and it was generally believed that the next generation from the university would continue to play a leading role in post-colonial Africa.

Some of the more Eurocentric writers on student politics even suggest that the influence of Western education on a group of Africans instilled in them the desire for freedom, democracy and independence.[25] However, an unintended consequence of the experience was to expose students to radical left-wing ideas, a key factor being the intellectual hegemony of Marxism in left-wing politics in European universities in the 1930s and 1940s. Along with these influences was the role black Marxists played in political struggles in the USA and Europe.[26] It is clear that student militants and intellectuals achieved an intellectual and organizational hegemony that was unparalleled in colonial Africa.

It is vital not to underestimate the role played by trade unions in the struggles for independence in many countries. In both Zimbabwe and Senegal it was national strikes – on the railways in 1947/8 in Senegal and the general strike in Zimbabwe in 1948 – that were key to initiating the nationalist movements.[27] The 1945 general strike in Nigeria crippled the colonial machine for weeks leading to a period of labour nationalism in the late 1940s and early 1950s. In Northern Rhodesia the Zambian trade union's official nationalist leadership agreed to an uneasy alliance, with the trade unions refusing to be completely subsumed into the Northern Rhodesian Congress.[28] Several commentators have argued that, rather than the period signifying the weakness of the organized working class, it was rather the 'lack of a visionary and strategic labour leadership' of this class.[29]

Many argue that the lack of such leadership was largely due to Stalinism's domination of the labour movements.[30] Stalinist-influenced politics insisted on broad alliances with nationalist organizations as part of the two-stage process towards socialism. The first stage was to be the democratic revolution, which included winning independence, and only afterwards would there be a sustained struggle for socialism, once the foundations of a national capitalism had been established. Most communist and communist-inspired students, trade unionists and intellectuals from the Third World believed they must proceed first to national independence, in broad class coalitions.[31]

Many had expected the working class to lead the struggle for national liberation, an argument advanced most convincingly by Trotsky.[32] Trotsky's theory of permanent revolution was predicated on the argument that the national bourgeoisie – historically responsible for the transition to liberal democracy – was incapable of carrying out these tasks. It would be too terrified that social forces would be unleashed on the very things it wanted to promote – private property, free trade and wage labour. If it had been unable to transform Russia, what chance was there in a colonial world setting that systematically enfeebled the development of an indigenous bourgeoisie?[33] Often under the influence of Stalinist politics, a generation of Western Africanists spent an eternity searching (largely in vain) for the emergence of an African bourgeoisie.[34] Seddon makes the essential historical point: 'In most of Africa, the colonial state (serving the interests of metropolitan capital and, where settlers became more strongly rooted, of local settler capital) was at pains to inhibit the development of an indigenous African capitalist.'[35]

In marked contrast to the absence of a nascent African capitalist class, the colonial state had succeeded in creating a significant stratum of functionaries who controlled many levels. Civil servants, teachers, nurses and clerks comprised a class that Poulantzas called a new petty bourgeoisie.[36] The colonial powers wished to train and 'civilize' a class of functionaries imbued with the superiority of Western values.[37] In the period of decolonization this process was speeded up in the hope that a willing and obedient intelligentsia could be handed the reins of state power in a peaceful transition that would, largely speaking, leave the colonial structures of power intact.[38] This was an inherently ambiguous (let alone risky) exercise for the colonial state, for it was from among these groups – intended to control the colonial states – that young educated radicals began to emerge. Many who were sent abroad on foreign scholarships would encounter and begin to engage in left-wing politics.[39] As Seddon reminds us, it is important not to see the history of class struggle in Africa in terms of a 'narrow definition of the working class … [but rather we] must recognize the crucial (but often problematic) role played by the radical elements of the new petty bourgeoisie.'[40]

Evidence of this has recently emerged in documents the Public Record Office released in March 2003 describing the emergence of radical and communist ideas in 'negro organizations' during the Second World War. Although the files concentrate on the consequences for the West Indian colonies, they betray the paranoia of the British secret services at the growth of a black consciousness linked to an embryonic civil rights movement in the United States. The documents stress growing radicalization among groups of West African students studying in America. In a prolonged correspondence with the Colonial Office, staff at the British embassy in Washington reported with growing anxiety the activity of West African students studying in the United States. In 1944 they were particularly concerned about two Nigerians, Nwafor Orizu and Ozumba Mbadiwe, who were to go on to play a prominent role in the radical wing of Nigerian nationalism.[41] A Colonial Office letter on 3 January 1944 noted: 'We have had a certain amount of correspondence with various Departments over the unsatisfactory position that tends to develop in the cases of many West Africans who have gone to America as students.' Quoting another letter received the previous year on the alarming state of African students permitted to study in the United States:

> between 20 and 30 students from West African [*sic*] have been permitted to come to this country, supported by the promise of profoundly inadequate allowances from their relatives at home. A few are all right, quiet, industrious and serious; others are anything but. They get into debt; they flit from one soft-hearted university to the next, piling unfinished course upon unfinished course. Gradually they learn there is a market value attached to the pose of the

exploited victim of British imperialism; they write books and they address meetings and they get taken up and used by groups whose interest is not at all any improvement to African conditions.[42]

The letter continued to the effect that Orizu and Mbadiwe were clearly from the latter category of unsavoury characters who mixed with dangerous (presumably left-wing) elements. The conclusion was often that these problems could be solved from a financial angle by ensuring that West African students did not find themselves without resources and so resort to the 'temptation to play to the anti-British gallery.'[43]

Although the student intelligentsia played a leading role, it could not do so without the mobilization of the popular classes. The role of the intelligentsia was disproportionately visible as the leadership of nationalist movements, but mass mobilizations of other social groups frequently fuelled these movements. A general strike in Zimbabwe in 1948 brought the nationalist struggle to the fore, but Bulawayo shop owner Benjamin Burombo came to epitomize the strike's leadership.[44] In the early 1950s the founding father of Zimbabwean nationalism, Joshua Nkomo, one of the country's first black graduates, headed the trade union movement.[45]

The first generation of African leaders after independence were often serious scholars, although this was frequently exaggerated. The presidential intelligentsia crisscrossed the continent. Kenya's first head of state, Jomo Kenyatta, was the country's first black anthropologist.[46] Uganda's Milton Obote changed his name to the author of the epic English poem *Paradise Lost*. While Julius Nyerere in Tanzania is famous for his writings on African socialism, he is less well known for his Kiswahili translations of *Julius Caesar* and *The Merchant of Venice* for Oxford University Press. Although Mazrui exaggerates the influence of this presidential intelligentsia, these self-conscious intellectuals helped contribute to campuses that 'vibrated with debates about fundamental issues of the days ... and the role of intellectuals in what was widely designated as "the African revolution"'.[47]

In reality, independence settlements compelled the student intelligentsia (now transported to the presidency) that had led the anti-colonial struggles to consolidate control in the existing state machinery. Many saw their role as liberators, taking their 'backward' societies into the modern (frequently socialist) world.[48] For Nkrumah, Senghor and Nyerere (the leaders of Ghanaian, Senegalese and Tanzanian independence) socialism was embodied in the state and in the state they felt themselves 'above class antagonism generally'.[49] As antagonism had no place in their newly founded societies, a classless discourse became a necessity in state control. The state in newly independent Africa became the means of carrying out state-capitalist development.[50] So, in Ghana's case, once independence had been achieved, the movements that had been mobilized in the anti-colonial struggles (and these had been considerable) were abandoned.[51] This left the state as the only lever of power. After the first decade of independence (the 1960s), First argued that the process of decolonization had been a 'bargaining process with cooperative African elites. ... The former colonial government guarded its options and ... the careerist heirs to independence preoccupied themselves with an "Africanization" of the administration.'[52]

Tony Cliff offered perhaps the clearest analysis of the role of the intelligentsia in the independent settlement, linking his theory of the 'deflected permanent revolution' to Trotsky's earlier arguments. He maintained that the failure of the working class to lead the movements for national independence and democracy in the Third World, as postulated by Trotsky, was due to the relative inexperience of the working class (often but not always paralysed by the politics of Stalinized communist parties). The leadership of nationalist movements was frequently taken up by a student intelligentsia in a process of deflected permanent revolution. The lack of strategic organization among the working class was in contrast to the high level of political and organizational coherence among students and intellectuals.[53]

Although Cliff's argument must be seen as an elaboration (and clarification) of Trotsky's original theory, he also provided a very clear critique of the role of the intelligentsia in developing societies, 'as the leader and unifier of the nation, and above all as manipulator of the masses.'[54] The intelligentsia, he argued, always attempts to separate itself and rise above society. He describes the Russian populist movement in the nineteenth century as led by an intelligentsia that saw itself as the unique liberator of the peasantry. However, a later intelligentsia, identifying itself with the emergent trade union movement, was forced to be accountable to the collective voice and organizations of the movement. The tendency towards individualism and elitism, Cliff argued,[55] is connected to the political and social milieu of the intelligentsia. The political milieu of Russian populist intellectuals was 'less restrictive, hence they showed clearer and much more extreme tendencies towards elitism, arbitrariness, as towards vacillations and splits'. In the period of nationalist struggles the revolutionary intelligentsia was a far more cohesive factor. The intelligentsia as a non-specialized section of society 'is the obvious source of a "professional revolutionary elite"'. It is ideally placed to do this because its members are able to pose as the radical (and neutral) arbiters of the nation, against sectional interests, but there is a further aspect to their role. The intelligentsia is the section of society with the clearest concept of national culture and identity, 'the peasants and workers having neither the leisure nor education for it'.

It is therefore not simply their organizational coherence but their status and self-identity as a student intelligentsia, and partly a self-perception as politically privileged actors. This group saw itself as the liberators of Africa and as uniquely representing the emergent nation. As Cliff wrote, 'They are great believers in efficiency ... they hope for reform from above and would dearly love to hand the new world over to a grateful people, rather than see the liberating struggle of a self-conscious and freely associated people result in a new world themselves.'[56] This is linked intimately to a vital aspect of student activism that has been analysed by a number of writers.[57] The distance students had to travel from their countries – described in the literature as pilgrimages – to colonial schools and colleges in Africa and Europe divorced them from the concerns and realities

31

of colonial life; they became aware of the distance between their situation and the communities they had left, but crucially of the gap between the West and the national marginalization of their as yet unborn or new nations.[58] This geographical element of the student experience remains key to their contemporary self-identity, expressed in the spatial separation from their family homes and lives in the modern and rarified spaces of the university campus (see Chapter 2). What effect did this have on student activism? It meant that as well as being forged into a 'national-bureaucratic caste'[59] by departing colonial powers, students regarded themselves and their activism as crucial to the development and leadership of the independent state.

The inherent elitism of the student intelligentsia simultaneously generates a feeling of guilt and debt towards the masses, 'and at the same time a feeling of divorcement from, and superiority to them. The intelligentsia are [*sic*] anxious to belong without being assimilated, without ceasing to remain apart and above.' Cliff argues that the heightened, one could say, exaggerated power of the intelligentsia derived directly from the 'feebleness of other social classes, and their political nullity'.[60]

For this book Cliff's model serves as a powerful description of how change actually occurred, and the role of the student intelligentsia in it. Indeed, Cliff gives an immensely useful analysis of the nature of student elitism, particularly in the first decade and a half of independence. The more student movements were integrated into broader structures and accountable to wider social forces, the more the elitism of their activism waned (and often the extent of their role in societal change clarified). Equally, the more isolated their activism – an isolation in which students frequently exulted – the more elitist they became.[61]

As we have seen, students believed they embodied the aspirations of national liberation; they saw themselves as the liberators of the emergent African nation. Mamdani has taken up many of the processes Cliff described. Mamdani claims that this liberation was undertaken by the petit-bourgeois intelligentsia through the levers of the colonial state:

Intellectuals ... saw the state and not the class struggle as the motive force of development ... socialism was turned into a strategy for economic development, and no more. Development, in turn, was seen as a technical, supra-political and supra-social exercise. It was assumed that this 'objective' historical process would erase the 'back-wardness' of the African people, rather than being itself the by-product of the struggle of that same people for social transformation.

From this perspective, it was difficult even to glimpse the possibility of working people in Africa becoming a creative force capable of making history. Rather, history was seen as something to be made outside this force, in lieu of this force and ultimately to be imposed on it.[62]

However, student activism was not limited to the actions of a diasporic student population studying in Europe and America. Anderson (1991) saw student pilgrims as an essential element in the construction of successful nationalism.[63] For a time Ecole Normale William Ponty in Dakar was the centre *par excellence* that received these student pilgrims from across West Africa; the Institut des Hautes Études (a teaching college), also in Dakar and founded in 1950, later served a similar purpose. It rapidly became a hotbed of anti-colonial agitation. As described in the principal study of the period, 'the Insitut des Hautes Études of Dakar absorbed all the graduates from French West Africa into four schools. ... Despite their small number and the surveillance to which these students are subjected ... they will play a very important political role.'[64] It provided colonial education for French West Africa, bringing together students from Guinea, Mali and Côte d'Ivoire. Students crossed Francophone West Africa until other secondary schools had been built. The impact on student identity was clear: the state was capable of creating solidarity between the pilgrims. Students acquired a specific identity that was linked to the colonial pilgrimage.[65]

Students were among the first to champion independence and question the political direction of self-appointed leaders of that independence. Still, as much of the literature cautions, student activism on the continent during the 1940s and 1950s was limited. Inevitably, as Federici explains, 'Africa had only a handful of secondary schools and universities; thus those who made it to a college were an absolute minority, who in most cases had to study abroad, often spending many years away from their countries.'[66] Diané makes the same point, noting that after more than 50 years of French colonialism, in 1946 not a single university had been created in French West Africa.[67]

The politically privileged position of students in much of the continent was linked to their exaggerated role in the movements for independence. To be a student at the time was to be alienated from the social world from which many had emerged. The sense of exclusion became the *raison d'être* of the student movement in the first decade of independence.[68] It was a key element in their politically privileged status. They saw themselves as the harbingers of European development, destined to bring about modernization.[69] These ideas formed the backbone of much of the political and theoretical thinking in the immediate aftermath of the first wave of independence in Africa.[70]

Cabral gave a thorough examination of the contradictory identity of the 'new petty bourgeoisie'. Although he reached the conclusion that independence had failed – 'we accept the principle that the liberation struggle is a revolution and that it does not finish at the moment when the national flag is raised and the national anthem played'[71] – he saw the student intelligentsia as uniquely equipped to bring about real liberation. He argued for the importance of class over ethnicity and believed that the revolution would require what he termed an ideal proletariat whom he saw as the 'petty bourgeoisie':

> the stratum which most rapidly becomes aware of the need to free itself from foreign domination. ... This historical responsibility is assumed by the sector of the petty-bourgeoisie which, in the colonial context, can be called revolutionary. ... In place of a 'real proletariat' an 'ideal' one would be comprised of a class of students and

intellectuals who would help create unity between the oppressed classes and combat ethnic divisions.[72]

The class suicide Cabral advocated required the ideal proletariat to make a conscious effort to see the world not as a nascent bourgeoisie but as liberators and modernizers. As Alexander explains, it necessitates 'a superlative act of the imagination ... by means of which they can consistently and consequentially view the world from the angle of vision of the workers and peasants, who constitute the overwhelming majority of the people of the continent'.[73] Students inherited a politically privileged role after independence that derived from their direct experience in the nationalist struggle and their subsequent role as a transitory group in the post-colonial state. Their world oscillated between visions of workers and peasants and urban privilege, contradictions that help to determine the nature of their activism in the first decades of independence.

Students: finding social position

As discussed above, students were central to the struggle to end colonialism, advocating and inspiring independence struggles from the 1930s. The university – the handful of higher education colleges and technical institutes that existed – became the contested ground where political leaders and democratic struggles found their voice. After independence both the student and university were transformed, often slowly and reluctantly, into national bodies with national responsibilities. Students could not continue to be part of a political vanguard contesting state authority; rather they had to become part of the project of reconstruction and development. The universities had to produce the elites that could power development.[74]

The university at independence in Africa was, in the words of one commentator, an 'implanted institution with largely expatriate staffs, metropole courses of study, and substantial political independence'.[75] For ten years it was at the centre of various attempts to Africanize the state, to disentangle the academy from its colonial past and to engage it with what were regarded as

African realities. It was also the crucial training centre for very limited sections of society dedicated to the needs of a tiny proportion of the population: in 1960 the entire university population in the Congo was infinitessimal.[76]

In the immediate post-colonial period these prerogatives were to demarcate the parameters of student activity. Some commentators have perhaps overstated the elitism of student activism.[77] Bianchini argues in the case of Senegal that a real student movement did not emerge until after 1966,[78] and Federici states that for much of the 1960s and 1970s student politics was limited in scope by the need for students 'to fill the empty spaces left by departing expatriates, and saw the expansion of higher education as a key condition for economic development'.[79] However, close attention needs to be paid to the processes at work.

First, it is important not to exaggerate the extent to which the university was simply an institution occupied by the society's elites (see Chapter 4). The university, though pulling in very few students, was one that reflected many of the class divisions in post-independent Africa. Van den Berghe, writing about the University of Ibadan in Nigeria, stated that 61 per cent of students came from the homes of farmers, traders or unskilled workers, while only 11.2 per cent had fathers who could be classified as professionals.[80] Zeleza makes a similar point about his experience at the University of Malawi in the early 1970s, 'many of my fellow students were from rural and peasant backgrounds, few were from the then minuscule middle class.'[81]

There was also nothing particularly new about how post-colonial regimes conceptualized post-independence African universities. The modern university in Europe was regarded as the principal arena for generating national culture in the eighteenth and nineteenth centuries. Philosophers and social reformers in the nineteenth century saw the university as the purveyor of cultural correctness in a modernizing state.[82] So it was not entirely surprising when President Nyerere of Tanzania explained in 1966: 'I believe that the pursuit of pure learning can be a luxury in society. ... Both in University-promoted research, and in the content of degree syllabuses, the needs of our country should be the determining factor. ... The real problem is that of promoting, strengthening and channelling social attitudes which are conducive to the progress of our society.'[83]

The university was seen as the force *par excellence* that could bring about the desired transformations. The effect of these ideas led to the direct control of university life by the state. In Tanzania it was relatively informal: research projects undertaken at the University of Tanzania had to be approved by the government. In the case of Nigeria, two years after General Gowon addressed the University of Ibadan, every university was under the direct control of the government. This saw federal government assume control over regional universities in 1973 with administrative command flowing from the head of state through federal governments to the National Universities Commission (NUC) and then to university councils and vice-chancellors. This led to the arbitrary appointments by the head of state of senior university administrators. In these circumstances Dibua explains that students soon assumed the 'vanguard of protest against military authoritarianism'.[84] At the university in Ghana repeated opposition and violence arose over the question of academic freedoms. Nkrumah struck what became a predictable pose: 'If reforms do not come from within, we intend to impose them from outside, and no resort to the cry of academic freedom ... is going to restrain us from seeing that our university is a healthy Ghanaian University devoted to Ghanaian interests.'[85]

Similarly, Mobutu yanked the university into his radicalizing project of authenticity, making his intention absolutely clear in the early 1970s. 'We need to emancipate the educational system in the Congo. ... It would be more desirable to have an educational system which shapes the youth according to our requirements. That would make them authentically Congolese.'[86] The idea of the university as a vital conduit of dominant ideas was emphasized repeatedly in the 1960s. The paradox, however, was that the university was also one of the principal arenas contesting authority during the decade. Universities were institutions of both control and contestation.[87] Althusser wrote directly to these themes: 'the true fortress of class influence is the university ... [it] is by the very nature of knowledge it imparts to students that the bourgeoisie exerts its greatest control over them.'[88]

For intellectuals and student militants in the 1960s the university was, therefore, the fortress *par excellence* where the *ancien régime* could be undermined (and in some of the more exaggerated claims even bought crashing down).[89] Rudi Dutschke and Jurgen Krahl, two leading student revolutionaries in Germany in the 1960s, asserted that students needed to become urban *guerilleros*. The university would be the shelter for this guerrilla war where they could 'organize the struggle against institutions and state power. The university was to be the garrison of the Extra-Parliamentary Opposition'.[90] The university was a space of great ideological and physical conflict.

These ideas received their most sophisticated exploration by Bourdieu[91] who regarded the entire education system, not just the university, as serving cultural reproduction. This was not the reproduction of neutral cultural values, however, but the transmission of those of the dominant classes. He saw these classes as being in a position to control the reproduction of cultural ideas in the education system, presenting them as legitimate and unbiased. Bourdieu was making an explicit statement against a superior cultural form; he labelled possession of the dominant culture as cultural capital. The distribution of cultural capital is not even across society, and only students from certain backgrounds had the necessary codes to unpick the messages transmitted by the education system. The university was a crucial instrument for the cultural reproduction of dominant ideas.[92] He also argued that the failure of those from working-class backgrounds to succeed caused them to internalize their sense of failure, making them feel personally inadequate rather than critical of the system that led them to fail in the first place.

This concept of the university was not lost on a generation of post-independent African leaders. However, there was a contradiction in the idea of independent academic endeavour at the university in an environment that Altbach argues tends 'to create a numerically significant group of dedicated and committed politicized students'.[93] After the first decade of independence the goals of national development were beginning to seem illusory as employment for graduates declined. The unravelling of the national dream was destined to intensify political unrest. Emmerson observed these tensions more than thirty years ago: 'As the student community within the nation expands ... as attempts are made to reorient higher education toward new national priorities and as the old anti-colonial consensus is fragmented ... the university tends to lose its former position of "splendid isolation".'[94] It was both the breakdown of the anti-colonial consensus and the disintegration of economic and political development of the new nation that saw student resistance escalate. These tensions gave way to a fractious relationship between the state and the university and impacted on the nature of political unrest on the campus and on the identity of the post-colonial students.[95]

In the first decade of independence writers describe a social pact between students and the state, seen as an implicit guarantee that ensured employment in the formal economy for university graduates. The state had been able to create a certain degree of solidarity between the institutions of the state and students, but this solidarity was premised on the reward of graduate employment.[96] It is also true that students were optimistic about the future social order. Inevitably, this resulted in a symmetry of interests between the newborn state and student identity. Although these factors had an important impact on student activism, they did not prevent the emergence of oppositional politics on the campus across Africa in the 1960s and 1970s.[97] Federici argues that in Tanzania in 1966 students defended their elitism against President Nyerere on the question of their participation in national service. He argues that similar confrontations were witnessed in Ghana and Mozambique.[98]

Indeed, despite the alleged social pact, student activism was a persistent (and irritating) feature of political life in the early process of decolonization, prompting a number of important investigations into the subject.[99] In Côte d'Ivoire students contested Houphouet-Boigny's vocal support for the Algerian

war while pan-Africanist protests demonstrated the political consciousness of student groups. In Senegal students demonstrated
outside the American embassy after Nkrumah was deposed in
1966, a factor that made their role in the revolt in 1968 possible.[100]
While much of the activism and many of the early demonstrations were about ending minority rule in Africa, in South
Africa and Rhodesia the issue of educational reform was also
key. The Africanization of university administrations that had
been dominated by white professors and lecturers became an
important demand.[101]

Student action was limited in the first few years of independence and more often than not it supported the state. Zimbabwe
was typical in that the students limited their activism in the first
half of the 1980s to protests against foreign embassies and even
gave vocal support to the regime in place.[102] But as the state
sought to increase the supply of trained personnel, civil servants
and bureaucrats, an expansion in the enrolment of students in
university followed. Although student enrolment was only just
hovering above 1 per cent of the age cohort in the mid-1960s, it
was going to reach 3 per cent.[103]

Small though it was, the expansion in student numbers meant
that universities were no longer simply training grounds for the
ruling classes. While the majority of the highest state functionaries and professors were still part of the post-colonial ruling
elite, increasingly many students (and their parents) were not.
However, the university had not become proletarianized, and
universities for at least the first decade and a half (from 1960 to
1975) were largely privileged institutions.[104] The overwhelming
majority of students were from professional and managerial
families, a section of the population, which at that time had far
superior lifestyles and opportunities than the great majority.[105]

How then should students be categorized after independence?
It would be misleading to give them a special social class, or
even allocate them to one that already existed. Rather, students
who had emerged from the social milieu of the student intelligentsia in the pre-independence period now became a transitory
grouping, 'young people whose final ... positions have not been

determined', as Harman put it.[106] However, this transitory category held for only a brief moment, for the economic crisis in the 1970s fundamentally altered their status. 'Students ... are only in transition, over which they have no control, because they have no impact on the socioeconomic stakes.'[107]

The idea of students as a transitory category and not a separate class was repeatedly raised in the 1960s. Many of the arguments arose as a result of the upsurge of student revolts on campuses in America and Europe; book shelves were filled with case studies, anthologies and calls to arms, often written by student activists and young members of the new left.[108] Many of these studies exaggerated the role of student revolts; Touraine[109] asserted that in post-industrial societies the working class, regarded as the force that could power social transformation, had ceded its position to university students who had become the new proletariat. 'Thus, is not the student movement, in principle at least, of the same importance as the labour movement of the past?'[110] Just as knowledge and technical progress were at the centre of the new society, like capital accumulation had been in industrial society, so universities had become the new factories (and students the new workers). Consequently, the rise in student revolts was not a transitory phenomenon, but symbolic of their new position in the forces of production (the production of knowledge and technical progress).

We should note, however, that the desire to find a new – or in Cabral's case ideal – proletariat was overwhelming among commentators and academics in the 1960s. Marcuse perhaps made the most thorough attempt to dislodge the old working class, which, he argued, had become incorporated into the system (see below). Attempts to find a new social agency to replace a co-opted and docile proletariat were not only linked to a sincere attempt to analyse new social movements, specifically student protest, but also represented a more profound political reality. As we saw in the previous section, the search for a new proletariat was related to the role played by a student intelligentsia in the developing world, which had appeared to supplant the political mobilization of other groups. For radical students in the 1960s and 1970s who looked to national liberation struggles for inspiration, the lessons of Cuba, China and of liberation movements in Africa were clear: a dedicated and devoted minority could bring about revolutionary change. Che Guevara's statement, 'if you are a revolutionary, make a revolution'[111] seemed to epitomize the period, and the role of student revolutionaries in social change.

A radical critique of these arguments highlighted three major weaknesses. Stedman Jones argued, first, that students did not constitute a separate class; while the situation for the working class is permanent – a life situation – the most important social characteristics of students is their transience. Second, students were also heading for senior positions in the job market, and that marked them apart from the working class: 'their social destination is either into professional groups or else into the managerial, technocratic class itself.'[112] The third argument centres on the nature of contemporary society, many writers at the time arguing that the centres of production had not been fundamentally changed and there were no grounds to characterize society as post-industrial.[113] While students might have become the centre of the political focus in the 1960s, it was not because 'they have stepped into the shoes of an obsolete proletariat'.[114]

Students do not have a privileged relationship with the productive process, for they neither own nor manage it. In this sense, student activism *per se* could never generate the necessary social force to transform society. On the contrary, their activism is determined by imponderables over which they have no control – graduate employment, price levels and economic policies, in short, society's vital socioeconomic stakes. Referring to student protest in the 1960s, Panitch reminds us that 'the class struggle was [never] going to be resolved at the university'.[115] This did not, however, protect students from the vagaries of social change. In one study they were described as an oppressed group isolated on campus and buffeted by economic forces they cannot control.[116] Students, though transitory, had no control over the curriculum, recruitment to the university, or how much they had to pay for accommodation, books and food.

Although, as many argued, students had not supplanted the proletariat this did not enfeeble their activism. Their elitism often powered their action and they sought to rise above society, which is still an important feature of student activism. The slogan of the Zimbabwe student movement today – 'voice of the voiceless' – expresses this elitism. Students still boast about being at university and not college or polytechnic.[117] Halliday noted that although students are a transitory social group they have the capacity to act as a political vanguard: 'Their relatively privileged social status ... often makes student protests possible, when all other social groups are shackled by military coercion.' This privileged role, however, has serious limitations:

> This vanguard role ... is an index of the restricted level of political development in any given country. For students are not a social class and cannot transform society. Their resistance to tyranny may often be heroic but there are constant limitations. Student consciousness is highly volatile. It is often hard to sustain a student movement beyond the initial provocation.[118]

A student's transitory status had an important impact on his or her activism. It meant that political and ideological conflict in society could become amplified in the politicized spaces of the university campus.[119] Harman writes, 'whole sections of the student population are expected to absorb the ruling ideology, so as to be able to transmit it to others when they graduate.' However, if those ideas stood in stark contrast to social reality, students are among the first to be thrown into 'intellectual turmoil and can react with indignation'.[120] Though material concerns might trigger student protests, as for example during periods of heightened activism in the late 1960s in Senegal, the movement would often rapidly develop an explicitly political agenda.

African university students, even during their so-called period of political vanguardism in the late 1960s and 1970s, were not always political. As Harman argues, it was their ambiguous status – caught between social groups – that caused students to react so powerfully when they realized the nature of the post-colonial state. Many activists had spent years believing (and defending) the state's progressive role, while being told that they were going to inherit and strengthen the nation. The sense of betrayal that student activists felt during this early period in Zimbabwe helps explain why they frequently reacted so violently.[121] The betrayal was about more than their personal well-being. It was also about the direction of the state and was seen therefore as an ideological treachery.

The anger and disillusionment many student activists from the 1960s in the United States and Europe expressed, often fuelled the ferocity of early student revolts during the period. Mario Savio was a leading figure in the Berkeley University Free Speech Movement (FSM) in 1964; 'many of us came to college with what we later acknowledged were rather romantic expectations, perhaps mostly unexpressed at first, about what a delight and adventure learning would be. We really did have unanswered questions searching for words, though to say so sounds almost corny. ... But once at college we quickly lost much of the romantic vision.'[122] It was this generation of angry and disillusioned students, Draper's non-ideological radicals,[123] who helped to energize the first student mobilizations.

Hal Draper, in a detailed study of the Berkeley student revolt, describes how this clash of expectations explained the volatility of early student activism:

This was the explosiveness of uncalculated indignation, not the slow boil of planned revolt. In many cases it was born of the first flash of discovery that the mantle of authority cloaked an unsuspected nakedness. The experienced radical on campus did not consider this to be news ... There is first love; there is the first baptism of fire; there is the first time that you realize your father had lied; and there is the first discovery of the chasm between the rhetoric of Ideals and the cynicism of Power among the pillars of society.[124]

It was in these circumstances, Draper argues, that non-ideological radicals became the most explosive element in the student movement. Paradoxically, it also explains one of the principal strengths of student action. Infused by a powerful indignation student activists were 'able to win so much because they didn't know it was "impossible"'. Older radicals and activists may feel oppressed by a careful analysis of the balance of forces, whereas student 'naiveté and inexperience was as a shield and a buckler to them'.[125]

The explosiveness of early student activism was combined with an explicit elitism. In their first serious mobilizations student activists in Zimbabwe saw themselves as revolutionary intellectuals fighting for the nation (even the one-party state). Their activism was often seen in terms of their unique ability to confront the status quo. While able to advance a critique of the regime – on realizing that 'their father [Mugabe in this case] had lied' – before the trade union movement, without the support from this movement they remained important, though ultimately peripheral, critics of the regime. And they regarded themselves as custodians of society, uniquely placed to change it.

The nature of student activism – a combination of seemingly explosive spontaneity and elitism – found a theoretical basis in the work of the Frankfurt school and Marcuse and Adorno. Their rather pessimistic arguments maintained that late capitalist society was closed and that the only serious systemic challenge could come from the Third World (and enlightened intellectuals). With the consciousness of the working class paralysed, only students and intellectuals could cut a hole in the closed and hegemonic system. As we have seen, this was part of the search for a new proletariat. Marcuse saw the student intelligentsia playing part of this role, and he was an important champion and advocate of student resistance in the 1960s and 1970s.[126] In an otherwise pessimistic conclusion to his chief work, *One Dimensional Man*, where the working class has become incorporated into the system it was historically destined to overturn, he sees a space for resistance. The agency for this transformation is made up of a 'substratum of the outcasts and outsiders', together with

45

elements of the intelligentsia, 'the most advanced consciousness of humanity'.[127]

At the end of the 1960s, Marcuse had become an even more forthright defender of the student movement. In a prolonged correspondence, he admonishes his former collaborator (and comrade) Adorno for his conservatism. The student movement was now, according to Marcuse, 'the strongest, perhaps the only, catalyst for the internal collapse of the system of domination today'. The student movement could act as a catalyst in the social struggles of much wider layers of society, that included agitation 'in the ghettos, in the radical alienation from the system of layers who were formerly integrated, and, most importantly, in the mobilization of further circles of the populace against American imperialism'.[128]

Although student activism might have been enfeebled by the students' separation from the production process, it was partly freed by their not having any connection to it. They could take action without worrying (excessively) about family and income. They could also meet and organize in substantial freedom without the discipline and punishment of a workplace. In addition, 'the initial outraged minority of students could take action on the campus without being held back by the indifference and even hostility of the majority – something rarely possible for workers in a factory or office'.[129] However, the illusion that the campus was a free (or at least freer) space was often bought crashing down when the police and army invaded the university during student mobilizations.

But it was the students' transitory character – their lack of socioeconomic stakes – that ensured that early mobilizations experienced explosive peaks and then sharp decline.[130] Although they could organize effective university-wide unions, these were unable to put the authorities under permanent (or paralysing) pressure. When their activism was most successful (1968 in Senegal and the 1990s in Zimbabwe) it was precisely because they were able to help unleash a more permanent and paralysing movement connected to the trade unions. The hit and run element of student activism did, however, ensure that they

frequently forced governments onto the defensive and to con-
cede to many of their demands. These cycles of mobilization
became a constant feature of student activism.

In addition, the decline of the movement did not mean that the
campus reverted to its old and apolitical self. On the contrary,
the upsurge in student action in the late 1960s and 1970s fundamentally altered the political environment on many campuses.
Although the wave of protest ebbed and flowed, actions drew
more students into an increasingly politicized environment.
What Harman writes about the European and American student
movements in the late 1960s applies equally to what was happening in many parts of Africa: 'The phase of "spontaneous"
upheaval and "charismatic" leadership gave way to a phase of
hard, and often bitter, arguments between those with different
views as to the way forward.'[131]

In the 1970s higher education (and consequently student activism) was transformed in Africa under the impact of economic
recession and structural adjustment.[132] But these processes were
not limited to Africa. In the 1970s, according to Bauman, the
Western university lost many of its functions, usurped by other
agencies (think-tanks, policy and research institutes and privatized consultancies). This has led to the commodification of
knowledge connected to a neo-liberal agenda that views education as a good, 'as procurable and securable "information",
rather than as a qualitative, experimental capacity for analysis
and judgement which must be cultivated through education'.[133]
In large parts of Africa the instruments of this commodification
were World Bank and IMF-initiated reforms. These polarized
higher education in Western societies, where a minority of
privileged institutions – the Ivy League universities in America
and Oxford and Cambridge in the UK – are able to remain
faithful to an earlier (idealized) world of intellectual endeavour
and educational pursuit (greatly assisted by private endow-
ments), while most institutions of higher education are caught in
a web of marketization. They have become client-driven, providing an increasingly self-funded service to larger bodies of
students.[134]

It is important to place the crisis in African universities since the 1970s in a global context.[135] Indeed, many authors see structural adjustment as a variant of a neo-liberal agenda that has not spared any region.[136] In Chapter 2 I argue that the crisis is symptomatic of the global drive for neo-liberal reforms that have had a catastrophic impact on higher education not only in Africa but also in the West.[137] The emphasis of these reforms in Africa has been on rising fees for students – cost recovery in the euphemism of the World Bank – and the reprioritization of educational provision to primary schools on the grounds of a higher economic return (and also as part of their anti-poverty agenda). In the Third World the discourse has been mediated through international development agencies, principally the World Bank and IMF, which see university education as a luxury that African economies cannot afford.[138] In the West the commercialization of higher education has seen both the reduction in state funding to universities and the enticement of private financing and sponsorship. While the crisis is a global one, there are vital elements to it that are peculiar to universities in Africa, specifically the colonial legacy that saw higher education as a way of civilizing 'native subjects'[139] and, as we saw in the years preceding independence, as a way of forging a national bureaucratic caste from the student intelligentsia.

In the next section I look briefly at the collapse of many post-independence dreams, when, with the onset of economic crisis, a process began that unravelled the elitism of university students. I identify the structural dynamics constantly limiting and producing social and cultural forms, while at the same time recognizing the ability of men and women to bring about social change in the transitions in the study.[140] The successive waves of protest are described alongside the macro (or structural) transformations of encountered circumstances.

Crisis and structural adjustment 1975–1990
The period from 1975 saw a combination of apparently contradictory features, including a deepening of the economic crisis that had started at the beginning of the decade and a series of

new struggles.[141] The first period marked the end to the long boom, and what now appeared to be the myth of rapid economic development directed by the state. In the early 1970s industrial production had slumped in the advanced economies by 10 per cent in one year, while international trade had fallen by 13 per cent.[142] The year 1973 was decisive. OPEC raised the price of oil, which, because commercial banks were flooded with petro-dollars, led to high levels of lending to African countries at low interest rates.[143] The recession had a catastrophic effect on Africa. Most countries were still economically dependent on their former colonial masters, relying on the export of one or two primary products. So in 1975, for example, Ghana and Chad depended on coffee and cotton respectively for more than two-thirds of their exports. Zambia depended on copper for half of its GDP, so the collapse in its price meant that by 1977 it received zero income from its most important export.[144] One study concluded that 'regions already marginal to international capitalism were further marginalized and even the protective edifice of state capitalism that was still being constructed in Africa was impotent to resist the violence of these slumps.'[145]

During this period, as the global economic crisis deepened and mounting debts drove governments to seek external flows of capital, usually under ever more stringent conditions of lending, the paths of autonomous national development adopted by existing African regimes were increasingly undermined. If the crisis of the late 1970s and early 1980s was an international one, much of the pain of adjustment was borne by the developing countries, particularly those that relied heavily on oil imports, agricultural exports and borrowing from the West.[146]

These developments are often reconceptualized today as elements of an emerging globalization.[147] Marxist geographer David Harvey, who was one of the first globalization scholars, described it as a speeding up of time–space compression. He saw the phenomenon, as Marx described it, as the 'annihilation of space by time'.[148] According to Harvey, this society is 'characterized by speed-up in the pace of life ... so overwhelming spatial barriers that the world sometimes seems to collapse inwards upon us'.[149] These processes have seen the uneven interconnection of economies, which many argue has historically characterized the development of capitalism.[150] Time–space compression has also seen the acceleration of movement and communication across space, which Massey colourfully describes as the extent 'to which we can move between countries, or walk about the streets at night, or venture out of hotels in foreign cities'.[151] Yet even these processes are geographically and socially bound, limited to relatively few privileged people. Massey thus insists on a power geometry of time–space compression that focuses on specific social groups with distinct relationships to these processes.[152]

Noam Chomsky[153] describes two phases that correspond broadly with the understanding of globalization in this study. Globalization represents Phase Two of capitalist development since the Second World War and consists of those processes that unpick the social democratic reforms characteristic of Phase One. Walton and Seddon identify how during Chomsky's Phase Two of postwar capitalist development, loans turned into debts and, as the process of global adjustment and restructuring required by the international capitalist crisis proceeded, more and more African states found their options severely restricted and their macro-economic policies increasingly shaped by the conditions imposed upon them.[154] This process received a boost with the election of the free market governments of Thatcher and Reagan. Both developed policies that shifted the focus to the market and private sector. The IMF and World Bank became the central purveyors of these policies. As the World Bank reported at the time, 'Africa needs not just less government – [but] government that concentrates its efforts less on direct intervention and more on enabling others to be productive.'[155]

For most African economies, structural adjustment preceded more far-reaching economic and institutional reforms associated with varying degrees of economic liberalization and privatiz-ation. SAPs were the conditions attached to IMF and World Bank loans. The terms of the loans required states to adjust their economies, privatize national industries, remove tariff barriers and open up to the outside world, exposing the economy to international competition and the free market – and hence dependence on the global marketplace.[156]

Protest and austerity

The social cost of economic liberalization and the austerity policies that followed fell disproportionately on what have been called the popular classes.[157] Seddon and Zeilig define the heterogeneity of these forces:

> They may include not only the urban and rural working classes (consisting of those who have little or no control or ownership of the means of production and only their labour to sell, whether in the formal or the informal sector) but also other categories, including on the one hand those whom Marx refers to as 'paupers' and on the other small peasants and tenant farmers, 'independent' craftsmen and artisans, small retailers and petty commodity producers, and members of the 'new petty bourgeoisie' (sometimes called 'the new middle classes') generally including the lower echelons of the public sector. Not only do these various social categories constitute, in effect, the relative surplus population, which may be characterized as a reserve army of labour, they often share a consciousness of their interdependency and common vulnerability.[158]

This motley social grouping is not an entirely new phenomenon in the sub-Saharan African political economy. Some commentators (like Ruth First) argue that African patterns of development had created a hybrid class (the peasantariat), founded on a twin rural and urban identity. The hybridity of the African social forms received a postmodernist gloss in the 1990s, in which ethnicity and culture came to be seen as more a determinant of social behaviour than alleged class membership.[159]

However, what is undeniable is that the crisis of globalization led to a reorganization of the continent's social worlds, though with great regional variation. As Harrison has argued, 'there is a real political economy of hybridization: the real import of culture within the workplace can only be understood within this defining context.'[160] These changes transformed the social forces that were active during the democratic transitions. The effect of reforms associated with SAPs was to unleash what some have described as waves of protests.[161] The first wave can be seen developing from the late 1970s until the late 1980s. Although there is much disagreement in the literature about the nature of the resistance against this austerity, there is little question about its actual occurrence. Some, for example, have argued that the role and reaction of the popular classes was defensive, only geared towards survival;[162] others have disputed this, arguing that these struggles have also been offensive – resisting, protesting and changing the policies and challenging those interests that they identified as affecting them.[163]

In more limited respects, popular protest had a political impact in all the countries; in virtually all cases it produced a rapid reversal of cuts in subsidies and a far greater awareness of the political limits to rapid structural adjustment and economic liberalization; in some cases it resulted in political changes and a greater degree of political openness. Even Saul admits that these struggles opened up 'further space for groups in civil society to openly practise politics'.[164] The focus of these protests were often the international financial agencies (particularly the IFIs), but also the governments that adopted the austerity policies and the representatives of the big corporations (foreign and national) that benefited from liberalization. Some have argued that in this way these struggles were a precursor to the contemporary anti-globalization movement.[165] It is widely acknowledged that throughout the continent during the late 1970s and 1980s, these popular struggles sought to resist the austerity policies of their governments.[166] The resistance was characterized by street demonstrations, marches, strikes and other forms of public action, often (and questionably) referred to as bread riots. It is important to make clear that the wave of popular protest during the late 1970s and 1980s was experienced across many countries in the developing world.

While it is important not to over romanticize the protests, it is misleading and patronizing to see them simply as desperate IMF riots taking place in 'wretched Third World cities ... where organization and democratic traditions of struggle are simply lacking'.[167] It is also unhelpful to try to divide, as inherently distinct and effectively antagonistic, workers' struggles and 'populist forms of socio-political movement'.[168]

The second wave of protest

The reality is that as economic reforms continued in sub-Saharan Africa during the 1980s, so too did popular protests, although by now they were becoming less spontaneous, more organized and more overtly political, fuelling what became known in academic literature as democratic transitions. But by 1989 Africa was about to undergo another wave of popular protest hardly noticed in the West but as far reaching as the changes that brought down East European communism, and sparking a renewed interest in democratic and popular struggle in Africa.[169]

From 1989 political protests rose massively across sub-Saharan Africa; while there had been approximately 20 recorded incidents of political unrest annually in the 1980s, in 1991 alone 86 major protest movements came into existence across 30 countries. By 1992 many African governments had been forced to introduce reforms and, in 1993, 14 countries held democratic elections. In a four-year period from the start of the protests in 1990, a total of 35 regimes had been swept away by a combination of street demonstrations, mass strikes and other forms of protest (but also under pressure from IFIs), and by presidential and legislative elections that were often the first held for a generation.[170] The speed with which these changes took place surprised many commentators, 'Compared with the recent experiences of Poland and Brazil ... African regime transitions seemed frantically hurried.'[171] Popular opposition reached a climax in Senegal and Zimbabwe during the 1990s. This dramatic increase in protest, connected to the pauperization of society, saw renewed and equally dramatic struggles on campuses across the continent. These protests were not limited to campus demands but frequently converged with wider social movements.

The collapses of the Berlin Wall and of the Soviet Union were cataclysmic for opposition parties and trade unionists across Africa. They were events that simultaneously inspired and weakened popular struggles on the continent. Within a very short space of time the politics that had helped sustain democratic resistance (and the thousands of activists across the continent) collapsed. Regimes that had used the cover of Marxism–Leninism were hugely weakened by the collapse of the Berlin Wall, which gave enormous impetus to the movements that sought to dislodge them. The opposition was left without any ideological moorings and student politics without a political *raison d'être*. Many commentators previously on the left rushed to proclaim a new faith in the market. André Gunder Frank was typical in arguing at the time that these policies resulted in 'enormous strides in the ... economic and political direction' of the Third World.[172] By the mid-1980s even regimes that had kept the banner of Marxism–Leninism flying were introducing programmes that mirrored IMF-led structural adjustment. The effect of these changes on the politics, organization and outcomes of the movements in the 1990s was large, and the ability of students to exercise effective political action was significantly weakened.

Two examples are presented here to illustrate what was happening in this period. In the West African state of Benin, the process started in 1989. Students demonstrated against the government in January, demanding overdue grants and a guarantee of public sector employment after graduation. The government, crippled by financial scandals, capital flight and falling tax revenue, thought it could respond as it had always done by suppressing the protest, but the movement grew during the year to incorporate the trade unions and urban poor. Halfway through the year, in the hope of placating the demonstrators, President Mathieu Kérékou invited a human rights campaigner into his government. In a pattern followed by other countries, he set up a commission that would eventually create a national reconciliation conference that included the opposition movement, trade unions, students and religious associations. Emboldened by events, trade unionists, led by postal workers and teachers, left the government controlled National Federation of Workers' Union of Benin. By the end of the year, mass demonstrations had convulsed the capital, Cotonou. When Kérékou attempted to befriend demonstrators during one of these protests he was jeered, threatened and forced to flee.[173] In February 1990, the National Conference of Active Forces declared itself sovereign and dissolved Kérékou's national assembly. Obstinately, he still insisted, 'I will not resign, I will have to be removed.' After his defeat in the presidential elections the following year he asked humbly for forgiveness and asserted his 'deep, sincere and irreversible desire to change'.[174]

In Côte d'Ivoire, severely affected by the drop in the international price of cocoa and coffee, violent unrest between March and May 1990 threatened the government's austerity programme designed to fill a £236 million gap in the budget (agreed the previous July with the World Bank and IMF) and shook the regime. Protests and strikes by workers in all sectors delayed the imposition of measures to cut public sector salaries and increase taxes, while student protests added fuel to the flames. The president of Côte d'Ivoire, Houphouet-Boigny, brought in the army to control the protests and rejected growing demands for a multi-party state. Pay cuts and higher taxes were imposed, along with some price cuts aimed at softening the blow of the salary reductions. But protests continued and businesses resisted the proposed reductions in prices. On 23 March soldiers used tear gas to disperse more than 1000 people protesting in the centre of Abidjan, bringing traffic to a halt.[175] Doctors voted for an indefinite strike and withdrew emergency cover in protest at mass arrests of demonstrators. A ban on demonstrations, imposed on 26 March, proved ineffective and in April the austerity measures were suspended after public protest and political pressure (from France as well as from within) forced a review of government policy. In May, demanding better pay and conditions, the lower ranks in the army began a series of demonstrations, which culminated in a temporary takeover of the main airport.[176]

Students played a vital role in both these cases. But student protests in the 1990s in Africa took place in a profoundly altered world, without an alternative to capitalism and facing a further onslaught from structural adjustment. The deployment of a discourse of democracy and good governance by the international lending agencies and the major capitalist states – despite their willingness in previous decades to support and even promote dictators and autocrats – coincided with what undoubtedly was also a movement inside Africa for democracy and legitimate governments.[177]

While these political movements have not always served to strengthen the formal structures of democracy, they have almost always helped to broaden and deepen popular involvement in the political process and even some quite hesitant writers are prepared to acknowledge their significance. Saul and Leys, who wrote despairingly of 'the tragedy of Africa', recognize that, in addition to the thousands of activists groups that constitute a vibrant civil society in Africa today, 'there are also resistances directed more broadly and self-consciously against the kind of parasitic governments that attempt to ride the African crisis to their own advantage'.[178] There is some consensus that the second part of the decade saw a deepening and widening of democracy, if not within the formal institutions of party politics, then in the informal arenas of urban politics – the slums, shanty towns, workplaces, schools, colleges, public spaces and streets of the major cities. Despite evidence that more than a decade of popular protest had created new space for democratization, it was still possible for analysts like Saul and Leys to ask 'to what extent might this climate of democratization also open up space for popular initiatives that could prove more transformative?'[179]

Although Saul has become far less sceptical about the significance of these waves of popular protest and political opposition, he still continues to highlight some of the undoubted weaknesses of these movements.[180] While accepting that the waves of protest prised open space for civil society to operate, he sees the developments as benefiting the middle classes – and the neo-liberal agenda – rather than popular interests. Saul claims that the best outcomes can be seen as empowering liberal democracy rather than genuine popular democracy. Together with Leys he was disparaging of the democratic transition, suggesting that in most cases it has done 'little more than ... stabilize property-threatening situations by a momentary recirculation of elites'.[181]

To a certain extent this has been the case, and the multi-party democracies that have often been established as a result of these transitions are enfeebled by the very processes that helped trigger the transitions in the first place. Abrahamsen is surely right when she identifies the liberalization of African economies as a crucial constraint on strengthening democracy rather than as a prerequisite for it:

> [A]lthough external pressure may have secured the survival of certain structures and procedures of democracy in Africa, the demand for economic liberalization has at the same time impeded the consolidation of democracy. Instead of consolidation, the result has been a fragile democracy, often little more than a facade, and this seems an almost inevitable outcome of the pursuit of simultaneous economic and political liberalization in conditions of poverty and underdevelopment.[182]

But this analysis is still blinkered; the economic liberalization she describes has had a far more ambiguous effect. While it has weakened the ability of the states now being urged to democratize, to control the direction and character of political movements, it has also directly generated the resistance that has given rise to many of the democratic transitions. Among activists it creates what many have criticized as bread and butter unionism (among students and trade unionists) – what in Senegal was dismissively described as *syndicalisme alimentaire* (economism)[183] – but that has the capacity to extend well beyond such immediate issues and take up broader matters of political significance.

The period also saw the powerful convergence of forces that plunged students into the general crisis. In Nigeria students spearheaded the fight against the government's home-grown structural adjustment programme in the 1980s. But students in the National Association of Nigerian Students (NANS) were no longer simply a political vanguard. The collapse of the conditions of study across the country's universities saw student status converge with a general societal meltdown. It was fuel price increases in 1988, demanded by the World Bank, that led students in NANS to initiate nationwide anti-SAP protests. Dibua explains: 'Students viewed that the increase in prices ... would visit untold economic hardship on the majority of Nigerians while making it difficult for impoverished parents to finance students' education.'[184] While the demand for economic liberalization may have weakened formal democratic structures, in some cases it created an extraordinarily explosive cocktail of social forces.

This period, as we have seen from the collapse of the Berlin Wall, can be regarded as marking the second wave of protests with more explicitly political aims and objectives than during the previous decades. In Chapter 2 I look at the period of student mobilization during the democratic transitions and examine how the newly adjusted world transformed their activism. In it I describe the broad canvas of political and economic change (the world directly encountered) and the historical evolution of student activism. The student activists we encounter later on in the study had to negotiate a world transformed by political and economic forces (and contested in waves of popular protest) that was discussed in the last sections of this chapter. We have seen that in the specific circumstances that pertained in sub-Saharan Africa the student intelligentsia had a specific political capacity. Changes that occurred from the 1970s brought together broad popular coalitions (that reflected the hybridity of a world liberalized by structural adjustment), which empowered the waves of protests that became more organized and wide-ranging throughout the 1980s and 1990s. As we shall see, students were a key element in initiating and organizing these movements. The extent to which a new (third) wave of protest in sub-Saharan Africa can be identified, and connected to the growth of the anti-globalization movement, will be examined in the conclusion.

Chapter 2

CONTEMPORARY STUDENT ACTIVISM IN SUB-SAHARAN AFRICA

University students in the period following independence were a transitory social group that held well-founded expectations of rewarding and high status employment after graduation. The 1970s began to erode many of these assurances as countries that had attempted to implement state-led development faced international recession and internal corruption and decay. State funding of higher education by the late 1970s was being targeted for restructuring. Student activism was affected: while students clung to a self-conscious elitism, the student poverty and financial crises of African universities affected their activism.[1] These processes, however, were inherently contradictory. As well as seeing their status as a privileged group collapse, there was an unprecedented convergence of forces between students and the popular classes. The austerity imposed by structural adjustment and national governments had turned the ivory tower inside out. This convergence was expressed in the waves of resistance from the mid-1970s and later the democratic transitions that swept the continent from the late 1980s and 1990s.

In this chapter I survey the role of students, their protest and their relationship with civil society in the processes that brought a wave of multi-party elections and democratic struggles in sub-

Saharan Africa. I focus specifically on the literature that relates to student activism and protest, although I acknowledge that this activism brings into play many other factors. The context in which students become political actors in contemporary Africa is tied to the transformation of higher education in sub-Saharan Africa, often under the auspices of IMF- and World Bank-led reform. These wider macro processes impinge on the ability of students to exercise effective and meaningful political agency.

In the first sections of the chapter I explore the changing nature of higher education in the political economy of sub-Saharan Africa, focusing on the changed circumstances that student activists have been forced to negotiate over the last 25 years. In the final sections of the chapter I discuss both the evolution of student activism and how it has been characterized in recent literature and the involvement of students in the convergence of forces and the popular protests that were typical of the democratic transitions. I intentionally present the broad political and economic changes to higher education in sub-Saharan Africa, and detail the role of students in the actual transitions that took place in the 1990s. The history of these transitions must be, in Thompson's word, 'embodied … in a real context'.[2]

Universities in crisis

Universities have been analysed as a site of contestation where the democratization process took place, incorporating a range of political forces and agency.[3] The literature, however, finds unanimity in the description of the university as a neglected institution, a crumbling edifice housing impoverished students and lecturers. The physical decay of higher education is a feature common in many sub-Saharan African universities.[4]

It is important not to generalize uncritically from Aborisade's observations (see Figure 2.1 below), although much of the literature tends to corroborate his observations.[5] In Malawi, Kerr and Mapanje note that the physical collapse of the University of Malawi, the non-payment of staff and declining facilities for students have helped to create an atmosphere of marginalization that has often led students to anti-social behaviour.[6]

Figure 2.1: A Nigerian academic and trade unionist, Femi Aborisade, describes higher education in Nigeria[7]

1. Inadequate infrastructural facilities

Classrooms are inadequate, both in terms of number and size considering increases in the number of students offered admission on a yearly basis. There is a trend towards phenomenal growth in the number of students without corresponding preparation for the growth. The management and government are concerned about the size of income to be generated from the students in terms of ... fees and other types of levies. Physical clashes occasionally occur between students in different classes as lecture timetables are often not observed – students scramble to outpace fellow students, in being the first to occupy classrooms.

2. Staffing situation

Higher education is grossly understaffed in many states. In the Department of Business and Public Administration where I was teaching in December 1999, for example, there were just 11 academic staff teaching 1109 students.

3. Libraries

Libraries are inadequate, in terms of size, number of books and the age of the books. Current literatures are hardly available. Yet, many students are too poor to buy books of their own. Thus the lack of reading materials tends to further strengthen the development of cultism among students and lecturers.

4. Payment of salaries

Salaries are never paid as and when due. Unfortunately, this situation encourages lecturers unlawfully to seek to pass the burden of their domestic problems on to students through the imposition of all sorts of levies, inducements and threats of failure. A common example is the practice whereby lecturers make it compulsory for students to buy photocopied lecture notes.

They describe the increase in sexual assaults on female students and lecturers from 1994 as a 'cowardly attempt among male students to find an easy scapegoat for a much broader set of frustrations'. Nkongolo described similar frustrations among students at the University of Lubumbashi in the early 1990s:

> Us, students and tomorrow's elite of Zaire, the youth of the Mouvement Populaire de la Révolution (JMPR) were compelled to go to the toilet in the bush, like animals. We went there every day, in the hot and rainy season. The night like the day ... even the 'largest library in central Africa' was not saved, and was used as a WC. ... The outside world must know the extent that Mobutu had humiliated us.[8]

It is clear that there is a remarkable symmetry in the decay of sub-Saharan African universities over the last 20 years: countries thousands of miles apart experienced the same erosion of higher education. Piet Konings writes about the crisis of the University of Yaoundé in Cameroon in the 1990s: 'first and foremost, there was growing dissatisfaction with [the] deepening crisis within the university and the lack of employment prospects for university graduates. Mockingly, students referred to their university as "the bachelors' cemetery".'[9] Konings goes on to describe how student numbers have swelled from 10,000 in 1982 to more than 42,000 ten years later, even though the university infrastructure was only built to cope with a maximum of 7000 students. Consequently, 'lecture rooms, libraries, laboratories, and office space for lecturers were inadequate and lacked necessary equipment. The university hostel could offer accommodation to a limited number of students, often on the basis of patronage or ethnic criteria, and the vast majority of students were compelled to look for accommodation themselves.'[10]

Even at Makerere university, regarded as a model for the rest of Africa, half the students questioned in a survey failed to make lectures because there were not enough seats.[11] Alternative private accommodation was invariably in overpriced mini-cities surrounding the university. Libraries have suffered acutely; Simui describes the decimation of Zambian university libraries since the mid-1980s: 'The records of journal holdings at UNZA [University of Zambia] library revealed that subscriptions to most journal literature stopped around 1984 and 1986. The few current titles the Library received are donor supported ... from development agencies like Book Aid International (BAI) ... and the American Association for the Advancement of Science (AAS).'[12]

The picture is almost exactly the same for Cameroonian university libraries.[13] Although the decay of library facilities is not universal, for example Ama and Ama's survey of student perceptions of library services across Nambia's seven tertiary educational institutions reveals widespread satisfaction.[14] Still, the overwhelming evidence is one of decline and collapse. The same pattern of decay affected Kenya's university system. Maurice Amutabi tends to romanticize student activism, yet his description of conditions in Kenya's universities is convincing: 'The lecture theatres and libraries are not only congested but also run down. The hostels have become overcrowded, sanitary conditions have worsened, and food quality has deteriorated. University buildings are dilapidated, making the university conditions not different from any slum or poor neighbourhood in Kenya.'[15]

Amutabi argues that the resulting impoverishment of student life has radically altered their position in Kenyan society, they are now, he maintains, bedfellows with the population as a whole. They share the same economic crisis and live the same poverty. Students, though, still have a role as societal watchdogs and only their vigilance will ensure that the gains of multi-partyism and democratization are maintained.

The conditions of higher education in Africa seen from the perspective of the university's physical infrastructure and the pauperization of staff and students declined steeply in the 1980s. A number of writers point out that SAPs have greatly exacerbated the withdrawal of state funding for universities, teaching staff and students.[16] They argue that these policies deprioritize higher education in Africa, forcing national governments to slash state support to university budgets and insisting on the introduction of tuition fees and levies on students.

Reform of higher education in sub-Saharan African

From the early 1980s to the early 1990s the World Bank produced a number of studies on the importance of higher education reform that advocated a dramatic reduction in expenditure in Africa. The most important of these reports, *Accelerated development in sub-Saharan Africa*, later known as the Berg Report, was produced in 1981. It focused on the general priorities for African development and prescribed policy reforms to unregulate national states. These reforms included the wholesale reconfiguration of university education in Africa. The report has become the subject of considerable and mostly hostile discussion.[17] It determined the approach of donor agencies to education in Africa. The problem was simple: too much money was being spent on education:

> Expenditure on schooling already claims a large part of GDP – around 4% in two thirds of the countries for which data are available. And, more important, they claim a sizeable share of public expenditure – about 16% of the total, on average, more than any other government function except general administration. In a significant number of African countries, recurrent expenditure on education is between 25 and 35% of total recurrent spending. In the 1970s, when government revenues rose rapidly in most of the continent, the average African country's incremental share going to education was 13% – again larger than any other single item except general administration.[18]

The report recommended fundamental reforms that centred on cost-analysis, which pitted the economic returns of primary education against those of the tertiary sector. The report explained the calculation:

> Given Africa's extreme shortage of fiscal resources and the many claims on revenue, all educational strategies must have a key objective of greater efficiency in resource use.

African education is expensive not only in the sense that it absorbs a significant share of public sector resources; it is expensive also in terms of average cost per pupil, especially at the higher level. African governments spend as much per university student as countries with per capita incomes at least three times and as much as eight times higher. By contrast primary education is cheap in comparison with industrialized countries. Primary education cost per student year as a per cent of per capita GNP in Africa are about as much as in other developing areas; secondary education costs are 4 to 5 times as much and higher education costs 5 to 10 times as much.[19]

While the report provided the blueprint for higher education reform in the 1980s, it was criticized by a World Bank report in 1989. On education the report recognized that tight budgets in the 1980s had led to a decline in primary to post-secondary education. Indeed, education had been the focus of an important report the previous year, *Education in sub-Saharan Africa*.[20] By the end of the decade it had become obvious to the World Bank that there was a need to improve human resources. The 1989 report even stated that donors should fund capital expenditure in tertiary education.[21] The effect of years of reform was clear: the rapid decline in salaries and the deterioration of higher education had led to shortfalls in doctors, managers, accountants and economists. The crisis even forced Babangida, the military ruler in Nigeria, to set up a presidential task force on the brain drain in 1988. As Sandbrook argued, 'A widespread decline in the quality of secondary and university education in the 1980s aggravated the problem of finding qualified staff. Economic crisis and budget cutbacks have deprived educational institutions of the resources they require.'[22]

Even so, the reforms did not go far enough for some. At the 1986 African vice-chancellors' conference in Harare, the World Bank questioned the very existence of universities in Africa.[23] Another conference two years later described the bleak state of higher education ravaged by structural adjustment. The conference – Human Dimensions of Africa's Economic Recovery and Development – noted that far from structural adjustment increasing the rate of primary school enrolment, the opposite was the case as all sectors of education had suffered:

> Primary school enrolment declined by 65% between 1980–5. Secondary school enrolment during the same period dropped from 13.7% to 10.9%. And in higher education, the annual enrolment declined by 66% between 1980–5. …
>
> The drastic growth in brain drain involving middle and high-level manpower is another disturbing trend. A joint ECA/ILO report estimated that, in six months to 1987, 70,000 Africans left the continent, up from 40,000 in 1985. This represents approximately 30% of Africa's skilled human resources. While the lucky ones flee to Europe, those less fortunate take up jobs as teachers and doctors in some of South Africa's homelands.[24]

The argument running through the reports was that reprioritization will ensure African countries a more equal distribution of resources across the education sector. Critics of the reforms following these reports noted after five years of SAPs, social spending in sub-Saharan African countries declined by 26 per cent (between 1980 and 1986). Governments already facing financial crisis were forced to cut subsidies to secondary and tertiary level students. The World Bank responded by claiming that it intended to reorganize funding on education because for too long governments had regarded universities as sacred cows, when in reality they were bloated, overfunded and inefficient.[25]

In a report for the World Bank, Kelly sought to describe the nature of postcolonial education typical of Africa. Zambia had suffered a severe economic crisis in 1977 with the collapsing price of copper, the country's leading export. The fall in copper prices meant that by 1977 Zambia, which depended on copper for half its GDP, received no income from its most important resource.[26] Despite the crisis the government continued to increase funding in higher education to the detriment of primary and secondary schools. This led Kelly to argue that 'too much was devoted to the refined needs of too few at the higher level, and too little to the general needs of too many at the lower level.'[27] In addition, the report concluded that higher education was inefficient, citing the tradition of not charging fees.

The World Bank argued that, unlike higher education, the primary sector had a higher return on investment, 28 per cent against 13 per cent for tertiary education. As Caffentzis explains, 'In other words university graduates received about two and half times more income over outlay than the government; and they received from the government thirty times more than ... primary students.'[28] Reports pointed out that while the white collar sector comprised 6 per cent of the population they received in state revenue more than 27 per cent of the education budget.[29] The World Bank maintained that the thrust of its policies was to ensure a more egalitarian allocation of funding: by reallocating funds from urban elites an educational egalitarianism could be achieved.

In Senegal, despite almost two decades of structural adjustment and a concerted effort in the 1990s from the World Bank and IMF to force the government to enrol fewer students into higher education, enrolment has increased (some estimate that there were more than 30,000 students at UCAD in 2006). The higher education sector was still absorbing roughly 27 per cent of the national education budget in 2001, whereas primary education received 38.4 per cent of the budget.[30] World Bank and IMF reforms have been unsuccessful.

There is considerable controversy over the number of university students in sub-Saharan Africa. According to one important study there are fewer than 500,000 students in higher education in the whole of Africa.[31] Considering that there is a continental population of about 500 million, that makes roughly one student per 1000 people. This figure is unreliable. Mama states that, 'Gross enrolment in African universities increased dramatically ... to over 1.75 million in 1995 and are still growing fast in most places.'[32] Caffentzis states that in 1986 the enrolment rates for higher education were about 2 per cent of the pertinent age group; this had reached 3 per cent by 1995.[33] This means that Africa has among the lowest enrolment rates in the world, much lower than Latin America's 12 per cent, and 7 per cent for the developing world as a whole. Moja summarizes the available data, 'participation rates overall still remain low in Africa ... based on the percentage of total population were reported to be 3 per cent'.[34] However, there are no reliable figures for sub-Saharan Africa, and Mama's enrolment numbers are contested by Teferra and Altbach.[35] This is largely because under the impact of World Bank and IMF reforms in the 1980s cash-strapped universities stopped producing their own statistics. But at the same time these organizations demanded figures on student enrolment in order to assess the progress of reforms. Often institutions were left to make up numbers that had previously been collated by the university administration. Enrolment rates rates for the first period of World Bank and IMF reforms can be seen from Tables 2.1 and 2.2.

But one fact escapes these statistics. Universities and student numbers have increased massively since independence. In 1960 the continent could boast 42 universities; by the beginning of the twenty-first century this number had increased to more than 400. Although this increase was fuelled by a growth in private educational establishments during a period of liberalization since the 1980s, the expansion is still significant. Student growth has also exploded. According to one study student numbers trebled from 782,503 in 1975 to 3,461,822 (a figure for the whole continent), this represents an increase of 17 per cent per annum compared with a global rate of 5 per cent.[36] Yet even here there is great national variation. In Egypt, for example, 22 per cent of the age cohort is in post-secondary education, while in Tanzania the figure is 0.3 per cent and in some sub-Saharan African countries, like the Gambia, São Tomé and Djibouti, there is either no university system or one with fewer than 10,000 students.

However, various reports disguise the huge discrepancies within the Third World so that the enrolment rates for Africa are lost in the figure for the Third World as a whole (see Table 2.1). This has the effect of disguising the stagnant and in some cases falling enrolment figures for Africa. Table 2.2 clarifies the situation on the continent.

Table 2.1: The evolution of enrolment rates, 1980–95

	Least dev. country%	*Less dev.%*	*World total%*	*Dev.%*
1980	2	4	11	36
1985	2	4	12	38
1990	2	6	13	48
1995	3	6	15	62

Source: World Bank 2000.

However, there are wide differences within sub-Saharan Africa. The university system varies widely across the region as the following examples illustrate. The two public universities in Zaire had a combined enrolment of approximately 2000 students in 1960 at the time of the country's independence.[37] Five years after independence the gross enrolment rate in the country was still bouncing around zero; at the same time the figure for Latin America was about 4 per cent (see Table 2.2). By 1995 enrolment on a single course offered at the university could exceed the entire number of students at the university 30 years earlier. The World Bank reports that in the academic year 1995/6 'nearly 2500 freshmen packed a single class in biomedical sciences'.[38]

Makerere University is an example of higher education in Africa celebrated by the World Bank. According to research,[39] the university managed to extricate itself from a crisis in the early 1990s, returning to its former pre-eminence as one of the foremost universities in East Africa. The World Bank highlights how the university has managed to increase enrolment rates and the number of students paying fees: almost 70 per cent of the student population were contributing towards their fees by the end of the 1990s. While previously the university was funded completely by the national government, today 30 per cent of revenue is raised internally.[40] The World Bank emphasizes the case of Makerere to stress the importance of releasing universities from state funding and control in Africa, 'The Makerere accomplishment has lessons for other universities in Africa that face similar resource constraints. It shows that expansion – and the maintenance of quality – can be achieved simultaneously in a context of reduced state funding. It puts to rest the notion that the state must be the sole provider of higher education in Africa.'[41]

Table 2.2: Gross Enrolment Rates

	Secondary		Tertiary			
Year	1965	'95	'65	'75	'85	'95
Low/middle income	21	55	4	7	7	10
Sub-Saharan Africa	5	25	1	1	2	3
East Asia/Pacific	23	64	5	5	4	7
South Asia	24	44	4	7	8	6
Europe/Central Asia	39	83	9	14	13	32
Latin America/Caribbean	19	55	4	13	16	18
Middle East/North Africa	20	62	3	7	11	15

Source: World Bank 2000.

Makerere would seem to be the preferred example of the success of neo-liberal reforms in higher education on the continent. Yet, in a devastating critique of these reforms, Obong asks 'In light of the fact that the reforms have yielded spectacular increases in the university's revenue, why have they not translated into a generally improved quality of teaching?'[42] Although there has been a massive growth in student numbers, from 7344 in 1993/4 to 26,700 by 2001, student grievances are typical of many on the continent: large class sizes, staff dictating or giving ready-made lecture notes to students, departments abandoning class tutorials and seminars and 'as many as 60 per cent of the students in some big classes failing semester examinations'.[43] Obong concludes that it is the neo-liberal 'fixation on costs and finances, they have emphasized quantifiable aspects such as the expansion of access ... introduction of "demand-driven" courses' and this has created a situation where staff have 'sought to adapt to the new changes in ways that directly enhanced their individual financial and material benefits. There was not much concern about what would happen to the students' learning and to the eventual output of the institution'.[44]

However, a series of academic studies have recently been published to emphasize the importance of higher education reform in Africa. They stress that higher education in Africa only has a future in emulating the liberalization of several key African universities.[45] As the preface to the series describes:

> Much of sub-Saharan Africa has suffered deep stagnation over the last two decades and is staggering under the weight of domestic and international conflict, disease, poverty, corruption and natural disaster. Its universities – once the shining lights of intellectual excitement and promise – suffered from enormous decline in the government resources for education. In the last half of the last decade however this began to change in a number of countries. … Our interest was captured by the renewal and resurgence that we saw in several African nations and at their universities brought about by stabilization, democratization, decentralization and economic liberalization.[46]

This quotation is remarkable for its absence of concern for the role of external factors in the sub-continent's decline. Indeed, the case studies that make up the series are highly contradictory.[47]

The World Bank envisaged the total transformation of the university system in Africa, from the reforms aimed at creating centres of excellence for a smaller number of students of high quality. For many students who would have previously gravitated towards higher education, a system of on-the-job training was envisaged that would be provided by the private sector and subsidized by the government, where worker students would receive training for lower wages. In primary and secondary education, schools would be run by local communities, religious institutions and private companies that would pay for the cost of teaching staff and the upkeep of buildings. In Senegal, Dakar has returned to being the educational focal point for the subregion, with students making pilgrimages to an almost entirely privatized pedagogical world. The city has been turned into a training centre; according to a recent pamphlet advertising *Enseignement supérieur* there are now 80 public and private establishments almost all based in the capital Dakar and offering an array of internationally recognized degrees, certificates and diplomas. Most of these schools, colleges and universities are private (65 are private and 15 public), and the majority of their students come from elsewhere in West Africa. The massive expansion in private colleges is connected to the liberalization of higher education in Senegal since 1994.[48]

The privatization of higher education is linked to these processes. In the last 15 years there has been a proliferation of private universities, colleges and polytechnics across the continent, offering a variety of internationally recognized diplomas, certificates and entrepreneurial training. In 2000 one study identified a total of 80 private universities in Africa. In her study of private education in six countries in Africa, Thaver argued that the decrease in state-sponsored higher education has promoted the rise of private institutions. She identifies two forms of private universities. First, not-for-profit private universities with an explicit religious orientation, 'the private universities in Kenya have a Christian affiliation, while the universities of Mbale (Uganda) and Zanzibar (Tanzania) have an Islamic orientation'.[49] The second category are explicitly for-profit institutions that have an entirely different approach; managed by groups of educational entrepreneurs they specialize in business courses that include 'marketing, administration, management, accountancy, banking and finance offered at certificate and diploma levels (in the case of Nigeria and Ghana) and degree levels (in the case of Kenya and Zimbabwe)'.[50]

Many of the premises that form the backbone of the World Bank proposals appear to make sense. Certainly, one cannot dispute that primary education in the context of limited national budgets should be a priority or that higher education should also aim for high quality. Some commentators have argued that World

Bank reforms and reshifting provision back to primary education are the only serious and viable options for African economies.[51]

A central question in considering these arguments is the effect of SAPs on social policy and economic development in Africa. SAPs have deepened the crisis that afflicts sub-Saharan society.[52] The reality for students and lecturers on much of the continent could not differ more from the image the World Bank presents of higher education as spoilt and over bloated. Higher education in Africa does not thrive, but in many places faces a battle for survival. If the objective is to streamline higher education then the question that needs answering is: where from? Africa has the lowest enrolment rates in higher education of any region in the world; further restrictions would limit access to higher education to an almost imperceptible minority of privileged and elite students.

As Caffentzis puts it, 'any policy that lowers enrolment rates – hovering now near zero – can be seen as a policy of academic exterminism.'[53] There is also a further dimension to the debate. The World Bank is correct to maintain that there is excessive demand for higher education in Africa. Young people see the university system as a crucial entry point to work and a way to escape poverty. The effect of the crisis that has gripped many African economies is to leave youth without any prospect of work. Politicized youth, or the youth factor,[54] has fuelled conflict in Africa, where youth have been recruited to movements of social breakdown in Sierra Leone, Ivory Coast, Senegal and Zimbabwe. Youth in this context has not, as Richards argued, supplanted ethnicity, but has often turned secessionist and political conflicts in Africa into ethnic-youth movements. The tendency to deprioritize higher education in the Third World has been an important contributing factor to these conflicts.[55]

If the World Bank advocates a system of loans and fees – introduced almost without exception across Africa – then there needs to be a pool of students able to take up and pay the loans. This is contingent on two factors, real wages that can sustain the loans and fees, and employment for students after graduation to ensure repayment of the loans. There is an additional problem connected to the relationship between primary and tertiary education. If the World Bank wants to expand primary education, then there must be a complementary expansion of teaching graduates from universities. Caffentzis argues therefore that the yearly influx from tertiary education must increase by 10 per cent a year but an enrolment growth rate of 1 per cent cannot keep up with the stated demands of expanding primary education and the World Bank is 'subverting its own alleged objective: the expansion and improvement of primary education.'[56]

The centrepiece of World Bank reform for higher education in Africa (and the Third World) was the economic return on educational provision. In resource strapped economies limited funds must not be diverted to the low returns of higher education but must re-emphasize the primary and secondary sectors where there are higher real returns on the money invested from state budgets. This approach has the effect of reducing education to a zero-sum game that places primary education in a competitive struggle with higher and university education. A World Bank funded report in 2000 included an important criticism of the approach previously taken by the Bank: 'Since the 1980s, many national governments and international donors have assigned higher education a relatively low priority. Narrow – and, in our view, misleading – economic analysis has contributed to the view that public investment in universities and colleges brings meagre returns compared with investment in primary and secondary schools, and that higher education magnifies income inequality.'[57]

The report notes that although 85 per cent of the world's population live in the Third World, less than half the world's 80 million students in higher education are from those countries. Another insider critique stressed the problems for students in the Third World: 'they are taught by poorly-qualified, poorly-motivated and (no surprise) poorly-compensated faculty, struggling with inadequate facilities and outmoded curricula. The secondary education system has often failed to prepare these students adequately for advanced study – and, once on campus, political activism, violence, cheating, corruption and discrimination can undermine their progress.'[58]

These are not reasons to undermine higher education but, on

the contrary, 'We have educated more and more young people to primary and secondary level – but, like Oliver Twist, they want more! They realize something that even the richest governments are only beginning to wake up to: in today's world higher education is basic education. Education that is needed by the masses – and can no longer be confined to a tiny elite.'[59] But this argument regards the university sector as a system to generate national elites, to respond to the challenges of globalization and 'to promote prosperity among people with talent and motivation, irrespective of their social origins'.[60]

Some commentators argue that these criticisms represent a major shift in World Bank thinking on the role of higher education. Moja cites a 2002 World Bank report by Richard Hopper that argues that higher education, contrary to almost two decades of Bank research, does have an important role to play in development.[61] This apparent shift in Bank thinking can, as Pithouse explains, 'best be understood as part of a broader shift by the Bank towards a rhetorical commitment to participation and empowerment',[62] as a way of seeking more effective ways of structural adjustment implementation. There are few signs that the World Bank or IMF are willing to help reverse the devastation wrought by 20 years of the reforms they orchestrated across the continent.

New student movements or the descent into corporatism?

There is a risk of exceptionalizing higher education in Africa, of seeing the university system as uniquely affected by catastrophe and crisis. The literature tends to emphasize the same tragedy, with students and youth seen as the quintessential lost generation.[63] Can we speak, as Barkan[64] did 30 years ago, of an African pattern dividing the behaviour of African university students and European and American ones? The implication in this example was that students in the West were driven by higher political ideals. Alidou et al. are unequivocal about the question: 'we can speak today of an international student movement, and that African students are paying by far the heaviest cost for the effort this movement is making to reverse the corporate agenda by which education is being reshaped worldwide.'[65] The argument finds a parallel in Boren[66] whose global survey of student resistance makes a case for the same pan-student approach.

There is an important divide in the literature on student activism that has ramifications for understanding student politics not just in the current period but historically. One strand of opinion is propagated by the editorial board of the important American newsletter Committee for Academic Freedom in Africa (CAFA) and summarized in *A Thousand Flowers*, a collection of essays by the same authors of the newsletter. Their arguments are very persuasive: they state their objectives in the introduction to the collection:

> Although the state is the immediate perpetrator, the ultimate responsibility for many violations of academic rights on the African campuses is borne by international financial institutions and more specifically, by the policy of 'adjustment' adopted by Washington and the European Union in the 1980s, that calls for the virtual recolonization of Africa's educational systems.
>
> The attack on the universities is part of a broader attack on the place of Africa in the International Division of Labor, on the value of African workers, and on the capacity of Africans to achieve self-determination, the still unrealized goal of the anti-colonial struggle.
>
> Defending the struggles of students and teachers in Africa is to defend the right of the African youth to study. This means the right to have equal access, with European and North American youth, and the youth of other countries across the world, to the knowledge and the wealth produced internationally, rather than being condemned to poverty and migration, the lot reserved for them in the plans of international financial institutions now ruling Africa's political economy.[67]

They have provided a running critique of the policies of the World Bank and IMF in Africa from the point of view of popular protest and student resistance.[68] They maintain that in the escalation of student protest since the introduction of SAPs in Africa from the early 1980s there has emerged a new 'pan-African student movement, continuous in its political aspirations with the student activism that developed in the context of the anti-colonial struggle, and yet more radical in its challenges to the established political power'.[69] The effects of SAPs have massively proletarianized the African student body, breaking them from their recent postcolonial past as members of the elite.[70]

The partial withdrawal of the state from higher education in Africa has altered the nature of elite formation at the university. Much of the literature confirms these arguments. Konings makes a similar point to CAFA in reference to the student rebellions in the late 1980s and early 1990s:

> As a result of such state withdrawal, African universities no longer appeared to be serving as centres of elite formation. ... Little wonder that they have been inclined to see corrupt and authoritarian regimes as responsible for their predicament and to perceive a 'democratic transition' as a necessary condition for change in society in general and in universities in particular.[71]

Equally, Mamdani has seen a similar development as part of a process transforming the African class system, where the limited expansion of the African middle classes after independence has been reversed as state directed initiatives receded from the 1970s onwards. The impact on higher education was clear: 'the growth in a state-financed higher and secondary education sector, whose enrolment came less and less from affluent families, went alongside shrinking opportunities for middle class advancement in a crisis-prone economy.'[72]

There has been a process of institutional liberalization that caused the explosions in student activism in recent years. The new proletarianized student population that has resisted SAPs, and their application to higher education, has created a qualitatively different form of student activism. This allows us to view the 'present phase of student activism not as a set of separate struggles but as one pan-African student movement'.[73]

Some writers and activists argue that there was a convergence of forces between previously privileged – now proletarianized – students and the urban poor. The case is put most forcefully by the former student leader at UZ, Brian Kagoro, referring to a period of activism in the mid-1990s:

> so you now had students supporting their parents on their student stipends, which were not enough, because their parents had been laid off work. So, in a sense, as poverty increases you have a reconvergence of these forces. And the critique started ... around issues of social economic justice, [the] right to a living wage ... students started couching their demands around a right to livelihood.[74]

Seddon raises similar themes, broadly defining these new popular forces as including the urban and rural working classes as well as other categories like the so-called lumpenproletariat, day labourers and the unemployed, workers in the informal sector, small (and sometimes medium) peasants, small retailers, craftsmen, artisans and petty commodity producers.[75] If we extend Kagoro's argument we can say that the social expectations (and pauperization) of students converged with these forces during the period of structural adjustment. However, to the concept of proletarianization we need to add a layer of meaning. It is not meant in the sense the authors of *A Thousand Flowers* describe, namely that university students come from increasingly proletarian backgrounds. That would seem to miss the essential point that university students have seen their status collapse, along with every social class. These are general processes that have seen the decimation of classes previously regarded as privileged – teachers, university lecturers, civil servants and white collar workers.

As Harrison noted, 'One can see the decline of corporatism and the increasing informalization of the urban economy [as] ... the reformulation of ... political identities into a realm of fiscal austerity and speculation.'[76] The hybridization of these social forces that bring together exceedingly motley groups has altered the mobilization and activism of students. An important study at Nairobi and Moi universities in Kenya reinforced these arguments. Mwinzi found that the majority of the 366 students in the survey were forced to engage in income generating activities (IGAs) because a wave of neo-liberal reforms since the early 1990s had forced cost-sharing onto students. Most of the respondents came from 'families where financial resources are insufficient to meet all their obligations'.[77] The majority ran businesses providing essential services to students, including foodstuffs (23.3 per cent) and computer services (16.1 per cent), while the sale of alcohol, cigarettes and drugs made up the overwhelming majority of IGAs, while nearly 40 per cent claimed they were forced to work to meet accommodation, food and transport costs. But, with mass graduate unemployment, such work fulfilled another function – it prepared students for a life in the informal economy. As the study concluded, 'the majority of the respondents resorted to running some form of business as a survival mechanism ... [but] also ... as a training ground and basis for future employment.'[78]

These arguments contrast with much of the commentary. For example, Bathily et al. reverse the categorization made by CAFA and *A Thousand Flowers*. It is necessary, they argue, to separate student activism from its perceived heyday in the 1960s and 1970s to the disintegration of the movement over the last 20 years. Today students are written off, 'left with their daily corporatism and the inefficiency of their fights'.[79] Yesterday they were harbingers of a brighter future. 'If prior to World War II students tacitly accepted being petty bourgeois with colonial linkages, up to the mid-1970s they claimed a left vanguard status.'[80] They make their argument by charting the evolution of student activism:

> But at the end of the day, they only managed some vigils with hardly any support. They appeared at most as the enlightened conscience of their people on the path to com-

plete emancipation and modernization. They managed to shift from their role as supporters of the Western system ... to that of rejecting it totally. ... By the late 1970s ... students saw themselves [as] ... political and economic failures.[81]

The argument asserts that with the collapse of the post-colonial social pact, student engagement has become corporatist and concerned only with bread and butter issues. In the case of Senegal, 'by the late 1970s Senegalese students saw themselves more modestly as symbols of the independent stalemate, of the political and economic failure of a regime which was unable to provide them with clear survival prospects.' Students, following this argument, have lost their status, 'from providers of modernity they became aid applicants'.[82] The respected scholar Donal Cruise O'Brien makes a similar point about students protesting in defence of their elite status: 'And students will riot for their privileges too ... defending their "right" to better scholarship.'[83]

While these arguments tend to avoid the heroic discourse of students 'counterposing and confronting the abuses of state power',[84] they miss the novelty in the wave of popular protest that has swept Africa in the last 15 years. Far from understanding the role of students in the democratic transition[85] as part of a generalized revolt, they tend to dismiss the significance of student revolt. Federici sees 'students struggle to defend education as "an inalienable right" they are fighting not in defense [sic] of a privilege or a corporatist interest, but against it.'[86] Students are, on the contrary, attempting to 'reverse the corporate agenda by which education is being reshaped world-wide'.[87]

There is, however, a tendency in CAFA and *A Thousand Flowers* to downplay the ambiguity of student protest. While they describe the significance and celebrate the resistance of the student population in Africa they miss the way student movements have been depoliticized and subject to manipulation and co-option. They capture the novelty of the new resistance among students but neglect the new directions that this activism can take. Students today are 'situated in a complex field of societal power, class interest ... and moral positions'[88] that create, in conditions of social breakdown, unique and challenging forms of activism.

Students and the democratic transition

In his popular history of student resistance, Boren notes that the last decade of the millennium saw students in Africa play a leading role in the democratic transition. 'In the wake of Eastern European revolutions against Communism, and the rampant local economic difficulties, many African students increased pro-democracy efforts and campaigned for the establishment of multiple-party political systems.'[89] Commentators celebrated the student revolts across Africa: 'political liberalization, starting at the end of the 1980s unleashed an unprecedented wave of student rebellion on university campuses in West and Central Africa.'[90] News reports of the day were replete with analyses of democratic struggles in Africa, often questioning the role of students.[91] Still, there is a recognized lack of serious research on the role of students in democratic transition.[92] Students were part of the broad and popular alliances that developed between opposition groups during and immediately after the processes of democratic change.

Perhaps it is advisable to express caution about the connection often (lazily) made between events in Africa and Eastern Europe. Boren makes the common assumption that the events in Africa in the early 1990s were a direct corollary of the revolutions that swept aside the Stalinist regimes in Eastern Europe. This idea received some support from incumbent regimes conscious of the events in Europe. Mazrui has questioned these assumptions: 'we cannot trace all democratic forces in Africa to the ... impact of Eastern Europe.'[93] Mazrui states that the origins of these move-ments can be properly traced back to earlier acts of democratic struggle – long predating the upheavals in Eastern Europe (see Table 2.3). Indeed, some commentators state that the origins of these movements are found in the first wave of bread riots in Egypt in 1977 and early anti-SAP revolts.[94]

Mazrui continues to press his point, 'What should be borne in mind is that the role model for Africa has not been necessarily the impact of demonstrations across the Berlin Wall. It has been youthful riots against armed apartheid.'[95] Although the influence of pan-African struggles has an important impact on the mobilization of student and trade union militants, it was the shared nature of the economic crisis gripping Africa that brought these movements together.[96] Still, it is important not to discount the effect of the changes in the Soviet Union and Eastern Europe. These countries had functioned as the ideological glue for generations of left-wing activists, students and intellectuals, as well as providing scholarships for students to the Soviet bloc.[97] The dismantling of these regimes undermined both the states in Africa politically connected and funded by the Soviet Union, and the political confidence of militants and intellectuals whose ideological moorings had been tied to Stalinism. Mazrui summarized the main points at the time:

> The speedy abandonment of one-partyism by Eastern European countries has made it harder for its African champions to carry adequate conviction on its behalf. It is in that sense that glasnost and perestroika in Eastern Europe and the Soviet Union have helped the cause of the liberal revival in Africa – though that liberal revival was already underway regardless of events in Europe.[98]

While these events might have broken the confidence of an older generation of activists, they gave new life to student politics, which many argued had collapsed irredeemably into corporatism and factionalism. In 1989 the movement started in the West African state of Benin when students demonstrated against the government in January, demanding overdue grants and a guarantee of public sector employment after graduation.[99]

Students at the University of Kinshasa in Zaire were the first to initiate the protests that almost unseated Mobutu, and led to a largely urban protest movement and transition that lasted into the mid-1990s.[100] They demonstrated on 5 May 1990 asserting that the reforms the dictator had announced ten days previously were irrevocable. The demonstration ended violently after security forces attacked it. The students immediately issued an appeal for other universities and colleges across the country to rise up in solidarity, 'Do not cross your arms. Follow our example. The dictatorship is finished. We cannot go back. Take on the state. Demonstrate! March!'[101]

The call to arms was answered. Students at the University of Lubumbashi responded to it by demonstrating daily in the city and at the university from 9 May. On 11 May a student uprising in Katanga (the southernmost region of Zaire) was brought to a swift and violent end when the president sent a squadron of death to the university.

Table 2.3: Incidents of student activism during the democratic transition 1985–95

Year	Number of incidents
1985	6
1986	5
1987	10
1988	6
1989	11
1990	11
1991	15
1992	15
1993	16
1994	22
1995	5

Source: Federici (2000, p. 112)

Dozens of students who had led the strikes and demonstrations were killed and their bodies disappeared. Their parents were unable to complain. Without wider protests the students could be picked off, killed and isolated. For thousands the massacre in Lubumbashi exposed the true nature of Mobutu's reforms. There was strong condemnation of the massacre from humanitarian organizations, and the Belgian government announced the immediate suspension of official bilateral assistance to Zaire. After some procrastination and strenuous denial of the reports, Mobutu authorized an official parliamentary enquiry, as a result of which a provincial governor and other senior local officials were arrested and charged with having organized the killing of one student and the injury of 13 others. Despite a news blackout, it emerged that the massacre had sparked serious clashes between students and government forces in other towns, including Kisangani, Bukavu and Mbanza-Ngungu. The massacre was in many ways pivotal to the early stages of the transition in Zaire, and it is still the subject of controversy and debate.[102]

Students were crucial to spearheading resistance in Zimbabwe. In 1989 a student leaflet denounced the investment code, which further facilitated foreign investment in Zimbabwe, 'as a further entrenchment of capitalism in Zimbabwe, ... an acquiescence to the IMF and World Bank sponsored programmes ... and incompatible with the doctrine of socialism'. Many students attended the May Day rallies in Harare, while the students' union condemned the suppression of a strike by doctors: 'The use of force which was exercised on Doctors while they were airing their clear, legitimate grievances is really an authoritarian and neofascist tendency and hence it has to be condemned.'[103] When the university was closed on 4 October 1989 following the arrest of student union leaders for organizing a celebration of the previous year's anti-corruption demonstration, the general secretary of the Zimbabwe Congress of Trade Unions (ZCTU), Morgan Tsvangirai, denounced the closure in strong terms and was detained for more than four weeks. At the 1991 May Day celebrations, the ZCTU organized the event under the theme 'Liberalization or Liberation'. Workers paraded with banners denouncing SAPs: 'Employers liberated, workers sacrificed'; 'Are we going to make 1991 the year of the World Bank storm?' ; 'The year of the people's misery'. Meanwhile, the Ministry of Labour distributed its own leaflets telling workers to 'Suffer Now and Benefit later'.[104] The criticism of the ZCTU mirrored that of the UZ students' union.[105]

In Mali, according to one important account, it was not university students but young unemployed college graduates who initiated the first protests on 15 October 1990 against the one-party state. The mobilization was small, roughly 15 young men marched through the centre of the capital with banners that declared 'Down with the UDPM [Union Démocratique du Peuple Malien]'. The demonstrators were attacked and arrested by the police. As Brenner contends, 'their initiative immediately preceded, and may well have helped to precipitate, the emergence into public of the clandestine opposition movement which had been actively organizing and plotting for some years against the regime of Moussa Traoré.'[106]

The collapse into sectarian factionalism affected the student body when the transition was frustrated or after it had been achieved. The examples of Mali and Cameroon are illustrative of these processes. Mali experienced a period of democratic transition at the same time as other countries in the region. There had been major demonstrations against Moussa Traoré's regime in January 1990, when thousands were involved in street protests demanding political reform and an end to Traoré's 22-year rule. The government was finally bought down in April 1991. The central role of students inside the Association des Elèves et Etudiants du Mali (AEEM) in the democratic transition is widely recognized.[107] A memorandum listing student demands in return for an immediate end to strikes was issued. It included a 50 per cent rise in the scholarship, followed by a further 25 per cent in six months, the increase of the scholarship to include secondary school pupils and physical improvements to the university and schools. While there was a widely recognized appreciation of the justness of these demands there was a similar understanding by the government that they could not hope to meet them. Within a short space of time the new government of Alpha Oumar Konaré confronted the wrath of his erstwhile political allies.[108]

By 1993 students in AEEM were calling for action against the government for failing to honour the promises made in the memorandum. Class boycotts, strikes and demonstrations punctuated the following years. In 1993 the AEEM leadership was divided between those supporting the government and those arguing for more militant action. The government was keen to exploit these divisions: 'In response to this unrest, the government attempted to manipulate divisions within the AEEM leadership by funding a "palace coup" in which a faction of the student leaders ... tried to replace the elected leader.'[109] One student expressed the dilemmas for many AEEM leaders with the recent experience of the revolution (democratic transition):

> I was young, I still am and I love Alpha and marched with ADEMA [Alliance pour la Démocratie au Mali] during the revolution to bring down Moussa. Imagine, I am a student leader and I am called by the president of my country, he invites me to his office and flatters me telling me how much potential I have. He then tells me that our activities are threatening democracy and asks for my help to save the country. I thought then what I did was in the best interest of democracy.[110]

The government carried on manipulating the student movement, providing scholarships to foreign universities for several leading members of AEEM. By 1995 the student union was so divided that it had lost the support of the population and could only rely on the fractured and intermittent loyalty of its own members. AEEM even split at one point with a new organization calling itself 'Friends of the Schools', which, amid accusations that it was funded by the government, argued in favour of opening schools and resuming classes. The rupture with the ruling party was complete by the time of the next elections, and the damage to the AEEM seemingly irreparable. Student protests were broken up by tear gas and students who had previously declared their love of Alpha 'burned campaign posters of Konaré and banners of the ADEMA party'.[111]

The experience of democratic transition in Cameroon contrasts with many of the examples already given. The process of political liberalization was protracted and violent, yet it provided students with a space in which to express themselves.[112] This expression took both a party and ethnic line. The government exploited these differences, which resulted in the emergence of two groups at the University of Yaoundé. The student body was divided between strangers, students organized in a student parliament aligned to the opposition, and indigenous Beti students loyal to the ruling regime and organized in the Committee for Self-Defence and the Beti Militia. The nature of the democratic transition led to the violence and disruption at the university that continued practically unabated from 1990 to 1996.

Students at the University of Yaoundé were deemed to be relatively privileged: the low level of political activism prior to 1991 testifies to this fact. Even in the late 1970s, when openings for university graduates began to shrink, President Ahidjo and then his successor Paul Biya forced vacancies for them in the state administration. Student numbers at the university exceeded 40,000 in 1992 although the conditions for students and staff were diabolical.[113] However, there was a high degree of political repression that outlawed student organizations, and police spies disguised as students repeatedly infiltrated the campus. The political liberalization of the 1990s combined with deep dissatisfaction at the deterioration of conditions under the impact of SAPs. The introduction of multi-partyism did not cleanse the regime of undemocratic habits but led them to use the liberalization to divide the student body. As early as March 1991, *Jeune Afrique* had noted the contradiction in the progress of the democratic transition in Cameroon; one article was titled 'Le pluralisme en marche au Cameroun, mais l'Etat est en panne'.[114]

The regional and ethnic cleavages became more prominent after the formation of the opposition SDF, which was founded in Anglophone Cameroon and received its initial support from the predominant Bamileke of the region. The reaction of the regime and Beti supporters was to form support groups, including the Commando Delta, Direct Action and the National Front for Beti Liberation. The support that the SDF did receive in the southern capital Yaoundé was frequently from the Anglo-Bami communities living in the city. National political cleavages found a similar expression in the political activism of students on the campus. The president exploited ethnic divisions, emphasizing his Beti origins and allying Beti students on the campus to the ruling Cameroon People's Democratic Movement (CPDM), explicitly opposed to Anglophone Bamileke strangers who often regarded the Anglophone John Fru Ndi in the Social Democratic Front (SDF) as their champion. Although there were historical roots to the crisis that now afflicted Cameroon and the university, they were not expressed so virulently in the period prior to political liberalization. Student MPs seeing themselves as revolutionaries were allied to militant elements in the opposition who saw the overthrow of the regime as the only answer to the political stalemate in the country and at the university. The Committee for Self-Defence attempted to respond to the perceived threat from opposition members on the campus, regarding the objectives of parliament as tantamount to the destruction of their university and country. Committee members – a small minority of students – were permitted to carry knives, clubs and guns to intimidate MPs and worked in tandem with other vigilante groups. Student parliament formed its own self-defence groups.[115]

The first political crisis at the university occurred in 1990, when students marched in favour of the SDF and multi-partyism. This led to the permanent presence of gendarmes – or *ninja*s as students called them – on the campus. Students used the political opening allowed in the country at the time to set up their first autonomous organizations, which, as we have seen, quickly became polarized. By 1991, along with the opposition, students called for a sovereign national conference, a political formation that was a popular demand during the democratic transitions in Africa. The year ended with a prolonged student strike at the late payment of scholarships. As the chaos on the campus escalated over the next few years the university authorities resorted to further desperate measures. In 1993 the university chancellor Peter Aghor Tabi ordered the Beti militias on the campus to step up their attacks on students.

By 1996 another group directly affiliated to Biya's party, PRESBY (President Biya's Youth), had replaced the self-defence groups. Like earlier formations, this group was a constellation of university students and other sections of the educated youth either engaged in informal-sector activities or unemployed, including university graduates. The process of political liberalization in Cameroon demonstrates diverse patterns of political behaviour and activism in the period of democratic transition.

Two more recent examples of student unrest illustrate again the continuity of state repression after the transition. The Ethiopian student movement has suffered particularly harsh repression, but no more so than in the recent period of transition. The overthrow of the Derg dictatorship in 1991 by the Ethiopian People's Revolutionary Front saw a continuation of violence directed at student unrest. Escalating during the border war with Eritrea between 1998 and 2000, student activists led a strike in April 2001 demanding academic freedom. The state's response was swift, 40 students were killed, more than 400 wounded and approximately 3000 arrested. Throughout 2002 student demonstrations, strikes and protest across the country's four regional universities were greeted with torture and killing. Predictably, international condemnation of this systematic rule of academic terror was stifled, Zeleza explains why: 'International protest against this regime ... became muted after September 11, 2001, as Ethiopia became a "frontline state" in the US war on terrorism'.[116]

Kenya's political transition was heralded by the victory of the National Rainbow Coalition in national elections in December 2002. The new government took a familiar path. Students inspired by the victory took their own action in January 2003, insisting the administration at the University of Nairobi reinstate the Student Organization of Nairobi University that had been banned since 2001. Following their lead, students at Kenyatta University staged a two-day sit-in calling for the resignation of the dictatorial vice-chancellor. The rising wave of student protests was greeted by the 'chagrin of the new government'.[117] Students do not appear, in these examples, as a permanent political avant-garde, but rather as contradictory social actors, prone to political manipulation and division. While the defining elements in student protests are the wider configurations of political forces involved in the democratic transition.

Conclusions

Students were not isolated political actors behaving simply as a democratic vanguard; they were neither demons nor democrats, as some commentary has expressed the distinction.[118] Their role in the democratic transitions was complex because it was inextricably tied to the liberalization of political space and the manipulations of these processes by incumbent governments and political parties. The success of student activism was linked to the wider social forces with which they could identify and help animate and this was tied to their ability to converge their struggles with broader popular forces. Mamdani is correct to recognize that when students were effective they succeeded in forcing an opening up even if they lacked an alternative strategy: 'Its possibilities depended far more on the character of forces that student action succeeded in mobilizing than its own internal energies'.[119]

Popular mobilizations were a response to widespread disaffection with the policies of austerity and structural adjustment, yet these movements were responding in new ways. Class structures in sub-Saharan Africa had been transformed, and resistance did not simply take old forms and often they confounded fashionable theories.[120] The processes of class alignment and resistance brought in new and heterogeneous forces.[121] In defining the role of popular classes in Africa, Seddon describes a shifting constellation of political forces that includes the unemployed, informal sector traders and trade unionists.[122] I hold that students and unemployed graduates are also an important part of the popular classes. As Harrison correctly formulates the issues:

> The salience of youth identities derives from a broader set of changes. Economic crisis has had a direct and negative impact on the postcolonial social political project of modernization. The ensuing ruptures of social life have impacted on ... urban society – notably they are part of the context in which the working class has become fractured and 'informalized'. ... But the particular situation of

youth, either leaving school to find employment, dignity and independence, or leaving university to join the middle classes, predominately through linkages with the state, gives a peculiarly sharpened twist to the experience of Africa's recent economic decline.[123]

This informalization or hybribization of the social structure is not the effect of indeterminacy of political identity[124] but the product of the political economy in much of Africa.[125] Zeleza explains in the context of the university how these changes have manifested themselves: 'The faculty becomes increasingly divided between an elite professoriate in the marketable disciplines ... and the plebs in the marginalized disciplines (including a growing mass of the lumpen-professoriate of part-time, poorly paid academics).'[126] These circumstances form the inherited structures that contemporary students have been forced to negotiate. Students are not free-floating above the political and economic crisis. The resulting hybrity of social groups in Africa has transformed their activism and identity and affected their ability to exercise political agency. We can say that students expressed their status as politically privileged actors in diverse forms during the political transitions, yet repeatedly they have sparked wider protests in a period that has seen the convergence of social forces.

Higher education, as we have seen, has transported student identity into the maelstrom of the structural crisis. In an important study on class and the intelligentsia, Mamdani has seen these processes at work: 'previously a more or less guaranteed route to position and privilege, higher education seemed to lead more and more students to the heart of the economic and social crisis.'[127] Students are no longer the transitory social group waiting to be allotted government employment; on the contrary, they have become pauperized, converging more and more with the wider urban poor – the social groups they historically saw as their responsibility to liberate. However, student activism is still instilled with an important element of elitism, though now tempered by the realities of campus poverty. They have a considerable ability to mobilize in relatively autonomous urban spaces, achieving an organizational coherence that is rarely matched by other social groups.

In this chapter I have concentrated on the neo-liberal reform of education across the continent in the 1980s and 1990s and the patterns of student resistance and activism. One of the central factors influencing student politics was the ability to contest the ideological foundations of structural adjustment. The capacity of student organizations to confront the world view presented by their governments (before and after the transitions) and the IFIs, helped shape their political agency. But their ability to do this was influenced by wider political forces in society, and they were disabled by the lack of a coherent ideological alternative to neo-liberal reforms. Students found themselves buffeted together with the popular classes, by the resumption of a more or less unopposed politics of adjustment and austerity.

Student activism has been affected by the vacillations in the popular movements they helped to mobilize. Once new governments had been installed (Senegal, Mali) or old regimes revived (Cameroon, Zimbabwe), the tempo of resistance and student activism receded, often returning to the corporatist and piece-meal demands many commentators have wrongly interpreted as representing a new phase in student activism. The corporatism – or economism[128] – of student politics is not symptomatic of a new and qualitatively different student movement, nor, as Bathily et al. imply, of a slide into irrelevance: 'students ... are only in a transition, over which they have no control because they have no impact on the socioeconomic stakes. So instead of being actors/ initiators of this change, they have turned into mere artefacts of this evolution.'[129]

According to this account, the only barrier students face in assuming their full role as actors/initiators is their temporality. However, the status of student – at university, as graduate, as a *cartouchard*[130] or part of the mass of unemployed – is not imper-manent. The crisis for students in sub-Saharan Africa is precisely because they are not in transition; on the contrary, they are increasingly permanent artefacts in the post-colonial impasse.

Their activism, which is always complex and contradictory, retreats into a routine of economic and factional contestation when wider popular and democratic movements in society decline or are frustrated.

In Malawi, students at the university and academic staff were important in the mobilizations that eventually toppled the Banda regime in the multi-party elections of 1994. As Kerr and Mapanje state, 'students and staff marched in protest against the regime during the demonstrations sparked by the Catholic Bishops' Pastoral Letter of March 1992 and during the riots of May in the same year.'[131] Although they note a wave of activism during the transition from 1991 to 1993, they also lament the decline of student politics into corporatist concerns after this period. By 1994 there were even cases of male students at the university attacking and ridiculing female students and lecturers.

After the victory of Bakilli Muluzi and his United Democratic Front, the Malawian government participated uncritically in the project of structural adjustment and economic liberalization that had given resistance to the previous regime such impetus. The University of Malawi continues to deteriorate: 'Research funding was available only for programs financed by donor communities with specific agendas. Government subventions for salaries and such essential resources as books, journals, computers, photo-copiers, paper ... remained pitifully small'.[132] The lassitude that Kerr and Mapanje claim affected students after the elections in 1994 was tied to the resumption of economic SAPs after a period of democratic transition. The same disillusionment and lassitude gripped student politics in dozens of campuses across sub-Saharan Africa as governments that had emerged from the transition committed themselves to implementing IMF and World Bank reforms. The predominance of neo-liberalism across the continent after the democratic transition ensured a quick death for the African renaissance and the movements that had heralded it.

Chapter 3

REFORM, REVOLT AND STUDENT ACTIVISM IN ZIMBABWE

In this chapter I draw on a wide range of sources, including interviews with student activists, to examine the political agency of university students in Zimbabwe, concentrating specifically on the post-1995 period. There is an explicit emphasis on the voices of student activists. Student voices are used in two ways in the chapter. First, in that they reconstruct historical events from the perspective of their activism, they are used as historical sources in conjunction with secondary data. Second, they are interrogated for the meaning of student activism they give us.

I have divided this chapter into three parts. In the first part I describe the country's political and economic history, focusing on the recent period of transition. In the second part I consider the evolution of the student movement from the 1960s and the development of the student intelligentsia. In the final section I make extensive use of interviews with leading student activists to reconstruct the history of the student movement from 1995 and the development of the opposition.

Part I: Political and economic background
Zimbabwe's recent political and economic crisis has seen the

Map 3.2: Principal institutions of higher education in Zimbabwe

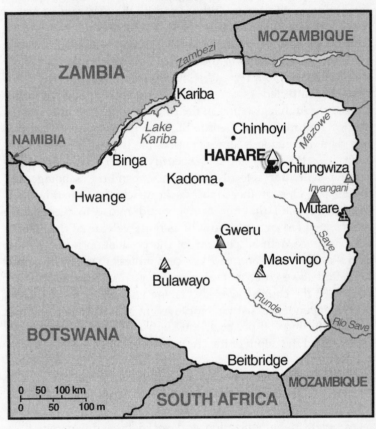

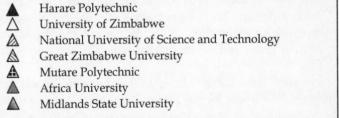

	Harare Polytechnic
	University of Zimbabwe
	National University of Science and Technology
	Great Zimbabwe University
	Mutare Polytechnic
	Africa University
	Midlands State University

Source: Adapted from the World Factbook (CIA).

politicization of youth and students, and youth have become one of the indispensable political forces supporting the regime. Most notably, communities are intimidated by the government-armed youth militia – the youth brigades – that have been central to the political upheavals in the country.[1] Elliot Manyika, a recent minister, set up camps to indoctrinate youth so that they 'fully appreciate their country and stand by it in times of crisis'.[2] The crisis has affected every aspect of society: the government pushed through legislation in the run-up to the 2002 presidential election that mimicked George Bush's legislation on the war on terrorism and made it almost impossible to oppose the government. The Public Order and Security Act (POSA) carries the death penalty for acts of 'insurgency, banditry, sabotage and terrorism'.[3] One of the country's army chiefs, General Vitalis Zvinavashe, said that the army would refuse to recognize a government led by a person who is not a veteran of the war for independence. With 36 per cent of the population living on less than a dollar a day and 64.2 per cent on less than two dollars a day, Zimbabwe confronts extremes of poverty and wealth.[4] By early 2004 the country was also facing its worst economic crisis since independence, with unemployment at over 65 per cent and inflation hitting 700 per cent.[5] In August 2006 one commentator summarized the depth of the crisis:

> Zimbabweans can no longer be fully described through terms such as inflation, percentage unemployment, GDP and so forth. Today one has to talk in terms of the complete dehumanization and social breakdown that is ripping the nation apart. ... In the ghettoes young people whose dreams have been mercilessly shattered are now preying on each other. ... On the other hand the Mugabe regime is in a state of thoughtless denial.[6]

For some time UZ has been at the point of general collapse. Employment in the formal sector has shrunk, leaving thousands of graduates without work or the prospect of getting any. Female students were reportedly pushed into prostitution to pay for their studies and food in UZ's privatized dining halls.[7] Fuel and food prices were forcing rural communities to move into over-crowded shantytowns on the outskirts of the two major cities, Harare and Bulawayo. In 2002, it was estimated that 33 per cent of the population aged between 15 and 49 years was infected with HIV, making Zimbabwe one of the worst affected countries in the world.[8]

In addition, the country was embroiled in a war in the Democratic Republic of Congo (DRC) from 1998, involving more than 15,000 troops, a quarter of the entire army. Army generals and businessmen were rewarded with contracts on mines and with logging companies. Mugabe's support for the government of the DRC was also rewarded by the gift of vast areas of land. One company, run by leading members of the ruling party, Zimbabwe African National Union–Patriotic Front (ZANU–PF), was granted what Global Witness calls 'the world's largest logging concession by gaining rights to exploit 33 million hectares of forests' – an area ten times the size of Switzerland.[9]

While the antecedents of this situation doubtlessly have their origin in the state structures inherited at independence,[10] it is the more recent popular protest movements that have shaped Zimbabwe's current political trajectory.[11] Since 1995 mass struggles have rocked Zimbabwe, threatening the regime and the agenda of structural adjustment the government had rather reluctantly been pursuing. These struggles have received almost no attention in mainstream accounts of the crisis, which prefer to see the current situation as arising out of Mugabe's autocratic rule. As one activist observes, 'The main point I want to make is that we were on the verge of a sort of revolution in Zimbabwe.'[12]

Out of these upheavals came one of the most powerful opposition movements on the continent. The MDC emerged from the Zimbabwe Congress of Trade Unions (ZCTU) in 1999 and became the most important force to challenge Mugabe since independence in 1980. The party almost won the parliamentary election in 2000, gaining 57 seats, despite widespread ZANU–PF violence that cost 31 lives. The fact that it came close to toppling the regime after having only existed for 16 months is an indication of the extent of the changes sweeping Zimbabwean society.[13] Recent events have confirmed the decline of the MDC, under the combined impact of state repression and the internal decay of the party. In parliamentary elections in 2005 – widely accused of being rigged – the MDC lost 16 seats to ZANU–PF, which secured the necessary two-thirds majority needed unilaterally to change the constitution. Norma Kriger observed before the election that the ruling party had already won the elections: 'The ruling party has already laid the groundwork to control the outcome and has honed its skills in terrorizing voters in by-elections.'[14]

The MDC is an enigma. While it was formed by ZCTU leaders Morgan Tsvangirai and Gibson Sibanda, it includes industrialists, white farmers and a constellation of smaller pressure groups and left-wing parties. Eddie Cross, formerly the party's spokesperson on economic matters, is a well-known entrepreneur who champions privatization and the policies of the IMF and World Bank. It has also received funding from the British Conservative Party, and when presented with the party's economic programme the World Bank reportedly said, 'We would have been proud to produce a programme like this, let alone have it handed to us'.[15]

In recent years, both state repression and the political turns taken by the MDC leadership (illustrated by the split in the organization in 2005) have paralysed the opposition. For some time there has been a disturbing truth in Zimbabwe: a predominant sense of political defeat coupled with a crippling economic crisis have led to an inability to mobilize for democratic change. Canwell Muchadya, president of the Zimbabwe Graphical Workers Union (ZGWU), powerfully described this in August 2006: 'for change to come in this set-up, it will not be by the ballot box, because this has failed dismally. Nor it is going to come through dialogue, that doesn't work in this country. It is only going to come by mobilizing but with the absence of resources during this economic crisis we cannot mobilize.'[16] I shall now describe, in part, how this disturbing reality could emerge from one of the continent's largest and most commanding opposition movements.

The rise and fall of Rhodesia

Zimbabwe emerged from the authoritarian and racist state the British established over a century ago. In 1890 the territory was marked out and handed to the imperialist adventurer Cecil Rhodes, who controlled it for his British South Africa Company. The British confronted wave after wave of resistance, culminating in the eventual defeat of the Chimurenga – the anti-colonial revolt in 1898. The next 40 years witnessed the mass expropriation of land from peasant farmers and communities, the repression of any form of resistance, and forced labour on mines and in factories. Thousands of Africans were forced off their land and herded into what were called communal lands, or reservations. The racial land division was consolidated by two pieces of legislation, the Land Apportionment Act of 1930 and the Land Tenure Act of 1969, both of which prohibited Africans from owning land in white areas. As late as the 1980s, approximately 4000 white farmers controlled almost 70 per cent of the most productive land, forcing more than seven million peasants onto dry and drought-ridden plots.[17]

In 1927 the Industrial and Commercial Workers Union (ICU) was established as the country's first trade union. It was founded principally by migrant workers from South Africa. Large numbers of white workers were recruited in both Britain and South Africa to work on the railways and mines. They were initially responsible for a high level of militancy, leading strikes and, inspired by the British labour movement, even forming a Rhodesian Labour Party.[18] In 1923 Rhodes's company rule was ended and limited self government was granted to Southern Rhodesia. The Reform Party, a coalition of British interests, dominated the political scene and sought to solidify an alliance between an increasingly militant white working class and the state. Only white workers were allowed to strike or belong to unions, although they were not allowed to form independent trade unions. White workers became wedded to the Rhodesian state, splitting the working class on racial and craft lines. Even so, a small Southern Rhodesian Communist Party emerged from a left-wing faction of the Labour Party. However, it was soon paralysed by following Russia's advice to form popular fronts and agitation among African workers was deemed too provocative to build these cross-class alliances.[19]

The state managed to force through a high level of industrialization from the 1930s onwards. By the 1950s, for example, annual growth was 10 per cent. But, as the economy expanded, so did the African working class. By 1950 the industrial working class, concentrated in urban areas around the industrial centres of what are today Bulawayo and Harare, had reached 469,000.[20] The 1948 general strike was the first major confrontation to threaten the state and give life to the nationalist movement.

Despite its militancy, the strike illustrated a weakness in the working class. Although there were African organizations in Southern Rhodesia by the late 1940s, there was not, in the words of one commentator, a 'single organization which was able to coordinate and unify the struggles of Africans'.[21] This meant that elitist, even conservative, forces could come to the fore. Benjamin Burombo, a local shop owner who became a leader of the strike, falsely assured a meeting of strikers that the government had increased their wages in line with their demands. He became a leading figure in the nationalist movement. Mkushi Khumalo, an activist during 1948, described Burombo in the following terms:

> Burombo was not an employee. Those who associate him with the strike are making a mistake. He was simply an opportunist. ... Burombo decided to join us and went about giving speeches as if he were an employee, and yet in fact he was a businessman, an employer. It was under these circumstances that Burombo became a participant in the strike.[22]

This example demonstrates an idea discussed in Chapter 1 regarding the organizational and political weaknesses of the emergent Africa working class. As we saw, this enlarged the political space for a petty-bourgeois student intelligentsia. Some have argued that the period demonstrated the failure, partly as a result of the political paralysis caused by ideas associated with

Stalinism, to build an independent organization that could develop and lead the black working class.[23] At each point of this failure, during the general strike in 1948 and later throughout the 1960/1 Zhii strike movement, other political forces and classes were able to capitalize on the organizational vacuum left by the working class. Benjamin Burombo managed to force himself on the movement, helping ultimately to return the country to the authorities.[24] Joshua Nkomo, the railway union leader, was also a representative of the same phenomenon. As a young graduate he had made his name in the 1948 general strike, sponsored by the railways in the hope that he could help offset the growth of radicalism. He rose to become the leading figure in nationalist politics in the 1950s and 1960s. The dearth of socialist politics, some commentators have argued, allowed a group of educated Africans, a petty bourgeoisie, to lead a movement that had the potential for far greater liberation.[25] As discussed in Chapter 1, this phenomenon was a key element in the pre-independence nationalist movements across much of the continent, which saw the predominant role played by a student intelligentsia that reflected the ideological immaturity of other social groups.

The 1948 strikes did, however, provide the impetus for the formation of the first trade union congress and the Southern Rhodesia Trade Union Congress (SRTUC), headed by Joshua Nkomo, was founded in 1954. This in turn precipitated the creation, three years later, of an overtly nationalist organization, the African National Congress (ANC). Trade unionists were the main source of support, and trade union leaders occupied most of the main positions in the organization. Nkomo became its first president. After the ANC was banned in 1959, Nkomo formed the Zimbabwe African People's Union (ZAPU).[26]

In 1962 the Rhodesian Front, a right-wing party headed by the racist Ian Smith, won power. Smith declared independence from Britain in 1965, in what was called a unilateral declaration of independence (UDI). The decision to declare independence was made in the context of growing resistance in Rhodesia and rising politicization across a continent resounding with independence movements. Nkomo sought active intervention against this decision from the UK government and, although the British courts condemned the UDI as treasonable, Labour Prime Minister Harold Wilson refused to sanction military action.[27]

Radical members of the nationalist movement, including Robert Mugabe, broke with Nkomo to form ZANU. Interestingly, when the party was first formed it was regarded as isolated from wider society. As Fay Chung has noted: 'when ZANU was first formed in 1963 it was labelled as a party of intellectuals cut off from the masses ... [and] intellectual and professional development ... were seen as necessary to overthrow the settler regime.'[28] By the 1970s a left-wing intelligentsia informed by Maoist and Stalinist ideas was leading the fight against white minority rule. It focused on guerrilla war in the countryside, and increasingly on a student leadership that had been expelled in the early 1970s from the University of Rhodesia. Arguably, this guerrilla war – conceived of as a popular liberation but in reality involving self-appointed leaders – was entirely consistent with the logic of student mobilization. Students were politically privileged actors transforming society in the name of the voiceless. In this respect, Cliff elucidates the action of this group: the intelligentsia as a non-specialized section of society 'is the obvious source of a "professional revolutionary elite".'[29]

These tactics were reasonably successful and by the end of the 1970s the Patriotic Front forces were between 35,000 and 40,000 strong. The government's forces were engaged on approximately six fronts, with martial law imposed throughout the country.[30] Although these tactics achieved some success, they failed to win a decisive victory over the Rhodesian Front.[31] Ian Smith was finally forced to negotiate and, under pressure from Mozambique, Mugabe accepted the Lancaster House agreement. In 1980 Zimbabwe held its first fully independent multiracial elections.

Land, independence and reconciliation

Zimbabwean independence involved one of the most spectacular and instant reconciliations in the history of armed conflict. The 1979 Lancaster House agreement, which led directly to independence the following year, guaranteed the property of the small white population. Ian Smith's regime conceded to black majority rule on the basis of a promise that the white minority's property rights would be safeguarded and that when land reform eventually came, white farmers would be fully compensated. At the same time Robert Mugabe and Joshua Nkomo, the two leaders of the independence war, were persuaded to adopt a new constitution that prevented the forced expropriation of white farms for ten years. This was a far cry from Mugabe's promise a few years before that none of the white exploiters would be allowed to keep an acre of their land.[32] The promise was extracted with a commitment from the Thatcher government to make millions of pounds available for land reform in the future.[33]

The only official commitment the foreign secretary, Lord Carrington, secured was that the first government would be unable to confiscate white property. Nevertheless, Mugabe went on to win the election with the pledge that thousands of black families would be settled on white land within three years. The initial resettlement figure was for 162,000 families. In the end only 70,000 families were resettled in that period. The 1980s did see a certain amount of successful resettlement, more than other resettlement programmes on the continent, but much of this was often popularly driven through illegal occupations. The period that followed was notable for its failure to continue the limited progress that had been made. Productivity even outstripped that in the communal areas on a hectare for hectare basis. For those who experienced the resettlement it transformed their lives, but for the thousands left landless and poor it was undoubtedly a bitter disappointment.[34]

Despite the lapse of the constitutional block on compulsory purchase in 1990, the regime failed to pursue redistribution with any seriousness for three main reasons. First, taxes on the huge profits white farmers made from export crops were a major disincentive to pursue large-scale resettlement. Second, at this time the priority was to expand black commercial farmland, an indigenization process, but this was coupled with confusion about whether the problems of communal areas could be resolved through expanded resettlement. Finally, and crucially, the adoption of a structural adjustment programme in the early 1990s led to a massive reduction of public expenditure on social programmes, which were essential to the resettlement projects.[35]

Another important factor was the relationship of the regime to white farmers. White farmers and the white community generally never integrated socially or politically with the black population after independence. However, they were not colonialists and imperialists (as Mugabe labelled them), but rather useful allies to the regime. As a consequence, 20 years after independence the percentage of white land resettled by black families was a small fraction of the total land owned by the white population, while most of the money promised at the gentlemen's agreement in London years before failed to appear. From the hundreds of millions the British had promised only a meagre £44 million ever materialized and, like all aid, it came with conditions, meaning that after the wrangling about what it could be used on, not even all this sum was spent.[36]

Some of the land redistributed in the early 1990s was used to create a class of black commercial farmers. Although there were certainly a number of questionable deals over its allocation to black commercial farmers, at this point not all the land went to political friends. Yet the combined effect of structural adjustment and the wave of popular protests after 1996 decisively shifted the pattern and use of land allocation. Some 200 farms were purchased and distributed to army officers and party officials whose loyalty could be guaranteed with the promise of land. One giant estate was parcelled into 27 smaller farms and presented to party figures, including presidential spokesman George Charamba. The military also benefited – General Vitalis Zvinavashe received his own estate, while thousands of poor Zimbabweans were ignored. In the recent land grab political patronage has again determined allocation. Loyal reporters, leading politicians and soldiers have been given land, but title deeds have remained with the government, ensuring continued loyalty to the regime. Still, the pattern of current commercial land allocation is a small part of the total picture and it is important to remember that recent land occupations have often been popularly driven, and the government has sought desperately to control them.[37]

The compromises, procrastination and ultimately failure to confront the issue of land redistribution are representative of the general approach of the regime. In the immediate aftermath of independence Mugabe made his intentions clear. He asserted that there would be no fundamental transformation of society and, despite the change in government, white businesses and farmers could rest assured that their living conditions would be guaranteed. On 17 April 1980, in front of an international crowd that included Prince Charles and Bob Marley. Robert Mugabe reassured the country: 'If yesterday I fought you as an enemy, today you have become a friend. If yesterday you hated me, today you cannot avoid the love that binds you to me and me to you.'[38] For a time, the desire to seek reconciliation and restore confidence to white farmers and businesses looked as though it would bring down the government.[39] As one writer observed: 'Despite its Marxist-Leninist rhetoric the ZANU-PF government tried to preserve the largely white-owned productive structures.'[40] The gross inequalities of ownership and control in the economy were maintained and shored up after independence.

It was not simply the inequalities that remained after independence, but much of the Rhodesian state. A great deal of the colonial legal system remained intact, ensuring unparalleled powers for the ruling party. The state continued to suppress dissent – it labelled oppositionists terrorists and massacred enemy communities. The recent violence expresses the continuity and escalation of state repression, not its first appearance. The worst examples of this brutality were the massacres in Matabeleland in the 1980s. The majority of the population are Ndebele speakers who were regarded as supporters of the rival liberation organization ZAPU, which was led by Nkomo. It has been estimated that between 1981 and 1988 between 10,000 and 20,000 dissidents were killed. Thousands more were herded into concentration camps, raped, tortured and starved.[41]

At independence, the union movement was fragmented and

disorganized. Yet, in the first years of independence there was an upsurge of industrial action, with 200 officially recorded disputes between 1980 and 1981. In many ways these strikes contained the grievances of a generation. Although many were concerned with low wages, others were against racist managers and the discrimination against trade union representation. The disputes helped to ensure that the government implemented a number of important reforms in the next few years. Later on the government urged the merger of unions into a central federation, the ZCTU. To start with, the ZCTU was tied closely to the government. It was packed with Mugabe's friends and even a member of his family. This relationship persisted while the government implemented limited reforms – a national minimum wage, legislation enshrining labour rights, and health and education provision.[42]

For a few years in the early 1980s the government increased spending on health and education, and picked up considerable support both in towns and the countryside. Between 1980 and 1990 primary and secondary schools were built across Zimbabwe. Enrolment increased in primary education from 1.2 million in 1980 to more than 2.2 million by 1989, and in secondary schools from only 74,000 to 671,000 in the same period.[43] However, by the mid-1980s the economy had begun to stagnate. From 1986 to 1987 per capita GDP declined rapidly.[44] Loans from the World Bank, which the government happily accepted, caused foreign debt to rise from US$ 786 million in 1980 to US$ 3 billion in 1990.[45] Having precipitated the crisis a group of neo-liberals gathered around the finance and economics minister, Bernard Chidzero. Thus, under some duress, but not without complicity, the government invited the World Bank in to provide proposals for the reorganization of the economy. Supporters of the state capitalist reforms of the early years became marginalized.[46]

Structural adjustment
Until recently Zimbabwe had one of the most important economies in Africa. Unlike most African countries, it had fairly

well developed industrial and agricultural sectors and a relatively developed infrastructure that produced a range of goods
in a number of industries. Manufacturing, at 24.8 per cent of
GDP in 1990, was about three times higher than in most African
countries.[47] The sector employed 16.5 per cent of all those in the
formal economy. Agriculture was also diversified, growing such
crops as tobacco, wheat and cotton. Coupled with this was a
massive concentration of ownership and control that originated
from the state set up by the British in 1890. Almost 60 per cent of
industrial production was controlled by foreign capital.[48]

The government introduced the first full economic structural
adjustment programme (ESAP) in 1991, although the IMF had
been pressing it to reduce expenditure and devalue the Zimbabwean dollar from as early as 1982.[49] Following similar – and
similarly disastrous – programmes in most of Africa, the World
Bank insisted on trade liberalization, the removal of import controls and export incentives, deregulation – including changes to
what was regarded as 'restrictive' labour legislation – and widespread public sector reforms.[50]

The government now pursued policies involving privatization
and the closure of state companies that Western donors, the IMF
and the World Bank deemed unprofitable. The year after, the
implementation of ESAP saw a huge 11 per cent fall in per capita
GDP.[51] More than 20,000 jobs were lost between January 1991
and July 1993. In 1993 unemployment had reached a record 1.3
million from a total population of about ten million.[52] Skalnes
reported 25,000 civil service jobs lost by 1995, while 'inflation
rose and exports declined'.[53] The new policies promoted by
Washington and the IMF had, it seemed, failed to stem, and by
all accounts helped to deepen, the recession that continued to
grip Zimbabwe.

A new militancy in civil society was born out of this turmoil.
By the late 1980s sections of society that had previously been
termed middle class (and loyal) were radicalized by the fall in
living standards. At the same time, opposition at UZ emerged,
criticizing the rightward shift in government policy. Most
significant was the rupture between the government and the

trade union leadership. The old ZCTU leadership that had followed and supported the government since independence was replaced by a new one that was influenced by the radicalization in society. In 1988 Morgan Tsvangirai – a mineworker and activist – became the ZCTU general secretary. The following year he supported student protests at UZ and was detained for six weeks on suspicion of being a South African spy. The period was crucial for a new generation of militants and trade unionists. As Tendai Biti, a leading activist at the time, argues: 'It was the first time people criticized the legitimacy of these heroes. It showed you can make noise and not get killed.'[54]

Gwisai[55] notes that while the role Mugabe had played in the struggle for national liberation carried some weight in the 1980s, those who had only been children during the struggle for independence (including the 'born-frees' born after independence in 1980) comprised a new urban working class and were less patient with the perceived failure of that liberation. Students were at the forefront of these new critiques and they saw through what appeared increasingly to be Mugabe's hollow promises. The trade union leadership even asked during the 1991 May Day rally, 'Are we going to make 1991 the year of the World Bank storm?'[56] Later, ZCTU produced an alternative economic plan, 'Beyond ESAP', which opposed some of the government's IMF-sponsored programme. But in the liberal rhetoric of 'Beyond ESAP' lay warning signs for those hoping for radicalism from the new union leadership.

The upheavals
It was not until the mid-1990s that Zimbabwe experienced its first significant upheavals against the austerity policies pursued by the government. Many activists regard the demonstration against police brutality in 1995, triggered by the murder of several people by the police in Harare, as a turning point. One young student activist, Luke Kasuwanga, who helped to organize the demonstration, recalls how it inspired him:

When I reached home I waited for the 8 o'clock news. The

news was read – Harare was burning! You could see fire
everywhere. The minister was interviewed and we could
see that he was sweating. He was saying, 'We know the
people responsible and we are going to get them. They are
going to pay for it.' And it all came under my name. ... At
first you have to deny that you are involved [but] later on
we are proud that we were at the forefront. And funnily
enough one of my workmates – who wasn't involved in
politics – he attended that demonstration, and that
demonstration made him solid from that period. ... Why
am I saying this? It politicized me. That was the first time I
was in the leading role as a worker.[57]

But it was not until the first national government workers'
strike in August 1996 that Zimbabwean society experienced a
much broader movement. Tens of thousands came out against
job losses, bad working conditions and government corruption.
Although health workers, nurses and doctors initiated the strike,
it spread rapidly to other workers – teachers, civil servants and
almost every branch of the public sector. It affected every area of
the country and crippled the government. As the strike continued it developed clearly political aims, eventually even
demanding a reduction in the size of the cabinet. An elected
committee of rank and file trade unionists directed the strike.
Flying pickets moved from workplace to workplace imploring
workers to join the movement.[58] Tafadzwa Choto, who was
active at the time, recognized the importance of the period: 'I
think the turning point was the government workers' strike in
1996. It really gave confidence to so many.'[59]

Trade union leaders found that they too were outpaced by the
dispute. Before long they persuaded strikers to accept a government offer. The strike ended in an agreement that included a
large increase in wages, the promise of a new labour act, a
guarantee that workers would receive bonuses, and the recog-
nition of public sector unions. However, the agreement did not
hold. By November health sector workers were on strike again,
staying out until February 1997. The strike also saw the active

intervention of the International Socialist Organization (ISO). Although at the time it had only 50 members, mostly at UZ in Harare, they were able to produce leaflets calling for indefinite action and had participated in the strikes in Harare and the second city, Bulawayo. As well as calling for the election of a strike committee to take the strike forward, they pressed for more militant action, including picketing government buildings.

The following year saw more demonstrations and strikes than at any time since independence. Many activists have noted how students combined with workers who linked the struggle in the city with the need to distribute land in the countryside. As Tendai Biti remembers: 'This was a momentous occasion in the history of this country because it brought confidence – you could smell working class power in the air.'[60] Rural labourers and peasants invaded commercial farms in various provinces and tried to resist the police who had been sent by the ruling ZANU–PF to evict them and restore law and order.

The previously marginalized war veterans broke onto the scene. They were, for the most part, former fighters from the guerrilla war against the Rhodesian state in the 1970s. They had been abandoned since independence and by the mid-1990s most of them were unemployed, without pensions or land. Galvanized by the mass upheavals, they joined demonstrations and started making their own demands. They denounced Mugabe at public forums, including the annual heroes' commemoration.[61]

Concerned by the threat the war veterans posed, at the end of 1997 Mugabe imposed a war veterans' levy, which he argued would be used to fund pensions for those who had fought in the war. The ZCTU's response was to call another strike, a two-day stayaway. Thousands of demonstrators converged on Harare and by the end of the strike the government had agreed to withdraw the proposed tax. The wave of militancy that had started in 1996 continued into 1998. The year started with a bread riot, led by housewives provoked by an increase in the cost of basic commodities. As the minister of home affairs commented immediately after the riots: 'The just-ended three-day food riots which came soon after the announcement of the general increase of prices of basic commodities, mealie meal, rice, cooking oil and bread, represent the most violent riots the country has experienced since independence.'[62] Eight people were killed, hundreds were injured and thousands were arrested. The riots quickly combined workers, students and the unemployed, while ZCTU leaders tried to dissuade workers from joining the demonstrations. Again the ISO helped to organize similar movements in other towns and produced a leaflet calling on others to join the struggle. Its slogan *'Shinga Mushandi Shinga! Qina Msebenzi Qina!'* – 'Workers be resolute! Fight on!' – has become the *de facto* motto of the trade union movement. Although there is a dispute about the role of the group in the existing literature,[63] Gwisai[64] criticizes the way the organization has been marginalized in Bond's work and almost completely ignored by Raftopoulos and Sachikonye. However, the organization was an important ideological tool in the student movement, equipping a layer of student activists with ideological resources that informed much of their political energy and hope.

The union congress was not completely wrong-footed. The general secretary, Morgan Tsvangirai, understood the importance of the new wave of militancy. He even called for a general strike without consulting the general council of the congress, and was almost removed as a result. Kasuwanga illustrates how the movement took the lead: 'When ZCTU was calling for stayaways, these stayaways were called after the housewives and the unemployed were rioting in the townships spreading around Zimbabwe. Even the 1998 bread demonstrations, which shook the whole of Zimbabwe [were] done by housewives on their own. Even Tsvangirai said he was nothing to do with it. It began spontaneously on its own.'[65]

The war veteran leader Chenjerai Hunzvi became a key loyalist to Mugabe during the period, even though his profile as a middle-class privileged member of the establishment could not contrast more with the peasants and ex-combatants he now claimed to lead.[66]

The ZCTU was mindful of events that had led to Kenneth Kaunda's removal in neighbouring Zambia in the early 1990s. A movement led and organized by the ZCTU had swept the old regime from power in elections held in 1991. The MMD came to power headed by Frederick Chiluba, the general secretary of the only trade union federation that had helped to coordinate strikes and demonstrations that undermined the old regime.[67]

What kind of opposition party?

Between 1996 and 1998 the ZCTU repeatedly sought to lead and direct a mass movement that persistently pre-empted their direction. Rank-and-file activists, often organizing in labour forums (where large groups of organized trade unionists meet to discuss politics) rushed ahead of union bureaucrats in organizing strikes and demonstrations. From 1998 a recurrent theme of the labour forums was the demand for the ZCTU to form a labour party, a demand that was repeatedly rejected on the grounds that a union's work should be limited to economic issues. However, as the crisis deepened so too did the urgency of these demands.[68]

Meanwhile, Mugabe seemed to be failing everyone. The international community, which had long regarded him as a reliable partner, and Zimbabwe as proof of the efficacy of IMF and World Bank reforms, began to ostracize the regime. He caved in too easily to an audacious trade union movement, which he was expected to have subdued. Gradually, various NGOs, academics, businessmen and lawyers added their voices to the calls for a new opposition. The demands now carried a contradiction. On the one hand they came from below, the labour forums, radicalized students and the streets that had been involved in mass upheavals since 1996. These forces insisted on a reversal of Mugabe's austerity policies. On the other hand pressure was mounted by the middle class – academics, lawyers and business people who were threatened by the movement they now sought to co-opt.[69] At its founding rally in Harare on 11 September 1999 (where 20,000 took part), the MDC announced that the party is 'a focused continuation of the ages-old struggle of the working people. The MDC is coming together, through a united front of the working people, to pursue common goals and principles that advance the interests of all people across Zimbabwe – workers, peasants, the unemployed, women, students, youths and the disabled people.'[70]

The South African based academic, Bond, notes that within a very short time the MDC adopted many policies antipathetic to their original goals. The party courted whites and international big business, as Bond wrote at the time:

> Is it not the case, as of February, that the MDC began to receive generous funding by (white) domestic and foreign capitalists, including white farmers? At that stage, didn't Zimbabwe's skewed land relations and abominable property rights simply drop off the MDC's campaign agenda? Wasn't a representative of big business put in charge of its economics desk, and wasn't his first major speech a firm endorsement of the International Monetary Fund and wholesale privatization for post-election Zimbabwe?[71]

Gwisai[72] notes how Mugabe began to realize that if he was to survive where Kaunda and Malawi's Hastings Kamuzu Banda, both ejected by popular resistance, had not, then he must be seen to retreat from the agenda of IMF reform he had enthusiastically defended. The regime moved quickly, and government rhetoric began to lambaste imperialism and Western racism. The effects of this shift helped to consolidate middle-class and foreign support for a new party, in opposition to Mugabe's new position. ZANU–PF did not move forward in one mass. Factions in the party, principally around Eddison Zvobgo, a longstanding advocate of neo-liberal reform, became a focus of opposition in ZANU–PF, trying and ultimately failing to resist Mugabe.[73]

Land was the key to this reorientation. For nearly 20 years the regime had failed seriously to redistribute land to the black majority starved of it. The government, which in the mid-1990s had ejected squatters from occupied white farms, a few years later sanctioned the occupation by squatters of the same farms.[74] Mugabe began to realize the potential of the war veterans and used Hunzvi – 'Hitler', as he labelled himself – to win their loyalty. Before long Mugabe had outmanoeuvred the opposition in his party and won most of the regime to his new stance. The collapse in value of the Zimbabwean dollar at the end of 1998 was symbolic of what was to come – the isolation and rapid demonization of the regime by international capital.[75]

The call for a new party was finally answered. In March 1999 the MDC, which was initially just a movement, was born through the National Working People's Convention (NWPC). The ZCTU had convened the NWPC, and invited NGOs, civic groups and residents' associations. However, the convention was not a friendly gathering, and attempts were made to exclude leading socialists. Tim Chitambure remembers: 'The guys were given special instructions, "You should not allow socialists in." But you know what we did? We are the leading people in locations, so some went under the banner of residents' associations; some went under the banner of other groups in the NCA [National Constitutional Assembly].'[76]

The aim for many of those present was to form a labour party committed to defending the interests of the working class, but the tension between these activists and the other participants was never far from the surface. As Chitambure recalls, 'So we were saying that ZCTU should form a workers' party. But they didn't like it – they wanted to separate economics from politics. ... They asked: "How come you are in here?" and you say, "I am representing Glenfield residents association." Those that did not get in were outside with some leaflets saying, "In this convention push these points"'.[77]

Until the organization's official launch in September 1999, trade unionists dominated the party, but a middle-class bloc representing local and international business interests quickly began to encroach on the leadership. In the parliamentary elections in June 2000, workers made up only 15 per cent of the candidates.[78] Policy also shifted, and the party courted Western leaders and committed itself in the election manifesto to policies of the free market, privatization, foreign direct investment and land reform that succeeded in being to the right of ZANU–PF, offering only very limited redistribution to the poor.

The parliamentary vote followed the MDC victory in a referendum held in February on a draft constitution proposed by the government. The MDC almost won the parliamentary elections. For a party less than one-and-a-half years old this was an extraordinary result. It attracted the core of the urban working class in all principal cities – Harare, Bulawayo and Chitungwiza. But the election also marked a decisive shift in policy and symbolized the end of what had seemed to be the inextricable radicalization of the struggle.[79]

Many commentators asked how the MDC could have fallen into the hands of the middle class.[80] The answer, some maintain, is the same weakness of the organized working class observed in the 1948 general strike. Although the ZCTU had jettisoned the old leadership in the late 1980s, its new leaders were still tied to Stalinist politics and an economism that maintained the congress should be limited to narrow trade union work. When the regimes in Eastern Europe and Russia collapsed, so did the ideological signposts for a generation of trade union bureaucrats, activists and leaders. This ideological collapse had a profound effect on student activism. At the same time there was no clear organizational or ideological force in the movement with enough influence to make sense of these events.[81] Although the period 1996–98 showed the power, initiative and creative force of the Zimbabwean popular forces, the strikes and demonstrations remained ultimately under the control of the trade union bureaucracy. In turn, they ensured that stayaways would only be used as a means, at most, to put pressure on Mugabe while keeping the interests of national and international capital on board. Bond,[82] however, argues that the reasons are far less elaborate, that it was the crisis of funding for the MDC in October 1999 that meant that the organization had to look beyond its natural constituency.

But there was another element to the participation of the middle class in the MDC, which was tied inextricably to the struggles that had marked the late 1990s. Kasuwanga, a member of the ISO, argues that it was the threat of mass revolt that marginalized and frightened the middle class. These tensions forced them to respond to the MDC, as he explains:

The main point I want to make is that we were on the verge of a sort of revolution in Zimbabwe. There was going to be anarchy, whereby revolts were going to be happening any time, any day. So I think some interested groups, to stop this, said, 'Why don't you form this NCA and later on the MDC?' ... Through ... the ZCTU calling for that dialogue thing [it] was trying to neutralize the power of workers. Because workers by then were calling [for] a five-day stayaway, the five-day stayaway was the one needed by workers. And Tsvangirai was calling for one day, two days, one day, two days, every Wednesday. It was a form of trying to control workers. If the MDC was not formed workers were going to revolt on their own. And the middle classes were scared. Do you know what was happening? People like me, I don't have O-levels, I don't have a degree. I was even more influential in my area. Our comrades, those who were putting up the barricades in the street, were having more influence. The middle class were losing influence because no one could hear them. They couldn't stand and talk to the people rioting because the language was different. But having that dialogue thing, they try to interpret all of those things to us – the rule of law, the IMF, economics, 'We want foreign currency. We want this and that.' They thought that they were talking to the uneducated: 'You cannot understand this. Do this and do that.' That is how the struggle was stolen from our hands.[83]

Whether the strikes and mass struggles between 1996 and 1998 amounted to Kasuwanga's revolutionary situation is highly debatable. There were never consistent political demands under an independent leadership that could have made the question of the forcible removal of Mugabe more than an issue among a minority of those active. But Kasuwanga is undoubtedly right that Zimbabwe went through a sort of revolution.[84]

Each step of the way attempts were made to stifle the movement's independent voice. Organizations that had built solidarity, organized labour forums, set up tenants' associations, and participated in strikes and demonstrations were obstructed in their work. Despite this, Munyaradzi Gwisai (the leading member of the ISO) won an important seat in a working-class area of Harare in the 2000 parliamentary elections as part of the MDC and, despite continued opposition from 'the party leadership, remained in the organization until December 2002 when it was expelled. However, regardless of the avowedly Blairite stance of the party, it was the product of the popular struggles that gripped Zimbabwe.

Conclusion
It was the largely urban struggles from 1995 that gave birth to the MDC but it was the very weakness of these movements that led to the party's failure to resist the pull of a layer of NGO professionals, the middle class, and foreign influence and finance. Although it was deflected from its founding purpose, it remains to many the crucial repository of the hope for social change of ordinary Zimbabweans.

Mugabe's partial withdrawal from ESAP was not a principled decision based on anti-imperialist politics, but a cynical move forced on him by a political crisis caused by popular resistance, which (as discussed below) involved the crucial agency of university students. The reality for most Zimbabweans has been a continuation of the same policies, while the regime mouthed platitudes about foreign powers and racist imperialism. Unemployment now affects much more than half the population – jobs in the formal sector for new graduates and students have disappeared. In the second and third parts of this chapter I examine the evolution of student activism from the 1960s.

Part II: Foundations
The University of Rhodesia became an increasingly militant site for student activism in the 1960s. From the university, students developed their nationalist politics and supported the wider struggle against the Rhodesian state. In many ways, the campus based organizations mirrored nationalist politics outside the

university. In the early 1970s, black students the university had expelled for leading demonstrations and organizing political groups on campus, became members of a student intelligentsia that helped lead the nationalist movement in exile and the guerrilla war inside Rhodesia. In this part of the chapter I track the growth of nationalist politics during the first days of the student movement.

Introduction: Students, education and the University of Zimbabwe
At an important conference on the role of the university and its future in Zimbabwe held at the newly renamed University of Zimbabwe (UZ) in 1981, Robert Mugabe gave the opening address. He underlined the centrality of the university to national development and quoted at length the academic Barkan:

> The world of the African University student is a rarefied one, for he lives in a realm which less than one per cent of his countrymen ever see. His time is monopolized by an institution, which is both physically and spiritually removed from the society which surrounds it. He attends class and resides on a campus that forms a self-contained community, segregated from the rural areas where he was raised, and often detached from the main urban centre of his country as well. With few exceptions, the university he attends has not attempted to create its own identity and academic traditions, preferring instead to imitate those found in the land of the former colonial power. Even though his country has been independent for several years, many of his teachers continue to be white expatriates.[85]

Mugabe was correct. The quotation expressed the reality for students at the one national university that existed at the time. Zimbabwe had achieved its independence the previous year and the university was an unreconstructed institution, dominated by white teaching staff and existing in a rarefied space. This space – self-contained and detached from the main urban centre – helped to determine the nature and extent of student activism in the first decade of independence. This is not simply an historical element to student activism in Zimbabwe. The rarefied spaces on campus at UZ were central to the successful mobilization of students and to political debate during the military repression from the late 1990s. Stephen Chisuvi, a student activist in Harare, explains the importance of this space to student mobilization:

> Students have played a significant part in the movement based on the fact that in Zimbabwe almost all students who go to higher institutions are at campus and so they have some togetherness and it adds some mass character to the activities of the students. Secondly, in the lecture rooms and the library students are in constant interaction with ideas; it's easy for them to have ideological development; they develop faster than those who learn from concrete experiences. The students engage with ideology on an abstract level so they can quickly raise their consciousness.[86]

But the university was 'rarefied' in another respect. As one student remembered, as late as the mid-1990s:

> The payout was too much for me. The first thing you do when you finish your first term is to go home and show off ... with the pocket money that you had from the pay-out. I could afford to drink beer daily and still have $3000 in my pocket for the vacation. Some of us even had enough to pay for our brothers and sisters to go through school.[87]

In the 1980s these payouts did not only allow students to indulge in beer and showing off, but as many former students note to build houses for their parents in the rural areas.

In the 1980s, though changing quickly, UZ still resembled the former University of Rhodesia. The vice chancellor's report in 1984 noted that the total number of full-time undergraduates had increased to 2705. As a result of recent reforms in 1983, 25 black lecturers had been appointed compared with just two in the past.[88] Overall, in the first five years after independence student enrolment at UZ rose from 1481 to 4741, reaching 7699 in 1988.[89]

The university – the only Zimbabwean university at the time – sat at the apex of the education system, as an institution that would forge the country's elite. However, the wider educational environment had a profound effect on the status and importance of university education. Education had played a central role in determining social status and class position, a situation that long predated independence. These points are well made by Bianchini who sees the diploma fetishism of sub-Saharan Africa as linked to what he terms the 'primitive accumulation of education capital'.[90] This was initially a colonial process that saw the forced education of a layer of *évolués* divorced from the mass of the population to whom they were destined to become the liberators (a bureaucratic elite running the colonial states). The accumulation of education capital became a central element in the post-colonial hierarchy, and competition to obtain diplomas a vital resource in accessing political and social power. Bianchini argues that it is only through appreciating this fetishism that the post-colonial crisis in higher education, which has seen the successive *dévalorization* of these diplomas, can be understood.[91]

These views of education had their roots in the colonial system. Education became fetishized in proportion to its scarcity, giving those who possessed it enormous status. It also had a peculiarly Zimbabwean twist: the incarceration of nationalist guerrillas saw the transformation of prisons into centres of learning and study, the prison university from which Robert Mugabe graduated with numerous degrees (often with the help of the Rhodesia Christian Council). Those not serving prison sentences were often the recipients of foreign scholarships for African students from the breakaway colony.[92] Nyamfukudza brilliantly expresses this obsession in his novel *The Non-Believer's Journey*:

> For as long as Sam had known him he had been studying by correspondence courses and had managed to pass the Junior Certificate exams, five O levels and, only recently, had had his fourth attempt at an A level subject. It had

become a hobby almost, failing repeatedly until he passed by virtue of mule-headed obstinacy. There was something abnormal in his generation's belief in the magic powers of education, Sam sometimes thought, verging on super-stitious, almost. They had had to make incredible sacrifices to be able to go to school for a few years and they seemed, throughout their later lives, to believe that it was the lack of educational certificates, those magic papers which were supposed to open up the world for one's taking, which explained all their privations. And all this despite the fact that the streets of every town were crawling with young black people, burdened with armfuls of certificates, who could not get jobs. The magic formula had long ceased to deliver the goods, but the myth remained, unshaken by the obvious, political fact that no white man, illiterate or otherwise, had any problems finding a supervisory job. It was a wonder that young people went to school at all.[93]

The story is about a cynical graduate from the University of Rhodesia who refuses to commit himself to the liberation war. The university's status in his narrative has another dimension: the rarefied world of university life has created an aloof and cynical generation that looks down dismissively at the society from which their education has excluded them. But the quotation expresses the social prestige of education that marks political and social discourse in Zimbabwe.[94]

In the next section I discuss the role of students in Zimbabwe as part of a student intelligentsia that helped to lead the national liberation war and, after independence, the first group to pierce the holy edifice of the regime. Later, in completely altered circumstances, they continued to play a politically privileged role in the frustrated transition in the late 1990s. The activism of Zimbabwe university students was forged in the liberation war, which was in part run and organized by university students who saw themselves uniquely placed to bring liberation, a process that saw, according to Astrow,[95] the marginalization of the urban trade union struggle by a petty-bourgeois leadership.

The student intelligentsia and national liberation: 1970–1980

The University of Rhodesia – as UZ was known before it was renamed in 1980 – was never a non-racial island of learning as the title of a study from the 1970s described it.[96] It was, on the contrary, regarded as a tense and politically charged place during the liberation war in the 1960s and 1970s.[97] However, in 1968, the year of student revolt across the world, the *Rhodesia Herald* proudly announced: 'Rhodesia is lucky in its University College.' Apparently, there was little evidence of subversive elements, 'in fact at the moment no evidence is visible at all'.[98] But within months of this article, black and white students at the university erupted in revolt against the proposed changes to the constitution that would have postponed black majority rule indefinitely. This marked one of the first occasions at the university when European and African students came together against attempts to entrench white minority rule.

Student politics on the campus mirrored the wider African nationalist movement in the country. In August 1963 the main party of African nationalism, ZAPU, split, leading to the creation of ZANU under the leadership of Reverend Sithole, who represented a more radical approach to independence and national liberation. ZANU plunged into the university milieu, recruiting student activists and addressing meetings in an attempt to win political hegemony on the campus. This led to the accusation of ZANU being nothing more than a party of intellectuals cut off from the masses.[99] Yet this strategy was consistent with ZANU's emphasis, at least in the movement's early years, on education and the political training of militants. However, ZANU's prescription for the student movement was very clear: students were to play an obedient role in the coming struggles, 'being part of the revolutionary movement you are to ... be directed by it,' and there was no space for an independent line.[100]

For some time the campus was torn in two by an internecine struggle between ZANU and ZAPU activists that was only brought to an end by the National Union of Rhodesian Students (NURS), which played an important role in 'coalescing the forces of African nationalism in campus' after the split.[101] NURS also managed to maintain a degree of political mobilization after the paralysis of nationalist politics caused by the banning of the ZANU and ZAPU in 1963. One student remembered that, as the leaders of ZAPU fled the country in 1963, 'the university student in that year became more conscious than ever of his role as a revolutionary'.[102] However, the period saw the marginalization of the urban struggle by a nationalist strategy that increasingly focused on rural guerrilla warfare led by an exiled political leadership. To a certain extent, this thrust the university and the student intelligentsia into the centre of urban politics, with students feeling an obligation to assume the leadership of the nationalist cause.

The pots-and-pans demonstration in 1973 was a high point in the pre-independence student movement, and the key turning point in the evolution of the student intelligentsia. Racial issues had exploded onto the campus: the main concern was the presence of a university delegation at the Association of Commonwealth Universities in Edinburgh. Because of the predominance of Rhodesian Front supporters on the university senate and council, many African students regarded support for the delegation as tantamount to accepting racism at the university. Most white students, however, saw the issue differently; they thought the delegation should be applauded for representing the university's multiculturalism. These issues were further heightened by the non-representation of African workers at the university, who turned to the student union to represent them. The president of the student union at the time explained that, 'workers have started coming to me not because I am the right channel but because they are both frustrated and desperate.'[103] African students occupied the principal's office in 1973 demanding the end of racial discrimination, the employment of Africans in all fields and an increase in the wages of catering staff. This act of solidarity was not accidental, but typical of the nature of early student activism. Black students at the one national university could see themselves as once removed from the realities of the black non-academic members of staff who had approached them with their complaints and also representatives of them.

Dissatisfied with the principal's response to the issue of wages for African non-academic members of staff, students launched the pots-and-pans demonstration, which Tengende, in his seminal study of the period, describes as 'the last significant confrontation between the students and the Administration and the Rhodesian state'.[104] A crowd of students proceeded to remove tea urns and other tea utensils and locked the property in a student union building before making their petitions to the university authorities. The identification of these utensils was not accidental; on the contrary:

> I thought it was the most exquisite demonstration that had ever been invented ... [taking] all the tea equipment from every department in the university before morning tea. They rightly recognized that in our [white] society, if you don't have morning tea, it's a fate worse than death! You can be raped, you can do nothing else, but you mustn't be deprived of your morning tea![105]

After a series of further consultations by the university disciplinary committee several days after the initial demonstration, a decision was made to expel a number of students. The decision inflamed student feelings. In the riot that ensued $70,000 worth of property was destroyed. The main target of their fury was the recently built – and much hated – senior common room. The university administration was also attacked and 150 students were arrested.[106] Most pleaded guilty and many were sentenced to six months with hard labour; several others pleaded not guilty and went through a lengthy trial. After serving their sentences the students faced further penalties and were restricted from coming within 20 kilometres of the city, making it impossible to continue their studies. The effect of these expulsions was dramatic. Tengende explains that many 'escaped to neighbouring countries *en route* to join the liberation struggle'.[107]

The effect of the liberation war on student consciousness at the time cannot be overestimated. The 1973 demonstration on campus coincided with the opening of a new Zimbabwe African

National Liberation Army (ZANU's military arm) northeastern front. After years of fratricidal struggles with ZAPU, this was regarded as a turning point in war and now, finally, liberation and independence were around the corner. Student militants and activists fed into and helped generate this renewed optimism. At the same time Rhodesian authorities intensified political repression on campus. The government had recently lowered the minimum age of conscription to 17 and it was not uncommon to see white students in military fatigues on campus. Students from rural backgrounds would also have had direct experience of the repression of the state at home: 'The university was now resembling the wider Rhodesian white society – armed and defiant.'[108] The 1973 demonstrations were the last effective resistance at the university. The mass arrests, imprisonment and expulsion of students, together with the militarization of the campus, effectively ruled out further open displays of resistance. The student representative committee was left impotently to issue press releases that the state media ignored.

Not only university students gave up their studies to fight in the liberation war; after 1973 secondary school students joined *en masse*, forcing at least six rural schools to close down.[109] One of the most prominent student leaders from the 1980s also emphasizes the role high school students played in the 1970s:

> They were the bedrock. Those who were in high school and who were old enough crossed from Mutambara Mission School into Mozambique, most of these ex fighters were actually high school students, who left form 4, form 6, they left the University of Zimbabwe [*sic*] to go to Mozambique. So the student movement has always been the basis of change in Zimbabwe, even internally ZAPU, ZANU ... students were the youth movement. But the fighters, I would venture to say that the 90 per cent of the fighters came from the colleges, high schools and the University of Rhodesia. People would leave in their first year, in their second year. People would go from St Augustine, Mutambara. ... All those fighters were students.[110]

125

University students were extremely important in the guerrilla struggle. After the 1975 assassination of guerrilla leader Herbert Chitepo, a large number of ZANU leaders in Zambia were arrested. An energetic student intelligentsia that had fled from the university and secondary schools in Rhodesia over the previous years filled the leadership vacuum. They took control of the struggle through the Zimbabwe People's Army (ZIPA), the product of a merger between ZANLA and ZIPRA (the rival military arms of ZANU and ZAPU) in the mid-1970s. ZIPA developed a reputation for being led by young leftist intellectuals.[111] Fay Chung, who was active in the ZANU–PF at the time, writes about how 'the university intelligentsia ... who had successfully established themselves in Zambia ... found an opportunity to take a more direct role.'[112] She notes that the university intelligentsia were not only students (or from Rhodesia), but also Zimbabwean intellectuals from across Africa, the UK and USA. 'Dozens of young university graduates followed, from Britain, Sierra Leone and Rhodesia.'[113] Education was at the centre of their approach, and they sought to develop coherent political training for political commissars. Groups of cadres were educated in the main tenets of Marxism–Leninism, but on an inherently egalitarian basis. Officer/recruit distinctions were eliminated and democratic procedures were, albeit briefly, introduced. When ZANU resumed leadership of the liberation movement, a populist authoritarianism that shunned independent thinking replaced this critical left-wing perspective.[114]

Today, a certain amount of political capital is made from these facts. The ruling party contrasts the true revolutionaries of the 1970s, who came from the university, with the 'fakers' of today. Mugabe used Zororo Willard Duri's funeral in 1996 to attack current activists, 'It was the dedication of cde [comrade] Duri's generation that led the ZANU–PF politburo to give him the status of a national hero. ... The new generation has to emulate that spirit in the new battles facing the country.'[115] This phenomenon is an important argument in the book. The role of the student intelligentsia reflected the weaknesses of popular social forces in Zimbabwe and the exaggerated (indeed fetishized) importance of university education. These combined processes turned an extremely small layer of the population into politically privileged (and deeply contradictory) agents of social change.

The development of a pre-independence intelligentsia has been discussed in a number of important studies,[116] all of which discuss the choices and dilemmas for a group of educated Zimbabweans that resulted from the expansion of secondary education in the 1950s and 1960s. Mandaza saw that this group wanted to rid settler society of the racial fetters to their own self-advancement, and so the principal issue was not to 'raise questions about the mechanisms of exploitation. This would risk exposing their own class position in relation to the African masses'.[117] However, another choice – that of self-denial – lay open to them: the intelligentsia was to immerse itself in the mass upheavals of the liberation struggle, and to perform a type of class suicide that, as we have seen in Chapter 1, was advocated by Cabral. 'Only when the petty-bourgeoisie itself decides to sacrifice its own class interests for those of ... a socialist Zimbabwe'.[118]

It is important to identify the weaknesses in the nationalist struggle, and in the student movement that was an adjunct of it, that marginalized the role of the urban poor and working class. In this context students at the University of Rhodesia failed to develop a clear political strategy that linked the rural revolt to an urban struggle, in the townships, factories and at the university. Student activists were ultimately paralysed by this failure, and their uncritical engagement in the nationalist movement gave them no alternative but to decamp from the university into exile and the guerrilla struggle, and not to the black townships or factories. Cefkin explains this paralysis brilliantly in his pioneering study of the student movement in 1960s Rhodesia:

> Expectation that the African townships might explode into popular rebellion rested upon fond hopes for spontaneous action: students did not undertake an analysis of the conditions under which uprisings occur. In the absence of effective nationalist organization in the townships which

could utilize campus demonstrations to touch off, spread and direct revolutionary actions the student initiative remained an isolated event of little impact within the African community.[119]

Cefkin reflects on the uncritical acceptance in the student movement of political tactics that derived directly from the nationalist leadership.[120] The failure of student activists, he argued, to focus on bread and butter issues that could have connected more immediately to the needs of black Rhodesians, hindered the potential to build a mass movement.

State-privileged activism: 1980–95
Between 1980 and 1995 there were broadly three periods of student activism. The first, a pro-government period, lasted until the anti-corruption demonstrations in 1988, with student activists still glorifying the national liberation struggle that had recently won independence. The second, an anti-government period, was followed quickly by the 'convergence of forces' in the 1990s with the struggles against privatization. A further period of activism emerged after 1995, with the consolidation of the ZANU elite around the IMF and SAPs, and the break up of revolutionary nationalism and the collapse of the Soviet Union. These three periods are discussed in turn below.

At independence student life could not have contrasted more with the rural and urban worlds from which students emerged. Most students received full grants from the state, which were, until the mid-1990s, more than adequate. In fact money allocated for grants increased by almost Z\$ 10,000,000 between 1993 and 1995.[121] Although there were frequent demonstrations about the late disbursement of payouts (grants), they were regarded as generous.[122] As late as 1995 a mature student, Talkmore Saurombe, who had been teaching for years in a rural school, fulfilled a dream to go to university to upgrade his teaching diploma:

When I arrived at UZ in 1995 it was a very exciting situation because life at campus was very different from life at work. So I was excited, you know, that I had come to university to help my ambition be fulfilled. You know because if I actually go back to my diploma days at college, I remember putting up a photograph of my graduation day at college, and I had this script at the bottom inscribed 'a pipe dream unfulfilled.' So, when I came to university it was actually the beginning of the fulfilment of that pipe dream.

Then we used to get a payout, which was a lot of money then ... to begin with it was 17,000 in the first year, then in my final year it went up to 32,000 and that was a lot of money. ... I know that it was something like even five times more than the salary of a diploma holding teacher at that time.[123]

This meant that students could sponsor other members of their family through school, send money home and socialize. As Gumbo said, they could 'drink beer daily'. Many students illustrated this by explaining that they had enough money to eat between meals, which is perhaps more an illustration of the crisis in the university sector today than a reflection of affluence in the past. Saurombe goes on to explain: 'We used to have full-course meals, you know. One could afford to get three meals a day and then it was nice. It was conducive to study. Because you had *nothing to worry about but your books*.'[124]

At the time most students were subject to a system of 75 per cent grant and 25 per cent loan. In the case of Saurombe who was returning to education, it was 100 per cent loans, repayable over five years when he returned to his teaching position.[125] The status of university students, privileged and cut off in many ways from the harsh realities of the rest of society, had profound effects on their activism. Activism combined a vanguardism – championing the cause of the poor and dispossessed – with an elitism that came from their privilege. It also meant – as student activists will tell you today – that students were not solely preoccupied with bread-and-butter issues.

Elites and vanguards

The most notable action among students in the early 1980s was a demonstration and rioting outside the South African embassy after the death of the Mozambican president Samora Machel in 1986. By the late 1980s, however, student activists could no longer ignore the blatant corruption in the government. The first anti-government demonstrations were only against certain members of the government and students regarded them as supportive of Mugabe's own anti-corruption drive. An anti-corruption demonstration took place in September 1988 at UZ. The demonstration – seen as a milestone in the movement – marked an abrupt fissure in the relationship between students and the ruling party – a party they had previously regarded as their own. The students called themselves revolutionary intellectuals and protested in support of Mugabe's drive to return the ruling party to the Leadership Code.[126] Students issued an anti-corruption document detailing ten cases of corruption within government circles. Mugabe's response, angrily dismissing the demonstrators who were protesting explicitly in his defence, was an abrupt and violent moment of truth for hundreds of student activists who had regarded the president as their hero. They also demanded that ZANU–PF be transformed into a vanguard party before a one-party state was introduced.[127]

The leadership of the Student Representative Council (SRC) at the university at the time was heavily influenced by socialist politics. The SRC president, Arthur Mutambara – whose period at UZ is now eulogized as the 'AGO era'[128] – recalls how the leadership would regularly visit the East German, Russian and Chinese embassies: 'I read *Das Kapital* in my first year. We used to go to the Soviet embassy to get books, from the Cuba embassy, and I had lots and lots of books and I read and read and read. So to me the first year at varsity was about politics.'[129]

The period was marked by ideological debates on Marxism. Another student from the 1990s argued that 'We were all dialectical materialists.'[130] Campus life was not only about ideological debate, for there was also a thriving social scene, of which the Zambuko Izibuko theatre company was an important component.[131] It staged political drama often on regional themes, the struggle in Mozambique and the battle against the apartheid regime.[132] As Mutambara describes campus life: 'another reason for our success was being able to combine a very good social programme with a good political programme, which meant that people would come to our political events because they were satisfied. We had cultural galas, we had bands, we had alcohol; although I didn't drink I would provide it.'[133]

By the late 1980s, students at the university were beginning to break with the government, opening up the second period of their activism: a process that saw their transformation from Mugabe's committed revolutionaries to an irritating oppositional force. The success of this period of student activism was linked to a changing relationship with the regime. First, it was a turning point for the regime and its attempts to impose a one-party state, an idea that was initially supported by students who, between 1988 and 1989, saw the true colours of the state they defended. Mutambara identifies this element as the key reason why: 'people are so keen on our period ... we were the first people, we have been vindicated. We looked very radical and extremist but everyone is doing it now. ... We were the first people to draw the guns and shoot from the hip.'[134]

But Mutambara disguises the pain and loss his generation of activists felt at the government's betrayal. This sense of betrayal explains the explosiveness of their subsequent action (declaring shortly after the demonstration in 1988 that the regime could be compared with apartheid South Africa). The student movement managed to lead the assault on the government, heralding a new and uneasy period of opposition and resistance in civil society.

ESAP and the collapse of the Berlin Wall
The trauma at the collapse of the Soviet Union was felt heavily across Zimbabwe's political scene. University professors who had educated a generation in a version of Stalinized Marxism were left without their ideological moorings.[135] The collapse coincided with the introduction of ESAP in 1991, a wide-ranging programme of economic reform promoted by the World Bank

and IMF. The sacred cow of university funding would be tackled through a policy of cost recovery.[136] The real casualties in the first five years of ESAP reform were primary and secondary education. The introduction of a new fee structure after the 1991 Education Amendment Bill modified the 1987 Education Act, which had provided the legal basis for free education. Real expenditure on primary education fell by 11.3 per cent in 1992/3, and between 1991 and 1993 secondary school enrolment fell by 10 per cent.[137] Between 1993/4 and 1994/5 funding for tertiary education increased by Z$ 74,605,000, with expenditure on the National University of Science and Technology (NUST) and on the UZ representing approximately 80 per cent of the total.[138] The withdrawal of grants and subsidized university-run facilities would occur later in the decade.

This third period of activism, many claim, marked a decisive break with an earlier and more political phase. Where previously students had fought corruption, now they sought only to see increases in their payouts and a crude economism came to dominate student politics.[139] The reality is not so neat. The literature tends to romanticize earlier periods of activism – as do ex-activists. The 1980s is a case in point. Mutambara sees that decade as marking a period of untarnished political struggle at the university. In fact, the 1987 SRC executive emerged as a reaction to a campus divided ethnically – reflecting the civil war being fought against 'dissidents' in Matabeleland – and riven by hooliganism, which affected all forms of political activism on campus.[140] This indiscipline[141] continued through the late 1980s and was partly reflected in the language used on campus. Nose-brigades was a derogatory term to describe students from formerly white only Group A schools who were regarded as speaking through their noses. The linguistic retaliation was similarly class bound and the Nose-brigades responded by calling rural students SRBs (strong rural background).[142]

These issues are central to the way student mobilization is viewed in many parts of sub-Saharan Africa. The literature on student movements[143] tends to make use of a false dichotomy that divides the student movement into distinct periods of activism. According to this categorization the early post-independence years coincided with a period of political mobilization (and it is no accident that the period coincided also with the student activism of the authors who often make these arguments), unaffected by the crude economism (and hooliganism) of students today.[144] The example of Zimbabwe points to a much messier reality. As Tengende documents, the 1980s were replete with moments of indiscipline and political action; similarly, the late 1990s, purportedly representing a degenerative collapse into daily corporatism, abound with moments of high politics.

Students continued to make explicitly political demands: perhaps the high point in this period was their involvement in the anti-police brutality demonstration in October 1995 and the anti-racist campaigns of the student union in the early 1990s. This also saw the emergence of the ISO (previously a study circle at the university) onto the public arena. The ISO would continue to play a vital role in the formation of student activists, attempting to fill the ideological vacuum the collapse of the Stalinist faction had left.[145]

Brian Kagoro, a leading activist at UZ at the time, describes the convergence of economic struggles – against the privatization of student services dictated by ESAP – and political ones, very much in the mould of the AGO era: 'we moved to the anti-racism campaigns, that's 1993, 1994, and then later on to the anti-police brutality campaigns. The mid-1990s were really around the student welfare issues particularly, because of the privatization that took place within the university system from 1994 onwards.' Kagoro also points to the contradiction that was at the heart of structural adjustment, seeing it as a process that unevenly gave birth to the opposition at the end of the decade:

> I think the contradiction of the structural adjustment programme was that whilst it presented political liberalization or appeared to for the rest of the country, it also killed the whole ethos of liberation, within student and worker struggles. And the focus was around issues of welfare ... they took ideology out of the [equation] ... [and

now it was] how much are we getting by way of stipends. Equally, if workers got a sufficient pay rise then there was no motivation to engage. And that informs why it took so long between the mid-1990s and the late 1990s for the emergence of opposition politics and also the nature and form in which that opposition politics emerged.

I think we have got to keep in mind that it was largely the same worker leadership and former student leaders who formed that opposition movement. If you read the founding documents, the intention is to make it a social democratic movement. And the triumph of neo-liberalism was such that there was a shame with which many regarded the old enthusiasm for the left. People consistently wanted to be seen as left of centre, but not sufficiently left to be called commies. So in a sense you try to sanitize ideological issues. People would easily engage with human rights questions devoid of politics ... progressively student unionism was reduced to student demonstrations and reduced to which students could hold off the establishment and for how long.[146]

Though this period was full of contradictions, student activism was still dominated by the politics of the left. These years saw the consolidation of the ruling elite, the (painful) exclusion of students from it, and the dramatic collapse of Stalinism. However, a new critique (and form of activism) began to emerge, at once powerfully critical of the regime yet weakened by wider political and economic changes affecting every level of Zimbabwean society. Kagoro again makes this point extremely well:

The issues were around class analysis to start off with. We are very much dialectical materialists and we saw an obscene accumulation of wealth by the political elite under the guise of people empowerment. And so the first critique was around issues of integrity. ... Whilst the rest of the country lived in abject poverty, you had an emergent class which was not based on production. It was not based on manufacturing, they were simply making money out of political positions and their children also were not being brought to local institutions. Their children were being shipped off overseas on some scholarships. So you saw a progressive privatization of the state. So in a sense most of us felt locked out of the independent Zimbabwe that our fathers had fought for. ... You can't still place whether it was out of bitterness or out of just a sense of exclusion. We were not recognized. We are not recognized as citizens because our parents were not amongst the political elite. So in a sense you could treat us like trash ... because we were not ministers' children. So the degeneration that occurred in the institutions, the degeneration that occurred within the fabric of academic offering at the university is something that we viewed with scepticism. We saw it as a conspiracy by the neo-political elite.[147]

Students took on what they described as the 'unrattled Rhodesian' establishment that had formed a *de facto* alliance with the obscene accumulation of the black political elite. As Kagoro explains, you 'had this totally undisturbed, unperturbed privilege of the former elite and what seemed to be an organic or strategic alliance between the two elites. The emergent black elite and what we often referred to as the conspiracy of silence because they were beneficiaries.'[148]

Students highlighted cases where government ministers became the owners of commercial farms, donated by their white counterparts. Connected to these protests was the identification of the university establishment and the police force as the pillars of strength for the establishment. The 1995 demonstration in Harare was something of a watershed: 'You will see at the anti-police brutality demonstration people demanding the resignation of the commissioner because a street vendor had been shot.'[149] The demonstration saw the crucial convergence of student and popular protest, and it opened up a new period of activism among students and in wider society after 1995.[150] The protest was organized by student activists at UZ, and specifically members of the ISO. It marked the convergence of forces that was a familiar feature across the transitions in sub-Saharan Africa, but highlighted the specific role of students in bringing about this juncture. Chisuvi makes the point in relation to Zimbabwe: 'the character of a student in Zimbabwe is such that whenever there is a movement, it is the students that act first, they act as that spark to the powder keg ... it is the role of students to act first, to act as torchbearers ... to instigate action.[151]

New activism: 'more sadza'

The period was replete with paradoxes, with many seeing student activism degenerate into crude hooliganism (an offshoot of the economism forced on students by structural adjustment). These were contradictions that characterized even the high activism of the AGO period. In an event that many saw as conclusive evidence of the degeneration of the student movement, students were arrested for raiding dining halls at UZ and urinating in freezers. The event occurred in April 1996 and the uproar – reported as headline news for several days – even led to one Zimbabwean in the USA to write that internationally 'all Zimbabweans have been tarnished by the incident of April last year.'[152] The ruling party also capitalized on the incident to condemn the new generation of activists. Typically, Mugabe led the assault. On 25 April the *Herald* reported a speech the president gave days after the events at UZ: 'President Mugabe castigated the so-called "warlords"[153] now emerging at the UZ whom he said called themselves revolutionaries but who fought for nothing more than more sadza and more allowances.' Mugabe argued that the current generation of students betrayed the 'true revolutionaries' who had emerged from the same institution during the 1970s.

Student representatives condemned the action and former student leaders set up an organization to liaise with the authorities and disaffected students called University of Zimbabwe Former Student Leaders. On 26 April the *Herald* reported: 'The association ... held its first meeting recently ... The association shall seek to provide an ongoing relationship with the university on a variety of issues, providing advice with a view to ensuring the existence of dialogue to curb unnecessary disruption of normal university activities and internal decay.'[154]

Part III: Transitions: resistance in civic society and student activism: 1995–2003

From 1995, under the impact of structural adjustment, Zimbabwe entered a period of deepening social crisis and prolonged revolt. Gwisai wrote that 'the urban masses have waged massive struggles that have shaken to the roots not only the post-colonial authoritarian state, but also the vicious neo-liberal paradigm imposed by our rulers. ... The struggles have gone further than most in challenging one of the continent's most entrenched and violent ruling classes.'[155] The anti-police brutality riot and demonstration was a key moment in student mobilization, for it brought students and popular forces together on a large scale for the first time (ISO militants at the university organized the demonstration). It also marked a new period of activism that led eventually to the political transitions in the late 1990s. The main national university, UZ, had also changed during this period. There was an increase in student numbers from 2240 in 1980 to 9300 in 1990 and to 10,139 in 2001.[156]

Students feed into resistance: 'the convergence of forces'
The rarefied existence of students began to break down when they were plunged into conditions at the university far removed from those experienced by the first post-independence gener-ation. Deepening privatization under a new programme for structural adjustment, Zimbabwe Policy Reforms for Social and Economic Transformation (ZIMPREST) introduced in 1996, meant that students faced hardships a world away from the heaven on earth Kagoro had experienced in the early 1990s. At the opening of parliament in 1997, Mugabe expressed new government thinking on tertiary education when he introduced ZIMPREST's second phase. 'It seeks to stablize the macro-economic environment ... enhance competition, promote equity in the distribution of

income and wealth and bring about further reform of the Civil
Service, parastatals and the financial sector.'[157] The country's
institutions of higher education would never be the same again.

Battles were now fought at the university over what was
commonly known as ESAP 2, the attempts to introduce 50 per
cent grants and 50 per cent loans in 1997, and privatization of
catering and accommodation at the university in 1998. The
government moved to scrap grants, Mugabe explaining in 1997:
'The funding of higher education programmes will continue to
take cognizance of equitable distribution of limited resources. It
is now Government policy that students are expected to contribute a proportion towards their education through payment of
fees, although care will be taken not to prejudice students from
poor families.'[158] These cost-recovery measures led to the government requiring students, in the words of Zvobgo, to 'provide 50
per cent of their university education costs'.[159] Kagoro describes
the convergence of student hardship during this period with
wider social disaffection and rebellion:

> The establishment came up with a more drastic ESAP 2. So
> [you saw] the alienation of labour from a possibility of a
> settlement or accommodation within social contract
> debates or discussions, and progressively as you moved
> from 1995, 1996, 1997 the rapidity with which the univer-
> sity privatized essentially meant that you no longer had
> student discontent, you had an outright student rebellion
> on your hands. You had the most violent demonstrations
> during the 1996, 1997, 1998 period and so curiously you
> then had a third thing that happened during that period,
> the prices for almost everything were liberalized: the fuel
> price, everything just shot up. The largest number of
> redundancies was created there, so you now had students
> supporting their parents on their student stipends, which
> were not enough because their parents had been laid off
> work. So, in a sense, as poverty increases you have a
> reconvergence of these forces. And the critique started off
> really being around issues of socioeconomic justice. Right

to a living wage you know, the students started couching their demands around the right to livelihood.[160]

ESAP had a profound effect on government thinking, specifically on how to offset student resistance. University students were recast to fit the new policy paradigm as spoilt, privileged and needing to show respect for their education. As early as 1992 the government considered reviving an earlier project of national service. It was cast explicitly within the new framework, as Brigadier Mutambara – charged with assessing the feasibility of such a scheme – explained:

the government pays most of the expenses of students going on to universities and other forms of advanced training. This practice may have to be discontinued however because of the economic situation. To gain these education benefits in the future, it may be necessary to do a period of National Service. Students may have to work on community programs during their holidays and when they obtain their degrees, may spend a period as National Service cadre where they train new recruits.[161]

Although the regime returned to the scheme under very different circumstances in 2001, it was the political dispensation instigated by ESAP and neo-liberal reforms that first resuscitated the idea of national service.[162] It is interesting to note that these changes occurred at the same time as an expansion of tertiary education, so by 2000 several new univerisites had opened, including the Great Zimbabwe University in Masvingo, Gweru University College and Africa University near Mutare, in eastern Zimbabwe. There was also a policy of devolving certain degree programmes to teacher and technical colleges.[163]

Formation of the opposition
From 1998 students made another decisive break with the government. After what some students claim was the reformation of the Zimbabwe National Students Union (ZINASU) in

1997, which was intended to mark a period of *détente* with the government, students again began to raise explicitly political demands.[164] Questions of the payout, traditionally a spark for student activism, were relegated and in their place student leaders argued that only by building a political movement would the government respect the right to free education.

On 4 June 1998 UZ was closed for almost five months after a period of intense activity over the late disbursement of the payout. However, former student leaders cite the influence of the revolution that toppled President Suharto in Indonesia, widely regarded as a student revolt, as significant.[165] Nelson Chamisa remembers songs on demonstrations at the time that made the link with the Indonesian revolution explicit:

> *Suharto aenda nengoro yemoto, Kana uchienda kuenda tanga wadhingura Mugabe* [Suharto has gone; he has been overthrown with fire. If you also want to move forward you must first remove Mugabe]. So ... students were becoming the vanguard of the struggle. You must know that students usually have this microcosmic approach to issues, they deal with campus issues, like payouts ... but on this one we were trying to nationalize the student agenda, to also be of consequential meaning to a broader body politic in the country.[166]

After the university resumed classes political activity continued. One important student activist at the time, Jethro Mpofu, a Ndebele student from Bulawayo who refused to hold office, remembers a crucial meeting with the ZCTU at the university:

> There was a deliberate effort on the part of students to forge an alliance with the workers' movement. So in my own humble judgements I'd say that the MDC was born out of the political efforts of the students at that time. I remember students encouraging ZCTU to take political action against the government.
> There was a public meeting at the Lecture Theatre 400 at

the UZ in 1998 where Morgan Tsvangirai attended and students were urging him to go on and form a political party and he was very reluctant. ... I put it to him that 'I urge you Morgan Tsvangirai to help our hard working parents by leading them in the struggle against this government. You need to represent them and be fearless because all of us will be behind you,' and I'm sure he remembers that very well.[167]

Student activists are not always the best judges of their historical role. When asked about what contributions students made to the formation of the MDC, many state that they were the central element in its successful emergence. Tinashe Chimedza, general secretary of ZINASU in 2001/2, perhaps exaggerates the role of students, although the dissolving (or merging) of student structures into the new movement did undoubtedly occur:

The first structures to be set up by MDC were set up by ZCTU leaders and ZINASU leaders all over the country: Nelson Chamisa, Tendai Biti, Maxwell Saungwema, Takura Zhangazha. All those former students union leaders who were then in ZINASU went over the country with ZCTU leaders setting up structures, and when the MDC did not have youth wings it was the students who were MDC youth wings. The first toyi-toying to be made, it was the students who toyi-toyied and raised the banners, it was the students who went into the high density suburbs to help set up the structures. In my view it is almost impossible for any history of the MDC to forget the inputs made up by the students. We talk about MDC national youth chairperson,[168] know the reason why he was expelled for life from Harare Technical College where he was studying was because he was called an MDC activist, that's why he was kicked out of Harare Poly. ... So in my view it is very, very unfortunate that anyone who decides to write the history of MDC can forget about the contribution of the Student Union.[169]

But there is more ambiguity about the contribution of students to the MDC than Chimedza suggests. In February 1999 the Working People's Convention (WPC) was held to discuss the possibility of establishing a political movement in Zimbabwe. It grouped together students, trade unions and NGOs. Student leader and ZINASU president in 1998, Hopewell Gumbo,[170] described the difficulties of raising purely political issues:

> In our day, in 1998, we had a serious fight with students who said, 'Why are we bothering with politics and not dealing with bread and butter issues?' Mutambara's period gave us confidence to criticize and take on the government. I was on a team that was moving around the country during the report back from the WPC. It was comprised of myself, Job Sakhala from ZINASU and others from the ZCTU. What we'd do is arrive in a town – we were visiting the district centres of the country – and contact every college SRC and trade union branch and invite them to a stipulated meeting that evening or later. Then at the meeting we'd explain the outcome of the WPC and set up a steering committee for the Movement for Democratic Change. These meetings were meant to generate feedback of what people felt of the WPC. Morgan was resistant, he did not want a party (or at least that is what he said) but the mood on the ground was so great. The groundswell was so great.[171]

These are important points. First, they corroborate Chimedza's description of the role of the student movement during this period and reinforce Jethro's arguments that cast Morgan Tsvangirai as a reluctant godfather to the MDC. What was the relationship between the ZCTU and ZINASU? Gumbo is clear about the relationship in the months after the WPC: 'Our bases were the ZCTU. While we as students were clear that the WPC was a movement of the ZCTU and ZINASU there was no reciprocal respect that students were equals. They considered that we could toyi-toyi and mobilize, although the senior leadership gave us respect.'[172]

While this was an intensely political period for students it was also influenced by the 'meat and sadza' politics that had permeated student activism. Former students complain about their failure to organize ideologically in universities and colleges, as Gumbo illustrates: 'We had no strategy to enter the movement and seek to make a serious difference. Our participation was then limited from being an ideological engine to being foot soldiers in the emergent party.'[173]

However, it is important not to misjudge the connection between workers and students. The 1990s had seen a convergence of their demands, both groups having suffered from the hammer blows of ESAP. On a daily basis students worked intimately with the trade union movement. Many student leaders were not even able to attend the WPC due to a wave of student demonstrations, but still the message that students conveyed to those demonstrations drew explicitly on events that were taking place at the WPC in Harare. Gumbo remembers the message given to student protesters: 'that while you are in the streets, the WPC is discussing these issues in Harare. In Bulawayo at the time students put money in a hat to hire a cab to drive a regional chairman of the ZCTU [Milton Gwetu] to address them and brief them on the progress of the WPC that was taking place.'[174] During this period students recognized that their activism became absorbed by the new political formation. John Bomba, SRC president at the NUST in Bulawayo for 2001/2, describes how the traditional student greeting, 'Ahoy comrades' became '*Chinja Miatiro*' [Change your ways], the MDC political slogan.[175] As Chimedza explained, the student movement became the MDC's youth structure.

Voting, students and the MDC
The year 2000 can be seen as the high point of the MDC's political fortunes. The party, together with the National Constitutional Assembly (NCA), campaigned for a 'no' vote in the constitutional referendum that year. Again students were reputedly an important element in the campaign teams, at university and national level. Student leader John Bomba characterized the

MDC during the period as 'the lion that roared in '99 almost defeating ZANU–PF in the 2000 elections'.[176] The effect of the constitutional vote – victorious for the 'no' campaign – had a dramatic effect on the ruling party: 'it woke the giant', as MP Job Sikhala put it, and accelerated a transformation of the country that had not been experienced since independence.[177] The MDC assumed it would achieve a similar victory in the parliamentary elections several months afterwards, and some activists talked about a mood of complacency that infected the party.

The government returned to the dormant concept of national service and launched the NYS. In 2001 the first camp was opened, named after the government minister who initiated the training, Border Gezi. This was an attempt to politicize sections of unemployed and rural youths and should be seen as only one part of the regime's effort to construct a social base to confront the emergent opposition movement. The war veterans and peasantry – politicized over the question of land – were the praetorian guards of this policy, but youth became a crucial third element of ZANU's social base.[178]

There is, however, a danger of regarding these processes as entirely new. In reality, there was a remarkable degree of continuity with pre- and post-election violence throughout Zimbabwe's post-1980 history. Kriger showed that: 'Organized violence and intimidation of the opposition ... has been a recurrent strategy of the ruling party before, during and often after elections.'[179] This violence, often justified as legitimate punishment against those audacious enough to vote for the opposition, has also frequently been instigated by a politicized youth: 'leaders mobilized unemployed youth, mostly males, and sometimes women to attack supporters and their property.'[180] However, in highlighting the continuity in these practices, Kriger loses sight of the vital break in Zimbabwean politics with the formation, and electoral success, of the MDC and the distinct ways that youth were mobilized. By 2006 NYS had opened eight training centres, in each of Zimbabwe's eight regions. In the first five years of the NYS more than 40,000 youths had completed training programmes.[181]

Unravelling the resistance

Student leaders, who had argued on campus, at demonstrations and in political meetings, that their issues could only be addressed with the formation of a nationwide political movement, faced serious problems. Not only did the transition they had sought not come, the opposite occurred; ZANU regained the initiative. The MDC's neo-liberal reorientation assisted the regime. It expressed a central paradox of the movement: the MDC had emerged from the resistance to privatization and neoliberal policies but rapidly came to advocate the same structural adjustment its activists had eschewed. The student movement is a case in point. Its political activism in the mid-1990s was predicated on hostility to neo-liberalism. Kagoro explains:

> The critical analysis ... done by some of our able minds in the students' union especially the information department within our SRC, consistently pointed to the structural adjustment programme. That was the same critique that labour had given and also contained in the alternative to ESAP document.[182] So in a sense everybody identified privatization and in particular ESAP as the problem.

The crisis, as it became known in Zimbabwe, unravelled the resistance movement that gave birth to the MDC. Student activism suffered greatly from this process. Students, however, continued to fight the effects of the privatization of education in 2001/2, at the same time as the MDC – the party to which they had given themselves – was advocating further privatization. Prominent student leader and member of the ISO John Bomba describes the formation of Students Against Privatization (SAP), which was set up to lead the 'war' against privatization and to provide students with an ideological framework through which to see their activism.[183] Bomba gives an excellent description of the tensions at the time:

> We thought for students to be proper combatants, to be really effective combatants in this battle, they were

supposed to be people with a proper understanding of what privatization was. The student movement at a national level did not have an educational policy at all, it did not have any educational policy on any specific issues it was just a question of saying: 'Thursday it's a demonstration and people, we want our payout.' You will find very reactionary arguments, we want payouts because we are good at school, we are academically up to it so we deserve a payout ... they are not proper ideological arguments to say: no, no this is a right, the provision of education is a right to us. It is the government's task to provide health, education things like that, social services, but some would say: 'No I deserve a payout because I am good at school. *I am not like those who fell out at form.*' So Students Against Privatization was built in an attempt to fill in the gap – the failure to properly grasp the ideological forces that were underlying the activities that we were carrying out, and also building up cadres that were ready to carry out a national programme.[184]

I remember when we were launching SAP we were moving around, it was a time [2001] of massive student struggles against privatization led by myself and Tinashe [Chimedza]. We led an invasion of the Ministry of Higher Education in Harare. It was after parliamentary elections. The people we went with were people who were linked up through the SAP programme. It is actually the programme that brought us in touch with comrades such as Chisuvi.[185] We distributed a lot of pamphlets, literature asking the question: What is privatization? We did a bit of writing here and there. That was the dream that we had then to say we have to develop students who have the proper ideological understanding of what is taking place and students who are ready to act. That's the way to build a full student combatant.[186]

These initiatives should be seen in the context of the ISO attempting to fill the ideological vacuum by advocating a clear anti-neo-liberalism that challenges both the government and the new opposition.

The privatization of campus facilities continued unabated from 1998. In that year UZ stopped providing catering services after the accommodation and catering departments were dissolved, meaning that students now depended on private caterers.[187] This led to the wave of protests in 1998 and subsequent closure of the university. In 2000 the government launched a project of cost-sharing associated with its Millennium Economic Recovery Programme, which in practice saw tuition fees at state universities increase as much as thirtyfold, and a further spate of privatization of student facilities. The government claimed that even with these increases, fees were still heavily subsidized, and to cushion the blow it would negotiate with private banks for a student loan facility for poor students.[188] Students did not believe these assurances.[189] From April 2001 until 2002, under the leadership of ZINASU, student protests were held in almost every university and college across the country in an attempt to resist the extension of loans, fee increases and privatization.[190]

In one early protest involving students from Harare Institute of Technology (HIT) and Belvedere Teachers' Training College (BTTC), ZINASU secretary general Tinashe Chimedza explained that the demonstrators wanted 'to correctly inform the country that the students of Zimbabwe are against the privatization process'.[191] The opposition *Daily News* described how the government's reaction was to 'unleash its trigger happy police force to bludgeon the students into silence'.[192] And bludgeon the police did. The worst violence came in early April after a demonstration at UZ when seven riot police attacked and killed Batanai Hadzizi.[193] In the proceeding months leading student activists in SRCs across the country were arrested, tortured and expelled. In June, 20 students from Mutare Technical College were rounded up in the middle of the night after rioting in the city against the hike in fees for purchasing training material.[194] On 4 July the *Daily News* reported that 60 students from Masvingo Technical College had been arrested after battles with riot police against the 'development levy' (a poll tax on students at the college). The same pattern was followed in almost every college. In October the High Court upheld the suspension of ZINASU leaders from UZ.[195]

Two important aspects of this rebellion need to be highlighted. The first, as Chimedza explained, the protests were explicitly fought against privatization, and one of the political engines in the student movement at the time was the recently formed SAP, described by Bomba above. This organization was an initiative of the ISO, which had been campaigning against privatization for years.[196] SAP (or more explicitly the ISO) helped to give the rebellion an ideological head. Leading ZINASU members, who often loosely regarded themselves as ISO members, were supportive of the initiative, eventually seeing it as their own. The existence of these ideas in the student movement made a marked difference to how far students were able to exercise meaningful political action. The rebellion's second aspect is more negative. After the suspensions and expulsions from colleges and universities of activists who had led the protests, NGO funds rushed in. New organizations, offering a dubious political home for expelled leaders, were founded on the back of this money. The consequences of this influx of donor money are described below.

But what shape did these struggles actually take and how did privatization manifest itself on university and college campuses across the country? John Bomba was instrumental in organizing this resistance, which often took the form of price controls enforced by the students. It is worth quoting at length the experience of these anti-privatization campaigns:

It was around, I guess, February [2002]. That's the time of price controls. So we had a general meeting and we simply decided that these guys were profiteering and students could not afford lunch. So what's the way out of this? ... the following day everyone wakes up to find posters all over the university written 'Presidential Declaration on Price Controls'.[197] And the staple food for students is buns so naturally buns were our main target, we said no one is going to sell a bun for more than a certain amount. No one is going to sell a plate of sadza for more than this much and a number of other things, *freezits*, which is the cheapest drink but that's what students get for their lunch so we put controls on *freezits*.

And the beautiful part of it was that the language was quite threatening. If anyone fails to abide by this, we said, they are not going to be able to exist here. We are simply not going to tolerate them and they cannot do their business here ... they knew that we didn't mince our words. ... We were not playing when we said we were going to come for them if they didn't stick to what we were declaring, so a number of them they changed, they put down their prices a bit. And I tell you, students were appreciative.

However one old man who was the main supplier of buns adopted our controlled prices but because initially he had shown some resistance, on the next demonstration he was punished. His shop was looted. People broke in and they looted. But later on he came to me after the looting 'I adopted the prices that you gave me but still you are looting my shop. I thought we were now coexisting well.'

In some cases like that you have to be a little bit diplomatic, you can't tell him that I was responsible for mobilizing students to loot your shop. You can only say that you will look into this. So this was part of the strategy that we had, you solve day-to-day problems this way.[198]

It can be argued, perhaps unfairly, that Bomba's organizational tactics combined elements of the newer desperate activism. The period saw widespread looting by a hardened core of male activists (the 'UBA *mulenge*')[199] as well as an attempt to politicize and mobilize the movement beyond the politics of meat and sadza.

Mugabe's youth: NYS and strategic studies
ZANU–PF students claimed to welcome the formation of the MDC but lament how the party has come to dominate the student movement. It is important not to sideline or dismiss

149

ZANU students as simply stooges of the ruling party; they are not. They are an eclectic, politically committed group and often critical of the ruling party. For example, as David Matsikidze, the ZANU–PF vice-chairman at UZ describes his political beliefs:

> I am a ZANU–PF activist, that's the truth and there are certain ideologies, certain principles that I cherish, certain principles that I believe in. For example, I believe in black empowerment, I believe in land reform, I believe in so many social programmes that protect the underprivileged, the poor, things like price control systems, I really believe in them, and many other policies that are targeted at helping the underprivileged.[200]

These principles coincided with a left shift in government policy, which has helped to galvanize ZANU students. The curse on the movement according to Matsikidze is the polarization on campus since the MDC was formed:

> Since the advent of the Movement for Democratic Change, student activism got so polarized ... some of the situations and some of the problems that we find ourselves in, we need to talk with the government, especially our parent ministry, especially when we come to issues like student funding, loans and all that. So because of that excessive polarization we ended up with a situation whereby student leaders can't sit down and solve student problems. So, because of that animosity, nothing was done and we ended up with a scenario whereby there was no dialogues and, you know, things can't happen if there is no talking.[201]

The hegemony of the MDC has led the ruling party to help initiate a number of important projects. In December 2002 a rival national union was formed. Although officially non-political, ZANU welcomed the Zimbabwe Congress of Student Unions (ZICSU), but most students who are aware of its existence dismiss it as a ruling party front. ZICSU was, however, only one part of the attempt to break up the MDC hegemony on campus, the most explicit attempt being the controversial formation of the NYS. While the six NYS camps established by July 2003 are not an overt attempt to enter the student body, they are linked to a wider strategy, that is a strategy that includes the introduction of national strategic studies (NSS) as a core course for students in higher education. Graduates from the camps have privileged access to tertiary institutions. Their role, though more ambiguous than the international media allow, is to act as a social buttress in support of the ruling party.[202]

Among certain graduates from the camps interviewed in Chegutu – a government stronghold two hours from Harare – there was an explicit commitment to the ruling party. A number complained that they should be taught in more detail about the functions of government, 'because we have become part of the government and the government now relies on us'. The diversity of their training expresses the government's uneasy commitment to state capitalism and neo-liberalism. One graduate described the courses, 'as a combination of things but mainly Marxism, socialism and business management'.[203]

The MDC's final push in June 2003 was illustrative of the role they play for the regime.[204] A large number of 'green bombers' – labelled such because of their green uniforms – were bussed into the city to maintain order. As one graduate from Chegutu spoke of how: 'In the recent mass action I supplied the police with information on what the MDC youths were planning to do, where they were meeting and at what time they were going to do their mass action. I also gave them names of activists. I think that it was not a good idea to march to State House.'[205] Other NYS graduates told of their municipal work in hospitals (five of those interviewed were working in the Chegutu hospital) and many described how they were more politically involved, for example, in controlling food queues.

Since March 2003 the government has been trying to introduce NSS at colleges and universities. This is a compulsory course on Zimbabwean history concentrating on the war of liberation. In June 2004 there was a scandal at Harare Polytechnic when only students who had completed NSS were allowed to graduate.[206] Many NYS students take a national orientation course that is intended to prepare them for tertiary education. It is advisable to avoid a simplistic interpretation of these programmes as simply intended to indoctrinate gullible youths. Although they are intended to undermine student activism and to act as 'young vets' defending the regime,[207] many of the students spoke with genuine enthusiasm about the courses, and after graduation from the course they are often given work for the first time.

The first public meeting in Zimbabwe to discuss NYS was in Harare in August 2003.[208] One graduate at the meetings justified the scheme on the grounds that it resolved the intractable problem of urban unemployment: 'NYS is trying to say this: that we don't need to create a nation of workers. We need to instil entrepreneurship in the minds of every Zimbabwean. For every Zimbabwean to own their own business. We are trying to say to every Zimbabwean youth to be a commodity broker.' While a nation of commodity brokers may seem far fetched, it expresses the complex reality of a country that has faced economic collapse, retrenchment and political crisis since the early 1990s. The Marxism and socialism come from a political strategy pursued by the regime in an attempt to outflank the opposition, and the emphasis on informal employment and business studies are economic facts that have emerged after years of adjustment and neo-liberalism. Although it is important to remember that ZANU–PF has always combined a public commitment to Marxism with a less ideological interpretation, the recent return to such radical and leftist rhetoric is consistent in many ways with the historical behaviour of the party.[209]

The students undertaking NSS invariably disliked the course and many questioned the history they were being taught. Also, divisions separate students in higher education from the rural youths who are the main target for the residential training. However, it is important to stress that these reforms have a long history in the Zimbabwean educational curriculum, with repeated attempts to introduce a more practical emphasis in education. For example, similar language was used to justify teaching the political economy of Zimbabwe in secondary schools.[210]

'Commodification of resistance'

The period of frustrated transition has created many distortions in student activism. The SAP policies the ZANU government pursued in Zimbabwe have had a contradictory impact on social movements and resistance. They have created conditions for bread riots and resistance in Africa and have diverted the struggles described in Chapter 1. As Zimbabwean socialist Gwisai explains, 'the crisis of neo-liberalism as well as creating massive revolts in peripheral capitalist countries has also led to the co-option of the middle class and a layer of the working class by donor agencies and NGOs.'[211]

The ISO has used the term 'commodfication of resistance' to describe how NGOs have privatized (or perhaps even 'bought') resistance in Zimbabwe. This is symptomatic of the frustrated transition, and the decline, in the movement that gave birth to the MDC, which has led to the massive distortion of social resistance by the introduction of donor money. This phenomenon has been described elsewhere in the world.[212]

Every political organization is sucked in. ISO members are drawn from party routine and activity to well-funded National Constitutional Assembly meetings that reimburse delegates with generous allowances and luxury accommodation. Delegates to a three-day NCA youth congress in Mutare in June 2003 were given expenses to the tune of Z$ 11,000–18,000 (for many the equivalent of a weekly wage). The full cost of the congress was eight or nine million Zimbabwe dollars. The effect of this on small grassroots organizations like the ISO can be catastrophic. Leading members flocked to the congress in Mutare. As John Bomba saw it:

> It brings in the question of how the international community has been able to assist us in advancing the cause and in some sense there has also been an element of some misplaced international support that has actually

drawn us back. With this asylum thing it has opened a massive window for opportunists.[213] ... It even links with the element of funding. With the crisis in Zimbabwe and the attention that has been focused there has been massive monies coming into Zimbabwe. You find a plethora of NGOs ... that do nothing that is relevant to the plight of Zimbabwe but nonetheless they are getting massive financial support. So there is this element, which we in the ISO call the 'commodification of resistance', people now selling the ability to resist.[214]

For example, in early 2003 the former executive of ZINASU established the Zimbabwe Youth Democracy Trust (ZYDT) with money received from the Norwegian Students' and Academics' International Assistance Fund (SAIH). It became a political base for students and ex-student leaders who were no longer office holders in the student movement, thus shifting the focus from grassroots programmes to building up superimposed organizations unrelated to political activism. Another such initiative was the Student Solidarity Trust (SST), originally established in 2002 after a wave of student expulsions, providing funds to expelled students to continue their studies through correspondence courses with South African universities. The funds are administered by the previous leadership of the student union and open to extensive abuse.[215] According to SST coordinator Mcdonald Lewanika, in 2006 the trust was supporting 72 students, most of whom had been suspended from polytechnics and universities in 2002/3, to study by correspondence degree courses with the University of South Africa (UNISA).[216]

There is certainly a question mark over the motives of certain donor bodies, and a new generation of critical student leaders have been attempting to counter the effect of this commodification. It is tempting to conclude that some organizations might desire to divert attention from the street to conferences and interminable public meetings. Public meetings are frequently held in hotels and conference centres across the country but with no political programme or serious linkages with the grassroots.

John Bomba's critique is reflective of the contempt many people now hold for the NGO community in Zimbabwe: they have 'disarmed the movement that was emerging from the ground, shifted people's focus from the real battles to some very fantastical arenas'.[217] But the real reason why civil society has been exposed to such distortions (disarming) is because the opposition – and the resistance that built it – has ebbed away since the formation of the MDC.

The final push: students and patriotic youth

On 2 June 2003 the MDC launched the 'final push', which was organized in universities by the ex-ZINASU executive, with SST support.[218] The political space the students occupy on campus meant that demonstrating at UZ was one of the only ways in which they were able to respond to the MDC's call. Instead of their activism arising from grassroots structures – the structures that were so active (and badly funded) during the highpoints of the student movement in the 1990s – the action committees set up by MDC members in colleges and universities in the run-up to the final push were mostly top–down distribution centres for *pitos* (the Shona word for whistles). And, crucially, these committees were not replicated in trade unions. Students, isolated without their traditional allies in the ZCTU, could easily be put down. Without the crucial convergence of forces the movement experienced in the 1990s, students were unable to sustain their resistance, thus proving again that they are easy to mobilize but even easier to sacrifice.

These failings reflect a weakness alluded to in Chapter 1, namely that students lack crucial 'socioeconomic stakes', which cripples their ability to paralyse political power. This is well illustrated in the case of Zimbabwe; the government with some impunity could close the principal national university in Harare for five months in 1998 without devastating consequences. It should, however, be remembered that student activists used this closure to galvanize support for their action and generate momentum for a new opposition party that emerged the following year. Still, Chisuvi's point about student action remains:

'students have one fundamental weakness, which is mainly that they are not located at the nerve centre of the system and no matter what action they do, the system can afford to ignore them. It can afford to have all the students out of colleges for two years without having any serious economic backlash.'[219]

At UZ on 2 June 2003, when almost 4000 students attempted to access the approach road from the campus that would have taken them to the city, they were viciously beaten. The following day the corridors in one student residence on campus, nicknamed Baghdad, were covered in blood.[220] One window of a ground-floor flat overlooking the courtyard was broken, and only the jagged glass left. The wall was drenched with blood. Students running from the military police hid in their rooms and corridors; the police then fired tear gas canisters into the rooms. In one room, the canister ignited the mattress. The two students in the room were prevented from leaving by riot police in the corridor. Struggling to breathe one student broke the shattered pane of glass; his head now partly exposed was repeatedly hit by police wielding batons in the courtyard; 45 students were admitted to hospital. By the end of the week Mugabe expressed regret at having to teach these youths a lesson.[221]

A number of female students were viciously beaten. One described the incident to me:

> Last Monday I was coming from home. I had gone home for the weekend. And when we arrived at the commuter omnibus rank there were soldiers and police and they ordered us to get down and lie on our stomachs and they started beating us. And inside, just beside that junction at the bus stop, there were boys who were singing and they were being assaulted by a group of police. And after we were beaten we were told to run and join the boys and the assaults continued, I think it was for almost an hour and half and after that a man came from the security office. The chief security officer of the university came and asked for permission to get the girls. It was granted and he took us to the security control room and then he later tele-

phoned the staff at the clinic. They came and gave us painkillers and treated us ... it was terrible.[222]

According to those attacked, the police and army were determined to humiliate them because of their own perception of being less educated. Philippa, the student quoted above, explains what army personnel were saying:

Murikuda kutengesa nyika nepito you want to sell the country for a whistle. And they were also saying that *ndozvamatunwa naTsvangirai*, that's what you have been sent by Tsvangirai to do. Go and tell him *kuti hapana zvaano tiita isusu*, that there is nothing he can do to us; we are the strongest army in Africa, and no one can do anything. And they were saying *munofunga tirimagrade four and imimi makadzidza sitereki munofunga kuti madzidza sitereki saka hamuna zvamunotiita saka tatokuwanirai ipapa. Tirikuda kukuratidzai kuti negrade four yedu tinogona kukukuvadzai.* You think we are grade fours and you are very educated, you think you are now so learned and there is nothing that we can do to you. Now this is our chance and we have got you. We want to show you that with our grade four we can still harm you.
  Against the women they said *imimi tikasangana nemi murodhi munotiita kunge tisina kudzidza sitereki. Saka hamumbofa makatida.saka munoda kuzviita masalad sitereki saka nhasi toda kuchibvisa chisalad chese ichocho* when we meet you on the way you treat us as uneducated people. So there is no way you can ever love us. You think you are special, so today we want to reduce you to size.

Many women faced the same treatment, victimized for being women and at university. Education, and the accumulation of diplomas, has long been a key symbol of social status and the ability to access the post-colonial state. UZ is at the apex of this fetishism and a crucial instrument for the distribution of what Bourdieu described as cultural capital.[223]

Summary
The causes of the malaise in the student movement are complex and ultimately linked to the regime's political orientation and the MDC's development. The formation of the MDC brought with it an avalanche of hope that came from the structures and movements that gave it life. The transition it promised, activists genuinely believed, would follow within months. A new government would be informed by the struggles that had taken place against neo-liberalism and the founding statements of the party indicated that these were not false hopes. These activists, including a layer of ex-student leaders who entered parliament as MDC MPs, had learnt their politics through combating the effects of privatization under ESAP. 'We were trained by leftists', Kagoro argues, often through the ISO. Their politics expressed a deep commitment to free education, which was anathema to the policy priorities of the government.

These same activists, who continued as MDC militants, MPs and supporters, were now championing a party that had swung under the banner of neo-liberalism. Students complained that they were not consulted during the drafting of the party's education policy, but this was symptomatic of a wider degeneration of the opposition. One ex-student leader, MP Job Sikhala, explains the extraordinary metamorphosis of the party:

> I remember last week [July 2003] I addressed a meeting in Mount Pleasant Hall [next to UZ], myself and the MDC president, we were the major speakers there. When the students asked my president questions about how much is the party concerned about the welfare of the students, he had to throw back the problem to the students themselves, that 'Why don't you find the solution on your own? You cannot think that the MDC can come and interfere at the university for you to remove privatization and the like.' They are no longer taking the student base seriously. ...
>
> I thought that the MDC was going to take over power in the year 2000, definitely. I was convinced. We were serious. We were all determined. Also, now the problem that we are

having today, that was not there in the year 2000, is the greed for economic riches within the party leadership and structures ... financial concerns have been put ahead of the struggle. The struggle now takes second place in the scrabble and fight for economic riches within the party.

The MDC was founded by a group of the poor; it was a group of totally the poor and a few middle classes. But now it is almost a party of the rich. Those who are within the core of the party, the inner core, are really fat and thick. You cannot look at a person who was with you during the foundation of the MDC as the person who is there now.[224]

While the MDC, which the dynamism and energy of the student movement largely formed, distanced itself from its social base, the ruling party transformed itself into a social movement. This movement animated the party more than at any time since the liberation struggle of the 1960s and 1970s. It included the politicization of the rural poor through the controversial land reform programme, the radicalization of war veterans who had been excluded from the political cake after independence and, crucially for this study, a political engagement with youth through NYS.

The regime was given space to pursue this strategy because of the opposition's failure. On each issue the MDC managed, with extraordinary consistency, to move further to the right, leaving the party disarmed and unable to articulate the frustrations and passions the ruling party sought to galvanize. This process was not inevitable. Many activists attempted to reverse the collapse of the opposition into the fatal grip of neo-liberalism, to prevent the party becoming what Sikhala describes as 'almost a party of the rich'.[225] In February 2001 the left-wing MDC MP Munyaradzi Gwisai (expelled from the party along with the ISO in December 2002) addressed a party leadership seminar. The blame for the party's current morass, he argued, was the 'hijacking of the party by the bourgeoisie, marginalization of workers, adoption of neo-liberal positions and cowardly failure to physically confront the

Mugabe regime and bosses'. Gwisai concluded: 'It is ... imperative that the party moves much more leftward ... in order to
realign to its base.'[226] The ability to hijack was linked to the trade
union movement's historically weak organizations and politics,
and the political coherence – even in a period of neo-liberalism –
of a middle-class intelligentsia. There was a strategy that may
have enabled the MDC to outflank Mugabe from the left, exposing, as Gwisai puts it, the government's 'fake anti-imperialism'.

After 2003 ZINASU became largely moribund, though it
continued to exist with student mobilization centred for a brief
period between 2003 and 2004 on a small group of ZINASU
office bearers and ex-student activists. Combat, an *ad hoc* group
of hardened militants who shunned mass mobilization, would
graffiti anti-privatization slogans on polytechnics and universities, stencil the group's emblem (a red clenched fist) and
organize cultural events. The MDC supplied Combat with
limited funds with which to buy stencils and spray cans. Theirs
were self-consciously guerrilla tactics, glorifying the activism of a
minority. Combat was influenced by autonomous ideas that
have played a role in the global anti-capitalist movement.[227] John
Bomba describes the context that saw the decline of ZINASU as a
mobilizing force, 'there are three elements to remember here,
firstly the massive wave of struggles from the 1990s was beginning to subside, while the commodification of resistance was
reaching crippling levels and lastly the 2001/2 student struggle
against privatization had been defeated.'[228]

Combat retreated when the Zimbabwe Social Forum (ZSF)
emerged. Though formed in 2002 by a number of activists and
NGOs inspired by the anti-globalization social forum movement,
the ZSF only really took hold in late 2003. ZINASU then re-
emerged as one of the formal structures to represent students in
the social forum. The youth camp was formed in tandem with
the ZSF and the first camp, where a range of political and
cultural events were organized, was held in 2003. As one rather
vague account puts it, the youth camp is 'a space and platform
for local youth activists, organizations and movements to
consolidate the local process of working towards social justice'.[229]

Neither students nor the university were at the centre of this mobilization. These youth camps achieved considerable success, pulling groups of youths who fell outside the transitional structures of student organization. But there is, according to one activist, another element to the ZSF, it 'represents the re-emergence of the socioeconomic agenda that had been completely lost by the MDC. The social forums respond more to the political and economic questions caused by reintroduction of structural adjustment'.[230] Still, the rise of the ZSF can be seen as occupying a space that emerged only after the real movements – of students and workers in the late 1990s and early part of the new century – were defeated.

Conclusion

From this chapter several critical themes have emerged that need to be linked to the general arguments being made in the study. Student activists in Zimbabwe were forged in the crucible of the struggle for independence: the student (or university) intelligentsia expelled from the University of Rhodesia in 1973 became leading members in the guerrilla war. After independence student activists saw themselves through the prism of the student intelligentsia and the historical role it played in the war. By 1988 student activists were describing themselves as revolutionary intellectuals, illustrating their politically privileged status in Zimbabwe. They advanced the first penetrating critique of the regime, proving to many people still under the spell of ZANU–PF, that it was possible to demonstrate against the government and not be killed (or at least not straight away). However, this was a time when they could draw on a political vocabulary of the left that was widely used in Zimbabwe – and globally – in the 1980s. Although Mutambara attempted to explain the collapse of the Berlin Wall as an 'attempt to restore the democratic and humanistic values of socialism lost through the vulgarization and distortions of the ideology since the Stalinist era',[231] his arguments were not entirely convincing. The Marxism–Leninism with which he continued to identify the student movement in 1991 was now being rejected internationally.

In the years that followed, under the impact of SAPs, students saw their status converge increasingly with broader social forces. However, even in this convergence students repeatedly acted as 'the spark that lights the powder keg'. Student activism in Zimbabwe cannot accurately be divided between a high politics of the early post-independent years and a crude economism of the 1990s. We find elements of both periods in the activism of students during the transition.

Yet there can be no sadder testimony to the ultimate failure of the opposition (and in turn the student movement) than the blunt response students received in July 2003 when they asked what role they had in the party.[232] Although it might be far-fetched to conclude that the MDC, 'are no longer taking the student ... base seriously', many students now (2006) argue that it is imperative that the student movement recover its autonomy and independent vigour from the political child for which it had laboured so hard to give birth. The contrast, as we have seen, with the heady days of the late 1990s could not be more dramatic. Bomba expresses this frustration extremely well: 'Those who remember 1997 to 2000 today feel like they are living in lost times. Every day activists ask what it will take to rebuild the confidence and idealism that drove us in the 1990s. ... One wishes for a return of the madness.'[233]

Chapter 4

POLITICAL CHANGE AND STUDENT RESISTANCE IN SENEGAL

Senegalese university students have always exerted a high degree of political independence. Over the last 30 years they have been seen alternatively as a vanguard for democratic change or as troublemakers manipulated by political elites. The high point in their activism is regarded as the student (and later trade union) uprising in 1968, which almost brought down President Léopold Senghor's government after only eight years of independence.[1] Student unrest was a continual theme throughout the 1970s and 1980s, and in 1988 students again dominated national politics and led the protests contesting the elections. In the recent election of President Abdoulaye Wade students were courted by the opposition to participate in the national crusade for *sopi* (Wolof for change). When this victory came, many students regarded it as their achievement. Before long, however, students were claiming to be the new opposition to the new government.[2]

Senegal was one of the first countries to introduce structural adjustment,[3] which dramatically affected higher education funding. In 1995 Senegalese students were written off, 'left with their daily corporatism and the inefficiency of their fights'.[4] Students in the mid-1990s were, according to O'Brien,[5] prepared to defend their elite status.

163

Map 4.1: Universities in Senegal

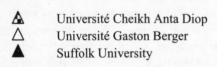

MAURITANIA

Podor

Saint-Louis

Richard-Toll

Matam

Linguère

Thiès

Diourbel

DAKAR

Nayé

MALI

Kaolack

Tambacounda

THE GAMBIA

Bignona

Kolda

Kédougou

Ziguinchor

GUINEA-BISSAU

North Atlantic Ocean

GUINEA

0   50   100 km
0   50   100 mi

Δ̂   Université Cheikh Anta Diop
△   Université Gaston Berger
▲   Suffolk University

Source: Adapted from the World Factbook (CIA).

In the first part of the chapter I look briefly at the political and economic trajectory of Senegal. In the second part I give a detailed account of the evolution of the student movement, and the growth of its opposition to successive post-independent governments. And in the final part, based on extensive interviews and archival research, I consider the role of students in the recent political transition. Students demonstrated both a *syndicalisme alimentaire* (economism) and an *avant-gardisme* associated with an earlier period of activism. The university was not peripheral to the new government, but a vital site for political reforms. The sections in this part of the chapter follow two important moments at the university. The first is student activism at the university in the run-up to the presidential elections in 2000, and the second is the key strike on the campus a year after the election. In the later sections I examine the nature of student participation in the new government and the ways in which the regime corrupted and co-opted many ex-student militants. By focusing on these years, I examine students and their (constrained) political activism during the *changement politique* in Senegal.

Part I: Political and economic background

To clarify the political background I briefly survey the main political and economic changes in Senegal since independence. The student movement that emerged in 1966[6] responded to tensions breaking through the relative calm of post-independence Senegal. I give a more detailed history of Senegal in Part 2, but through the prism of an increasingly buoyant and oppositional student movement.

Political and economic change in the 1960s and 1970s

Léopold Senghor's Union Progressiste Sénégalaise (UPS), which was founded in 1958, dominated the political scene following independence in 1960. Senegal secured a certain degree of political calm through state-led development in the early years of independence; this was rapidly eroded as the country was struck by an international recession that forced down the prices of Senegal's main agricultural exports. The new regime had inherited, and was committed to maintaining, colonial structures of political and economic control. In particular, the government was determined to guarantee an intimate relationship with France. In addition, the political fate of Senghor's party (and the political trajectory of the state after independence) was tied to the control of groundnut production by religious leaders known as *marabouts*.

The central role of religion in Senegal requires some explanation. Mouridism is the most influential of Senegal's Sufi brotherhoods and is linked to the historical figure of Ahmadu Bamba. Bamba was a spiritual leader and fervent commitment to his teachings has made the Mouride brotherhood a potent social force. Bamba lived at the turn of the twentieth century and was forced into exile by the French for refusing to renounce his beliefs. Stories abound of his heroism (and miracles) during his exile in Gabon. His miracles, told and retold in Senegal today, include escape from feeding lions and praying on ocean waves, though his true charismatic appeal stems from his perceived anti-colonialism. By resisting the colonial authorities he was, according to O'Brien, presented as a saviour of Islam in Senegal and the defender 'of African cultural pride'.[7]

Mouridism is organized in urban areas through the *da'ira*, which hold weekly religious singing but also act as an important social forum. While members' fees sustain the group's activities, mainly funding the annual pilgrimage to the religious capital of Mouridism in Touba, through the Khalifa general they also cover the expenses of the brotherhood as a whole. The political reach of Mouridism is largely connected to the brotherhood's commercial activity, which extends far beyond Touba and Senegal. Powerful and wealthy international networks of Mourides exist in many major cities.[8] Many of these groups have been established by students. In 1977 Paris students formed the Association des Etudiants et Stagiaires Mourides d'Europe (AESME), which quickly established branches in most of France's main universities.

Typically, in the 1970s, Donal Cruise O'Brien saw a worrying sign of Islamic revivalism within Mouridism:

Mouride student enthusiasm and the mobilization of the younger generation appeared at one time to be heading in dangerous directions. Aggressive Mouride proselytism among the urban young, spreading outwards from the university and the lycée, heightened popular awareness of differences between Senegal's Sufi brotherhoods; thus an explosive communalist politics was prepared in the late 1970s. ... Mouride student self-righteousness, with a more or less explicit critique of other brotherhoods ... awakened the spirit of communalism.[9]

Although Mouride groups proliferated in this period and continued to grow in the 1980s and 1990s, they did not present the danger O'Brien expected.

By the end of the 1960s the economic situation had begun to deteriorate as a result of a number of interrelated factors. The French abolished the price guarantees on oil seed in 1967 and between 1968 and 1969 Senegal experienced the worse cycle of drought since independence.[10] As we shall see, political calm was finally destroyed in 1968 when the government faced its first major crisis. Originally starting as a student revolt in May – in tandem with events in France that year – it rapidly became generalized as trade unions raised their own demands and called for a general strike. French troops stationed in the capital Dakar helped to suppress the demonstrations and strike.

The year 1968 brought a crisis of great economic and political significance for the new state. For a start, with the country's economy largely dependent on revenue from agriculture, particularly groundnuts, and with the price of the commodity falling throughout the decade, the government was forced to tighten public finances. Concurrently, between 1959 and 1968 unemployment rose by 450 per cent, with most of the job losses concentrated in Dakar.[11] Second, political spaces were closed off because the main trade union federation, the Union Nationale des Travailleurs du Sénégal (UNTS), formed in 1962, became tied to the state in the name of national unity and cooperation. While members of the federation elected the general secretary, the UPS appointed an additional post in the UNTS. Students were among the first to question the government's political control. By 1966 the student leader of the UPS admitted that in the university 'it is difficult to organize for the UPS. ... Students say that they cannot get involved and seal themselves in a certain neutrality.'[12] To an extent the radical Parti Africain de l'Indépendence (PAI) could fill the political vacuum on the campus.

Athough a student strike was called in May 1968 to oppose the government's decision to reduce student grants, students came to express a general urban malaise. The university had seen a growth in student numbers, almost tripling from 1018 at independence in 1960 to 3047 in 1968.[13] Frightened by the possible onset of an economic recession, the UPS aimed to pull in the university. On 28 May a demonstration in support of the students was estimated to have attracted between 20,000 and 30,000 protesters. With support for the strike spreading beyond the university, on 29 May police were sent onto the campus and students were attacked. Official figures record one death and 80 injured;[14] 600 student were interned in an army camp until 9 June and foreign students were expelled from the country. But by 31 May the UNTS had already declared a general strike.

UNTS national bureau members and leaders of several independent unions were placed under house arrest in Dodji in the north of the country. A state of emergency was declared in Dakar, with any demonstration of more than five people forbidden. The regime even called on the *khalife général* of the Mourides to diffuse the movement and for workers to return to their factories and offices, but the khalife's message fell on deaf ears. One minister, Magatta Lo, describes how as the police and army attempted to hammer the movement into submission, the president had given the French ambassador permission to plan his possible evacuation by helicopter from the Palais and then by aircraft to France.[15] In increasingly hysterical tones, Senghor pointed to a foreign influence:

In reality this insurrectional movement has come from Peking. ... It is the future of Senegal that is in question. It confirms the intentions of foreigners. Unfortunately there are French people who are up to no good. There are also left-wing civil servants. The choice for us is not difficult. We will resist until the end. ...

For the students, those responsible will do their military service. Foreigners will be sent home. Sadly it is the Mauritanians who are the most relentless. ... I believe that the university will need to close for two or three years.

The existence of Senegal is at stake. If the opposition triumphs, the country will be plunged into catastrophe.[16]

On 12 June the movement was defused. Once the UNTS had been assured that its comrades would be released it entered into discussions with the government. The eventual deal involved important concessions to both students and trade unionists. The minimum wage was increased by 15 per cent, while privileges to parliamentarians were slashed. But the most significant result of the crisis was the sense that the ruling party's (and the state's) invulnerability had been irrevocably shattered. Thioub summarizes the main effect of the uprising on Senegalese society:

May 1968 was the midwife of the 'democratic opening', that saw Senegal return to a system of political pluralism at the start of the 1970s. .. If the movement ... could play this role it was because the regime had never succeeded in spreading its political project. ... Activists trained in the ranks of the PAI judiciously exploited this weakness and gave to the movement a radical orientation.[17]

Senegal then entered a period of political turmoil. Several political parties were born, helping to determine the political trajectory in the 1970s and 1980s. Perhaps the most significant of these was the PDS, created in 1974 and led by the lawyer Abdoulaye Wade. There was also a proliferation of left-wing Maoist and communist groups, including the Mouvement des Jeunes Marxiste Léniniste (MJML). A more radical anarchist-inspired group emerged from the MJML, partly as a reaction to the group's perceived conservativism. The group attempted to attack the cortège carrying the French president Georges Pompidou with Molotov cocktails during his official visit on 5 February 1971. One student, Omar Blondin Diop, was arrested and sentenced to three years, only to be tortured to death in prison in 1973.[18] Nevertheless, Senghor managed to remain largely unopposed from within his party, renamed the Parti Socialiste (PS) in 1976. By 1980 – after 20 years as president – he was able to choose his political heir. Abdou Diouf replaced him that year and held power until 2000.[19]

Political change and structural adjustment in the 1980s and 1990s
Abdou Diouf presided over hardening economic realities that had been developing throughout the 1970s. The country has been crippled by an economic crisis since the late 1970s, linked to the international collapse in commodity prices. Rising costs in the public sector worsened the fall in the price of primary goods. Senegal was one of the first countries in sub-Saharan Africa to introduce SAPs through the World Bank and IMF with the stated aim of restoring equilibrium to the country's finances. However, one of the most commonly felt effects of these reforms, lasting for almost 20 years, was the austerity targeted at the public sector, regarded as over-funded by international lending agencies. In 1985 it was estimated that the civil service consumed 60 per cent of the government's expenditure.[20] That year, under the aegis of the IMF, the government launched a programme of reform aimed at correcting these distortions by reorienting the economy through a reduction in the role of the state in economic affairs.

Wade's PDS rose to prominence in the 1980s. Although the PS easily won elections in 1983 and 1988, on both occasions many claimed the voting had been rigged. The year 1988 saw the country plunge into another major political crisis closely resembling the political turmoil it had faced 20 years earlier. Wade fled to France after his arrest that year. Yet, following this crisis, calls for political reform were much more widely heard.[21]

The 1988 crisis was triggered by a dispute the previous year over the reform of employment law. The dispute went to the heart of how structural adjustment – advocated by the IMF and World Bank – was attempting to transform Senegalese society. The result was a confrontation between the Confederation Nationale des Travailleurs du Senegal (CNTS), formed after the 1968 events, and the National Assembly. In July 1987 the National Assembly was in extraordinary session called by the president Abdou Diouf to examine certain legislative changes that would affect the Code du Travail (work code). The government had earlier adopted certain changes to the code that would, in the words of the law, 'repeal articles 35, 193, 199 and 250 of the Code du Travail, with the aim of adapting the Code to the objectives of the New Economic Programme of the state, in particular softening the conditions for hiring labour and the employment of casual labour in enterprises'.[22] The trade union movement saw this as a frontal attack on the rights of workers.

Behind these changes lurked the IMF and World Bank. The government's decision to convoke the National Assembly in order to adopt these revisions (and two further legislative changes on investment and privatization) was forced on the government by the IMF and World Bank. Both institutions demanded these changes before 31 August as a condition for their financial assistance.

The CNTS convoked a general assembly on 21 July. The huge crowd that turned out, according to one account, made a simple demand: 'the pure and simple rejection of the law'.[23] Trade unionists also demanded the CNTS threaten the government with a boycott of the presidential elections in February the following year. But the mobilization exposed the federation's close relationship with the government. The general secretary of the CNTS, Madia Diop was also vice-president of the National Assembly. He announced to the crowd that he had had a meeting with the president and was confident that the law would not be passed.

Finally, a compromise was reached, which was an attempt to trick the trade union movement. Offending article 35 was repealed only to be replaced by an amendment to the same code (labelled 'amendment of the CNTS') and presented by Madia

Diop personally. The new reworded article ensured the same flexibility for hiring labour. One commentator was scathing about the federation's complicity: 'On 31 July a further *Assemblée Générale* was called and Madia Diop tried to explain himself, but remained vague and confused. Workers left the *Assemblée* with the sentiment of having been cheated from beginning to end.'[24] The revolt of 1988 was the movement's riposte.

Another problem for the government began to emerge in the south. Calls for independence increased throughout the 1980s in the fertile region of Casamance, populated largely by Diola people. The Mouvement des Forces Democratique de la Casamance (MFDC) was formed in 1982, but by 1990 it had become more aggressive and was launching offensives against military posts in the region. The regime responded in kind and the army attack MFDC bases in northern Guinea-Bissau. The school student strikes in 1980, which the police attempted to put down violently, helped to trigger the calls for independence in the region. Described in one account as the *'grande insurrection'*,[25] the strike in the regional capital Ziguinchor in January led to countrywide disturbances. Large solidarity demonstrations were held by school and university students across the country. In Dakar on 18 January 15,000–20,000 students marched carrying slogans supporting the movement in the Casamanse: 'Vive la lutte des scolaires casamançais.'[26]

In 1990 Abdoulaye Wade returned from exile and back to politics, welcomed by crowds shouting *sopi*, which had become the slogan for the movement for democratic transformation. Eight political parties signed a declaration that demanded the president's resignation and fresh (and free) elections. The following year the National Assembly officially sanctioned the involvement of opposition parties in the government and Wade was made a minister of state.[27]

In the presidential election of 1993 Wade resigned his position in the government and stood against Diouf. He won only 32 per cent of the vote, so Diouf entered his third term. In the legislative election held the same year the ruling party secured more than two-thirds of the votes. Soon after the election the government redoubled its efforts to implement further economic adjustment that was to have a dramatic effect on university reform. The devaluation of the CFA franc in 1994 deepened the political and economic crisis in the country. Continued privatization of the economy led to serious clashes with the trade unions, including the imprisonment of several leading trade unionists who were particularly vocal (and active) in their opposition to the rapid extension of privatization.[28] The devaluation also led to a significant adjustment in bilateral relations with France.

The legislative election in 1998 saw yet another victory for the PS and confirmed Senegal's title as a semi-democracy.[29] Still, with the economic crisis grinding inexorably on and the government lacking real legitimacy, by the end of the 1990s the picture remained bleak. According to World Bank figures, the industrial sector lost more than 21 per cent of its workforce in the 1990s.[30] The trade unions also saw new legislation restrict their room for manoeuvre and capacity to contest the changes. More than 20 years after the first SAP was introduced, the crisis SAPs were implemented to resolve was regarded by most to have deepened.

Support for the opposition continued to rise in the run-up to the presidential election in 2000. A short general strike the previous year, while not directly related to the political situation, was further evidence that the government was without urban support. Wade was finally victorious and Diouf stepped down. The result shocked the public and commentators alike, many of whom had previously dismissed the notion that the PS could be defeated. The democratic transition was confirmed the following year when a new constitution – limiting presidential terms to five years – was passed with 90 per cent approval. In the legislative election in April that year the presidential result was confirmed with extraordinary finality. Wade's eclectic coalition of 40 parties (*coalition alternance*) swept to power, winning 89 seats to the PS's 10. These changes cannot be over-estimated, but in the analysis that has emerged since the *alternance* there has been a remarkable silence on the role of students.[31] In the second part of this chapter I examine the evolution of the student movement in Senegal.

Part II: Aspects of Senegalese student activism 1950–98

Surveys in 1960, the year of independence, show that Senegalese students had a stronger political identity than their counterparts elsewhere in Africa.[32] They provided support for both the opposition and government, leading some to observe that 'national political leaders ... view student activists as rival politicians rather than as students.'[33] In the last 30 years they have been seen alternatively as a vanguard for democratic change or troublemakers manipulated by political elites. In the presidential election in 2000, students were courted by the opposition to participate in the national crusade for *sopi*. When this victory came, many students regarded it as their achievement. However, the state of the university and the corruption of the state gave way to a realistic assessment of political change and demands for opportunities for personal advancement.[34] Before long, students were claiming to be the new opposition to the new government, an issue that is taken up in Part 3 below.

Shaped by the politicized and rarefied spaces of the university campus in Dakar, the Senegalese student movement has played a vital and contradictory role in the country's political transformation. After examining some historical antecedents of the student movement before independence. I argue that, contrary to some historical literature,[35] students are not a pampered elite motivated solely by corporatist (or what are disparagingly referred to as 'bread and butter') demands. Several moments of student activism in Senegal are highlighted to illustrate continuities and change in their activism; in the final section I return to the problem of how we understand student mobilization.

Early students

Student politics in Senegal emerged as much from outside the country as from within. One vital element was the role of an exiled student intelligentsia who were among the first militant anti-colonialists. The role of the Parti Communiste Français (PCF) in the 1920s was an important influence on activists like Lamine Senghor. The Communist Party expressed an anti-racism that was also internationalist and attracted many of the best militants. In 1933 Léopold Senghor created and ran the Association des Etudiants Ouest-Africains. However, it was not until the 1950s that Senegalese students began to participate directly in the nationalist struggle.

The main organizations to emerge in the 1950s, the Association Générale des Etudiants de Dakar (AGED) and subsequently the Union Générale des Etudiants d'Afrique de l'Ouest (UGEAO), remained limited despite their attempts to extend their influence. Students in the 1950s were often linked to radical nationalist parties, particularly the Parti Africain de l'Indépendence (PAI)[36] and the Parti du Regroupment Africain (PRA).[37] Students played a central role in both these organizations and in the ideological and political mobilizations of the time.

UGEAO was noted for its radicalism. The colonial authorities were worried that it had fallen under the influence of Marxism, and saw in the radical statements it issued 'the desire of African students to enter into the political arena'.[38] These fears seemed to be confirmed when the UGEAO president declared in 1957 that 'we will organize and demonstrate, and we must place ourselves at the head of the movement of the anti-colonial struggle in Africa. We will win our independence and fight like our comrades in South East Asia and North Africa.'[39] UGEAO became involved in the creation of the Université Populaire Africaine (UPA), an initiative to raise literacy rates among the population. In the regional referendum organized by the French in 1958, UGEAO campaigned for immediate independence. The Senegalese government finally dissolved the organization in 1964. According to Thioub,[40] it was UGEAO's continued hostility to French interests in Africa after independence and particularly its support for Guinea that forced the new regime's hand.

The history of the movement is vital to the identity of the student movement today. There is a remarkable historical consciousness among students, as Bianchini comments: 'when one observes African student movements in relation to their northern counterparts, one is struck by the constant references to past mobilizations through ... various "commemorations".'[41] In addition one is struck by the historical memory of students in determining and defining the movement. Although it is not possible to rely entirely on students for the demarcation of the movement, their self-identity is formed in part by repeated references through *des commémorations diverses*. The press regularly covers student politics (often even its minutiae), which is an aspect of this process. In a period of research for this study (January to April 2004) the movement and its demands were frequently mentioned in the press and at political meetings (dinner debates) held on campus.[42]

The Association Musulmane des Etudiants d'Afrique Noire (AMEAN) also played an important and underestimated role in the development of the movement. The association was established in the early 1950s during what might be called the first Islamic revival. The period saw an increasingly self-confident Muslim world that included the violent liberation struggle in Algeria and the rise of Gamal Abdel Nasser and the 1956 Suez crisis in Egypt. AMEAN was at the vanguard of this ideological and religious revival in Senegal. One was the Catholic and Christian bias of the colonial authorities and the presence of an active Catholic youth organization. AMEAN stated that first priorities were issues of religious practice, diet and holidays. The first issue of *Vers l'Islam*, a journal set up by members of the association, was uncategorical about the need for AMEAN: 'Superstitions, prejudice and lies distort the perception of our religion ... , the lazy Islamic practice from the streets so different from the vivid dynamic of the Qu'ran ... the creation of AMEAN confirms our successful effort to break away from the monstrous [distortions].'[43] These demands were doubtless antagonized by what Ciré Ly called 'eucharistic imperialism' where the French celebrated the emancipatory potential of Christianity yet lambasted the vices of Islam.[44] Student Islam emerged in confrontation with the colonial state and as a precursor to the role students would play in the new state.

The explicitly political dimensions to the association's activities are the most revealing. AMEAN tirelessly opposed the authorities' attempts to divide the Muslim community, arguing that the 'meddling Bureau des Affaires Musulmanes' must be scrapped. The association's newspaper *Vers l'Islam* concentrated on friendly foes, the *marabouts* (religious leaders) whom they saw as collaborating profiteers. Many leaders of the brotherhoods 'strut about today, covered with all their decorations for "services rendered". ... These very same people agree with the administration on how to eradicate Islamic movements agitating all over black Africa.'[45] Yet there was another element to their radicalism; as well as seeing *marabouts* as accumulating scandalous wealth, they saw the need to build alliances with other forces in the nationalist struggle.[46]

AMEAN collaborated with secular student groups. Although the leading student organization, AGED, expressed disquiet about the association's political credentials, these were quickly allayed; AMEAN had links with the Union Générale des Etudiants Musulmans in Algeria. The 1956 AMEAN congress went on to pass a motion supporting the Algerian struggle and, in an interview with an Algerian student activist, the association expressed a desire to 'come together with the people in their struggle'.[47] These commitments were not simply in the realm of ideas and good intentions, a number of AMEAN members were trade union activists and members of left-wing groups, including the Union Démocratique Sénégalaise (affiliated to the Rassemblement Démocratique Africain). The extent of this radicalization is conveyed by one member, Modibo Diallo, who attempted to bring to light the links between Islam and socialism: 'We Muslims support a human orientated socialism allowing freedom of conscience. ... We encourage a type of socialism which would secure the full development of every faculty in the individual, in the sole interest of society.'[48] Another leading member of AMEAN saw the need to develop a radical programme for liberation: 'It is time to think again about Socialism and Marxism ... to keep the dynamic and constructive scientific enquiry of African politics.'[49] One study even concluded that, 'AMEAN seems to have been somewhat instrumental in the intellectual movement which led to challenging the ideological bases of the colonial system.'[50] It is certainly true that on the eve of independence the association helped define a socially radical Muslim identity, an identity that students would continue to hold.[51]

When the university of Dakar was founded in 1957 it was (and remained until 1971) a French university. In the first decade of independence its management and department curricula were under the control of the French, who provided 70 per cent of the institution's finances.[52] Two important factors are connected to this. First, for the first decade after independence Senegalese students were a minority at the university: Europeans, Lebanese and other African students were far more numerous. Second, to a large extent, students at the university were *choyés* (pampered) by the authorities, eager to avoid making the university a site of contestation. The university did not become a space for collective mobilizations for a number of years.[53]

According to Bianchini, student activism in the independent period emerged only in 1966. He claims it is possible to identify the roots of the student movement among students in the Fédération des Etudiants d'Afrique Noire en France (FEANF), the pre-independence organization, and among Muslim student groups in Senegal, but neither constituted for him a student movement; the social movement was evolving from the associations of students in exile. Prior to the mid-1960s he speaks only of student organizations.[54] For Bianchini, to be defined as a movement it must have 'a sufficient influence in time and space'.[55] 'Consequently, a spatially limited mobilization confined to a few individuals does not correspond to the definition used here.'[56] Bianchini dates the origin of the student movement to 28 February 1966 when, following the coup that removed Nkrumah, a figurehead of radical pan-Africanism, students demonstrated against the USA and British embassies. As a consequence, the existing associations were overturned and the Union des Etudiants de Dakar (UED) emerged in their place. The government violently opposed the demonstration. But ironies abound. When the military overturned Nkrumah's government on 24 February, students celebrated in the country's capital, Accra. University of Ghana students immediately issued a statement in support of the newly formed National Liberation Council (NLC), which was read out every 30 minutes on national radio. The day after the coup students left the campus at dawn and demon-

strated until dusk and the 'psychological booster this demonstration gave to the coup was tremendous'.[57]

Students and elites
In the 1960s and 1970s Senegalese students were seen as a
privileged and transitory social group waiting to be allotted
employment after graduation, often as members of the new state.
An early study noted that 'university students are disproportionately elite in background, mature and urbane in experience,
and likely members of their country's social (and perhaps
political) elite.'[58] The statistics support this view. There were only
1018 students in higher education in 1960–61.[59] A survey at the
University of Dakar showed that more than 27 per cent of the
student body had fathers who worked in the civil service and 22
per cent in business, but less than 30 per cent had fathers in
either of the country's two main occupations, farming and
fishing. While it is debatable whether any of these professions
were elitist it is certainly true that university students were part
of what have been called the *évolués* (the educated).[60]

The University of Dakar was an adjunct of the French system
of higher education. Gross described it as 'Dakar's Sorbonne
South'[61] and observed that students received a monthly stipend
of 22,500 CFA francs (US$ 90), which was substantially higher
than the average monthly income in Dakar. The study showed
that this situation was maintained by a close partnership with
the French government, which contributed 80 per cent towards
the administrative costs. Even the rector at the time of the 1968
uprising was a French civil servant. This was consistent with
Senghor's desire for a university at the crossroads of African,
Islamic and Western civilization, 'essentially a European, French
university at the service and disposition of Africa'.[62] This
relationship was borne out in enrolment figures: of 3047 students
in 1967, 737 were French, by far the largest foreign contingent.
But it also represented a broader continental trend. Although the
1960s and 1970s were far from a picture of harmony, there was a
degree of mutual dependence: 'African states were vitally
dependent on students to fill the empty spaces left by departing

expatriates, and saw the expansion of Higher Education as a key condition for economic development.'[63] If graduation from the university in the 1960s did not guarantee gainful employment there was certainly a strong probability of it. In Senegal, like much of the continent, this picture began to unravel quite quickly.

It is problematic to assume that Senegalese students were simply recruited from the nation's elites, for a closer look at the statistics reveals a more complex truth. Many of the students at the university in the first ten years of independence had been sponsored, with part or the full cost of their education and maintenance being met by future employers, government scholarships or private organizations. This was the pattern across many African countries. In Senegal, 72 per cent of students were sponsored.[64] Students received funding from businesses, government departments and community organizations. The expansion in university education was determined by a government demand for qualified functionaries that far outstripped the supply of children from elite backgrounds.[65] William and Judith Hanna found that most students could expect to become 'respected residents of the localities in which they live'.[66] More than three-quarters of university students aspired not to be members of the political or business elite, but on the contrary to go into a profession or work as a government official.[67]

In surveys of Senegalese students at the University of Dakar they emerge as extremely confrontational. A total of 74 per cent of students from the university (higher than any other country) stated that they had basic disagreements with the leaders of the country.[68] One study asserted that this figure could not be generalized across Africa, as students in Dakar have a particular penchant for disruption.[69] The revolt in 1968 that spread from the university to the trade union movement must have presented a mystery for academics, who have traditionally seen African universities as the centre of producing the national ruling class.[70] Hanna was even forced to admit: 'Students at the University of Dakar were able to influence the Senegalese government in part because of the support received from labour unions.'[71] The trade union movement joined the student movement because of the rise in the price of basic commodities and high unemployment. These were real concerns shared by both groups.

The number of students in higher education in Senegal had also expanded; by 1978/9 it had reached 10,000.[72] Still scholars insisted on beating the same old drum, and even in the mid-1990s Senegalese students were being characterized as spoilt youths, long after their material conditions had collapsed: 'The students' aspiration is to gain government employment, membership in the ruling elite, privilege.'[73] The reality of student life in Senegal and the nature and meaning of their activism could not contrast more with these stereotypes. The events that took place in 1968, could not demonstrate this more clearly.

The spirit of 1968

According to most authors, the student movement now entered a period of anti-imperialist struggle.[74] It is not possible to regard the experience of 1968 in Senegal in isolation; a wave of protest movements, strikes and political activity gripped the international political scene.[75] In Senegal the signs of political change had been present for some time, notably with the formation of UED in 1966 and the Union Démocratique des Etudiants Sénégalais (UDES), which had replaced the two former organizations of the student body. As we have seen UED was founded on 30 March, a month after the student demonstrations in support of Kwame Nkrumah.

The university was at the centre of the crisis that shook the regime in 1968. Student strikes and demonstrations even managed to detach the trade union movement from its traditional base inside the structures of the ruling party. This rupture did not last long and by 1969 the regime had managed to reorganize the trade union federation. However, the effects of 1968 were colossal.[76] From mid-April that year students had explicitly linked their struggle at the university to wider social demands: the movement was not simply a reflection of events in France. Bathily notes that the first student strike in March started before events in France, although the two movements were very closely linked. Students explicitly drew attention to the high prices of food staples, the fall in the standard of living, graduate unemployment and the extent of foreign ownership and control of domestic industry. On 1 May the organized working class in the officially recognized trade union congress, UNTS, adopted the political slogans of the student movement.

On demonstrations the crowd declared: 'Power to the people: freedom for unions', 'We want work and rice.'[77] The collision of student and working-class demands culminated in the general strike that started on 31 May. Between 1 and 3 June 'we had the impression that the government was vacant ... ministers were confined to the administrative buildings ... and the leaders of the party and state hid in their houses!'[78] Students precipitated and galvanized the action: 'everybody seemed to agree with the students, the cost of living had become so expensive.'[79]

In a society often regarded as conservative, the movement produced unity that perhaps had not been seen since independence. National radio for the first time became regarded as 'an ideological device in the service of the government'.[80] The government reacted to the strike by ordering the army onto the university campus, with instructions to shoot on sight. During a demonstration after these events, workers and students decided to march to the presidential palace, which was protected by the army. French troops openly intervened, occupying key installations in the town, the airport, the presidential palace and of course the French embassy. The university was closed, foreign students were sent home and thousands of students were arrested. The *Daistes*, students who supported a leading and imprisoned figure of the opposition, Mamadou Dia, were put under tight surveillance. At the same time, as we have seen, Senghor alluded to the foreign manipulation of the movement, as France was gripped by a similar crisis, a peculiar accusation from someone who had just called on the support of a foreign military force.

Politics, reorganization and structural adjustment

The events of 1968 transformed Senegal and produced personalities and parties that went on to dominate the country's political scene. The period was marked by traumatic changes in student organizations: the dissolution of the UED in 1971 led to the creation of the Association Générale des Etudiants Sénégalais (AGES) in 1972 and its rapid dissolution in 1973, the year of an important student strike. The experience after 1968 was a direct consequence of the social turmoil the year had caused.[81] Even after the formal dissolution of AGES, it managed to exist underground until 1976. The generation of university students that had experienced political mobilization from 1968 was influenced (and inspired) by external politics, forces and actors. Bianchini sees the decade of 1977–87 as the *'patriotique'* period, which saw the emergence of initiatives for the reorganization of the student movement.[82] The 1977–84 period was marked by a high degree of political in-fighting among student groups.[83]

A university strike in 1984 managed, to some extent, to bring together various unions that had emerged within the Comité de lutte (Action Committee). It was not wholly effective: different organizations had different views on the negotiations with the government and this weakened the representatives of the unions.[84] These confusions were very real. One organization called for a return to class before negotiations, and when the Comité de lutte called for an end to the strike the base refused to follow the instruction (*mot d'ordre*), considering that their representatives had sacrificed the student demands for vague promises. The strike continued from below for a few days longer.

According to a principal study of the period,[85] Islam was not present as a political force on campuses. However, by the end of the 1970s, the *mourides*, the main Muslim brotherhood in Senegal, influenced important activists. By the 1980s groups like the Association des Etudiants Musulmans de l'Université de Dakar (AMEUD) emerged, though it is doubtful they had an influence on the direction of the movement. By 1987 a mosque had been built on the campus, but this was mainly to do with the government's relationship at the time with Muslim countries. Yet, it seems that Muslim activism did not directly engage with the student movement and the defection of student leaders to the *dai'ra* (religious associations) was very rare.[86]

It was not until 1987 that the movement was relaunched. The Coordination des Etudiants (CED) emerged from the January 1987 university strike and rapidly became the effective representative body between the students and government during the strike. On 26 May that year an order was sent demanding the dissolution of the various unions to leave the field clear for the CED. As one student leader at the time, Mamadou Bocum, recalls, 'Thinking about it, we realized that the existence of a national union was a hindrance ... for the reorganization of the movement.'[87]

This represented an important development in other ways. The CED was founded on the General Assembly – mass general meetings of the student body that became the main organizing body of the student union. It also marked the emergence of the PDS onto the student scene (formed in 1974), a political world that had previously been dominated by parties of the left (notably And Jeff and the Ligne Démocratique). It is important to emphasize that students remained militants in political parties, even in the period of unity under the CED. Membership of political parties was always a feature of student politics. While often crippling political mobilization, it frequently animated and organized student activism.

The development of the CED was good preparation for 1988. Students played an important role in the protests against the disputed election results in February 1988, appealing to the wider society that: 'our claims only reflect those of the masses.'[88] However, the claim that external forces were manipulating the students was repeated, with their demand for the release of political prisoners seen as proof of this manipulation. Certain activists have identified the role of school students and, in this contest, the leading role of the university. Oumy Ndour questions Bianchini's assertion that the movement started at the university: 'historically school students have taken a leading role. In 1988 we were radicalized in Thiès and it was there that the strike spread to other schools and colleges.'[89] Before long the government moved to ban the general assemblies, leading to the establishment of neighbourhood committees to relay information outside the university, which continued to exist until the summer. A connection was also made with school students who established the Coordination des Elèves du Sénégal (CES).

An ex-student leader from the time recalls the vitality of the movement and the crucial role university students played. Even when the university was officially closed, students played a crucial role in setting up and organizing neighbourhood committees. Assane Dia explains how 'we were going to the neighbourhoods and we rallied the people; we met politicians, trade unionists and we explained our movement. We also visited the imams, the notables through which to pass on information. We even went into the mosques to discuss with people, to speak to them, and to the markets to explain our position.'[90]

Students played a key role in disseminating the movement's objectives from their own claims to wider social demands. Dia explains how they organized demonstrations, 'We decided to go to the streets, for example, to demonstrate. There were people in charge of smashing cars, others in charge of leading the rally, others indicating the presence of cops.' Students acted repeatedly as *provocateurs* during the crisis, stirring up trouble:

> There is a very important element, a very useful strategy; I remember that we used to go to the stadiums ... like Demba Diop stadium, during the night, because there were matches at that time. When there was a match, we used to arrange to be as a group. After the match we used to follow the defeated team because they were upset and together with the mass we shouted 'fed up with Abdou Diouf' ... as the defeated team were angry following their defeat it increased this anger. The policemen in charge of security when they heard that ... immediately they were throwing grenades. ... Really, it was very important. The movement was so intense that even Abdoulaye Wade was scared it would go beyond his objectives.[91]

The success of the CED extended to the organization of the university, where students were able to influence the election of the vice-principal and influence elections of departmental *amicales*. However, a combination of factors presented the CED with a number of problems. These included the evolution of the political opposition in Senegal and, most significantly, the effect of the World Bank on higher education, which explicitly regarded the 'opposing power of students [as] ... one of the causes of the blockage of the university system'.[92]

Let us start with the first of these two issues. The role of the PDS in the university was significant in the evolution of the CED and in the development of opposition to the ruling party. The growth of the PDS in the student movement was linked to the fact that the party had emerged as the principal opposition to the PS. An important factor in the growth of the PDS on the campus was the centrality of its popular and charismatic leader, Wade. Wade had long identified students as an important constituency and would repeatedly appeal to them, making much of his own background in student politics years before.

The second factor in the decline of the CED was the central issue confronting the movement in the 1990s. The main World Bank report in 1992 launched the reforms at the university. The aim was essentially to reduce the cost of the university for the state, but it realized this would not be easy: 'It is clear that implementing such a strategy would meet a lot of resistance from those who currently profit from the generous policy of access and subsidies ... it would be wiser to adopt a more conciliatory strategy of transition.'[93]

The report stressed that it was necessary to launch a marketing campaign that would have the benefit of hiding the real nature of the reform agenda. At the heart of the reform and typical of World Bank thinking across Africa (see Chapter 2) was the need to limit the intake of students into higher education: 'it is better to exercise control over student access to higher education rather than through internal efficiency plans.'[94] As Bianchini observed, this meant that the baccalauréat – the normal pathway to higher education – would not automatically open doors to the university. The World Bank was targeting what had been the core demands of the student movement over 30 years – grants, accommodation, cost of food and medical insurance.

Among the measures suggested were the privatization of certain restaurant facilities and their annual closure for a month, the reorganization of student accommodation – where rooms were to be allocated according to academic results – and the general increase in the cost of enrolment. While many of the reforms were marketed as experimental, they soon became central features of the university. Student canteens were to undergo a period of limited and experimental private management, but before long the measure had become generalized across the university system. By December 1993 the government had decided to implement many of the reforms.

The two principal forces opposing the creeping privatization of the university were the CED and the independent trade union, Syndicat Autonome des Enseignants du Supérieur (SAES), which had been created in 1985. Teachers in SAES went on strike in May 1994 against the implementation of these reforms, and the CED supported them. The government 'invalidated' the academic year, which was the equivalent of making all students retake the year. On 2 August, as a result of continuing unrest, the government gave students 24 hours in which to evacuate their accommodation at the university.

The government had taken the initiative and managed to disorient the opposition. When students returned in October the CED attempted to relaunch the action, but after the evacuation of the university in August the student base was poorly organized. When leading activists attempted to mount a final confrontation they were quickly dispersed by a heavy police presence. The result of the defeat was catastrophic for the CED, which was unable to recover from the crisis and dissolved several months later. The teachers' union, while managing to survive, emerged weakened and divided. For the government and World Bank it was an unqualified victory.

Even members of the university who had initially not been hostile to the pact the World Bank made with the government – the Programme d'Amélioration de l'Enseignement Supérieur (PAES) – began to see it in a critical light. It appeared that once the World Bank had obtained its reform – to reduce the number of students admitted to the university[95] – it failed to carry out its side of the pact by refusing to rehabilitate the university.[96]

In the late 1990s the movement began to show signs of revival. A lecturers' strike over housing expenses in 1997 breathed life into it and gave it the space and confidence to re-emerge, this time reorganized as the Comité de Gestion de la Crise (CGC). By 1998 students had started to mobilize again and the strike at the Ecole Normale Supérieure (ENS) marked the movement's recovery. Students in Dakar and Saint Louis brought forward a series of demands regarding the grant and university fees. On 5 May police firing live rounds seriously injured several students in Saint Louis. Then, for the first time, an additional factor emerged when administrative, technical and scientific staff organized under the Coordination des Syndicats des Travailleurs du Supérieur (CSTS). Against this background the university authorities convened a general assembly on 10 June 1998, which declared a '*réforme de la réforme*', referring to the reforms initiated by the World Bank six years earlier. Opposition to PAES succeeded in bringing together a considerable force opposed to the continued restructuring of the university.

Two issues impinge directly on the study: first, the effect of the World Bank reforms on the student movement and second, the impact of the student movement after 1998 and the election of Wade. The second issue is taken up below, but it is clear that the cycle of mobilization started again with the 1997 lecturers' strike that helped to rally students and university workers the following year. On the first point the picture is uneven. The success of the World Bank's *concertation nationale* (national dialogue) disorientated the movement and wore down student and trade union opposition. Students were effective in defining corporatist interests but less successful in mapping an alternative strategy to the crisis. They did, however, manage to ameliorate the World Bank's worst proposals.

The rise and fall of student mobilization in Senegal
The most recent and important work on the student movement in Senegal[97] shows there have been three broad phases: the confrontation led by the UED from 1965 to 1975; the UNAPES-led period from 1979 to 1986; and the years 1987 to 1995 under

the direction of the CED. Specific demands and a specific type of student organization, determined partly by the political context, mark each phase. Then, according to Bianchini, follows a period of decline until the cycle of mobilization resumes. Within these phases are periods of great repression and acute crisis. There is an important generational element to Bianchini's demarcation: 'From the viewpoint of the older generations who "made" the student movement, there is a natural inclination to valorize the movement of their own youth to the detriment of the one that followed.'[98] This is an important consideration because a former generation of students will see the movement as having become corporatist, lacking the ideological and political clarity of their period, while today's students regard the former ones as having been integrated into the political establishment. As Bianchini puts it, 'To attempt a "geological" metaphor, the action of the Senegalese student movement can be compared with an eruption, in which materials in fusion end up cooling down and add up to the pre-existing bedrock of power.'[99]

A principal problem of this categorization is also one of its strengths, namely the evident resilience of the movement and its ability to recover from internal and external crises by forging new organizations to unify mobilization at the university. It also undermines certain generational critiques of the movement that regard the current mobilization as irredeemably corporatist, depoliticized and in some analyses without a future.[100] Student action has proved more resilient; students still play their role as politically privileged actors. However, in showing the cycles of student mobilization, Bianchini fails to illustrate the divergence between each phase. While there are elements of corporatist demands at each stage of these mobilizations, the prevailing political situation has a profound effect on the direction of the movement. There is a danger of conflating the experiences of 1968 and the 1990s, for example, which downplays the impact of structural adjustment and the collapse of the Eastern bloc. Soviet communism, after all, sustained the political motivation of most political parties active on the campus in the 1970s and 1980s. The rise of the PDS and the domination, especially after 1993, of

Wade's supporters in the student movement was possible because of the political disorientation after the collapse of the Berlin Wall. This is of central importance to the re-emergence of the movement after its decline in 1995.

Yet the strength of Bianchini's analysis is unquestionable. There are two vital and related aspects to his work. First, as we have seen, he criticizes the generational approach that denigrates the contemporary movement by looking at student mobilizations through the prism of a golden age of activism. He is dismissive of the way history has been written to justify contemporary and partisan events: 'We then see the 1968 student movement in Senegal presented as an introduction to the "democratic" wave of the late 1980s.'[101] Second, he stresses the centrality of corporatist demands throughout the movement, criticizing the argument that these are a contemporary feature of the degeneration of the movement. This argument was also made against the student movement in Zimbabwe (see Chapter 3).

This requires some explanation. The question of the grant has been central for the movement. Students were not immediately galvanized into political action in 1968 to effect revolutionary change, or because they had been reading Lenin. On the contrary, it was the reduction of the grant, or more specifically its *fractionnement* (splitting up), that triggered the action. Almost 20 years later it was the late payment of the grant that led to the strike in January 1987. The reality is that economic demands have always been central to mobilizing students, and even more so since the economic crisis.[102] Yet the generation of 1968 (and 1988) still denigrate the movement and students today.[103]

Conclusion

As we have seen in much of the literature, there is a tendency to search for clear demarcations in student activism. A typical caricature is the separation of student activism from its perceived heyday in the 1960s and 1970s to the disintegration of the movement over the last 20 years. Today students are written off: yesterday they were harbingers of a brighter future but today symbols of failure.

It has been shown that it is not entirely satisfactory to divide the Senegalese student movement into its political vanguardist phase and a later economist one. After the collapse of the Berlin Wall in 1989, a generation of intellectuals and leaders lost their ideological signposts. This applies as much to the political left in Senegal as it does anywhere. This has left its mark on social movements across the world. Although the political and material world at Cheikh Anta Diop University in the late 1990s and early part of the new century was notable for the lack of political debate, the celebrated vanguardism of the 1970s was a consequence of the collision of forces that are not present today. This neither precludes the development of these politics today nor explains the important role students continued to play in 2000 as privileged political actors in the historical victory of *sopi*, even without the old ideologies.

In an unpublished text that is generally very disparaging of student action, Deme Abdoulaye, a student leader in the period of *alternance*, admits that 'if the students are organized, it can constitute a danger for the state if they do not take their claims into account ... it can even lead to the fall of the system.'[104] In the following part of the chapter I analyse the experience of students after 1998, examining the tensions and pressures on the movement in a period of intense political change; the system certainly did not 'fall', but it was shaken.

Part III: 'Changement politique':
student protest and activism in Senegal 1998–2004

In this section of the chapter I concentrate on the experiences and role of students in the election – the democratic transition – that took place in 2000. I analyse how students reorganized their university union in preparation for the elections and the campaign trail – the *marche bleue* – of Abdoulaye Wade in 2000. In the following sections I address three important moments at the university – a university strike in 1999 that precipitated the collapse of the union; student action at the university in the election of Wade in 2000; and a key strike on the campus a year after the election. Further on I look at student participation in the new government and how many ex-student militants were corrupted and co-opted by the regime. The years 1998 to 2004 involved the culmination of years of political change, encapsulated in the popular slogan of the movement, *sopi*.

The 'silent' revolution

In recent years Senegal has undergone a silent revolution that is hardly mentioned, let alone analysed, in the international media. It has come in two parts. The first came with the victory of Abdoulaye Wade after a bitterly fought two-round presidential election in March 2000. This was one of the few times there has been a peaceful transition of power in sub-Saharan Africa. Despite widespread fears of another crisis, former president Abdou Diouf stepped down, thus signalling the end of 40 years in power of a party renamed the Parti Socialiste (PS) in 1975. The second came with the legislative elections held on 29 April 2001, when the former ruling party was reduced to a handful of seats. It was left without the control of a single region or department, even in areas regarded as its strongholds.[105]

Since independence Senegal has been regarded by commentators as a semi-democracy and by most Senegalese as a one-party state.[106] The movement for political change, in which youth and students in particular played a leading role, was often regarded as facing insurmountable opposition. The political class was tied inextricably to leading *marabout*s who held the allegiance of much of the rural population and the groundnut industry. The break with these traditions holds significant lessons for democratic change beyond Senegal. But one must look behind the election to see the forces responsible for this change, notably the general strike in 1999 that continued despite the attempt of Madia Diop, the general secretary of the CNTS, to call off the strike. But clearly the role of students before, during and after the presidential elections has been a significant force in the silent revolution.

The commitment of students to the movement for *sopi* is seen as crucial to the election of the new regime; in fact the alliance between the student movement and new president Wade was a vital element in the politics of the government after his victory. In the anniversary celebrations commemorating four years since the victory of the *alternance*, one of the principal achievements highlighted by the government was university reform: 'In the area of education the new government has achieved an important victory. We have been able to give to all students a grant or, at least, assistance equivalent to a grant. This is proof of the importance we attach to education.'[107] This meant breaking from the World Bank's advice to limit the intake of students into the university sector.

However, these reforms were wrung out of the regime in the aftermath of a university strike in January and February 2001 that led to the death of law student Balla Gaye. This was the first major crisis the new government faced and it still divides national life. The strike was fought over issues that student leaders claimed Wade had promised to resolve after the presidential election in 2000. The national newspaper, *Le Matin*, noted in the aftermath of Balla Gaye's death: 'No one can predict what the stars will hold for students in the next few years. However, everyone remembers that May 1968 started like this.'[108] So, within a year, students were boasting that they were the new opposition to the government. The astonishment was tangible: 'last year ... the same students who today have been attacked by the police ... had rallied to Abdoulaye Wade.'[109]

Preparing the structures: striking in 1999

Although the student movement had been unsuccessful in contesting World Bank reforms, it succeeded in limiting their more harmful effects. By 1999 students were organized in the CGC, a university-wide union, grouping together department *amicales*. However, for a number of student leaders the CGC was already a moribund organization that needed to be replaced with a new union that would be able to respond to the rapid political changes that were taking place in Senegal.

A strike that students organized between February and April 1999 crucially shaped the nature of their participation in the *sopi* campaign and helped mould a new national student union that would organize student activism in the coming year. A number of very significant events impacted on the political consciousness of students and led many to conclude there was now a good chance of removing the PS from power. The PS had been severely damaged by the resignation in 1998 of two of its political heavyweights, Mustapha Niasse and Djibo Ka, who went on to form their own parties. These events weighed heavily on student activists in 1999 as they became aware of the need to forge unity in the student body (and if necessary a new union) to help secure *changement politique* the following year.

The desire to find the right candidate to contest the presidential elections in 2000 dominated the first three months of the year. Abdoulaye Bathily, the university professor and leader of the left-wing Ligue Démocratique–Mouvement pour le Parti du Travail (LD/MPT), led the charge, heading the coalition of opposition parties determined to find a single candidate. The Alliance des Forces du Changement pour l'Alternance (AFCA) and the Bloc Républicain pour le Changement (BRC) were set up to organize the opposition, with many arguing that Wade was the only candidate with sufficient support to beat the ruling party.[110] Reports of the opposition regrouping around Wade monopolized the newspapers – *'Six partis votent Me Wade'* (six parties vote for Wade) reported the headline in the *Sud Quotidien* on 8 February 1999. The youth organizations of the nation's major political parties, organized in the Coordination des Jeunesses Politiques de l'Opposition (CJPO), failed to agree on a single candidate. Instead, at its meeting on 6 February 1999 the organization split along party lines. However, the youth and student groups of Mouvement pour le Socialisme et l'Unité (MSU), And Jeff–Parti Africain pour la Démocratie et le Socialisme (AJ–PAD), the LD, the PDS and the Union pour la Démocratie et le Fédéralisme (UDF) voted to support Wade, while the youth wing of the Union pour le Renouveau Démocratique (URD) rejected the choice and proposed its own party leader Djibo Leyti Ka. This political split among youth, students and political parties continued throughout the presidential campaign with Djibo Ka and

Mustapha Niasse of the Alliance des Forces du Progrès (AFP) standing in the presidential elections.[111]

The student strike started on 24 February with a number of key demands. At its general assembly the CGC demanded an increase in student grants (from 18,000 to 25,000 CFA francs for half grants and from 36,000 to 45,000 CFA francs for full grants), and an increase also in student assistance and the distribution of grants for all those currently without state support. The strike was called alongside a day of action to hit the authorities fast and hard (*frapper vite et fort* – the CGC slogan). The strike demands were also linked to the work of a commission at the Ministry of Education responsible for analysing the situation at the university. CGC leaders were angry at the commission's lack of progress.[112] The daily *Sud Quotidien* also referred to the explicitly party political dimension motivating the strike: 'But there is also a political factor ... because according to our sources the students who, for the most part, organize politically do so to accompany the activity of the parties of which they are members.'[113]

The question of a single candidate continued to dominate the press. Again Bathily, pressing Wade's candidature, took this to his supporters at their congress on 5–6 March.[114] The youth wing of the PDS also initiated its first caravan for change (*caravane pour le changement*).[115] This involved hiring local minibuses to take trips into the rural areas to 'sensitize the people'. The first caravan would be used to crisscross the country on 18 March to 'raise the awareness of the population, even in the most remote areas, on the necessity for political change in 2000'.[116] Students were the first to participate in these caravans.

By mid-March there were two important developments in the strike. First, on 12 March the recalcitrant Faculty of Medicine, which had been on the margins of the strike, joined the movement. Second, the first signs of a split in the CGC were beginning to show. Accusations started to circulate that some CGC members had received bribes from the Ministry of Education. One CGC member, Ali Fary Ndiaye, made a name for himself as spokesperson for the opposition: 'certain members of the CGC are suspected of having received money (5 million CFA francs) from the authorities. We insist they explain themselves at the general assembly. Otherwise, we will have to take action at the general assembly on Wednesday 17th.'[117]

The worst crisis in the strike was when the forces of law and order, the notorious Groupement Mobile d'Intervention (GMI), entered the university on 15 March. One lecturer, Penda Mbow, expressed the general attitude: 'This situation is scandalous. You cannot violate university space like this and under any old pretext. The inviolability of the university sphere is something that has been acquired after years of struggle by humanity since the Middle Ages.'[118] The event created a small political storm, leading to widespread condemnation of the violated university.[119] Five students were seriously injured; four rooms in the university were destroyed and the campus restaurants ransacked. Boubacar Diop of the lecturers' union, SAES, joined others in declaring that the union was determined to shine light on the incident.[120] By 17 March the CGC had almost completely lost control of the strike. When a rumour circulated that a first-year medical student, Mouhamadou Dieye, had died of injuries inflicted on 15 March, students cried '*à mort les flics*' (death to the cops) and organized an impromptu general assembly.

Meanwhile, the Union des Jeunesses Travaillistes Libérales of the PDS organized its own caravan. Mbaye Diack of the LD spoke to the union, insisting 'If young people do not want to suffer, they must break with the PS, which has been in power for too long.' The caravan organizers made it clear that they would start with Dakar before going into the interior of the country.[121]

By 19 March the university strike, which had been limited to the university, had spread to Université de Gaston Berger and a number of schools. Yet, as the strike spread and gained support, the CGC decided to call it off, a decision the students almost totally ignored. The CGC was divided, with some members pressing for further radicalization of the strike.[122] The sense of disarray dominated the CGC, which asserted at a press conference (held at the SAES headquarters) on 20 March that the strike would end on Monday 22 March. It did not and its continuation signalled the death of the union.

As the opposition struggled to forge a coalition for *sopi*, the political differences over the country's radicalization tore the CGC apart. The decision to end the strike was a product of these divisions. Meissa Touré, who was active as a representative for his faculty, explains that it was the political divergence within the union that led to its disintegration at the time of the strike:

> we had political problems because there were those from the URD and others from the PDS. Those in the PS who were there [meant that] we had political differences when the strike was lifted. There were problems in the leadership. The death of the CGC was declared in 1999 ... students were divided. One could not mobilize the student body around this organization.[123]

Yankhoba Seydi, another leading member of the CGC and a militant of the PDS, recalled five years later, 'I was among those who signed the death warrant of the CGC.'[124]

Despite the CGC's collapse, the strike spread to more schools and colleges. UGB declared that its strike in support of students in Dakar would continue at least until 8 April 1999.[125] While schools in Rufisque, where Dieye, the injured medical student, had taken his baccalaureate, issued a similar strike order.[126] Tension continued to mount in the country as opposition parties attempted to come together around one candidate. The 30 March was declared the decisive day in this quest; opposition parties of the AFCA and the BRC met in Wade's Dakar home, but failed to agree on a single candidate. Djibo Ka of the URD emerged as the main splitter, refusing to support Wade's candidature. Students were quick to condemn the opposition: a geography student Khady Gning made it clear that with the 'failure of the negotiations to find a single candidate, the opposition has little chance of winning the presidential election in 2000'.[127]

Students were centrally organized in the structures of opposition parties seeking to find unity. They were not simply puppets of their political masters, but a political force that had been involved since the beginning of the year in the debates that had taken place across the country. It is in this context that the strike and subsequent disintegration of the CGC must be seen. While the strike was fought over corporatist demands (an increase in grants) students were also openly engaged in national politics, not simply as cheerleaders of their political parties but in agitating for the unity the opposition as a whole sought.[128] The CGC disintegrated partly through the realization that new structures were needed to forge the same unity among students.

Meissa Touré of the CGC made it clear that students would return to their courses after the Easter holiday. He argued that the police would now be responsible for investigating the accusation of corruption made by Ndiaye, while Ndiaye, predicting the eventual dissolution of the CGC later in the year, argued for the creation of a new union and the resumption of classes: 'in my role as spokesperson of the students [and] who at the beginning was against the lifting of the strike ... I think that there are no viable reasons not to return to our courses. Students must remain vigilant in ensuring that the promises are upheld.'[129] Within days of the strike being called off, a reception committee was organized to welcome *papa du sopi* (father of change) from his semi-retirement in France (where he had been for seven months). The welcome was regarded as the first test for the new coalition that had come together to support his candidature, and a crucial gauge of his continuing popularity.

It was not, however, until August that students finally consolidated the reorganization of their national union. Seydi recalls how the process came about:

> We invited all the other student movements in other faculties to a general assembly and afterwards called the dissidents of the CGC. We moved to the rectorat, met the rector[130] and we gave him a declaration, it was clearly mentioned that the CGC was dead and from that day it was replaced by a new movement called the Union des Etudiants de Dakar (UED).[131]

However, the reorganization of the student movement was

more complicated than Seydi suggests. The decision to dissolve the CGC formally was taken at a seminar on 11 August at the Ecole Supérieure Polytechnique de Dakar. The name of the new structure was going to be communicated after the Comité d'Initiative et de Pilotage (CIP) had held a special workshop made up of students, many of whom were ex-members of the CGC. The intervention of the rector, Mustapha Sourang, was important because it was through his patronage that the seminar took place. These decisions did not go uncontested; on the contrary, certain students at the seminar questioned the CIP's legitimacy. One complained that it was simply 'a group of friends, fervent activists in political parties ... members who have never been elected, they want to politicize the movement as always'.[132] While making his contribution, the student pointed a finger at Pape Birahim Ndiaye (a PDS deputy) in the lecture theatre demanding a justification for his presence.

Only afterwards – contrary to Seydi's tidy categorization – was the new movement created. Partly due to the important role that the union was going to play in the following two years, student leaders of the period perhaps exaggerate their involvement in its formation. Aliou Sow,[133] a student activist initially in the PS, remembers, 'It was in fact in my room at the university that we made the decision to form UED, and replace the CGC.'[134] Sow also illustrates another important feature of the period. As opposition parties regrouped, individual politicians formed new alliances and changed political allegiance. Students went through the same processes as old political allegiances were cast off and new ones found, often referred to disparagingly today as *transhumance politique*.[135] Sow changed political allegiance so dramatically that he was attacked by former comrades and had to be hospitalized, a story that has entered into student mythology.[136]

Election year: sopi *and students*
Most student leaders argue that the student movement played the key role in the election. However, others argue more realistically that the election was in fact the culmination of more than 25 years of political activity by Wade's PDS, political

mobilization around *sopi* and the crucial support of a coalition of mostly left-wing political parties, the private press, students and certain powerful and autonomous trade unions.[137] However, students did play a privileged – and indeed leading – role in ensuring that the rural population was mobilized to support Wade: in registering voters in rural districts and generating support for change during the second round of the election and in the caravans organized by students in the year before the election. As one student, Idressa Gassama, put it: 'During the campaign the university was empty. Students went to their villages and around the country. ... They wanted the change and students I can say made the change.'[138] Even when students were funded to campaign for the ruling PS they often used the funds to build further support for *Papa Sopi*.

National debate in January and February 2000 was monopolized by the scandal of false electoral cards. The PS allegedly printed these cards – made illegally in Israel – without informing the opposition.[139] This scandal rumbled on throughout the campaign, threatening at one point to derail the elections and on 2 February the Front pour la Régularité des Elections (FRTE) – grouping the main parties supporting Wade – organized a demonstration in the centre of Dakar against the fraud.[140] However, between the two rounds of the election the question of youth became the predominant theme in the election.[141]

Students at the ENS were at the centre of this focus and received most national attention during the campaign. The central issue was over their recruitment upon graduation into the teaching profession, questions that had preoccupied students from the ENS for some years.[142] Their plight was raised to national prominence during a violent confrontation with the police on 18 January, when one student was stabbed in the back by a police officer and 13 others were injured. Their demands occupied a significant place in the election campaign throughout both rounds of the presidential election, with candidates being interrogated on the plight of the ENS students.[143]

While these issues dominated the press, the PDS launched the *marche bleue*, initiated by the party's second in command

Idressa Seck as the most efficient way of disseminating the party's message. It was a campaigning road show for Wade to meet the people.[144] The university welcomed the *marche bleue* on 12 February and Wade addressed hysterical students who were shouting Alpha Blondy (a radical Ivorian singer) lyrics. He set out his credentials, 'former student, former professor and former dean. No one knows your problems better than me.'[145]

In January, however, students were still contesting the legality of the new structure that had been created the previous year. Students voiced disquiet about the new union and its capacity to mobilize students. Mor Diankha – a member of the Amicale of the Faculté des Lettres – explained: 'the Union des Étudiants de Dakar (UED) is not built on a democratic base. This is why it is unable to mobilize students. We are really eager to see the birth of the Union Générale des Etudiants de Dakar (UGED), an organization in which all students will come together.'[146]

The university campus erupted into political action in mid-February 2000, and the strike was again ostensibly corporatist, limited to receiving the promised reforms won by the movement the previous year. As leading UED member Yankhoba Diatara explained: 'The principal point of the agreement that we signed last year with the authorities is connected to the allocation of a two-third grant to students in the "second cycle".'[147] Many student leaders at the time testify to the way the politics of the movement were disguised under a thin veil of bread and butter demands. Yankhoba Diatara[148] explains how politics were frequently hidden in the student mobilizations at the time:

> We did not lead a political strike. The strike movement was not launched to say that Abdou Diouf must leave power. No, the strike was based on legitimate and legal demands. Because it was necessary to increase the numbers receiving grants, and in negotiation with the minister it was these issues that we discussed. If it had in fact been demanding the removal of Abdou Diouf, the minister would not have spoken to us.[149]

Diatara goes even further in saying that 'there was never any talk of the election or even of Diouf or Wade during the general assembly.' He explains: 'we were a lot more subtle than those in 1988. In 1988 they said "free Abdoulaye Wade", when he was imprisoned after the events of 1988. However, we wanted the change but we never said it ... we were able to lead more subtly and [as a result] students had confidence in us.' As we shall see, the claims of political neutrality in the public domain of the general assembly did not last. The desire to limit the strike to corporatist demands – the typical platform of demands – was a strategy frequently used as a reaction to the hostility towards political parties, but also as a way of keeping the university open during a political strike.[150]

On the eve of the first election the atmosphere at the university was ecstatic. *Walfadjri* recalled that 'students demanded the *alternance* as the condition *sine qua non* of a return to class.'[151] The first vote of the election failed to secure Abdou Diouf the required majority, forcing a runoff for the first time in Senegalese history, between Wade and Diouf. The effect of the vote further radicalized students at the university. The vote also broke open the political debates and tensions that had been simmering under the surface. Between the elections students in MEES (Mouvement des Elèves et Etudiants Socialistes) composed a letter they claimed had been written by PDS campaign director Idressa Seck. In the letter Seck congratulated both Sow and Diatara for having brought the students out on strike at a critical moment during the election. Socialist students distributed copies of the letter during a general assembly. Diatara continues the story: 'students read it, then looked at us. They thought that it was true ... [but] if they had no confidence in us they would have killed us. They didn't, they had learnt by now. They said "Oh it's those socialists" [and] they ripped up [the letter].'[152] This incident illustrates both the extent to which student leaders sought to avoid stepping on overtly party political territory and the tensions that were then gripping the campus.[153]

After the first round of the election student leaders were forced directly into making political declarations. Despite Diatara's claims to the contrary, he made perhaps the most political statement from the university, challenging the president to close the university. As he remembers:

> Abdou Diouf had said ... that it was necessary to close the campus; otherwise it would not be possible to control the student body. After this I made a declaration on the radio – you can even get it from *Walfadjri* – saying that 'If Abdou Diouf closes the campus, I will close the presidential palace,' and that was a political declaration.[154]

Meissa Touré – another PDS militant from the period – concurs with Diatara. He argues that the strike that had begun with student demands became openly political in February: 'in February everyone, all the political forces in the country, at the university and in education were united around the idea of getting rid of Diouf. But before we did not dare say this, during the general assembly we spoke of the problems of grants and teaching issues.'[155]

Many student leaders describe the strike as the most widely supported at the university for years, comparing it with the movement in 1988 and 1993. Touré describes the students' passion, with thousands of participants at every general assembly. On one occasion in February a student who had been part of a delegation to the Ministry of Education was asked to present a report on the negiotations before the general assembly. Touré describes what happened:

> We asked a comrade to make a report of our meeting with the Minister of Education, who had responded positively to the questions posed. The comrade said to the general assembly: 'Comrades I think that we have reached a turning point in the strike. Yesterday we met the minister who is in agreement on several problems. All the students cried "corrupted, corrupted, corrupted", then when I took the platform I said that beyond our official demands that we had advanced there was a preamble, which was the

departure of Abdou Diouf. Everyone cried *"Sopi, Sopi, Sopi"*. And we said that students today are in agreement that there is only one point on our list of demands, the departure of Abdou Diouf and they cried that Diouf *"Na dem, na dem, na dem"* [that he go].' ... This is why there was such a popular frenzy around the strike.[156]

After the first vote commentators and politicians celebrated the victory for youth. Bathily gave some idea of the historical significance of the vote in an interview between the two elections:

It is true that this election has assumed an historical character, exceptional from all points of view. We have never seen such enthusiasm for political change in Senegal. ... Those who voted on 27 February 2000 represented an electorate essentially composed of the young, who had cut the links with traditional forms of political engagement, based on a dependence on some or other local or national leader. These young people have a more independent spirit coupled with a commitment to ensure transformation.[157]

The PS also responded to the youth vote, which it claimed made the difference in the first round of the vote on 27 February. However, there is no avoiding the desperation in its attempts to engage the youth and students. In its ten-point plan issued after the first round, four points were dedicated to youth and students. Point five promised to increase by 50 per cent the number of those receiving grants and to recruit all graduates from the ENS and EFI (Ecole de Formation des Instituteurs).[158] These promises did not convince university students; on the contrary, they were seen for what they were, last minute bribes. One student questioned on the proposals probably spoke for most of the student body when he said: 'these last-minute promises do not interest us.' ENS students confirmed their support for *coalition alternance 2000* before the second round when they met Wade and defined the conditions of their support.[159]

Meanwhile, negotiations with the minister of education

Andre Sonko had reached a clear impasse. When students met him on 4 March he doubted his ability to resolve their grievances: 'At the moment I cannot involve myself in finding a solution to your problems as I might not even figure in the next government.'[160] Given the uncertainty in the country, it was hard to disagree.

Wade won the second round securing 58.5 per cent of the vote to Diouf's 41.5 per cent. According to the result 43 per cent of those registered to vote were aged between 18 and 35, or 1,127,100 of the 2,618,176 Senegalese registered to vote. As *Sud Quotidien* correctly observed, 'This age group seems to have voted most heavily in the two rounds of the presidential elections in Feburary and March 2000 to ensure the victory of the *alternance*.' However, those between 18 and 26 made up only 13.55 per cent against 29.49 per cent for those between 26 and 35.[161] Yet these statistics conceal the mobilization of the youth – and particularly students – in the campaign. Youth were not simply the backbone of Wade's electoral victory but also among the principal organizers and propagandists of his campaign.

Madiop Biteye – the secretary general of the Mouvement des Elèves et Etudiants Libéraux (MEEL)[162] – recalls how student activists began to radicalize youth from August 1999: 'we decided to go into schools in the region and to mobilize youth ... To organize and prepare the polling stations ... and to supervise the registration, to help the population obtain identity cards to register on the electoral rolls ... we ensured that the population received their voter cards.'[163]

During the election, students were also present at the polling stations, and several student leaders identified the presence of student activists there as the reason why there was no serious electoral fraud. They were also active after the votes, during the counting of ballot papers. They scrutinized the procedure and even – according to certain reports – accompanied the military to ensure that the ballot boxes were not tampered with.[164]

However, most students participated directly in the campaign by travelling in minibuses commandeered by student groups and frequently paid for by political parties.[165] Ibrahima Bâ says that students used hundreds of vehicles in the run-up to the two elections and organized the 'caravans' for two main reasons – to vote themselves because many were registered in their home localities, and to raise awareness about the vote in their home towns and villages. Bâ gives a good sense of the fervour surrounding one of these caravans:

> I voted in conditions where I could have lost my life ... on the eve of the elections I travelled in a vehicle that didn't have any headlights, and we took these risks because all those who were in the vehicle wanted to vote. It was between the two rounds of the election. ... We said to ourselves that it is essential that we arrive, because tomorrow an historical event will take place ... and we travelled with only one headlight for a distance of 45 km between Tambaçouda and Koussanar. I live in Koussanar and therefore I accepted to travel in these conditions to realize my dream: to change the regime in Senegal.[166]

Coudy Kane was living in Dakar with her family throughout the election. She describes how she organized voter registration in Peking, a large neighbourhood in the north of the city: 'In my neighbourhood I raised people's awareness. ... They were invited to register, as we had done, then they were encouraged to vote. ... They were registered on the voter's roll ... and on the day of the vote we pushed them to get there.'[167]

Other students explained how they encouraged villagers and their families to vote by describing conditions at the university. Meissa Touré, one of the main student leaders at the time, spoke of the responsibility they felt for mobilizing their parents, 'it was necessary to engage in the campaign and we did it by raising our parents' awareness of the conditions in which we lived.' Touré says it was necessary to convince their parents because of the influence Diouf and the PS had in the rural areas:

> They did not believe in President Diouf. [Students had to] say to our parents that today 'I am at university and I

don't have either a grant or room, I live in incredibly difficult conditions. ... I don't eat or I only eat one full meal a day. And you don't have the means to help me. Therefore to change these things it is necessary to get rid of Abdou Diouf ... and if you continue to vote for the president ... after we have finished our Masters we will not be working ... and our parents understood. They voted for President Wade and we were responsible for the result.[168]

All political groupings on the campus organized transport for students to travel across the country. MEES arranged a dozen minibuses to take its militants around the country on 15 March. However, Idressa Gassama argued that students used the buses organized by PS students to campaign for *sopi*. For the second tour the opposition organized buses through Wade pour l'Alternance avec la Coalition 2000 (WAC).[169]

The students' support came at a price. First, they regarded the victory as a pact with Wade who would agree to improve conditions at the university in exchange for their support. Second, if he failed to deliver on the pact he would face the same intransigent opposition from a movement he had rallied to his cause.[170] Students also felt a keen sense of ownership of the elections, an historical justification for their demands and an understanding that they were involved with the opposition, in Gassama's words, 'to stir things up'. This did not give them a sense of gratitude for the change, but an authority over it. As Nar Ndoye argued in 2001: 'The points we were struggling for have been there for a long time, even under the socialist government. So the question I ask: Why not when Abdoulaye Wade comes to power? Why not ask the same question?'[171]

Euphoria swept over the campus after Wade's victory in the second round on 19 March.[172] One student who had been active in Kaolack describes the ambiance: 'It was euphoric, people were happy. They believed in the change. They believed that their lives would improve and that young people would have work. There was hope, euphoria ... we danced.'[173] The concert Wade had promised the students in the event of his victory was held on 22 March in Dakar. Pape Birahim Ndiaye, a student deputy for the PDS, spoke from the podium: 'if today we see that *sopi* has achieved power, it is especially thanks to the youth.' At the same time he warned students that Wade would not bring them paradise on a silver plate. But, retreating to familiar territory, it was necessary to 'tighten one's belt and work to ensure that Senegal finds a way out of its misery'.[174] Thousands wore T-shirts with Wade's effigy and, when he arrived, the chant went up in the stadium, '*Papa ñëwna, Papa dikkan*' ('Father has come, father has arrived'). Wade repeated the message of his campaign, explaining that 'the youth of Senegal liberated me from prison and today it is the same youth who have elected me.'[175]

Walfadjri commented after the final victory that perhaps observers had been right to see the hand of political manipulation behind student action, noting that almost all university students and school students in Senegal were engaged in the campaign. However, pure independence in the student movement is a myth frequently used to debunk their activism.[176] Their action is always a complicated interaction between political parties and the dynamic of campus activism. This symbiosis of forces was exemplified in student participation in Wade's election campaign.

Although the strike at the university continued until almost the end of the month – returning to class on 27 March – UED quickly signed an agreement with the new government. It claimed to be aware that, though Wade would be unable to resolve all its issues with a magic wand, according to Diatara students would at least have a more attentive ear.[177] Wade inherited the culmination of more than a decade of demands, notably the reduction in the price of meal tickets and rent for student accommodation on campus and the increase and extension of student grants.[178] His political honeymoon lasted less than a year.

The death of Balla Gaye and the student strike 2001

Perhaps the first fact to note about the university strike that shook the campus (and country) between January and February 2001 was how quickly the university returned to being an arena of confrontation with the government. The strike and death of student Balla Gaye sparked the first major crisis for the Wade government, and a rupture with students who had been almost unambiguous supporters and campaigners of the *coalition alternance* the previous year. The strike can be seen as the regime's first *naufrage* (shipwreck)[179] and its aftermath triggered other developments that determined the fate of the student movement.

The immediate background to the strike was illustrative of the tensions and problems in higher education in Senegal throughout the 1990s. The government's national plan for education, Programme Décennal d'Education et de Formation (PDEF), which the World Bank was partly funding, was the source of well-known resentment. At a national conference held immediately before the start of the strike the minister for higher education threatened to find other sources of funding if the conditions attached to the World Bank loan did not coincide with domestic priorities for higher education in Senegal. The conference included student representatives and members of SAES who made their opposition to the proposals clear, with students issuing a threat of their own if the government went ahead with certain reforms. They strongly opposed the planned increase in university inscription to 35,000 CFA francs. The daily newspaper *Sud Quotidien* reported that student representatives saw in the proposal a possible source of disruption at the university. The student delegation insisted the minister make it clear that the new Bank reforms were contrary to the *gouvernement de l'alternance*. Déthié Diouf, a student representative, said they could convoke 'a general assembly of students to launch an indefinite strike in response to the measures announced'.[180]

The strike started on 15 January and was limited to several departments; two days later it had spread through most of the university. According to Alioune Diop, a student delegate: 'We participated a great deal in the *alternance* ... and we thought that the era of strikes was over. We see that the current leaders who are still deaf to our grievances are those who used us and promised us better conditions of study and life on the campus during the election campaign.'[181] Student representatives stated at the general assembly on 17 January that until they heard from the authorities they would refuse to pay for food at the university's restaurants.[182]

The strike was eloquent testimony to the fact that many regarded the pact broken. The central demands centred on what came to be called the *cercle magique* – a reduction in rent and the cost of meal tickets; financial help for students without a state grant; grants for second and third year students; and the abolition of half grants in the second year. Although these points formed their core demands, other issues arose during the course of the strike that varied between departments, including internet access on campus and improved student facilities. Idressa Gassama expressed how the strike generalized discontent: 'There are no phones here. So if our mothers need to call us it isn't possible. Look at where we watch TV we are crowded into one room. And we didn't even ask for these things!'[183]

In the first weeks of the strike there was a general assembly every 48 hours. Student representatives from UED addressed students in front of the COUD. Although most of the university was brought to a standstill, there were a number of incidents at the Faculté des Lettres et Sciences Humaines, which houses the semi-independent Institut Français pour les Etrangers (IFE) at which foreign students are taught French. No effort was made to explain the reasons for the strike and, as a consequence, there were for a time tensions and misunderstandings. A student activist recalls that for the first week of the strike no clear set of demands were formulated: 'I participated in all the meetings and for a lot of the time certain students were saying that it was necessary … that we showed President Wade … that not everyone was with him. That it was necessary that we came out before the referendum[184] … we came out on strike without a list of demands and it was during the strike that we tried to present the demands to the students.'[185] Biteye argues that certain students used the strike to get known. Serious divisions within MEEL had also begun to emerge.[186]

Several thousand students demonstrated during the course of the month. The general assembly often sparked off the demonstrations, with students marching into town singing their battle song: '*Nous disons non, nous disons non, camarades élèves, camarades étudiants, il est temps que nous disions non*' (We say no, we say no, comrade pupils, comrade students, it is time to say no). Although a number of vehicles and shops were damaged in the events leading up to 31 January, every protest was peaceful.

On 31 January, at the end of a general assembly that renewed the strike for a further 48 hours, 'We decided to demonstrate to ensure the authorities heard our voices ... we said to ourselves that this march must be peaceful.'[187] In a crowd of about 4000 students, almost half continued on to the demonstration. Later a group of students decided to close one of the main streets. Students throwing stones forced the police out of the area. At about 10 a.m. students took control of Avenue Cheikh Anta Diop, a major road linking the university to the centre of Dakar and to most of the adjacent streets. When it became clear that the police had retreated, the mood changed to one of jubilation. The '*Nous disons non*' cry went up, then riot police returned in greater numbers. Students took up position again, but suddenly shots could be heard and demonstrators ran for cover, though doubting they were real bullets. Their doubt did not last for long; dozens of students were wounded and Balla Gaye, a 24-year-old law student, was killed inside the university campus.[188]

Within hours the university was the dominant issue in the country. The national media expressed disbelief that *Papa Sopi*'s government could have been responsible: 'The first year of the new government registers the first student killed by security forces within the university compound.'[189] Parallels were immediately drawn with 1968; national television and every newspaper interviewed old militants of that era.[190] The opposition PS did not lose the opportunity to attack the government. The general secretary of the party, Ousmane Tanor Dieng, was clear who was to blame: 'These facts are illustrative of an authoritarian and dictatorial power currently running the country.'[191]

The president agreed to meet a delegation of students, but the most significant concession made to them was the demotion of Madior Diop, the minister of higher education, whose resignation had been the students' first demand in the aftermath of the demonstration. Libasse Diop, a member of the coalition AFP, replaced him.[192] The decision was announced to students at the general assembly on 5 February. UED press officer Amadou Ndiaye claimed: 'This decision taken by the head of state will not change our struggle because we are only concerned with the full satisfaction of our demands.'[193] Nevertheless, students still cheered the announcement.

Even before these events the media reported a radicalization of the student movement. This was, to a certain extent, very real. For the first time student participation in the general assemblies included the majority of the campus-based student body. The national media now followed every movement on campus and support came from school students and the general public. One student captured the mood, a mixture of anger and confidence, commenting on the appointment of a new minister: 'another huge salary while poor students do not have enough to eat, drink and continue to suffer ... this decision of the president compels us to go to all lengths to win our demands'.[194]

Student representatives, sensing the change in mood across the country, added several more demands: students must be represented on the commission of inquiry; Balla Gaye's family has to be compensated; and the police should not be allowed on campus. The *révolte universitaire* had triggered the first major crisis for the new regime, and accusations, denials and counter-accusations filled the air in the days after 31 January.

Wade even questioned the shooting: 'The police are not armed. I have to remind people, who assume the police have weapons, that our police are not armed.' He said it was impossible for the police to have been responsible given their location far from the university at the time. Moreover, 'this sort of thing has happened in the past in Senegal, but we are in a new era now.'[195]

The interior minister General Mamadou Niang went further, maintaining that the police had never violated the interior of the university, an area that was considered sacrosanct. Niang fuelled speculation that some other 'fifth column' had been responsible for the murder: 'the boy has been killed; by what and where?'[196] Many now asked if it had been a student assassin paid for by the opposition to cause mayhem for the government before important legislative elections in April. Although the majority of students on the campus dismissed these claims, the commission of inquiry claimed that the government's failure to give them adequate access to relevant information was hampering their investigation. As we shall see, the silence of the inquiry continued to fuel speculation of a student assassin. This in turn has given rise to bitterness at the university.

At the time political groups on the campus were united over a desire to see the demands met and the strike resolved, even if it required further militant action. Even the MEEL stated: 'We ask the authorities ... that light is shone on the circumstances of this event.'[197] Students from the coalition party AFP held a meeting and made a similar demand.

More significant was the level of support from students across the country. For the first time students from UGB in Saint Louis, the second university in the country, made their support clear: 'The authorities are not taking things seriously, just as the case is in the process of escalating.'[198] They decided to boycott lectures until the following week and organized sit-ins and demonstrations. Other students at the university requisitioned vehicles to take them the ten kilometres into town to spread the strike among pupils in local schools, while others marched into town shouting *'policiers assassins'*. They added their voices to the demands made by students in Dakar by calling for the dismissal of the minister of higher education.[199] School students in the Malick Sy lycée in Thiès, the second city in Senegal, joined the university in three days of mourning, sending delegates to other schools in the region to ensure that they too closed as a mark of solidarity with the university. Even primary schools were empty of pupils. By 11 a.m. on 1 February, 'every pupil was in the street and in the main roads of the town returning calmly home.'[200]

Student representatives from UED met Wade at the presidential palace on 6 February after four days of national mourning. They maintained a hard line on the *cercle magique* of non-negotiable demands and, while the negotiations were taking place, the strike was extended from 48 to 72 hours. The next general assembly was held on Thursday morning. 'I have a question to ask you: are you satisfied?' shouted Matar Seck, nicknamed Kabila, after the contents of the meeting had been explained. The president was reported to have agreed to their platform of demands: 'we have obtained everything we have asked for.'[201] The agreement included setting up a commission of inquiry; recognizing that 31 January would be acknowledged as the 'day of the martyrs'; compensating Balla Gaye's family; and satisfying all the points in the *cercle magique*.

Before 31 January, participation in the strike had been limited and only a minority of students attended the general assembly meetings. The strike was dominated by leading members of UED and younger students. Decisions to extend the strikes were never voted on and no contributions were invited from the floor. It was a male dominated event with limited active support. As Jean-Claude Kongo observed:

> Before the death of Balla Gaye, the campus was practically divided in two. One felt that there were two sides, one being the supporters of the president and the opposition who would do everything to combat this. There were those, of course, who wanted the strike to be 'pure' – under serious demands. But it is the two main parties that are in control.[202]

On the 31 January everything changed. As Amadou Dieye Wade noted: 'What changed events was the death of Balla.'[203] Gassama agreed: 'When I heard that Balla Gaye was wounded and then that he had died we started to riot. ... No one slept ... if students themselves found you in your room, they would tell you to get out and go to the front. Everyone participated, throwing stones, marching.'[204]

Balla Gaye's death was a catalyst to students who had not been active: 'everyone, even those who were not excited by the desire to go on strike, now became active.'[205] Others who had not noticed or been interested in the university strike, over the next few days supported and participated in demonstrations and rallies. Oumy Ndour – a student representative at CESTI – commented, 'the students became interested in the movement after the death of Balla Gaye.' Before this she noted 'most of the work was conducted by a group of students ... although it was a different matter when it came to the demonstrations.'[206]

A vigil was held outside Hôpital Principal, the military hospital in the centre of Dakar to which the body had been taken. Thousands of students were joined by pupils from local schools and colleges in a march to the hospital through the city centre. Market sellers and bystanders watched and many cried. When the crowd passed the Ministry of Interior, sadness turned to anger – '*Assassins, Assassins*' it shouted at the police officers guarding the building. When they reached the presidential palace, the same cries were heard 'under the embarrassed gaze of the police'.[207] There were no obstructions to their progress past the palace, and they shouted *Woye Wete, Cheikh Anta moungui dioye, Balla Gaye deme na* (Balla Gaye we miss you, the Université Cheikh Anta Diop cries).

At the hospital, where thousands of students and pupils had already gathered, a poem that the politician and former student leader Talla Sylla distributed to students and dedicated to Balla Gaye lay torn on the floor as students declared, '*Nous refusons la manipulation politique.*'[208] When the minister of interior Mamadou Niang arrived, sent by the president to express his condolences to the students and Balla Gaye's family, the anger of the crowd exploded. After he had spoken to the family he tried to leave, but students blocked his cortège. One shouted: 'How can you leave without meeting the student leaders?' Student leaders lost control and pleaded with the others to let the minister pass. In the middle of this scene Niang declared: 'I want to say to you that we share this pain. You are our children. The enquiry into who injured Balla Gaye leading to his death will be carried through to the end.' Students were furious that he had referred to Balla Gaye as being hurt and they forced him to repeat '*Balla est mort.*' As he entered the car, anger rose and his path was obstructed by students who hit and kicked the side of the car. As one newspaper reported, 'the government representatives just escaped being lynched.'[209]

Balla Gaye's body was carried to the university and followed by a procession that stretched through the city. The palace gates had been reinforced by the time students moved past them, they shouted again at the police and one woman watching the cortège expressed what many were thinking: 'They are capable of forcing the doors of the presidential palace.'[210] Outside the university the cortège carrying the body stopped for Balla Gaye's father to address the crowds. According to BBC correspondent Natalia Antelava: 'all the streets were blocked, there were perhaps more than 100,000 people.'[211] The father, El Hadj Babacar Gaye, addressed the crowd, calling his son's death the divine sentence and asking students to remain calm.[212] When he finished, people dispersed quietly, with many students making their way to the waiting vehicles to take them to Touba, the religious capital of Senegal where Balla Gaye was finally buried.

The immediate aftermath of the strike seemed to suggest that nothing had changed, but the reality was quite different. The government reaction to the crisis – accepting the entire *cercle magique* – led to a series of profound university reforms and the eventual disintegration of the UED. Yankhoba Seydi, who boasted about having been instrumental in forming the union in 1999, now claimed that he delivered the *coup de grâce* in 2003: 'I was head of the Amicale at the Faculté des Lettres.[213] I didn't send representatives to the UED because I found the movement not only corrupt but also ineffective. If you don't have the five faculties present it cannot exist and those who were there ... we knew they were corrupt.'[214] Meissa Touré argues that the reasons for the strike lie in the failure of those who had led the movement during the election:

> I say it often to Minister Sow ... we are largely responsible because after having ... elected the chief Wade we all left the movement and 'nature abhors a vacuum' ... [and] other students who are only involved for their own interests filled the vacuum ... because we said at the time –

euphoric with the victory – that instead of ... arranging for our members to fill the vacuum ... we said it is finished.[215]

Corruption, reform and the Balla Gaye affair
When students are interviewed about the effect of the *changement* on conditions at the university they typically respond by referring to the reforms introduced after Balla Gaye's death. Hamidou Bâ speaks for many students when he explains:

> Wade did two positive things for students: he generalized assistance ... that is every student who does not receive a grant benefits from a sum of 60,000 CFA francs from the state. That is a very good thing. Second, he allocated grants to the second year of the 'second cycle'. When you come directly from school you don't automatically have a grant, but you do receive assistance. If you get through to the second year ... you get a full grant. This was not the case with the former government.[216]

Wade said he saw the university reforms as one of his main achievements,[217] first because all students now receive either a grant or assistance on entering university and second, because with the university entry exam abolished, all students can go directly on to higher education after the baccalaureate.[218] Between 1992 and 2002 the government recorded a 41 per cent rise in student numbers at UCAD and UGB, namely an increase from 22,052 to 31,172. UGB stubbornly continues to resist government pressure to increase student enrolment, with student numbers still below 2000. But to see the real effect of Wade's reforms, the comparison has to be made between the intake of students between 2000 and 2004. Here the statistics show an increase of approximately 2500 students from 28,585 in 2000/1 to 31,172 in 2002/3.[219] The government also advocates establishing *collèges universitaires régionaux* (CUR), which will 'decongest universities in Senegal and promote professional training'.[220] But in the context of the university in Dakar it is inevitably an attempt to reduce overcrowding.

217

The effect of these reforms, Wade argued, was to create a rupture with the World Bank . He explains that it was necessary to 'fight to make the institutions of the World Bank accept this improvement to the conditions of the student body that we had for a long time wanted to bring about.' The World Bank had long considered state expenditure on grants as an unnecessary and costly waste of the state's resources. Wade explains well the thinking of the World Bank: 'the grant was considered to be in the social domain, in other words as "consumption". When they looked at the statistics they deduced from them that most of the money allocated to the university goes to this "social element" and very little to teaching and training.' Wade disagreed with these arguments, insisting that the grant was not a luxury but an investment: 'It is why today I do not have any problems giving out grants to every student who registers at the university. It is one of our greatest victories.'[221]

But it was the result of the strike – and the death of Balla Gaye – that forced the government's hand on university reforms. One of the greatest victories of *alternance* was forced on the government in an attempt to pacify the university. Deme Abdoulaye relates how the president 'signed the agreement with a quick hand' after Balla Gaye's death.[222] Even Madiop Biteye of MEEL concedes that these reforms emanated from the strike and subsequent death of Balla Gaye: 'it is true that it coincided with the death of Balla Gaye.'[223] The decision to grant these demands compelled the government to borrow from the following financial year.

Subsequent developments connected to the strike led to the dissolution of the UED. By the end of the academic year almost all the student leaders who had organized the strike had received scholarships to travel abroad. Abdoulaye claims that the decision to send the leadership abroad 'killed the student movement that had taken years to construct'.[224] PDS militant Yankhoba Seydi made the same observation and with some fury listed the names of UED members who led the strike in 2001 and subsequently left the country on government-awarded scholarships.[225] Madiop Biteye of MEEL describes the same shame at the layer of student leaders who 'benefited by going abroad on the backs of students'.[226]

In an unpublished text, Deme Abdoulaye describes the immediate aftermath of the strike. Some students congratulated the delegation as heroes, he notes, for meeting their demands while forgetting that their success had come from the death of their comrade. After the strike was lifted, students resumed their courses. At the same time, Abdoulaye argues: 'The corrupt students negotiated their trips abroad.'[227] He notes that 'at the start of the following academic year 15 delegates had already left' despite the commission of inquiry having forbidden delegates to leave the country until it had concluded its work. Yankhoba Seydi claimed he made a public statement during the second anniversary of Balla Gaye's death that 'the delegates who had left the country must return to assist in the inquiry'.[228] In 2005 it was still a popular demand of the student movement.

However, both Abdoulaye and Seydi fail to apportion blame in the most obvious place – with the government. The government followed a clear strategy that combined introducing the reforms the students demanded while systematically buying off the student leadership with overseas scholarships. Abdoulaye fails to condemn it mainly because his text is targeted at student corruption, which, by his account, is of endemic proportions.[229] He does, however, write: 'Can the authorities give the reasons why they pushed for them to leave?'[230]

The 'Balla Gaye affair', as it is now called, rumbles on. It is both the cause of frequent student demonstrations, normally students from Gaye's old department (Faculté des Sciences Juridiques et Politique), and a continual humiliation for the government.[231] His death, which is still unresolved, is the subject of frequent exposés in the national press. In a front-page feature *Walfadjri* asked why is the Balla Gaye so affair difficult to resolve?[232] The initial inquiry identified a policeman, Thiendella Ndiaye, whom they claimed was their primary suspect. However, he was declared innocent of the murder after being tried and acquitted by a military tribunal in 2003. Today it is often argued that he was a scapegoat, used to hide the identity of the real murderer.[233]

The remarkable fact in the multiple hypotheses that are advanced today is how little has changed since the murder. Then, each day brought new and more far-fetched explanations, as accusations and counter-accusations were flung at students, the government and the police. In this sense *Walfadjri* is wrong when it states that: 'One hypothesis not accepted is that the murderer of their comrade is one of their own. Students even demanded that the state repatriate students who left to study abroad.' A student assassin was among the first hypotheses politicians and the media put forward. It is now even thought that there might have been a rapid intervention brigade of armed students on the campus before Balla Gaye's death. A witness at the inquiry who had been in charge of security at COUD seemed to confirm this, and testified that indeed there were 'certain elements that moved around with firearms'.[234] Student leaders today are united in demanding that those ex-student leaders responsible for leading the strike are repatriated to answer questions about the murder.

In the *Walfadjri* report Minister of Justice Serigne Diop justified the failure to resolve the case by appealing to what he termed 'similar' cases: the assassination of John F. Kennedy and the Moroccan political leader Ben Barka, 'the real authors are still being looked for today.'[235] How can the most notorious assassination in the world more than 40 years ago be the political equivalent to a student killed on a demonstration in Senegal three years ago? The comparison that at first sight may seem absurd illustrates both the enormous importance of students in Senegal, but also the cynicism of a government that has failed to solve the 'assassination'.[236]

Balla Gaye's death determined the course of student politics in the years to follow, and was the key juncture in the movement after Wade's election. What was Wade's relationship to youth and students after his election? How was this relationship affected by the student strike in 2001? Madiop Biteye gives the 'party response' to the question:

Just after the election he named a young man to head the

newly created Ministry of Youth. In the same way he nominated many young directors. He advocated for 13 young deputies in the National Assembly and equally in the recent government there are at least three ministers who have not reached 35, and one minister [Sow] who is 26 years old. That is an indicator of the importance that he accords Senegalese youth and he always says 'Youth is worth more than the millions from abroad' because he knows what young people did for him. Therefore youth played a central role in the realization of the *alternance*.[237]

Wade has used students in the government as deputies, advisers and ministers. Ex-students from the *alternance* period were key militants in the student movement during the presidential elections (and to a lesser extent the legislative elections the following year). There are several key factors in this process. Many ex-student leaders retain a close, even intimate, relationship with the university after they have ascended to government. The minister of youth, Aliou Sow – who is 26 years old and referred to in the press as the student minister – is also a part-time lecturer in the English department, or more accurately a guest lecturer. He was also completing a Ph.D in 2004.[238] Yankhoba Diatara, like his friend and fellow PDS member Aliou Sow, is also completing a Ph.D. at the university. Both regard the university as the key base of their political power beyond the uncertainties of political office. The university secures them a tenuous independence from their political masters and an independent source of authority. Sow, often regarded as the youthful mouthpiece of Wade, demonstrated this during a controversial government reshuffle in April 2004. To the astonishment of many observers he defied the president by threatening his own resignation if Modou Diagne Fada[239] – another ex-student leader with widespread support on the campus – was not given a post in the government. *Walfadjri* could not disguise its shock and indignation that 'never has a minister of the republic dared to be so impertinent to the head of state.' The reasons these acts went unpunished are close to the mark, 'the president does not want to have a group of youth from his party on his back, especially after the eviction of Idressa Seck who carries with him an important part of the PDS youth'.[240]

This process reveals a further important factor in student politics. Student activism at the university is the arena *par excellence* where politicians are formed. It is not foreign-educated students who become political leaders, but those who have been baptized by student politics in Senegal. This serves the political establishment, in that ex-student leaders are able to deliver the university to the government and to a certain extent demobilize the campus after *changement politique*. It is not only rich foreign-educated sons and daughters of politicians,[241] returning from Harvard or the Sorbonne, who become leading members of the political class, but those who were involved in the grassroots mobilizations in the student movement.

This observation can be extended into some general conclusions. While UCAD is a vital site for the acquisition of political capital, there is an important further source: the expatriated student who acquires a foreign and technical training enters the Senegalese political scene and frequently achieves high office. However, the importance of the national university cannot be exaggerated. While some students might pursue their studies abroad, for many their relationship to the university and the collective memory of their activism at the university is an essential element in their future political trajectory.

These are common facts on campus and repeated frequently by student activists. Diatara makes the same point: 'But it must be said that today all political leaders ... have been leaders in their time at university. In Senegal ... the university has played a formative political role ... of political education.'[242] Ibrahima Bâ makes a similar point by referring to students as intellectuals: 'It is not possible to bring about a large project without intellectuals ... who make and remake the governments of Senegal. It is something that must not be forgotten. They play a very important role in the elections.'[243] For the government, therefore, we can identify a twin-pronged approach that included the exile of troublesome (though ultimately compliant) student leaders and the co-option of others with a proven track record in campus politics. Both strategies serve the same purpose – to placate the student population and demobilize student organizations.

While corruption, as Abdoulaye claims, is widespread on the campus and permeates many levels of student politics, it is in many ways a logical reaction to the crippling poverty on campus. It is also an equally logical strategy to the permanent crisis of graduate unemployment. If changing political allegiance – *transhumance politique* – was rife among *les grands* before and after *alternance* then it also existed at the university[244] and secured employment for a number of student leaders. As Seydi comments: 'If you come from a poor background and you are a member of the movement, you have connections and access to money ... that can be hard to resist.'[245] But many students resist both the co-option and corruption on campus.

The strategy the government employed fatally crippled the UED and by 2002 it had been rendered impotent: by 2003 it was killed off by the refusal of faculty unions to send delegates to it.[246] As Hamidou Bâ summarizes, 'at the time of the death of Balla Gaye, there was a union that brought all students together ... [after his death] members of the UED all left for France ... the government judged it necessary to keep them at a distance from the country ... to calm the situation ... those who stayed did not have much influence.'[247] Although in early 2004, again under the guiding hand of the rector, a new initiative was launched to establish UGED. The effect on student participation was clear: in the legislative elections in April 2001 it fell from the high of the previous year and was negligible in the local elections in 2002.[248]

Students: intellectuals and turncoats
Long-time PDS militant Pape Birahim Ndiaye,[249] while proclaiming the virtues of student activism, could not disguise a certain irritation at their incessant opposition to all governments, parties and authorities – even those they helped to put in place. 'But you must understand that students have their own characteristics,' he declared, 'even if students have elected someone they will not issue a blank cheque ... if you are elected

today, and tomorrow you do not do what they want ... they will attack you, take you on. That is the general characteristic of students.'[250] There are few I suspect who would disagree with his account of their characteristics. But there is also a slight complacency in Ndiaye's analysis. This centres on the notion that all students, in all places in the world, have the same characteristics and essentially the same activism. Ndiaye's argument is typical: 'You must see ... that everywhere in the world ... students [are] ... the most enlightened group of society.' This is the common-sense understanding of student activism. If this were indeed the case there would be no need to analyse their activism; it would suffice to write 'students all struggle and demonstrate in the same way. Students in Tiananmen Square in 1989, apart from some local nuances, are the same as those in Senegal.'[251]

To determine what is unique about the activism of students in Senegal we have to return to the testimony of student activists. Central to the conception of a student is their self-identity as intellectuals, as Mor Faye – the general secretary of MEES – describes, students are a *jeunesse intellectuelle* (intellectual youth). Faye explains that as students:

> We struggle ... to understand economic, political, scientific and intellectual mechanisms so tomorrow, when we are adults, ... the country will have need of us. ... Today as an intellectual and as a student, if I visit my family, I say to everyone, 'here you are; for these reasons support the Parti socialiste.' They will do this for me alone [and] I convince thousands of people. If each student [says] ... to their parents ... you put me in school so that I can help you tomorrow therefore I ask you to support this candidate because with their political programme I am sure that I will be able to reach my objectives and to help you.[252]

Students played a crucial role in spreading the ideas of *sopi* across the country during the elections. Certain student activists have a keen sense of their ability to shape the political choices of others. Hamidou Bâ, who was active in *alternance* at the university, explains why students were so effective in disseminating the message of the election:

> Students represent a very important force for the political system ... even if he could have won without students you must recognize that they constitute 40 per cent of the vote that brought him to power. Understand that there are 40,000 students and each one of them raised the awareness of people in their village or neighbourhood to vote for Wade. Each student is connected to a family network in Senegal and these networks are made up of between 30 and 50 families. For example, I am from the region of Kolda; I can go to my family and I tell everyone to vote for Wade, [and] because it is Hamidou who comes from Dakar who tells us, it is advice that is followed. That is why I said that students made up a fundamental pillar in the victory of Wade because they are the conduit of information across the country. They have been the pillars of communication. Without students it would have been difficult for him to have won.[253]

Linked to their capacity to sensitize the population is their recognized position as privileged political actors informed about national and international affairs and belonging to an urban world. A central element to Hamidou's influence in Kolda was that, as he explained, he came from Dakar. As Hamidou said, students 'are listened to and regarded as people who are ... the most well informed; they are considered to be the enlightened of the villages ... of the localities... therefore when students arrive they are listened to [and] one waits for their opinions on political life, the economy and the social situation of the country.'[254] This element of student identity made them ideal political actors during the electoral campaign in 1999 and 2000. As we have seen, they were sent into rural areas 'to convince their parents and their region of the necessity of voting for the change'.[255]

Mor Faye makes a similar point: 'Our parents speak of culture, religion and other things typically African, but about politics and

the government for example ... it is us [students] who have
learnt about them at school and university. It is us who
understand what a computer is. Our parents understand well
that we know some things that they do not.'[256] In this sense the
university – even more so than the school – is a foreign space: in
Faye's terms a European one. It is located in an urban world far
from the culture and geographical universe of the student's
parents. There is therefore, 'an African culture and a culture that
comes to us from Europe and that we have learnt. We have
learnt this culture and through us they will accept it'.[257] Students
are transformed into the purveyors of a foreign world that exists
far from their parents, and yet one that dominates their
interaction with them. Faye's use of Europe and Africa expresses
the real division that separates the two worlds.[258] This division
illustrates how students could be used to transport the foreign
world of urban politics to the countryside.

But how does the conception of students as enlightened
political actors sit with the corruption of student activism? Cherif
Bâ describes the university as a space of heightened political
emotions, 'the university space in political terms is not a neutral
one. In fact this space is over-politicized.' But the kinds of
politics and activism that exist on campus – according to Bâ – are
cynical, corrupt and unprincipled. Contrary to an early generation of student leaders – Bathily and Savane are examples
frequently cited (often by themselves) – today's students are
irredeemably corrupt. And most students:

> launch themselves into politics for other reasons. Question
> a student from the PDS about 'liberalism'; ask him what
> are the foundations of ... political liberalism ... they will
> know nothing about it. They don't read economic theories.
> ... Rather they think: 'there you are. I am in a party, I will
> remain there, I have my card, there is a small meeting
> called, I go to it. Political leaders must see that I am there
> and that I am active. ...' This is all there is to it.[259]

There is undoubtedly an element to Bâ's account that is true; a deep layer of cynicism exists in student politics. But his argument has to be qualified. He is speaking specifically of the activity of political parties on campus, so if an older generation of student leaders and politicians condemns student activism as corrupt then they too must take a share of the blame. Who, after all, helped to corrupt it? Bathily – the quintessential Senegalese intellectual–politician – has been forthright in criticizing the ideological weaknesses in contemporary student activism. However, in his capacity as the leader of an influential party of the left, he must share at least some responsibility for this degeneration. After all, as Bâ explains: 'political parties must take responsibility for raising the political level of their activists. But what party does this? ... Therefore, activists don't get the basic training they must ... political involvement is simply engaged in ... to welcome the president.'[260]

While the corruption of political activism is an undeniable feature of campus life it has to be seen in a wider context.[261] First, the systematic co-option and corruption of an important layer of student activists has strangled the movement,[262] which was to a large extent powerless – ideologically and organizationally – to resist this co-option because it had been formed as part of the nationwide campaign for *sopi* in 1999. To a certain extent its *raison d'être* predetermined its subsequent dissolution into the structures of the PDS. It is undoubtedly a source of weakness that the movement was unable to survive the Wade experience; however, many student activists were able to remain free of the party's grasp.

Summary: virtual power and virtual universities
There was a sense of great disappointment among many of the participants in the *alternance* in 2005. For some it was an historic opportunity that has been tragically scuppered. In the first half of 2004 militants of the two main left-wing political parties – LD and AJ – were raising questions about their participation in a government of the neo-liberal right.[263] 'What are we doing', asked one delegate in a meeting in March, 'supporting a government that advocates further privatization of our national

heritage?'[264] While it might have been possible for Bathily to convince himself for a short time that Wade was a closet socialist posing for the international community as a neo-liberal,[265] it was impossible to believe this by the end of 2003. In October 2003 he complained about being stopped constantly on the street and forced to justify the government's behaviour: 'Each day I am stopped in the street and asked, 'Why have you done this or that?' The contrast with the euphoria of victory could not be greater – 'this great enthusiasm, this immense mobilization, the huge expectations from everyone'. Yet the historical moment was missed by a government that quickly resumed the old politics: 'It is in these moments that a country can make great advances. Among the masses, we could have made enormous strides. But in its place the worst habits of the former regime are being recycled.'[266] The government has recycled the old elites, who willingly came under the umbrella of the PDS.

When Wade was asked to account for his government's achievements he boasted that today he was 'one of the principal interlocutors of the Western world ... today when African leaders are spoken of there is ... a francophone'. But even more than this, Wade now claimed to have established a close relationship with George Bush, who 'has been kind enough to consult me on large problems'. Wade's role as international mediator, consultant and middleman was apparently assisted by Chirac 'he [Chirac] has fought for me to become an interlocutor'.[267] This is a clear demonstration of the role of compliant African leaders in the international pecking order: if they obey orders from their geopolitical bosses they may be permitted to give advice. Wade's celebration of this role is illustrative of the impotence of post-colonial political power in Africa: a world of virtual power.

When Wade returned to the university for the first time since his election victory for the inauguration of UCAD II in March 2004,[268] he received a decidedly mixed response. Although crowds of bussed-in school students dutifully shouted *sopi, sopi*, university students were visibly absent. They left complaining that there were too many unsolved problems at the university to celebrate.[269] The inauguration resembled a Hollywood award ceremony with elaborate police escorts heralding the arrival of the prime minister and then, with even greater pomp, the president. However, the centrepiece of the inauguration was the demonstration by Wade of the Université Virtuelle d'Afrique (UVA) where courses will be taught 'virtually' through satellite links with French, American and Canadian universities. This will ensure, according to Wade, that 'the diploma in the end will not be equivalent but the same'.[270] The UVA will mean students no longer need to travel overseas as the world will have come to Senegal: 'Those who will have the diploma from this university will not need to go to the USA to study.' Appropriately, in a world of virtual power here is the virtual university.

As the chances of obtaining visas and scholarships are shut down in the West, students in Senegal turn to a virtual universe and Wade's globalization offers young people a tantalizing illusion. The paraphernalia of this illusion – mobile phones, the internet, the UVA and advanced technology – reinforce the frustration of a global community, a community that seems to offer them access to the world while simultaneously confining them and restricting their real opportunities. Even the classic demands of the student movement become strangely virtual. Today students often mobilize not for government employment – long regarded as a pipe dream – but visas to escape.

This is linked directly to the arguments advanced in Chapter 2. Globalization exposes the simultaneous confining and restricting of certain regions and social groups, at the same time as others benefit from the contraction of space through improvements in mobility and communications.[271] Massey describes the contradiction in the context of the export of Brazilian music:

> The people who live in the favelas of Rio ... who gave us the samba and produced the lambada that everyone was dancing to last year in the clubs of Paris and London; and who have never, or hardly ever, been to downtown Rio. At one level they have been tremendous contributors to what we call time–space compression; and at another level they are imprisoned in it.[272]

These contradictions lie at the heart of a cosmopolitan and globalized capitalism and reveal a highly complex pattern of geographical inequality. The global economy has led to the spatial imprisonment of huge numbers of the world's poor, who are perhaps more confined than they have ever been. Students in Senegal are imprisoned in a world that boasts an apparent acceleration across 'space'.[273]

Conclusion

In conclusion, the first point is the importance, indeed centrality, of student politics in Senegalese society. The student movement has the ability to dominate the political scene. Although the campus is often riven by political differences, students are politically privileged actors who see their mobilizations magnified onto a national canvas. In this context their voices – of complaint and resistance – are amplified far beyond the campus. Yet the weaknesses of the student movement are enormous. Student activists lack, as Cherif Bâ would have it, training in the shape of independent ideological or organizational structures. These weaknesses left them powerless to resist the domination of the UED by Wade's liberalism and the eventual liquidation of the movement under the twin pressures of co-option and corruption.[274] Still, if these are criticisms of the student movement, then they are also valid for almost every political formation in Senegal over the last seven years. However, students' amplified status and activism ensured that despite the corruption, poverty and political cynicism that frequently dominate life on campus, they were able to unite around *alternance*, forge their own organization between 1999 and 2000 and make a decisive contribution to the victory of the *changement politique*.

Although the conclusions from both case studies are discussed in more detail in the next chapter, it is important to examine briefly how the experience of Senegalese students directly relates to arguments being made in this study. There are two factors particular to the activism of students in Senegal that are discussed in Chapter 1. Students described their activism during the *alternance* in much the same way as Cliff explained the consciousness of the 'student intelligentsia'.[275] They see themselves within a modernist paradigm, as vectors of social change. In Cliff's words 'They are great believers in efficiency.'[276] Senegalese students referred repeatedly to the distances (both geographical and metaphoric) that they travel to university, leaving a distinct and 'African' world for the 'European' one represented by the university. These journeys have been described in terms of pilgrimages in the academic literature.[277] These have important consequences for the activism of Senegalese students. It reflects an explicit elitism (that exists as part of their identity if not in their material conditions) that heightens the importance of their activism. Mor Faye described how students have learnt to operate in a modern world, replete with computers, the internet and political debate: 'We have learnt this culture and through us they [our parents] will accept it.'[278] Their status as politically privileged actors derives directly from this exaggerated notion of themselves, at once alienated from and connected to the social world of their parents. These ideas formed much of the political and theoretical thinking after independence.

The direction the Senegalese student movement took in the 1990s reflects an important theme. The weakness of their organizational forms (and ideas) – partly as a result of the collapse of the Berlin Wall – contributed to the disintegration of the movement described above. If students as political agents act to change their inherited conditions, then they also construct organizations, parties, unions (ideological and organizational tools) to assist them in these transformations. These are at once reflections of their inherited circumstances (Senegal's case replicating the failures of the left) and an attempted rejection of them. The student movement's inability to protect itself from Wade and the PDS is illustrative of these tensions and of the student activists' capacity to exercise meaningful agency. While these were obstacles for students in Zimbabwe there were several important differences. The next chapter reflects on two case studies.

Chapter 5

STUDENTS OF THE TRANSITION SPEAK: THE MEANING OF STUDENT PROTEST

In the immediate post-independence period students, privileged by a state able to play an influential role in economic development, moved away from being a transitory social group. Later, when conditions in universities rapidly deteriorated, they still clung to an earlier elitism. Processes of pauperization across Africa during this period battered students' privileged access to the state. However, the increasing convergence with other social groups brought about a new and dynamic relationship between students and wider social forces in the successive waves of protest and political mobilization in the 1980s and 1990s. These transitions, often led by an opposition that advocated neo-liberal policies, which had galvanized the protest movements in the first place, were elusive and contradictory. In these confusing times, student activism retained characteristics from its earlier transitory phase, still regarding its activism as privileged and frequently couching it in an elitist discourse. However, the collapse of state development and the onset of structural adjustment had in many respects substantially transformed student activism (see Chapter 2).

The aim here is to explore the students' role in the waves of political unrest and protest since the 1980s, specifically in the political transitions in the 1990s, in an attempt to discover how this activism can best be understood. Students in post-colonial Africa have had a politically privileged status that is linked to a number of factors described in earlier chapters. A range of changing circumstances over the last 30 years has affected their capacity to act as meaningful agents of political change. These are linked to wider global changes that have impacted on graduate unemployment and privatization. Student movements in sub-Saharan Africa had long drawn on a political tradition that derived from a Stalinized Marxism, but the collapse of Stalinist regimes, linked to changes in the global economy,[1] brought about a profound shift in the ideological and political landscape. Although a student avant-garde that frequently set off a wider convergence of social forces characterized the democratic transitions, these movements were marked by political confusion, an opposition that promised democratic change (literally *sopi* and *chinja* in Senegal and Zimbabwe) and a return to a version of the neo-liberal reforms of the incumbent regimes. Still, even without coherent political philosophies, students were able to play a part in changing governments and achieving changes in national policy. In this chapter I examine how students in the altered and peculiar circumstances of the transitions in the 1990s were able to exercise *meaningful* political action.

In this chapter I also bring together the principal conclusion from the study, namely that the meaning of student protest in sub-Saharan Africa can be understood only in the context of the historical evolution of student action. In the first section I reconceptualize student activism in Senegal and Zimbabwe before going on to examine the experiences of Zimbabwean students and some of the principal – and revealing – differences between the two case studies. I then attempt to draw out some of the historical and theoretical ideas described in earlier chapters. In the final sections I re-examine the inherently contradictory nature of the democratic transitions and the transformation of student activism in an era of globalization.

Dividing lines: student activism, politics and mobilization

Much of the literature on student politics in Senegal divides the student movement into distinct periods. Perhaps the most common is the categorizations given to student activism by an older generation of student leaders, who are now part of Senegal's political and intellectual elite. Bathily et al. claimed that the student movement reached its zenith in the 1960s and 1970s, declining in the 1980s to reach its current impasse.[2] Today students have lapsed into a 'daily corporatism' devoid of ideological debate and fighting over the scraps handed out by the state: increases in grants, reduction in the price of restaurant tickets and other economic demands. This approach has not, however, gone uncontested; Diouf presents a far more positive description of the evolution of youth activism in Senegal.[3]

Bianchini[4] advances the most concerted attack on the idea of the irrevocable decline of the student movement. Such arguments, he claims, are typical of a generational critique that valorizes the activism of the authors while denigrating the present. Against these ideas he advances a notion of cycles of mobilization, where student organizations periodically regroup to form university-wide unions to organize the student body over a set of defined objectives. Once the mobilization has peaked, however, these structures decline and break up.

Student mobilization in Senegal, Bianchini says, has always proceeded under the cover of economic demands; these have frequently been related to the level and distribution of the grant. In addition, students have never acted with pure independence, free from external control. On the contrary, their mobilization has always included external forces; students belong to political parties. It is as unsatisfactory to say that student action is always the result of outside manipulation (for the press normally howls during university strikes), as to say that students manipulate 'outside' political parties. Bianchini's arguments have the advantage of explaining the consistency in student action. Students have continued to play a prominent role in national politics that has not irrevocably changed since their perceived heyday in the

1960s and 1970s. Bianchini outlines these argument in his ground-breaking book, *Ecole et Politique en Afrique Noire*:

> The hypothesis of a certain depolitization of the campus ... can be seen as relative. What is obvious is that the international ideological context is not the same. But the dynamics of student mobilization mean that it can never become totally pacified ... the cycles of mobilization have always been linked to the appearance of new organizations. ... Equally, when a new crisis grips the campus the spectre of political manipulation is always the privileged interpretation of commentators. Therefore the thesis of the depolitization of the student universe is regularly challenged by new developments of conflict between ... [students] and political power.[5]

There are two obvious benefits to this approach. First, he acknowledges the ideological context, which affects student mobilization, and second he criticizes the dominant notion of the depoliticization of student activism. These both represent enormous advances over the predominant commentary. There are, however, serious problems with Bianchini's counter position in that he fails to distinguish between the real differences that separate the cycles of mobilization to which he refers. Do these cycles simply repeat themselves again and again? Is it only a question of identifying the next cycle? What both Bathily et al. and Bianchini fail to do is develop a serious categorization that links student activism to the political economy of post-independent Senegal and that identifies the contours of economic and political transformation, from the early state-led development through economic crisis to neo-liberalism and structural adjustment.

There are periods in Senegal's political and economic trajectory since independence that have made an impact on and helped to determine student activism. Between 1960 and 1975 the Senegalese government advocated state-led growth, which, in keeping with the economic orthodoxy at the time, was regarded as the key to development. Linked to these ideas was the idea of university students as an affluent social group destined to become senior members in the new state apparatus, and they were not pipe dreams. Graduates from the University of Dakar during this period could be fairly certain of work in the expanding civil service.

Although students at the university were excluded from the material hardship of the overwhelming proportion of the population, these 'benefits' were being continually undermined and by the early 1970s they had come under sustained attack. Still, the students' status gave them a degree of political autonomy with which to champion the cause of the poor and the working class without being poor or hungry themselves (even though they may have claimed they were). Students championed social change in the revolt of 1968 – and the unrest that continued throughout the early 1970s at the university. These revolts were animated and propelled by the ideological debates of the left at the time. This should not be surprising given that the left was ascendant internationally and the university was awash with political parties, clandestine groups and 'external forces' debating the direction of the movement, and the future of revolution and social change in Senegal (and the world).[6]

The erosion of state-led development marked the period that followed. Between 1975 and 1990 Senegal was crippled by an economic crisis linked to the international recession in the early 1970s. The fall in the price of commodities severely affected Senegal, while rising costs in the public sector meant the country faced years of recession. Senegal was one of the first sub-Saharan African countries to introduce SAPs through the World Bank and IMF in the early 1980s. In addition, the corruption and inaction of the political class helped to paralyse the country further.

During this period the assurances of graduate employment given to university students quickly disintegrated, as did their material status. Students started to face increasing hardship, for they often had to support their parents on diminishing grants while themselves facing uncertain and frequently jobless futures. Though the political left dominated the campus in the early

1980s, the disorientation (and disorganization) of the left in the face of the onslaught of structural adjustment (and crucially the collapse of the Stalinist regimes at the end of the decade) saw the influence of Wade's PDS grow on campus.

Processes that had been underway in the previous decade were consummated between 1990 and 2000. The result of SAPs was clear for anyone who cared to draw the lessons. According to the World Bank's own figures, the industrial sector lost more than 21 per cent of its workforce in ten years. The restrictive legislation also affected the trade union movement by reducing its capacity to contest the job losses implemented to 'adapt the tools of production to the norms of competition'. Though the PS claimed that these changes would help to attract international invest-ment, as we gave seen, one writer argued, 'Fifteen years after the adoption of the first structural adjustment programme, the crisis is far from being solved.'[7]

Similar processes were at work in other African universities. In the Congo (Zaire) students had been able to advance some of the first and most powerful criticisms of the regime in the late 1960s and 1970s; they continued to resist the regime throughout the 1970s and in the lead up to the democratic changes in the early 1990s. Nzongola-Ntalaja identifies the importance of the student movement, which was, 'the single most important civil society organization to challenge the Mobutu regime at the height of its power'.[8] However, like their counterparts in Senegal and Zimbabwe, by the early 1980s students who had been privileged recipients of state patronage in the 1960s and 1970s suffered from the SAPs that systematically bled resources from the state uni-versities, institutions that were now regarded as over-bloated and mismanaged. Munikengi and Sangol describe the collapse of student status at the University of Kinshasa: 'Until the 1990s, students believed that their university diplomas were equivalent to titles of nobility. ... By the early 1990s ... degrees still consti-tuted social capital ... [but] if a job opportunity did miraculously present itself, they no longer ensured automatic recruitment.'[9]

What is remarkable in the case studies is not so much the variations – significant though they are – but the convergence of both student movements. In many ways Zimbabwe bucked the continental trend, coming to independence 20 years after Senegal. After independence in 1980 the country embarked on an ambitious and widely supported programme of state provision of education and health. To many progressive activists and campaigners, the first years of independence seemed to confirm the progressive nature of the liberation struggle that had taken place in the 1960s and 1970s. Between 1980 and 1988, while these reforms were sweeping Zimbabwe, university student activists were largely supportive of state-led development, seeing themselves as the new student intelligentsia or revolutionary intellectuals[10] who would continue the work of those who had fought for independence. However, by the end of the decade the sheen had rubbed off many of the former heroes of national liberation. Students – privileged and largely cut off from the rest of society – were the first to criticize the regime publicly. From 1988 to 1995 they became trenchant critics of the government, identifying and attacking what they saw as a ruling trinity linking a corrupt regime, an 'unrattled Rhodesian elite' and the introduction of the first of the SAPs in 1991 (see Chapter 3).

By 1995 university students were no longer lone rangers but increasingly one element in an alienated and radicalized civil society. Their rarefied life at the university, which one student leader described as 'Christmas every day', rapidly unravelled. By the late 1990s students – though still regarding themselves as politically privileged – had started to describe their lives at university in very different terms. Far from being Christmas every day, students now suffered from 'Buns-itis' (an illness caused by eating too many buns – the only food they could afford). Dining halls had closed, with catering now provided by private outlets at prices many students could not afford.[11] Zimbabwe's university students had been dragged in a remarkably short period into a pauperized world, no longer able to support their parents (who faced the same hardships). These processes, which were happening across the continent, affected and transformed Zimbabwean and Senegalese student activism.

Students in Senegal and Zimbabwe maintained an identity that was redolent of an earlier elitism. Students of the transition were in many ways the direct inheritors of a former activism. They still saw their movements as privileged, crossing the divide from a traditional (African) society to a modern (European) one symbolized by the university. Similar to Cliff's student intelligentsia, they were acutely aware of the divide between their parents' social world and their newly discovered one. Their activism cast in this mould was still regarded as the means by which development (and democratization) could be achieved.

It is this sense of escape from the social world from which they came that has eroded in the last two decades. The *raison d'être* of the student movement in the first decades of independence was the student activists' alienation from their country's political economy. They saw themselves as the unique vectors of change. The students involved in the transition, while often conceptualizing their activism within the prism of the 1960s and 1970s, became more modest agents of social change.

However, the unique space of the university, often identified as a crucial element in the effective mobilizations of students in the 1960s,[12] still played an important role in the transitions. In Zimbabwe, students at UZ had a freedom to act (and be beaten up) that was far more difficult in the constrained spaces of the city. In 2003 students were the only group that could mobilize in the week of action – the final push – in June 2003 when the rest of urban society had been militarized.[13] In this context, Halliday's argument, more than 25 years ago, is still valid: 'Their relatively privileged social status ... often makes student protests possible, when all other social groups are shackled by military coercion.'[14] But this action is limited, and without the crucial convergence of forces students, though able to engage the regime in heroic acts of resistance, are unable to bring about the transitions. As we shall see, it was only when students were able to unleash a more paralysing movement connected to the trade unions that these transitions could emerge. However, even then, this transition (see Chapter 3) returned to a familiar rhythm of structural adjustment and neo-liberal reforms.

These developments are connected to the ascendancy of neo-liberalism and private capital, which the collapse of the Berlin Wall facilitated. The left, which since the 1960s had dominated opposition politics in Senegal and empowered the national liberation movement in Zimbabwe, was suddenly without an ideological head and conceded that there probably was not an alternative to capitalism, only strategies to reform its hard edges. In Senegal, the PDS did not have to make any such concessions. Bianchini makes this point well:

> During these years the parties of the Marxist left underwent the effects of an ideological crisis ... while a new era presented itself with the involvement in the government of leading members belonging to parties like the PIT in 1991, then the LD in 1993. Teaching unions suddenly found themselves in the position of having a minister from their own ranks, now in charge of applying 'educational adjustment' that together they had fought against in the previous years. The basis of the debate on the collapse of political demands in the 1970s to social ones in the 1990s can only be understood in this way, as the loss of ideological bearings for the Senegalese left. This explanation does not, of course, only apply to Senegal ... where the parties of the left were only able to play a secondary role within a game marked by the rise to power of a political alternative embodied by the PDS.[15]

In this context *sopi* emerged as a slogan that brought together the collective grievances of students, workers and the poor – grievances that had arisen out of the austerity of structural adjustment. By the 1990s it was also (similar to *chinja* in Zimbabwe) a slogan that partly expressed the ideological vacuum left by the collapse of the Berlin Wall. Both these slogans were simultaneously a rejection of the politics of neo-liberalism and a general statement for democratic change that could be brandished by almost any opposition force, including parties that advocated the same neo-liberalism. The 1990s also ushered in a second wave of popular protest, often explicitly political and with far-reaching aims and objectives. As we have seen, these movements were motivated by the rejection of the Washington consensus, but often led by forces loyal to this consensus. Political change in the 1990s in Senegal and Zimbabwe was part of the same pattern of social struggle.[16]

What had happened to student mobilization in both countries? To some extent student life was dominated by a daily struggle to survive on campus; by the end of the millennium most students sought to leave their countries, a desire that was coupled with increasingly draconian visa restrictions placed on Third World countries by the West. Students fought over the few university-allocated scholarships to study in the West, or in Zimbabwe often tried to leave for South Africa. Their self-identity and the world they inhabited had fundamentally changed. These changes influenced their political demands and the frequency and levels of their participation in student action. While students had not collapsed into apolitical corporatism, they were forced to negotiate a world that was collapsing under their feet.

To return briefly to the argument made earlier. Students in both Zimbabwe and Senegal had been members of a transitory social group whose final social position had not been decided.[17] Correspondingly, students regarded their activism as uniquely privileged, where they alone could effect social change. By the mid-1980s students were no longer passing through university on the way to rewarding graduate employment, but frequently only to unemployment. University students became increasingly fixed features of the social world, no longer in transition to another place. In Senegal the suicide of Cheikh Tidiane Fall in 2001 tragically expressed the frustrations of this failed transition. His profile is strikingly similar to many students in Zimbabwe and Senegal: an excellent student at school, the only child in the family to have reached university, but 'failure' at university forced him to repeat the same year several times. The university failed him repeatedly and as he tried in vain to find work at the age of 32 his will to live collapsed. The campus had become a hurdle he could not cross.[18] However, the generalizations about the unemployment of graduates and the transformation of student identity are reflective of the paucity of social science research on higher education in Africa. Mkude et al., in a study of higher education in Tanzania,[19] are right to insist on further research into areas such as the employment of graduates.

Comparing the case studies: the scale of mobilization

In many ways the case studies occupy very different worlds. The differences between the case studies reveal some important features of student activism. The first most striking difference is the scale of political mobilization. From 1995, Zimbabwe saw what one activist described as a 'sort of revolution', with urban (and rural) protests increasing year after year. With each new wave of protest new layers of society would be galvanized, deepening the political movement that was tightening around the government.

The crucial element during this period of student rebellion was that they were not rebelling alone. While their activism displayed an important avant-garde (and elitist) role in the late 1980s – advancing the first serious critique of the regime – by the mid-1990s they were one part of a widening convergence of protest and resistance. By the late 1990s their action, while important, had become essentially subsidiary to that of the trade union movement. This observation can be extended to make a general point: as the level of mobilization and unrest across society increases, the significance of student activism – now accountable to a wider movement – diminishes. Although students might have initiated the first daring protests or advanced the first scathing critique of the regime, they soon become just one element of the general movement. The irony of successful student protest is, therefore, that it becomes less visible and less significant. This inevitably enfeebles student activism, for students have historically regarded their activism as being apart from and above society. So, where students could no longer see their activism as deriving from the 'feebleness of other social classes',[20] their visibility in the transitions declined. We can say, therefore, that the political agency of students varies according to the role and visibility of other social forces. Students in post-colonial Africa, as privileged actors, have continually played the role of a political avant-garde. However, the political agency of students is greater in the early stages of popular mobilization.

In many respects, the experience in Senegal could not have been more different. The period running up to the presidential election in 2000 was not marked by urban protest and ferment. On the contrary, the political elite, which, though drawn from the ranks of the opposition was not directly accountable to a wider movement, made most of the political decisions themselves, including the formation of the *coalition alternance*. The election victory was the result of a much longer process that had seen students protesting against World Bank and IMF reforms throughout the 1990s. Although students played an important role in generating the groundswell of support for the transition, they were not operating in conditions of widespread political protest, let alone rebellion. They did not, as a result, reach the dizzy heights of euphoria and political development that activists in Zimbabwe experienced.[21]

There are striking differences between activists in the two countries. In Zimbabwe student activists talk about the euphoria of having been involved in massive social mobilization. Often they conceptualize this activism in general terms of liberation and revolution, terms that do not seem transplanted onto their activism, but a product of the scale of the protests in which they have been involved. In Senegal, while students remember the excitement of the campaign and the exquisite joy and hope that Wade's victory generated, they have a much weaker level of political analysis. Their horizons are fixed on more parochial concerns, having never been stretched by a wider movement.

Undoubtedly, one reason why the movement was weaker (yet in narrower terms more successful) in Senegal, and why student activists are animated less by broader ideologies, is what Cherif Bâ described as the failure of *la formation des militants*. It is important to repeat his argument (see Chapter 4) that: 'political parties must take responsibility for raising the political level of their activists. But what party does this? ... Therefore activists don't get the basic training they must ... political involvement is simply engaged in ... to welcome the president.'[22] However, most of the political left, disorientated after the collapse of Stalinism, became immersed in Wade's political circus. In this circus student activists are relegated to the status of cheerleaders, with no real responsibilities except as uncritical supporters of their political leaders.

In Zimbabwe, a culture of political discussion and ideology permeated the student movement from the early 1990s. Many of the leading activists – many of whom are now MPs – credit the strength of their activism and political vision to their political 'formation' inside the ISO. Although a small organization, it provided indispensable political debate and ideas to a significant layer of activists, providing them with theory (in the monthly newspaper *Socialist Worker* and the anti-privatization pamphlets written and distributed on campuses) and political practice. Though the group was unable to sway events, it demonstrated the significance of the two most important and frequently missing elements to student activism – organization and ideas.

This phenomenon is linked to an important theme in the book. If students can act to bring about social change, they do so with the available organizational and ideological tools. These resources, fashioned by the student movement and conditioned by inherited conditions, inform beliefs, loyalties and activism. However, such ideas neither act by themselves – independently of the social context – nor simply reflect this context. The case studies show us that ideas and organizations (or their absence) can have a vital influence on events.

Students, agency and political change

It is the argument of this study that students in Zimbabwe and Senegal – and more broadly in sub-Saharan Africa – are crucial agents of social change. Their historical status – described in Chapter 1 – as politically privileged actors gives them an ability to shape political change, which is disproportionate to their numbers and distinct from their counterparts in developed capitalist countries. The study has explored the way students have exercised political action, and the ways that opportunities for activism are shaped by historical and political circumstances.

However, certain elements of this student activism need more careful reflection. The case studies tell stories of students playing a part in overturning governments, creating opposition movements and achieving changes in national policy. But, despite highly energetic student activism, both Zimbabwe and Senegal are resolutely pursuing neo-liberal agendas. Does this mean that students cannot exercise meaningful action in the face of global pressures? And does political activism require a coherent political philosophy? If so, to what extent are students able to achieve this, constrained as they are by highly structured worlds?

What is meant specifically by the term 'meaningful'? In one respect this is a highly misleading word, for we are concerned with the politics and activism of university students and regard them as politically privileged agents. Student activists in both Senegal and Zimbabwe were in this respect able to affect political transformation. However, the desire to stress the meaningfulness of political action emerges from the distinguishing features in the case studies. The impact of student agents on political and social change is highly variable. It could be argued, for example, that students in Senegal made more impact on the political and economic trajectory of the state after the official transition in 2000, by forcing the government to break with the World Bank (see Chapter 4). Still, as discussed in Chapter 2, after the second wave of democratic struggles new governments across the continent more or less obediently followed the IFIs' advice. This resumption of neo-liberalism stemmed from a common failure, which was linked to the inability of protest movements to develop independent organizational and ideological alternatives that could have offered a sufficient counterweight to the global momentum of neo-liberal forces. In this study I argue, therefore, for the need to distinguish between the effectiveness of political activism, against the extreme relativism of much social theory.[23] University students in Zimbabwe attempted to exercise meaningful action through a conception of social transformation that linked the democratic struggle outside the campus, principally in the trade union movement, with the struggle of students. They also made hesitant steps towards constructing organizational tools (like SAP) to question not only specific economic reforms but also the prevailing worldview of the local and global elite.

We saw the dramatic contrast between the case studies, with an important layer of student activists (many of whom went on to lead the student movements and later become opposition politicians) in Zimbabwe being trained by a political organization with an explicitly socialist philosophy. Many of the student activists acknowledge the role of the ISO, Brighton Makunike, chair of the MDC at UZ in 2003, for example, is clear about the continuing role of the organization: 'What I like from ISO is their issue of *jambanja* [resistance]; they don't beat about the bush trying to come up with some alternative; they always have the way forward at their disposal.'[24]

It is important to emphasize the role of the organization among a wide group of activists who have had contact with the party as one-time members, sympathizers or simply fellow travellers. Among students, however, the organization is not simply the forum for the political formation of militants. The example of leading ISO member Munyaradzi Gwisai deserves more than a passing mention. Students singled him out not only as one of the student movement's historical leaders but also as a consistent and intransigent opponent to the regime. His political identity is inextricably tied up with the organization and he is regarded as someone who can be trusted to train other activists: he is a principled activist rather than a political weather vane. Among students this has never meant uncritical support for a political hero, rather as Jethro Mpofu explained:

To me there was something particularly striking about Munyaradzi Gwisai. I found him concerned about the poverty of the people, the interest of the students at the time. He was not absorbed by his position as a lecturer who earns a lot of money and who is comfortable but thinking and empathizing with other people in a different social structure than his. I saw a missionary and revolutionary in such actions and I think he inspired me a lot. We differed in other issues but he inspired me by his selflessness.[25]

This quotation expresses a typical aspect of student action, the importance of setting an example as champions of the poor and underprivileged. From the mid-1990s (and to a limited extent before this at UZ) the ISO organized and trained through militants in cadre schools, meetings, newspapers, pamphlets and endless political discussions. This was not a hierarchical model of political organization and leadership,[26] rather one that endeavoured to lead, not principally through representing people in existing political institutions, but by seeking to mobilize. As Barker argues, it is a model of organization based on the desire 'to win fellow-militants to a common framework of understanding and intervention. Far from promoting passivity, they encourage activism; instead of neglecting education ... [it is] their very *métier*, their be-all-and-end-all.'[27]

In this respect we have the answer to Cherif Bâ's scathing criticism of political parties in Senegal that simultaneously lambast the student movement for its empty head but undertake no political formation of their own. These are not political accidents but aspects intrinsic to the character of these organizations. For the most part they are political bodies fixated on parliamentary and presidential elections, which require no fundamental alternative to pre-existing social relations and identities. Historically, these organizations have been categorized as reformist.[28] Michels wrote critically about how the Social Democratic Party of Germany, the SPD, at the turn of the twentieth century neglected political education: 'Devoting all its energies to the imitation of the outward apparatus of power characteristic of the "class-state", the socialist party allots no more than a secondary importance to psychological enfranchisement from the mentality, which dominates the same class-state.'[29]

These political formations, Michels argued, confirmed his belief in the inherently 'oligarchical tendencies of modern democracy'.[30] In reality, this conservativism and oligarchy are logical consequences, according to Barker, of their 'acceptance of the broad framework of capitalism, the state and its constitution and procedures, etc. Michels did not grasp this argument, for he did not distinguish between forms of parties.'[31] This concept of political organization and leadership contrasts sharply with the one the ISO employed in Zimbabwe, which emphasized self-activity and collective decision-making. This did not turn the organization into a talking shop of endless debates but, by its own admission, decisions were 'reached through the democratic process of the majority' and then acted on.[32] The party's stature rested not only on its pamphlets and debates but also on action, namely 'generating facts' (collecting for striking workers, organizing demonstrations).[33]

Even activists with only slight contact with the ISO commented on the clarity of the organization's political perspectives. ISO members were able to link specific questions and perspectives to more general issues of neo-liberalism and regional development. They were involved in a 'dialogical engagement' with the wider movement, a process of constant political debate and discussion with other movement militants; similar experiences are described in other contexts.[34] Ultimately, the ISO was unable to stop both the neo-liberal turn of the MDC (the MDC had consumed the student movement) because, according to Gwisai, 'it lacked the necessary size and penetration ... to offer a sufficient counterweight to the might of local and international neo-liberal forces.'[35]

Although students were able to exercise political change in the absence of a 'coherent political philosophy', 'political ideas' impact on their ability to exercise *meaningful* action. In the period following the collapse of the Berlin Wall, which signalled the final death of state-led strategies for development, ideological confusion consumed many of the social forces that had looked to progressive and left-wing political change. Yet, in much of the Third World, students remained important agents of the political transitions, frequently initiating wider social protests. However, the collapse of state-led development meant that the student intelligentsia drew on a myriad of confused political and ideological ideas, which gave them a decidedly hybrid identity. They were often at once Guevarists and Islamists, drawing on a peculiar mixture of Islamist teachings from Pakistan or Sudan fused with ideas classically associated with Third World revolutionaries. This student intelligentsia often acted out of despair; as Derluguian says of the student intelligentsia in Chechnya, 'they have neither the resources nor a real programme of socio-economic reform'.[36]

The political transitions in sub-Saharan Africa in the 1990s occurred in a world fundamentally altered by global geopolitics. The struggles of students in periphery capitalist societies have been profoundly affected by the collapse of ideas of national liberation linked to state-led development.[37] What Derluguian writes about the northern Caucasus could apply equally to the students in this study, 'an increasingly desperate search for a renegotiated identity and a dignified position within the reconfigured world-system'.[38] Countries such as Senegal and Zimbabwe were seemingly faced 'with the impossible choice between the competitive discipline of global markets and the prospect of total marginalization'.[39] These ideas are examined in more detail in the conclusion.

The collapse of vibrant protest movements into a familiar pattern of neo-liberal reforms reflects a failure of the protests and rebellions described in this study (see Chapter 2). Students are clear about their failure to organize ideologically in higher education. In Zimbabwe, as we have seen, Hopewell Gumbo explained that during the formation of the MDC students had no clear strategy for entering the movement so as to influence the new party and maintain their independence from it: 'Our participation was then limited from being an ideological engine to being foot-soldiers in the emergent party.'[40] These weaknesses in student agency are identifiable historically. In the war for national liberation in Zimbabwe, student activists again failed to 'undertake an analysis of the conditions under which uprisings occur'.[41] These problems typically derive from the same source, namely the failure of the student movement to distinguish itself clearly and independently from the political weaknesses of wider political forces; and the absence of an effective organization that organizes in a broad political and social milieu (in townships, factories and universities). In the presence of such organizations students may indeed be able to 'touch off' wider radical actions that could lead to lasting political transitions; without such political leadership and organization 'the student initiative remained an isolated event of little impact within the African community'.[42]

These issues are connected to other concerns for the study. Harman, in an important essay, stresses the centrality of political and ideological structures in the historical process. As he writes, 'Economic development never took place on its own, in a vacuum. It was carried forward by human beings, living in certain societies whose political and ideological structures had an impact on their actions.'[43] These structures, in turn, were the products of a confrontation between social groups.

Social development is propelled by ideological and political conflict between rival social groups, and not simply economics. The resolution of these conflicts 'is never resolved in advance, but depends upon initiative, organization and leadership'.[44] Initiative, organization and leadership (and to some extent Michels's 'psychological enfranchisement') are the raw materials through which human beings are able to make history, but not on a level playing field (or in a vacuum). We do not choose the circumstances in which these struggles take place.[45]

Historical progress proceeds under such contradictions. Amin argued that western Europe's economic backwardness gave it an advantage in the development of capitalism.[46] Other Eurasian African societies experienced similar developments in production, but existing state structures ultimately suffocated them. The Chinese empire – the most economically advanced in the Middle Ages – was able to block these developments while in the least advanced areas of western Europe the social forces unleashed by these changes could break down the old superstructures.[47] But the capacity to 'break down' old institutions was not simply a matter of economics, but crucially of politics and ideology. It was not only a question of struggling against the economic control by old social groups but also the prevailing worldview. Where the social forces associated with the new forms of production were unsuccessful, or too closely connected to the old states and institutions, 'they were defeated and the old orders hung on for a few more centuries until the battleship and cheap goods of Europe's capitalists brought it tumbling down.'[48]

Female activists
One of the most dramatic observations that can be made about the activism of students in this book is the near invisibility of women. Among more than 90 student activists interviewed over five years, only a handful have been female. One of the rare female activists who held office in the otherwise male-dominated SRC at UZ was Commercie Mucheni. She explains the significance of her election, and the difficulties for women on campus (from September 1997 to March 1998):

> I made history to become the first female student secretary general. A lot of people questioned if I could handle the position ... they didn't know that a woman could actually come out in the open and say, 'I am taking a leading role.' ... At the time you would hear guys shouting to female students, 'why bring those big breasts on campus, do you want to breast-feed everyone here?' You would see such kind of verbal threats, verbal abuse towards women ... it was oppressive and as a consequence female students often could not enjoy life on campus. Physical abuse also occurred. They could strip naked women seen wearing mini skirts or what they would describe as indecent clothing.[49]

The lack of leading female activists did not exclude their activism at other levels of the university, though student demonstrations in both case studies were largely male activities. There are repeated appeals for the unity of UBAs (University Bachelors' Association) and USAs (University Spinsters' Association) at UZ, although in recent years the relationship between the sexes has been strained by attacks on female students.[50] Even the terms UBA and USA have come to represent the largely male frustration at being unable to have relationships with university women. Because of the paralysing poverty on campus, there is a belief that only NABs (non-academic bachelors or male professionals outside the university) have access to university women because they are in a position to take them out. The question of gender and political activism in Africa has received some important recent attention.[51]

But the relative silence of female activists also reflects their poor access to higher education across Africa. In 2000, for example, gross enrolment ratios for sub-Saharan Africa were 5.1 per cent for men and 2.8 for women. There are, however, important national variations. Female admissions at Makerere University in Uganda increased massively in the 1990s, up from 27 per cent in 1990/1 to approximately 40 per cent in 1999. Over a similar period at the University of Dar es Salaam in Tanzania, female student enrolment increased to 24 per cent from 13 per cent in the six-year period from 1994.[52] Still, as Zeleza argues, 'women remain largely under-represented in African institutions of higher learning'.[53]

Negotiating the democratic transition

Much academic literature has questioned the extent of the democratic transitions that have taken place across Africa, casting doubt on the depth of the transition and the extension of democracy. Although John Saul has become far less critical of the protest movements in recent years,[54] he still highlights some of their genuine weaknesses. There are serious and important problems, not so much to do with the waves of democratic struggle as with the limitations of democratic advance under conditions of structural adjustment. Abrahamsen is perhaps the most penetrating critic of the international community's shallow calls for good governance. She rightly identifies how popular resistance, frequently against IMF and World Bank policies, dovetailed with the international community's demands for more democratic openness (and a greater drive towards neo-liberalism).[55] This is, perhaps, one of the central paradoxes of the period since the collapse of the Berlin Wall. Most members of the international community do not fear popular mobilization and protest in the same way. Indeed, they have come to regard them as useful ways of removing certain particularly corrupt or intransigent governments that have failed to implement SAPs successfully. As Callinicos explained, 'The method of velvet revolution has become a technique of imperial rule – more effective, arguably, than the US Marines – through which American funds and émigré expertise are deployed behind the local politicians most likely to set up a pro-Western regime'.[56] This should not be interpreted as an argument that sees all protest movements manipulated by American power, but an appeal for the careful analysis of the forces behind national political change. However, the reality is that in sub-Saharan Africa, during the 1980s and 1990s, as economic reforms continued, so too did popular protests. The two transitions in this study, frustrated in Zimbabwe and successful in Senegal, were part of these waves of change, but also subject to the same enormous contradictions.

In the post-Stalinist world the struggles that have erupted as consequences of neo-liberal reforms and structural adjustment have often taken on the appearance of movements for democracy and human rights (and even further liberalization). This is frequently because the governments implementing these reforms rely on increasingly draconian measures to suppress popular discontent. Harman describes these processes well: 'The path that began with neo-liberalism ends up in quasi-dictatorship ... the effect is to turn social and economic issues into political struggles around demands for democracy and human rights. In the process people can lose sight of the social and economic roots of these political issues.'[57] This is what has happened in Zimbabwe.

The dynamics of protest and change were very different in Senegal and Zimbabwe, though the same contradictory situation prevailed. The *sopi* movement had it roots in the anti-neo-liberal protests of the late 1980s and 1990s, specifically the World Bank and IMF reforms the regime had been implementing since the

1980s. In the course of the 1990s it came to be epitomized by a party (and leader) that saw further liberalization and structural adjustment as the solution to Senegal's woes. Similarly, the desire for widespread economic and social transformation became a movement, led by an opposition elite from above, for democratization and citizenship. In both cases the cycle of neo-liberalism resumed: in Zimbabwe when Mugabe dropped his popularist pro-poor price freezes and in Senegal the day after Wade's election. However, a note of caution needs to be sounded: as we have seen, Wade's higher education reforms necessitated the government breaking with the World Bank, yet these were changes forced on the government by Balla Gaye's murder (see Chapter 4). As argued above, this implies that students do, in certain circumstances, have sufficient political agency to negate the will of the World Bank.

The effect on student activists was devastating. In Zimbabwe they saw their unions and political hope expire as the government recovered momentum and the MDC resorted to courting the international community by promising to return the country to neo-liberalism and seized land to its rightful owners. Student activists were politically disarmed, and were used increasingly for set-piece confrontations with the regime. In Senegal the new government, which had promised heaven and earth to university students, only granted reforms after the student strike in 2001, and then proceeded to co-opt and corrupt leading student activists (a process that did not pose too many difficulties for the government). Student activism had been softened up by the hammer blows of neo-liberalism, and though students maintain a privileged political role they have seen their activism transformed. Their capacity to act independently has been drastically undermined by the twin pressures of poverty and the commodification of resistance.

Student activism and the commodification of resistance
Student activism has been dramatically affected by the so-called donor syndrome. The effect of structural adjustment, to enfeeble national government, has led to the emergence of a plethora of

NGOs over the last 20 years. Some authors distinguish between different types of NGO. Klein argues[58] that NGOs were part of the 'swarm' that was going to paralyse multinationals, while Bond[59] makes a distinction between co-opted and non-co-opted NGOs, regarded as important allies of popular struggles. The great majority of NGOs, however, have in many countries assumed traditional state functions. Foley of the Norwegian Refugee Council explains that they 'have assumed responsibility for state-type functions such as the provision of public services, health and education'.[60] The growth of NGOs from 145,000 worldwide in 1990 to more than 250,000 in 2000 has increasingly directed the distribution of foreign aid.[61] NGOs have stepped in to fill gaps created by the impact of structural adjustment and neo-liberalism on basic social services, often using the language of empowerment and community participation.

It is among Bond's NGO allies that problems for many activists start. The ISO uses the term 'commodfication of resistance' to describe how NGOs are commodifying resistance in Zimbabwe, yet it is a feature of many sub-Saharan African countries. In Zimbabwe the commodification of resistance is a symptom of the frustrated transition, and the decline in the movement that gave birth to the MDC. The general effect is the massive distortion of resistance by the distribution of donor money to activist groups and NGOs. The result for the student movement in Zimbabwe was the creation of the Zimbabwe Youth Democracy Trust in 2003 by ex-members of the executive of the national student union, ZINASU (the Student Solidarity Trust is another example). A Norwegian NGO provided the money for the trust and student activists were diverted into fighting over positions in the trust and for control of the organization. Donor money also flowed into ZINASU because the union was incapable of funding its own activities through student subscriptions (see Chapter 3).

Some writers have seen the connection between NGOs and neo-liberalism as proof of their collaboration with imperialism; indeed, this is an argument ZANU–PF used to justify the legislation constraining the activism of Zimbabwean-based NGOs.

James Petras argues that the funding of NGOs by Western governments exposes their so-called apolitical approach, revealing them as 'grassroots reactionaries'.[62] They act, according to Petras, as an emergency service disorienting discontent to ensure that capital accumulation can continue unabated. There is, undoubtedly, an historical case for these assertions. For example, a principal NGO in Zimbabwe is the Friedrich Ebert Stiftung Foundation, linked to the German SPD, which operated across Africa during the cold war and sought to undermine the 'influence' of communism in trade unions.

Increasingly, NGOs do not reinforce grassroots initiatives but create a climate of dependency. Activists are not obliged to 'find their own resources for struggle, and union meetings and seminars are held in the comfort of expensive hotels'.[63] This stems from a profound failure to understand the momentum of activism (and not always an explicit desire to work as an 'agent of imperialism'). Rather than seek a solution to political change and agitation in the self-organization of activist groups and organizations, NGOs divert these energies to the scramble for funds. The case of Thailand applies equally to Zimbabwe (and Senegal): Ungpakorn explains that here NGOs 'look to foreign networks and the internet for help. This can be seen by the way they teach striking workers to chant slogans and write placards in English – a language which most Thai trade unionists do not understand.'[64]

These distortions have had a similar effect in Senegal. Although the principal conduit of the commodification of resistance has been through funds made available to student activists by political parties, the result is the same. The ubiquitous poverty on campus has severely eroded the students' capacity to resist such co-option. Harman writes that these NGOs 'have money which other grassroots activists lack, getting it from foundations run by western multinationals or from governmental bodies. This means they can go into an area from the outside and offer local people the finance and resources they need to advance their campaign.'[65] However, these are not grassroots initiatives but ones with clear limits prescribed by the donors. They distort local activism by sucking in militants who become cut off from the struggles they were involved in generating. The pull of donor money under conditions of widespread poverty is hard to resist, and activists are now drawn into a spider's web of regional conferences, national meetings, organizing committees, training days and interminable public meetings – or *diner-débat* at UCAD in Dakar.

The commodification of resistance is linked to twin phenomena, namely the neo-liberal pauperization of sub-Saharan Africa and the political collapse of the left in the 1980s and 1990s. 'Disillusionment, especially after the disintegration of the Eastern bloc, led many of its members to retreat from any idea of total confrontation with the world system and turn to single issue campaigns.'[66] This explains the proclivity of single-issue campaigns among NGO activists who see new possibilities of empowering communities through donor funds. In these contexts it is not the co-opted NGOs of Bond's dichotomy that pose the real threat but his non-co-opted allies who are able to ingratiate themselves in movements and campaigns. Bomba's seemingly harsh treatment of these allies (discussed in Chapter 3) now seems a reasoned critique, they 'disarmed the movement that was emerging from the ground, [and] shifted people's focus from the real battles to some very fantastical arenas'.[67]

Conclusion

Perhaps the most remarkable feature of contemporary student activism in much of sub-Saharan Africa is not its distortions and transformation but that under often crippling poverty students were able to make important contributions to political transitions on the continent. They have tenaciously clung to their status of privileged political actors, occasionally using an elitist discourse to make sense of their activism. This status gives their political actions a particular intensity unavailable to other groups. This is still linked, as in the years immediately after independence, to both their organizational coherence (living in a rarefied or hyper-politicized university space) and the relative organizational weaknesses of other social groups in society. However, student activism has followed the political and economic trajectory of the continent. From their role as a student intelligentsia in national liberation movements, to articulating the first systematic critiques of the new nations and then, when their privileged access to the state was shut down, students helped to galvanize the convergence of forces during the democratic transitions. The transitions in Zimbabwe and Senegal betrayed the hopes of countless activists, but remind us of the centrality of political organization and ideology to combat the cacophony of cries that there are no alternatives to austerity, neo-liberalism and Wade's 'you must work, work again and always work.'

It is clear that the importance of activism is not simply as a topic of research, but also as an important element in social and economic development. Economic development without the intervention of ideological and social struggle (political activism) can lead to stagnation or worse 'the common ruin' of contending social forces.[68] Therefore, to make and remake our circumstances, requires a social group with 'its own ideas, its own organization and eventually its own ... leadership. Where its most determined elements managed to create such things, the new society took root. Where it failed ... stagnation and decay were the result.'[69] The inability of students to consider the 'impossibility' of social change[70] ensures the continued necessity and vibrancy of their agency, as an important element in the organizations that will seek a 'transition' to a world not dominated by neo-liberalism, austerity and underdevelopment.

In the Conclusion I shall consider the contemporary student intelligentsia introduced in Chapter 1 and describe how this group, deflected from its post-independence trajectory and cast adrift by globalization, has responded through a variety of movements and organizations. I shall also return to the idea of waves of protests, and consider the evidence that a 'third wave' linked to the international anti-capitalist movement is emerging on the continent.

CONCLUSION: THE RETURN OF THE STUDENT INTELLIGENTSIA?

In this chapter I intentionally broaden the conclusions of the study, so the ideas discussed are preliminary and provisional. I simply mean to illustrate some of the important areas that deserve further careful analysis. So far I have charted the evolution of university students and considered their uneasy membership of the intelligentsia, which informs much of their activism. Former student activists in Zimbabwe described themselves in the 1980s – as they started to formulate the first critique of the ruling party – as 'revolutionary intellectuals'; one way of understanding this self-identity is in relation to a historically derived status as politically privileged actors. However, in the context of the austerity and adjustment on the continent, do students maintain this position? Has student activism become fragmented and less influential with the privatization and diversification of higher education? This tension divides much of the commentary.[1] The contemporary activism of students takes place in a highly structured world where students frequently struggle to survive at the university and to secure a future in an uncertain post-university job market.[2] Still, students have repeatedly demonstrated a capacity to 'touch off' wider social protests during the transitions.[3]

In this book I regard the neo-liberal project of the corporate university and higher educational reform in Africa, and the struggle of students against it, as a global one. But in Africa, in

259

the midst of a deep-seated economic crisis, these reforms take on a more violent aspect. It is argued that there was a 'glory period' in continental higher education, but that it was extinguished not long after independence. Soon Africa became the guinea pig for the project of market-led rationalization of higher education. This study has reflected specifically on the peculiarities of the African experience, and this experience, I have argued, is connected to the evolution of the student intelligentsia, which has responded to the crisis on the continent in diverse ways. In this chapter I briefly look at some of these responses. While the student intelligentsia often triggered a 'democratic revival' linked to the convergence of social forces in the transitions, its members have also been among the leaders of secessionist and rebel movements on the continent.[4]

The reforms that have impoverished the continent and pulverized higher education have not gone unanswered. But the ideological response of the opposition through the transitions was muted, disorientated by the collapse of Stalinism. Activists across the continent were left believing that there was no genuine alternative. The triumph of neo-liberalism, and Bush senior's 'new world order', was seemingly without response. Student agency was enfeebled at exactly the time when a radical ideological alternative was needed. The euphoria of the 'end of history' profoundly affected individuals. I was finding my political feet during the short-lived triumph of capitalism in the early 1990s. I remember a family holiday in 1991, when a right-wing uncle scoffed at a copy of the *Communist Manifesto* I was studying. 'Leo, capitalism has vanquished its foes; there is nothing more to fight for.' I was stunned, but my riposte was not as fierce or as quick as it would be today. Today the scoffing belongs to the activist. The language (and organizations) of social transformation, prematurely buried in the fall of Soviet communism, is returning. This crucial element in the capacity of students in this study to exercise meaningful political agency is, to a certain extent, answered in the rise of global resistance.[5] Those seeking to build on the movements described in the study must draw on this resistance.

The student intelligentsia

As we saw in Chapter 1, university students, graduates and foreign educated and organized students were able to play an important, some say vital, role in leading national liberation movements in the 1940s and 1950s. Frequently organized in exiled student groups, they fraternized closely with a left-wing and communist milieu that converged and fed into their anti-imperialism. When this student intelligentsia returned, often after years overseas, they helped set up, lead and organize the nationalist forces that were gathering momentum. Their status as a student intelligentsia ensured they could gain authority over movements with very different social roots. They occupied a unique position between two social worlds, one represented by the West and symbolizing modernization and development, and another world that they had escaped in Africa. They rejected the latter and believed that independence would herald rapid state-led development of their backward societies and confirm their historical role in bringing this development to fruition. In many ways this explicit elitism – derived from their unique organizational and political coherence in colonial Africa – was the mantle handed to post-independence students.[6]

An important element of this elitism continues to generate student activism. Students still see themselves as privileged in terms of their proximity to a European world – a world of technology, development and globalization. It is this contradiction – a heady mix of poverty and elitism – that motivated student activists in Senegal and Zimbabwe during their recent political transitions. University students in sub-Saharan Africa have maintained a politically privileged position in society despite the almost total collapse of their material conditions from the heyday of the 1970s.

But there are other perhaps more dramatic examples of the continued importance of this group in contemporary Africa. One of the secrets of the student intelligentsia was its capacity to organize in national and international student unions and politically through access to a conceptual and intellectual world denied to most sections of society. The student milieu generated

261

conditions that were at once internationalist – giving them access to international organizations and funds – while pulling students into hyper-politicized spaces, in college and on university campuses (see Chapter 2). Organizations could flourish without the rigid discipline of the workplace or the state-controlled streets. Over the last 20 years the student intelligentsia has been propelled into new roles, under very different circumstances. Although they are no longer advocates of state capitalist development – that was an elusive goal long before the collapse of the Stalinist regimes – they have become new political actors in diverse movements and groups across the continent.

During this period there has been an unprecedented transformation in Africa's political economy, often connected to structural adjustment, which has seen state industries and businesses collapse. These changes have often exacerbated processes of state decline leading in some cases to total collapse.[7] Under these conditions, the only group able to maintain a degree of cohesion is often that of university students. The transition is often rapid, from participating in democratic struggles in civil society, a student intelligentsia is able to organize and lead rebel movements that follow (and help precipitate) state collapse.[8]

The cases of Liberia and Sierra Leone are revealing. Richards describes an alienated intelligentsia composed of ex-students who made up Sierra Leone's rebel armies.[9] One fighter explained: 'Most of the rebels are students, the majority are students. ... After an attack they write a message and drop it. These are the reasons they are fighting they say. The government doesn't give any encouragement to people to get land or to go to school.'[10] In Liberia the same processes have taken place. The wave of resistance to Samuel Doe's brutal and corrupt regime saw students act as the *de facto* opposition from 1980 to 1984, when all opposition parties were banned. Students helped to organize Firestone workers but their leaders, together with trade unionists, were viciously repressed. Many spent years on death row. With the collapse in the rubber market in 1985 and the end of the cold war, Liberia had lost its strategic importance. The economy was destroyed, and the USA, which had been the country's chief backer, could ignore the war that descended on the state. The war did not represent the 'primitive' or 'barbaric' nature of societies in West Africa (as some commentators would have it).[11] On the contrary, it demonstrated how the region was connected to a globalized economy that was at the same time criminal and informal.[12]

Behind the war and rebel groups was a student intelligentsia that had been active in the anti-Doe opposition in the early 1980s. The Liberians United for Reconciliation and Democracy (LURD) was a rebel group that fought Charles Taylor's government after elections brought him to power in 1997. It had been a faction in Taylor's original war against Doe. The majority of the rebel leaders were also former student activists who had been involved in resistance to Doe in the 1980s.[13]

The student intelligentsia played numerous roles during the period of state decline and collapse. Perhaps, most notably, university students have been active in the resurgence of Islamic fundamentalism. They have been key players in the Islamic movements that are now demonized around the world, partly as a result of the collapse in graduate employment and the erosion of the same certainties that undermined the status of students in sub-Saharan Africa. Harman explains that Islamism has arisen in 'societies traumatized by the impact of capitalism'[14] but it is the crisis in the world economy in the last 30 years that has seen a rapid increase in these ideas. Harman emphasizes that it was frequently students who formed the backbone of Islamist movements:

> [These were] students, the recent Arab speaking graduates and above all, the unemployed ex-students who formed a bridge to the very large numbers of discontented youth outside colleges who find that they cannot get college places. ... And through its influence over a wide layer of students, graduates and the intellectual unemployed, Islamism is able to spread out to dominate the propagation of ideas in the slums and shanty towns as a 'conservative' movement.[15]

It was the control and domination of Islamic ideas on the campuses of Algeria in the 1980s and 1990s that ensured that the Islamists were able to step into the 'impoverished streets of the cities where students and ex-students mixed with a mass of other people scrabbling for a livelihood'.[16] The convergence of forces – between an impoverished student and ex-student body and the mass of other people – has manifested itself in a multiplicity of movements.

Similarly, student suicide bombers carried out the 11 September attack on New York. The leading figure in the attack is illustrative of these trends. Mohammad Atta was born in Kafr el-Sheikh in the Nile Delta, in what one report called the 'slightly down at heel Cairo suburb of Giza'.[17] His family belonged to a branch of the intelligentsia that was angry at Anwar Sadat's opening out to the West in the late 1970s. Atta graduated from a university that had, by the early 1990s, become a ferment of fundamentalist activity. He joined the Engineers Syndicate, one of the few Muslim Brotherhood-controlled professional associations in Egypt. He became appalled by the creation of what he regarded as a new class of Egyptian 'fat cats'. Volker Hauth, who studied with him in Germany, remembers 'One of the main points of his critique was the contrast between a few rich people and the mass of people with barely enough to survive.'[18]

Mohammed Atta is portentous of the movements for Islamic revival, inspired by the desire to reverse real injustices that have emerged violently across the Third World in the last 30 years. A student intelligentsia has played a pivotal role in these movements as the ideological champions of Islamic reforms and of rebel movements during state collapse.[19] In each case they act as disgruntled victims of the economic and political disintegration going on around them. While students in the Muslim association of Senegalese students, AMEAN, in the 1950s could envisage a radical Islam, and a revivalism linked to a progressive agenda for radical social change, today the collapse of this agenda has transformed student activists. As Diouf has written, these students, rather than being the agents of progressive social transformation, see themselves as the custodians of tradition: 'Certain sections of youth assign themselves the role of guardians of a Muslim morality which justifies punitive expeditions against drugs, drunkenness and thieves.'[20]

In general, Senegalese students have not assumed the ideological mantle of religious change that has characterized North African and Middle Eastern universities, nor have they spearheaded a Senegalese version of the Islamic revival. They have, however, played a crucial role in the separatist movement in the Casamance.[21] Out of the economic crisis that has gripped the country, religious associations have grown substantially. Today there are many active Islamic groups. The country is full of Islamic schools teaching Arabic, in wealthier suburbs and in poor neighbourhoods, in makeshift wooden huts and any improvised spaces. At the university a number of associations claim to instil the pure tradition of the Prophet Mohammed.[22] What is striking about the associations that are active on campus, however, is their relative invisibility in the political life of the university. What connects most university students across the continent is their economic trajectory; as promises to students were shattered in the economic crisis, they were left without a secular or progressive agenda.[23]

When the Berlin Wall collapsed in 1989 a generation of intellectuals and leaders lost its ideological hold on the world, and this has left its mark on social movements everywhere. Although much recent student activism on the continent is notable for its lack of political debate, the celebrated vanguardism of the 1970s (or the 1980s in the case of Zimbabwe) was a consequence of the collision of forces that are no longer present. This does not preclude the development of these politics today.

Converging forces

Higher educational reforms, as we have seen, have brought student identity to the centre of the structural crisis. This is a point that is worth reiterating. Mamdani, in an important study, has seen these processes at work: 'previously a more or less guaranteed route to position and privilege, higher education seemed to lead more and more students to the heart of the economic and social crisis.'[24] Students are no longer the transitory social group waiting to be allotted government employment; on the contrary, they have become pauperized, converging more and more with the wider urban poor: social groups that they had historically regarded as their responsibility to liberate. They are a marginal social group in so far as the whole of urban society has become marginalized from the formal economy, forced increasingly into a precarious world of casual and informal employment. In an important sense they have become less marginal to the social word they sought to change in the 1960s and 1970s.[25]

There is an international dimension to these developments that should not be ignored. The neo-liberal processes that have led to the privatization and commodification of university education in sub-Saharan Africa have had a global reach. Across the world student movements have grappled with the changing nature of university education. Nowhere is this clearer than in France, where globally the student movement is perhaps at its strongest. Here there is a direct symmetry in the lives and experiences of students and the working class. This is explained brilliantly by the Marxist writer Daniel Bensaid, when he describes the differences between the current period and the so-called highpoint of student unrest in 1968:

> The present movement is directly based on a social question – the destruction of workplace regulations and the generalized casualization of employment, which is common both in education and to workers. The question of the link, and not just solidarity, between the two is therefore immediate.
>
> Finally, the fundamental difference is with the general context and in particular with the way unemployment weighs on things. In 1968, the unemployed were counted in tens of thousands in a period of great expansion, so students had no worries about the future.[26]

This is a central issue. Students were a privileged part of this stable economic world. However, in France today, Bensaid continues, 'six million people are either without work or casually employed.' This has impacted enormously on the identity of students, who require no ideological leap to connect their activism to the labour movement. The link, as Bensaid argues, is immediate. Students do not simply dabble in the social world outside the university campus – committed as they might have been in 1968 to building the bonds of solidarity with the labour movement – they are a central component of it. Often this connection is explicit in terms of student involvement in the labour force, but there is also a political dimension to these changes:

> The link is natural, and the labour movement is less closed, or even hostile, than it was towards students in 1968.
>
> At the time this hostility, or wariness, was fostered in particular by the workerist demagoguery of the Communist Party. ...
>
> Today relations are not so closed. On the one hand the ability of the bureaucratic machines to control things has been considerably weakened.
>
> On the other the overall expansion of secondary and higher education means it is no longer possible to portray students as an exclusively middle class layer.

Today students can be redefined as a 'student mass' within the workers movement, and not as a separate or distinct class. Kouvelakis has powerfully made this argument in the context of France. 'This "great transformation" has, of course (in comparison with 1968) not only made easier the link with workers, but, above all, has given this an "organic" character, the character of the building of a common struggle, and not of an alliance or solidarity between separate movements.'[27] These comments could as easily have been made about much of Africa, buffeted by the same blows of globalization. However, student activism internationally is still instilled with an important element of elitism, though now tempered by the realities of campus poverty. They have a considerable ability to mobilize in relatively autonomous urban spaces, achieving an organizational coherence that is rarely matched by other social groups. The power of students to set off wider social protests was again vividly demonstrated by French students in 2006, though no longer as an alliance between separate movements.

A third wave? Protest in the twenty-first century

Considering that this study is concerned with the transitions that took place in two countries at the end of the 1990s and early part of this century, it is essential that we return to the notion of waves of protests discussed in the first chapters. Is a third wave of protest emerging on the continent? It is argued that the antecedents of the anti-capitalist movement have their roots in waves of protests across the world, associated with the restructuring of the world economy in the 1970s, 1980s and 1990s, but the rise of global dissent in terms of an explicit anti-capitalism is a much more recent phenomenon. For the first time popular protest and dissent are not merely national and international (in the sense of occurring in many places simultaneously across the world) but transnational and potentially global. As the process of globalization continues to break apart the flimsy structures of national capitalism in favour of global capital and its agents and parasites, the popular forces encountered earlier have resisted this process.

Popular protest against illegitimate and undemocratic regimes, and against antisocial policies, continues to take place. There are still bread riots, and forms of protest reminiscent of the first wave (of the 1970s and 1980s) continue to erupt; there is still unfinished business as regards the replacement of illegitimate regimes in many countries, and the establishment of new and more broadly representative governments is still likely to be the immediate objective of most popular movements in Africa, Asia and Latin America, as it was in the second wave of the 1990s. But finally, there is now emerging a variety of movements and groupings that are explicitly – ideologically and politically – linked to similar movements of protest elsewhere in the world, and that draw strength and vitality from those international links to form the beginnings of a truly global movement of dissent against the dominant form of global capitalism.[28]

Important developments in political protest on the continent are taking place in South Africa. Although limited in scale, over the last few years new groups have emerged in the struggle against the government's essentially neo-liberal agenda. Frequently, this has taken the form of community-based protest movements. In Johannesburg, relatively disparate actions have fallen under the organizing umbrella of the Anti-Privatization Forum. Most notable of these is the Soweto Electricity Crisis Committee (SECC) that has campaigned successfully against disconnections by the electricity supplier Eskom that were occurring at a rate of 20,000 per month in Soweto in 2001.[29] Action includes marches, meetings and sit-ins, as well as the illegal reconnection of electricity by SECC militants.

Activists and militants have emerged from these new social movements, many of them identifying explicitly with the anti-capitalist mobilizations in the north and elsewhere in the south. However, there are vital questions over the nature of leadership and of the working class in South Africa. Desai and Pithouse make a familiar argument about the collapse in the organizing power of the working class:

> Clearly it is true that in a context where full-time employment is part of the everyday life of just one-third of the African labour force, and with unemployment estimated as high as 45 per cent ... the forms of solidarity that had once translated insertion in waged employment into popular expectations for citizenship and democracy are facing a slow and dramatic decline.[30]

Similarly, on the question of leadership, there is often hostility to any organizational form regarded as 'Stalinist'. Certain activists eschew leadership and instead advocate direct democracy (often under the influence of 'autonomism'). Ngwane summarizes well the main objections to this: 'My concern is also that the ideology of no leadership means, by default, the principle of "self-selection" and thus encourages a lack of accountability. There is also the danger of some social movements "drowning in their own militancy" because of the failure or the refusal to develop long-term political projects in favour of immediate short-term militant actions.'[31]

In this study I have argued that ideas and organizations – the ideological tools – are crucial elements in social change, and that the failure of these organizations and the ideological weaknesses of the movements discussed in the study have contributed to the collapse of vibrant protest and activist movements. The agents of political transition must engage with some of the ideas emerging from the anti-globalization movement that reject the Washington consensus. If students, as part of the 'reconvergence of popular forces'[32] are to change their circumstances, then the political direction and trajectory of popular protests in Africa must advance through an interchange across countries and even across continents. The anti-capitalist movement (for all its weaknesses) offers the possibility for such an interchange. It is vital, however, to be cautious about South African social movements. The nature of the movements sketched above has in many respects been extremely ephemeral, and they seem to have failed to evolve into a serious and systematic political opposition. This in itself, perhaps, expresses the level of trade union activity, and the ideological confusion and divisions within the South African left that have prevented groups that animated these movements from engaging critically with the ANC and the Congress of South African Trade Unions (COSATU). It is also the case that in South Africa, as elsewhere across the continent, there are other, arguably contending traditions of resistance and protest. There are, of course, important counter tendencies on the continent that make use of religious commitment and community to engage in organized and orchestrated violent action, which have demonstrated their vitality over the last decade.[33]

While a third wave of popular protest has yet to emerge in Africa, the future success of mobilization on the continent as the basis for far-reaching progressive social and political change will depend, in my opinion, on the serious re-engagement by activists and political movements in Africa in both analysis and action at the grassroots, and also on the debates and discussions of the so-called anti-capitalist movement in its many manifestations. As we have seen in Africa there was a developed anti-neo-liberal consciousness that stretches back to the national anti-SAP demonstrations organized by the National Association of Nigeria Students in the mid-1980s. Yet these movements were demobilized by the collapse of Stalinism and the hammer blows of neo-liberalism.[34] Larmer and Dwyer in their study of southern African social movements summarize well the challenges for an emergent anti-capitalism on the continent: 'Glimpses of wider social movements – opposing privatization, environmental degradation and against gender-based violence – are visible in the countries under study. Without consistent and considered efforts by activists to generalize and coordinate these campaigns into a wider movement, they tend to remain temporary outbursts of anger at injustice that rapidly dissipates.'[35]

The student activists who have spoken in this study must heed the lessons emerging from these movements. In Zimbabwe there is evidence that this process is going on. Stephen Chisuvi – a student activist and ISO member in Harare – described the effects of the anti-capitalist demonstration on a core group of student militants in Zimbabwe: 'I remember the excitement students had when there were demonstrations in Seattle and Genoa, and when our comrades went to South Africa for the WSSD summit last year [2002] ...when they came back they spoke of the international experience.'[36]

Although questions remain about the pattern of resistance and the nature of popular struggles in Africa, there is a sense that the debates that preoccupied so many people in the 1980s and 1990s – about a new diffuse post-colonial identity that had displaced class, resistance and liberation – have finally been shown to be somewhat beside the point. As Callinicos writes: 'less because of some decisive theoretical refutation of postmodernism (the most damaging philosophical critiques were produced during its heyday and seemed to have little effect on its influence) than because the world-wide rebellion against capitalist globalization has changed the intellectual agenda'.[37]

Those who would wish to promote and spread that worldwide rebellion must learn from the experiences of protest and resistance in Africa and pay close attention to the nature and composition of the popular forces that have emerged in recent years. The voice of students in this reconvergence of forces is a vital witness to the reorganization of protest and activism in sub-Saharan Africa.

Students of the transition speak
Students will continue to play contradictory and ambiguous roles in the movements that emerge across the continent. This will rest as it has always done on their peculiar status in society. On the question of elitism, student Jean-Claude Kongo illustrates this ambiguity:

> If you think how few members of society actually gain access to university in Senegal ... students are privileged; they are in a better position to help and ultimately control the nation. But every student I know has the problem of money although students are here for themselves and for society in general.
>
> Materially they certainly aren't a privileged class, that's not possible. I know a student with a scholarship who can't live at the university but has to live in the suburbs. The price of transport, accommodation everything, I know two students who committed suicide because life was impossible for them.[38]

And, like their predecessors, students often have an inflated idea of their role in society. Amadou Dieye Wade states: 'The election of the president [Wade] was only possible with ... students. This is why we can say that President Wade owed his election to students and youth.'[39]

Yet, the same students also have the capacity for unleashing political change which, if tied to wider social forces, can bring about these transitions. The origin of the MDC (once the great hope of the opposition in Zimbabwe – and the progressive left across southern Africa) emerged in large part because of the frenetic energy of the student movement. There is no better example of student militants than Jethro Mpofu. During the heady days before the MDC was created, Jethro was one of the key militants at UZ. He refused to stand for office, preferring to stay in the background, and is remembered for his incredible capacity to galvanize students into action. As an Ndebele he was welcomed by a student movement that is often accused of being dominated by Shona activists. Interviewing him (and being arrested with him shortly afterwards) in 2003 was to hear an echo from the late 1990s of the political euphoria and hope that finally *chinja* (change) was coming. Jethro remembers the role of the student movement in this period of rapturous expectation:

> There was a deliberate effort on the part of students to forge an alliance with the workers' movement. So in my own humble judgement I'd say even the MDC was born out of the political efforts of the students at that time. I remember students urging the ZCTU to take political action against the government. ... I put it to [Morgan Tsvangirai] that ' ... you ... help our hard-working parents by leading them in the struggle against this government.'[40]

The agency is forgotten by the 'enormous condescension of posterity'[41] and only the successful remembered. The voices of students – the crucial agents of this study – so often missing from the literature, will remain the best witness of student politics in sub-Saharan Africa and a guide to further action.

NOTES

Foreword by David Seddon

1. David Adelstein was 20 and a student of sociology at the LSE in 1967–68. He was suspended in February 1967 for his activities as President of the Union but reinstated after a ten-day student occupation.
2. Daniel Cohn-Bendit was a member of a group of students and junior faculty at Nanterre that helped found the 22 March Movement, and who visited and spoke to the student body at the LSE during the course of the 'disturbances' there.
3. See, for example, Alexander Cockburn and Robin Blackburn (eds) *Student power: problems, diagnosis, action* (London: Penguin Books, 1969).
4. Herbert Marcuse 'Repressive tolerance', in Robert Paul Wolff, Barrington Moore Jr and Herbert Marcuse, *A critique of pure tolerance* (Boston: Beacon, 1965); and Herbert Marcuse, *One dimensional man: studies in the ideology of advanced industrial society* (London: Routledge & Kegan Paul, 1991, first published 1964).
5. F. Halliday, 'Students of the world unite', in A. Cockburn and R. Blackburn (eds) *Student power: problems, diagnosis, action* (London: Penguin Books, 1969) pp. 287–326.
6. P. Armstrong, A. Glyn and J. Harrison, *Capitalism since World War II: the making and break up of the great boom* (London: Fontana Books, 1984).
7. Armstrong et al., *Capitalism since World War II*; W. Brandt et al., *North–South: a programme for survival. The report of the Independent Commission on International Development (The Brandt Report)* (London: Pan Books, 1980); A. G. Frank, *Crisis in the world economy* (London: Heinemann, 1980); A. G. Frank, *Crisis in the Third World* (London: Heinemann, 1981).
8. J. Walton and D. Seddon, *Free markets and food riots: the politics of global adjustment* (Oxford: Blackwell, 1994).
9. E. P. Thompson, *The making of the English working class* (London: Penguin, 1991).

10.	D. Seddon and L. Zeilig, 'Class and protest in Africa: new waves', *Review of African Political Economy*, 31 (103) pp. 9–27, 2005. See also P. Dwyer and D. Seddon, 'The new wave? A global perspective on popular protest', paper presented at the eighth International Conference on Alternative Futures and Popular Protest, Manchester Metropolitan University, 2–4 April 2002.

Introduction

1.	C. Harman, *The fire last time: 1968 and after* (London: Bookmarks, 1988).
2.	E. Cleaver, *Soul on ice* (New York: Dell Publishing, 1970).
3.	A. Cockburn, 'Introduction', in A. Cockburn and R. Blackburn (eds) *Student power: problems, diagnosis, action* (London: Penguin Books, 1969) p. 7.
4.	G. Stedman Jones, 'The meaning of the student revolt', in A. Cockburn and R. Blackburn (eds) *Student power: problems, diagnosis, action* (London: Penguin Books, 1969).
5.	Herbert Marcuse, *One dimensional man: studies in the ideology of advanced industrial society* (London: Routledge & Kegan Paul, 1991) p. 256.
6.	Such as F. Halliday, 'Students of the world unite', in A. Cockburn and R. Blackburn (eds) *Student power: problems, diagnosis, action* (London: Penguin Books, 1969).
7.	A. Bathily, *Mai 68 à Dakar ou la revolte universitaire et la democratie* (Paris: Chaka, 1992).
8.	M. N. Nkongolo, *Le campus martyr* (Paris: L'Harmattan, 2000).
9.	Chris Harman's otherwise good book on the period (*The fire last time*) excludes any reference of the Senegalese events, and unfortunately presents a rather Northern perspective on 1968. Mark Edelman Boren's *Student resistance: a history of the unruly subject* (New York: Routledge, 2001) gives the event a fleeting mention.
10.	Interview with Femi Aborisade, 24 September 2004.
11.	T. Moja, 'Policy responses to global transformation by African higher education systems', in P. T. Zeleza and A. Olukoshi (eds) *African universities in the twenty first century* (Pretoria: CODESRIA/UNISA Press, 2004) volume 1, p. 37.
12.	B. K. Banza, 'Ignorance of rights to health or lack of health promotion initiatives? The case of the University of Kinshasa', *CODESRIA Bulletin* (1–2) 2005, p. 16.
13.	See P. T. Zeleza and A. Olukoshi (eds) *African universities in the twenty first century* (Pretoria: CODESRIA/UNISA Press, 2004) vols 1 and 2.
14.	O. Alidou, G. Caffentzis and S. Federici, *A thousand flowers: social struggles against structural adjustment in African universities* (Trenton, Asmara: Africa World Press, 2000).
15.	From the French verb 'cartoucher' literally cartridge. When a student

is given another year to obtain his or her exam. A 'cartouchard' is someone who has exhausted his 'cartridges'.

16. Harman, *The fire last time*.

17. '*Lubov*: So Pyotr why've you lost your looks? Become so old? You were just a boy then, a dear little student. And now your hair is thin and you are wearing glasses. Are you really still a student? *Trofimov*: I suppose I am going to be a perpetual student' (A. Chekhov, *Chekhov's plays*, London: Penguin Classics, 2002).

18. In the mid-1990s in Dakar for example 20,000 students had to make do with 5000 university beds.

19. R. Abrahamsen, *Disciplining democracy: development discourse and good governance in Africa* (London: Zed Books, 2000).

20. D. Harvey, *A brief history of neo-liberalism* (Oxford: Oxford University Press, 2005).

21. L. Zeilig and D. Seddon, 'Marxism, class and resistance in Africa', in L. Zeilig (ed.) *Class struggle and resistance in Africa* (Cheltenham: New Clarion Press, 2002).

22. J. Walton and D. Seddon, *Free markets and food riots: the politics of global adjustment* (Oxford: Blackwell, 1994).

23. P. Dwyer and D. Seddon, 'The new wave? A global perspective on popular protest', paper presented at the eighth International Conference on Alternative Futures and Popular Protest, Manchester Metropolitan University, 2–4 April 2002.

24. C. Monga, *The anthropology of anger: civil society and democracy in Africa* (Boulder: Lynne Reinner, 1996).

25. Interview Luke Kasuwanga, 8 July 2001.

26. Alidou et al., *A thousand flowers*.

27. Boren, *Student resistance*.

28. For example, P. Bianchini, *Ecole et politique en Afrique noire: sociologie des crises et des réformes du système d'enseignement au Sénégal et au Burkina Faso (1960–2000)* (Paris: Karthala, 2004); F. B. Nyamnjoh and N. B. Jua, 'African universities in crisis and the promotion of a democratic culture: the political economy of violence in African educational systems', *African Studies Review*, 45 (2) 2002, pp. 1–26; and R. Pithouse (ed) *University struggles in post-apartheid South Africa* (Trenton, NJ: Africa World Press, 2006).

29. For example, P. Konings, 'University students' revolt, ethnic militia, and violence during political liberalization in Cameroon', *African Studies Review*, 45 (2) 2002, pp. 179–204.

30. D. Mills, 'The "new" African higher education?' *African Affairs*, 103 (413) pp. 667–75, 2004, p. 671.

31. A. Olukoshi and P. T. Zeleza, 'Conclusion', in P. T. Zeleza and A. Olukoshi (eds) *African universities in the twenty first century*, volume 2 (Pretoria: CODESRIA/UNISA Press, 2004) p. 610.

32. A. Bathily, M. Diouf and M. Mbodj, 'The Senegalese student

movement from its inception to 1989', in M. Mamdani and E. Wamba-Dia-Wamba (eds) *African studies in social movements and democracy* (Dakar: CODESRIA, 1995).

33. Mills, 'The "new" African higher education?', p. 671.
34. L. H. Siegelbaum and D. J. Walkowitz, *Workers of the Donbass speak: survival and identity in the New Ukraine, 1989–1992* (New York: SUNY Press, 1995) p. 1.
35. L. Zeilig (ed.) *Class struggle and resistance in Africa* (Cheltenham: New Clarion Press, 2002).
36. L. Zeilig, 'In the age of Wade: political change and the student strike in Dakar 2001', in N. Akam and R. Ducasse (eds) *Quelle université pour l'Afrique* (Bordeaux: Maison des Sciences de l'Homme d'Aquitaine, 2002).
37. L. Zeilig, 'Crisis in Zimbabwe', *International Socialism Journal*, 2 (94) 2002, pp. 75–96.
38. L. Zeilig, 'En quête de changement politique: la mobilisation étudiante au Sénégal, 2000–2004', numéro spécial sur le Sénégal pour *Politique Africaine*, 96, 2004, pp. 39–58.
39. L. Zeilig, 'Student politics and activism in Zimbabwe: the frustrated transition', *Journal of Asian and African Studies*, 41 (6) 2007.
40. D. Seddon and L. Zeilig, 'Class and protest in Africa: new waves', *Review of African Political Economy*, 31 (103) 2005, pp. 9–27.
41. G. Williams, 'Political economies and the study of Africa: critical considerations', *Review of African Political Economy*, 31 (4) pp. 571–83, 2004, pp. 576–7.
42. See M. Dawson, 'Students: activism and identity', in P. Alexander, M. Dawson and M. Inchharam (eds) *Globalisation and new identities: a view from the middle* (Johannesburg: Jacana Press, 2006); Pithouse, *University struggles*.
43. Alidou et al., *A thousand flowers*.
44. Bianchini, *Ecole et politique*.
45. N. Ansell, *Children, youth and development* (London: Routledge, 2005).
46. P. Anderson, *In the tracks of historical materialism* (London: Verso, 1983).
47. M. Keith, 'Conclusion: a changing space and a time for change', in S. Pile and M. Keith (eds) *Geographies of resistance* (London: Routledge, 1997) p. 284.
48. K. Marx, *The eighteenth Brumaire of Louis Bonaparte* (London: Lawrence & Wishart, 1984) p. 10.
49. C. Ginzburg, 'Microhistory: two or three things that I know about it', *Critical Inquiry*, 20, pp. 10–35, 1993.
50. D. Harvey, *The condition of postmodernity: an enquiry into the origins of cultural change* (Oxford: Basil Blackwell, 1989); H. Lefebvre, *The production of space* (Oxford: Blackwell, 1991).
51. A. Blunt and J. Wills, *Dissident geographies* (London: Prentice Hall, 2000) p. 77.

52.   C. Hill, *A nation of change and novelty: radical politics, religion and literature in seventeenth century England* (London: Routledge, 1995) p. 245.
53.   E. P. Thompson, *The making of the English working class* (London: Penguin, 1991) p. 11.
54.   Ibid., pp. 11–12.
55.   Bathily et al. 'The Senegalese student movement'; J. L. Cefkin, 'Rhodesian university students in national politics', in W. J. Hanna and J. L. Hanna (eds) *University students and African politics* (New York and London: Africana Publishing Company, 1975).
56.   In Zimbabwe two excellent recent examples of *history from below* are referred to extensively in Chapter 4. These are B. Raftopoulos and I. Phimister (eds) *Keep on knocking: a history of the labour movement in Zimbabwe 1900–1997* (Harare: Baobab Books on behalf of the Zimbabwe Congress of Trade Unions and the Friedrich Ebert Stiftung, 1997); and B. Raftopoulos and L. Sachikonye (eds) *Striking back: the labour movement and the post-colonial state in Zimbabwe, 1980–2000* (Harare: Weaver Press, 2001).
57.   Thompson, *The making of the English working class*, p. 12.
58.   See also L. Zeilig, 'Zero, zero, zero pito formation: student activism in Zimbabwe', *Debate* (10) 2004.
59.   Hill, *A nation of change and novelty*, p. 245.
60.   See P. Routledge, 'River of resistance: critical collaboration and the dilemmas of power and ethics', *Ethics, Place and Environment*, 6 (1) pp. 66–73, 2003.
61.   Siegelbaum and Walkowitz, *Workers of the Donbass speak*, p. 1.
62.   S. Terkel, *Working* (New York: Avon Books, 1975) pp. xxv–xxvi.
63.   Interview with Job Sakhala, 30 July 2003.
64.   *Walfadjri*, Senegalese online news agency, various articles between 1999 and 2005.

Chapter 1: Politics, students and protest: the making of the student intelligentsia

1.   W. J. Hanna, 'Students, universities and political outcomes', in W. J. Hanna and J. Hanna (eds) *University students and African politics* (London: Africana Publishing Company, 1975) p. 13.
2.   A. Bathily, M. Diouf and M. Mbodj, 'The Senegalese student movement from its inception to 1989', in M. Mamdani and E. Wamba-Dia-Wamba (eds) *African studies in social movements and democracy* (Dakar: CODESRIA, 1995); D. C. O'Brien, 'A lost generation? Youth identity and state decay in West Africa', in R. P. Werbner and T. O. Ranger (eds) *Post-colonial identities in Africa* (London: Zed Books, 1996).
3.   L. Zeilig, *Class struggle and resistance in Africa* (Cheltenham: New Clarion Press, 2002).

4.   G. Caffentzis, 'The World Bank and education in Africa', in O. Alidou, G. Caffentzis and S. Federici (eds) *A thousand flowers: social struggles against structural adjustment in African universities* (Trenton, Asmara: Africa World Press, 2000); D. Seddon, 'Popular protest and class struggle in Africa: an historical overview', in L. Zeilig (ed.) *Class struggle and resistance in Africa* (Cheltenham: New Clarion Press, 2002).

5.   T. Cliff, 'Deflected permanent revolution', *International Socialism*, 1 (12) pp. 15–22, 1963.

6.   F. Cheru, 'The silent revolution and the weapons of the weak', in L. Amoore (ed.) *The global resistance reader* (London: Routledge, 2005) pp. 74–83.

7.   J. Walton and D. Seddon, *Free markets and food riots: the politics of global adjustment* (Oxford: Blackwell, 1994).

8.   Cliff, 'Deflected permanent revolution'.

9.   T. Mkandawire, 'African intellectuals and nationalism', in T. Mkandawire (ed) *African intellectuals* (London: Zed Press, 2005).

10.   This is partly because many of the contributors to the collection – for example Ali Mazrui and Joseph Ki-Zerbo – are from the original student intelligentsia. They were politicized students in the 1950s and 1960s, whose lives were animated by the pre- and post-independence struggles. The collection suffers from an uncritical nostalgia for the immediate post-independence period.

11.   R. Flacks, 'Youth intelligentsia in revolt', in H. Becker (ed.) *Campus power struggle* (New Jersey: Transaction Books, 1973) p. 126.

12.   Ibid., p. 131.

13.   A. Mazrui, 'Pan-Africanism and the intellectuals: rise, decline and revival', in T. Mkandawire (ed) *African intellectuals* (London: Zed Press, 2005) p. 56. Are these suitable definitions of the 'intelligentsia'? Searching for an adequate definition is no simple task. R. Desai, *Intellectuals and socialism* (London: Lawrence & Wishart, 1994) p. 21, for example, comments, 'definitions of intellectuals are ... notoriously difficult'. Perry Anderson, *In the tracks of historical materialism* (London: Verso, 1983) argues that intellectuals are those concerned with 'social reality' but some, for example, have argued that real intellectual work involves the political engagement with this social reality (R. Debray, *Teachers, writers, celebrities: the intellectuals of modern France*, London: Verso, 1981).

14.   Flacks, 'Youth intelligentsia in revolt', p. 126.

15.   It is important to stress the fluidity of this category because members of the colonial civil services and trade union leaders were also frequently recent graduates. See Chapter 3.

16.   B. Davidson, *The black man's burden: Africa and the curse of the nation-state* (London: James Currey, 1992).

17.   C. Diané, *La FEANF: et les grandes heures du mouvement syndical étudiant noir* (Paris: Chaka, 1990).

18.   S. Federici, 'The new student movement', in O. Alidou, G. Caffentzis
       and S. Federici (eds) *A thousand flowers: social struggles against structural
       adjustment in African universities* (New York: Africa World Press, 2000)
       p. 90; see also W. J. Hanna and J. L. Hanna (eds) *University students and
       African politics* (New York and London: Africana Publishing Company,
       1975).

19.   H. Adi, *West Africans in Britain: 1900–1960* (London: Lawrence &
       Wishart, 1998) p. 34.

20.   Diané, *La FEANF*; A. Diaw, 'The democracy of the literati', in C. M.
       Diop (ed.) *Senegal essays in statecraft* (Dakar: CODESRIA, 1993); M. C.
       Diop, 'Introduction: from "socialism" to "liberalism": the many phases
       of state legitimacy', and 'Student unionism: pluralism and pressure
       politics', both in M. C. Diop (ed.) *Senegal essays in statecraft* (Dakar:
       CODESRIA, 1993).

21.   While these communities might not have been very numerous, their
       national unions certainly were. Diané (*La FEANF*, pp. 55–64) notes that
       14 African student organizations in France formed between 1947 and
       1956, many with their headquarters (and leading activists) in France.

22.   M. E. Chambrier Rahandi, 'Introduction', in C. Diané, *La FEANF: et les
       grandes heures du mouvement syndical étudiant noir* (Paris: Chaka 1990) p.
       16.

23.   A. Olukoshi and P. T. Zeleza, 'Conclusion', in P. T. Zeleza and A.
       Olukoshi (eds) *African universities in the twenty first century*, (Pretoria:
       CODESRIA/UNISA Press, 2004) vol. 2, p. 598.

24.   Quoted in S. Cissé, 'De la provenance des espèces', *Comprendre le
       Sénégal* (Dakar: Le Soleil, 2001) p. 36.

25.   Hanna, 'Students, universities and political outcomes'.

26.   D. Georgakas and M. Surkin (1998) *Detriot, I do mind dying: a study in
       urban revolution* (New York: South End Press, 1998).

27.   See S. Ousmane, *God's bits of wood* (London: Heinemann, 1986).

28.   M. Larmer, 'Resisting the state: the trade union movement and
       working class politics in Zambia, 1964–91', in L. Zeilig (ed.) *Class
       struggle and resistance in Africa* (Cheltenham: New Clarion Press,
       2002).

29.   See Femi Aborisade, 'Interview', in L. Zeilig (ed.) *Class struggle and
       resistance in Africa* (Cheltenham: New Clarion Press, 2002) pp. 93–7.

30.   J. Molyneux, *What is the real Marxist tradition?* (London: Bookmarks,
       1985).

31.   L. Zeilig and D. Seddon, 'Marxism, class and resistance in Africa', in L.
       Zeilig (ed.) *Class struggle and resistance in Africa* (Cheltenham: New
       Clarion Press, 2002).

32.   L. Trotsky, *The history of the Russian revolution* (Michigan: University of
       Michigan Press, 1964).

33.   A. Blunt and J. Wills, *Dissident geographies* (London: Prentice Hall,
       2000) pp. 60–70.

34. J. Sender and S. Smith, *The development of capitalism in Africa* (London: Methuen, 1986).
35. Seddon, 'Popular protest and class struggle', pp. 28–9.
36. N. Poulantzas, 'The problem of the capitalist state', in J. Urry and J. Wakeford (eds) *Power in Britain* (London: Heinemann, 1973).
37. Ngugi, wa Thiong'o, *Decolonising the mind* (Harare: Zimbabwe Publishing House, 1987) pp. 69–71.
38. F. B. Nyamnjoh and N. B. Jua, 'African universities in crisis and the promotion of a democratic culture: the political economy of violence in African educational systems', *African Studies Review*, 45 (2) pp. 1–26, 2002.
39. Nkrumah, the future Ghanaian leader, was a case in point, boasting that while in London in the 1940s he would read the British Communist Party newspaper on the London underground. Nkrumah's role in relation to students and the radical nationalist movement generally cannot be exaggerated and extended beyond Anglophone Africa. Diané (*La FEANF*, p. 29), for example, writes that, among students active in FEANF, he exerted a profound influence, not simply for his radical statements but as a politically engaged intellectual.
40. Seddon, 'Popular protest and class struggle', p. 30.
41. Nwafor Orizu later became the first president of the Nigerian Senate.
42. PRO CO 968/121/4 Letter Colonial Office, 3 January 1944.
43. It is interesting that the solution was seen as 'better funding' to prevent students falling in with anti-imperialist groups. How it could conceivably have been financially beneficial to fall in with the anti-colonial left is not made clear in the files (PRO CO 968/121/4).
44. B. Raftopoulos and I. Phimister, *Keep on knocking: a history of the labour movement in Zimbabwe 1900–1997* (Harare: Baobab Books on behalf of the Zimbabwe Congress of Trade Unions and the Friedrich Ebert Stiftung, 1997).
45. See Chapter 3.
46. Mazrui, 'Pan-Africanism and the intellectuals'.
47. Ibid., 59.
48. Adi, *West Africans in Britain*.
49. K. Marx, *The eighteenth Brumaire of Louis Bonaparte* (London: Lawrence & Wishart, 1984) p. 45.
50. Cliff, 'Deflected permanent revolution'.
51. Davidson, *The black man's burden*.
52. R. First, *The barrel of a gun: political power in Africa and the coup d'état* (London: Allen Lane, 1970) pp. 57–8.
53. Cliff, 'Deflected permanent revolution'.
54. T. Cliff, *Trotskyism after Trotsky: the origins of the international socialists* (London: Bookmarks, 1999) p. 67.
55. Cliff, 'Deflected permanent revolution', p. 20.

56. Ibid. These ideas were inextricably connected, as Cliff argued, to the attraction of the Soviet model that appeared to indicate that independence and development could be achieved by 'delinking' from the capitalist world (S. Amin, *Delinking: towards a polycentric world*, London: Zed Books, 1990).

57. Federici, 'The new student movement'; M. Mamdani, 'The intelligentsia, the state and social movements in Africa', in M. Diouf and M. Mamdani (eds) *Academic freedom in Africa* (Dakar: CODESRIA, 1994); and M. Mamdani and E. Wamba-dia-Wamba (eds) *African studies in social movements and democracy* (Dakar: CODESRIA, 1995).

58. V. Foucher, 'Les "évolués", la migration, l'école: pour une nouvelle interprétation du nationalisme casamançais', in M. C. Diop (ed.) *Le Sénégal contemporain* (Paris: Karthala, 2002) and V. Foucher, *Cheated pilgrims: education, migration and the birth of Casamançais nationalism, Senegal*, Ph.D. thesis (University of London, 2002). An enormous amount of post-colonial African literature deals with the experiences of educational separation and ambiguity. Three examples illustrate this well. In *No longer at ease* (London: Heinemann, 1960) Chinua Achebe describes the difficult homecoming in newly independent Nigeria of a recent graduate. In 2002 Gani Fawehinmi wrote about the hardships he faced as a student trying to survive in London in the early 1960s. Students in Europe and America clearly faced some very uncomfortable realities. Nigerian writer J. P. Clark in *America, their America* (New York: Africana Publishing Company, 1962) brilliantly relates the racism he confronted during his first year in the United States.

59. D. Boyer, 'The African crisis in context: comparative encounters with educational rationalization', *African Studies Review*, 45 (2) pp. 205–18, 2002.

60. Cliff, 'Deflected permanent revolution', p. 20.

61. T. Adorno and H. Marcuse, 'Correspondence on the German student movement', *New Left Review*, 233, pp. 123–36, 1999.

62. Mamdani, 'The intelligentsia', pp. 253, 255.

63. J. L. Anderson, *Che Guevara: a revolutionary life* (London: Bantam Books, 1997). The idea of the pilgrimage to Europe and America brought together African students who organized intellectual and cultural movements that shaped political consciousness for generations – notably the Harlem Renaissance in New York and Négritude in Paris. But we should also note that the pilgrim is a student who makes a journey to the university or school. Like a religious journey it is both physical, the student is separated from his or her community of origin, and spiritual, he or she undergoes intellectual development and transformation. The student becomes a committed member of a modern nation, and is able to identify with it. It

was this class of pilgrims in Senegal that was crucial in carrying out the project (or idea) of national construction.

64. Diané, *La FEANF*, p. 38.
65. See Foucher 'Les évolués' and *Cheated pilgrims*.
66. Federici, 'The new student movement', p. 90. See also W. Rodney, *How Europe underdeveloped Africa* (Washington: Howard University Press, 1981) pp. 238–61.
67. Diané, *La FEANF*, p. 38.
68. Bathily et al., 'The Senegalese student movement'.
69. This idea is still an important one to student activists today. As one student described to me, 'our parents speak from an African culture ... whereas ours comes from Europe' (Mor Faye interview, 5 February 2004). These ideas are also discussed in Ngugi's (1987) classic, *Decolonising the mind*.
70. A. Cabral, *Revolution in Guinea: an African people's struggle* (London: Stage 1, 1969); F. Fanon, *The wretched of the earth* (London: Penguin Books, 1963).
71. Cabral, *Revolution in Guinea*, p. 87.
72. Ibid., pp. 88, 89.
73. N. Alexander, 'New meanings of Panafricanism in the era of globalization', Centre for Civil Society, 2003 http://www.nu.ac.za/ccs/default.asp?3,28,10,853.
74. Mamdani, 'The intelligentsia'.
75. Hanna, 'Students, universities and political outcomes', p. 11.
76. Caffentzis, 'The World Bank'.
77. O'Brien, 'A lost generation?'.
78. P. Bianchini, *Ecole et politique en Afrique noire: sociologie des crises et des réformes du système d'enseignement au Sénégal et au Burkina Faso (1960–2000)* (Paris: Karthala, 2004).
79. Federici, 'The new student movement', p. 91.
80. P. Van den Berghe, *Power and privilege at an African university* (Cambridge, MA: Schenkman Publishing Company, 1973).
81. P. T. Zeleza, *Rethinking Africa's globalisation: the intellectual challenge* (Trenton, NJ: Africa World Press, 2003) p. 69.
82. T. Ziolkowski, *German romanticism and its institutions* (Princeton NJ: Princeton University Press, 1991).
83. J. Nyerere, *Freedom and socialism* (London: Oxford University Press, 1968) pp. 179–84.
84. J. I. Dibua, 'Students and the struggle against authoritarianism in university governance in Nigeria', in P. T. Zeleza and A. Olukoshi (eds) *African universities in the twenty first century* (Pretoria: CODESRIA/UNISA Press, 2004) vol. 2, p. 460.
85. Quoted in Hanna, 'Students, universities and political outcomes', pp. 12–13. These were not uniquely African trends. In many developing countries the university was seen as well placed to provide the exact

needs of 'national development'. Cuba went through a similar transformation of higher education after 1959 (Anderson, *Che Guevara*; A. Hochschild, 'Student power in action', in H. Becker (ed.) *Campus power struggle*, New Brunswick, NJ: Transaction Books, 1973). The university in the developed world displays many of these characteristics today. In the UK the current emphasis is on 'employability' and the needs of employers.

86. Cited in Mkandawire, 'African intellectuals', pp. 22-3.
87. It is interesting to note that early post-independent regimes relied heavily on intellectual support from the university-based scholars. Some of the more radical regimes made use of a large number of left-wing academic advisers. Julius Nyerere had a group of 'Fabian socialists' around him and Kwame Nkrumah pulled in pan-Africanists from Africa's diaspora, such as George Padmore and C. L. R. James (see D. Renton, *C. L. R. James*, London: Haus, 2007).
88. L. Althusser, 'Freud and Lacan', *La Nouvelle Critique*, 161, December 1964, quoted in P. Anderson, 'Component of the national culture', in A. Cockburn and R. Blackburn (eds) *Student power* (London: Penguin Books, 1969) p. 214.
89. A. Cockburn, 'Introduction', in A. Cockburn and R. Blackburn (eds) *Student power: problems, diagnosis, action* (London: Penguin Books, 1969).
90. E. Leslie, 'Introduction to Adorno/Marcuse correspondence on the German student movement', *New Left Review*, 233, pp. 118–23, 1999, p. 120.
91. P. Bourdieu and J. C. Passeron, *Reproduction in education, society and culture* (London: Sage, 1990).
92. P. Bourdieu, *Bourdieu et le Marxisme* (Paris: Publications L'Etincelle, 1999).
93. Quoted in M. O. Nkomo, *Student culture and activism in black South African universities: the roots of resistance* (Westport: Greenwood Press, 1984) p. 6.
94. D. Emmerson, *Students and politics in developing nations* (London: Pall Mall, 1968) p. 407.
95. Hanna and Hanna, *University students*.
96. Foucher, *Cheated pilgrims*.
97. Hanna, 'Students, universities and political outcomes'.
98. Federici, 'The new student movement', p. 105; see also J. D. Barkan, *An African dilemma: university students, development and politics in Ghana, Tanzania and Uganda* (Nairobi: Oxford University Press, 1975).
99. W. J. Hanna and J. L. Hanna, 'Students as elites', in W. J. Hanna and J. L. Hanna (eds) *University students and African politics* (London: Africana Publishing Company, 1975).
100. P. Bianchini, 'Le mouvement étudiant sénégalais: un essai d'interprétation', in M. C. Diop (ed.) *La Société sénégalaise entre le local et le global* (Paris: Karthala, 2002); and Bianchini, *Ecole et politique*.

101. A. Bathily, *Mai 68 à Dakar ou la revolte universitaire et la democratie* (Paris: Chaka, 1992).

102. See Chapter 3.

103. World Bank, *Higher education in developing countries: peril and promise* (Washington, DC: World Bank, 2000).

104. Federici, 'The new student movement'; and Hanna, 'Students, universities and political outcomes'.

105. Federici, 'The new student movement'.

106. C. Harman, *The fire last time: 1968 and after* (London: Bookmarks, 1988) p. 41.

107. Bathily et al., 'The Senegalese student movement', p. 401. It is important to stress that although their status as a 'transitory group' has now changed, their relationship to 'socioeconomic stakes' has not.

108. See, for example, A. Cockburn and R. Blackburn, *Student power: problems, diagnosis, action* (London: Penguin Books, 1969). To make a slightly frivolous point, the average age of the 13 contributors to this collection was 24.3 (the student radical David Widgery was only 20). See also, B. Crick and W. A. Robson, *Protest and discontent* (London: Pelican Books, 1970); S. M. Lipset and G. M. Schaflunder, *Passion and politics: student activism in America* (Boston: Little Brown & Company, 1971); and G. R. Weaver and J. H. Weaver (eds) *The university and revolution* (Englewood Cliffs, NJ: Spectrum Books, 1969).

109. A. Touraine, *Le mouvement de mai ou le communisme utopique* (Paris: Éditions du Seuil, 1968).

110. Quoted in G. Stedman Jones, 'The meaning of the student revolt', in A. Cockburn and R. Blackburn (eds) *Student power: problems, diagnosis, action* (London: Penguin Books, 1969) p. 26.

111. Quoted in Harman, *The fire last time*, pp. 36–7.

112. Stedman Jones, 'The meaning of the student revolt', p. 28.

113. P. Sweezy, 'The future of capitalism', in D. Cooper (ed) *The dialectics of liberation* (London: Pelican Books, 1968).

114. Stedman Jones, 'The meaning of the student revolt', p. 29.

115. Quoted in A. Beckett, 'In the house of the rising sons', *Guardian*, 28 February 2004, p. 20. Panitch is referring to Ralph Miliband's position on student action in the 1960s. Miliband wrote about the lack in the student movement of 'any culture which is even approximately Marxist ... which no doubt sounds square, but is nevertheless the case. Sit [- in] they can but think is another matter' (quoted in Beckett, 'In the house of the rising sons', p. 20).

116. A. Callinicos and S. Turner, 'The student movement today', *International Socialism*, 1 (75) pp. 9–15, 1975.

117. John Bomba interview, 22 May 2003.

118. F. Halliday, 'Students of the world unite', in A. Cockburn and R. Blackburn (eds) *Student power: problems, diagnosis, action* (London: Penguin Books, 1969) p. 323.

119. See Chapter 2.
120. Harman, *The fire last time*, p. 42.
121. See Chapter 3.
122. M. Savio, 'Introduction', in H. Draper, *Berkeley: the new student revolt* (New York: Grove Press, 1965) p. 5.
123. H. Draper, *Berkeley: the new student revolt* (New York: Grove Press, 1965).
124. Ibid., p. 162.
125. Ibid., p. 163.
126. He appears in many of the student compendiums of the time, and students regarded him as the theorist of their revolts (D. Cooper (ed.), *The dialectics of liberation*, London: Pelican Books, 1968). It should be noted that his arguments were always more nuanced and sophisticated than many of his latter-day critics maintain. Harman (*The fire last time*) is particularly hard on him, ignoring the brilliant critique of contemporary capitalism provided in *One dimensional man* (1964). In a later edition he warned inexperienced student activists that the 'pre-condition for the efficacy of a serious opposition remains the political revitalization of the working-class movement on an international scale' (H. Marcuse, *One dimensional man: studies in the ideology of advanced industrial society*, London: Routledge & Kegan Paul, 1991, p. 368).
127. Marcuse, *One dimensional man*, pp. 256–7.
128. Ibid., p. 133.
129. Harman 1988, p. 47.
130. T. Cliff ('Nothing so romantic', in D. Widgery (ed.) *The left in Britain*, London: Harmondsworth, 1976, p. 439) described student mobilization as rising like a rocket and falling like a stick. In an interview in 1970 he described students as 'manic depressives', acting swiftly and angrily but unable to sustain their action. However, students do have a special capacity to act: 'It is easier for students to act because a minority of students can act on their own to start with. Workers cannot go on strike in a minority – for students it is much easier to act. But their impact is far more limited, and therefore students rise like a rocket and fall like a stick.'
131. Harman, *The fire last time*, p. 49.
132. See Chapter 2.
133. Boyer, 'The African crisis in context', p. 207.
134. There has been controversy in England about the increase in tuition fees for students in the government's 2003 White Paper on education. The argument centres on the increase in annual fees, allowing universities flexibility to levy £3000 a year. The argument is that graduates will earn £400,000 more in their life times as a result of having been to university. Some have disputed this reasoning, maintaining that these figures are based on assumptions from

students in the 1960s, when a small percentage of young people went to university compared with more than 43 per cent today (*Socialist Review*, Editorial, February 2003).

135. Boyer, 'The African crisis in context', p. 213.

136. For example, P. Bond, *Against global apartheid: South Africa meets the World Bank, IMF and international finance* (Cape Town: University of Cape Town Press, 2002); and N. Klein, *No logo: no space, no choice, no jobs: taking aim at the brand bullies* (London: Flamingo, 2000).

137. While writing sections of this book in Paris in 2005 I witnessed an extraordinary movement of 'lycéens' (high school students) who demonstrated across France against 'la loi Fillon' of the Education Minister François Fillon. The reforms include the reorganization of the national education system, and they were widely criticized as adapting education to the exigencies of the business world (see 'Education: Raffarin tente de prendre les lycéens de vitesse', *Libération*, 17 February 2005). In completing the study in South Africa France erupted again in student protest against the Contrat Première Embauche (CPE), which saw huge protests and a series of public sector general strikes. The protest movement expressed the same 'convergence of forces' described in this study, between a precarious world of work and student politics.

138. Nyamnjoh and Jua, 'African universities in crisis'.

139. Fanon, *The wretched of the earth*.

140. See also D. Seddon and L. Zeilig, 'Class and protest in Africa: new waves', *Review of African Political Economy*, 31 (103) pp. 9–27, 2005.

141. Walton and Seddon, *Free markets and food riots*.

142. E. Hobsbawm, *The age of extremes* (New York: Vintage, 1995) p. 405.

143. G. Hancock, *The lords of poverty* (London: Macmillan, 1989).

144. P. Marfleet, 'Globalisation and the Third World', *International Socialism Journal*, 2 (81) pp. 91–130, 1998, p. 104.

145. Zeilig and Seddon, 'Marxism, class and resistance', p. 10.

146. Ibid.

147. See P. Alexander, 'Globalisation and discontent: project and discourse', *African Sociological Review*, 5 (1) pp. 55–73, 2001.

148. Quoted in D. Massey, *Space, place and gender* (Cambridge: Polity Press, 1994) p. 146.

149. D. Harvey, *The condition of postmodernity: an enquiry into the origins of cultural change* (Oxford: Basil Blackwell, 1989) p. 240.

150. G. Capps and P. Panayiotopoulos (eds) *World development: an introduction* (London: Pluto Press, 2001); D. Harvey, *A brief history of neo-liberalism* (Oxford: Oxford University Press, 2005).

151. Massey, *Space, place and gender*, p. 147.

152. Ibid., pp. 149–50.

153. N. Chomsky, 'Anti-capitalism: what next?' *Socialist Review*, 245, 2000.

154. Walton and Seddon, *Free markets and food riots*.

155. Quoted in R. Sandbrook, *The politics of Africa's economic recovery* (Cambridge: Cambridge University Press, 1993) p. 3.

156. Bond, *Against global apartheid.*

157. Seddon, 'Popular protest and class struggle'.

158. Seddon and Zeilig, 'Class and protest', p. 12. To which, we argue, should also be added university students.

159. H. Bhabha, 'Signs taken for wonders', in B. Ascroft, G. Griffith and H. Tiffin (eds) *The post-colonial studies reader* (London: Routledge, 1995).

160. G. Harrison, *Issues in the contemporary politics of sub-Saharan Africa: the dynamics of struggle and resistance* (New York: Palgrave, 2002) p. 113.

161. P. Dwyer and D. Seddon, 'The new wave? A global perspective on popular protest', paper presented at the eighth International Conference on Alternative Futures and Popular Protest, Manchester Metropolitan University, 2–4 April 2002; Walton and Seddon, *Free markets and food riots.*

162. J. Saul and C. Leys, 'Sub-Saharan Africa in global capitalism', *Monthly Review,* 51 (3) pp. 1–23, 1999.

163. Harrison, *Issues in the contemporary politics.*

164. J. Saul, 'Africa: the next liberation struggle', *Review of African Political Economy,* 30 (96) pp. 187–202, 2003, p. 192.

165. P. Dwyer and L. Zeilig, 'Shinga mushandi shinga! Qina mSebenzi qina!', in L. Zeilig (ed.) *Class struggle and resistance in Africa* (Cheltenham: New Clarion Press, 2002); see also Conclusion.

166. B. K. Gills (ed.) *Globalisation and the politics of resistance* (Basingstoke: Macmillan, 2000).

167. P. Bond and M. Mayekiso, 'Toward the integration of urban social movements at the world scale', *Journal of World Systems Research,* 2 (2-c) pp. 1–11, 1996, p. 6.

168. J. Petras and D. Engbarth, 'Third World industrialization and trade union struggles', in R. Southall (ed.) *Trade unions and the new industrialization of the Third World* (London: Zed Books, 1988).

169. C. Allen, 'Democracy development and defence', *Review of African Political Economy,* 22 (64) pp. 147–50, 1995; M. Bratton, *Democratic experiments in Africa: regime transitions in comparative perspective* (New York: Cambridge University Press, 1997); J. A. Wiseman, *The new struggle for democracy in Africa* (Aldershot: Avebury, 1996).

170. Bratton, *Democratic experiments.*

171. Ibid., p. 5.

172. Quoted in C. Harman, 'Where is capitalism going?' *International Socialism Journal,* 2 (60) pp. 77–136, 1993, p. 79.

173. S. Decalo, 'Benin: first of the new democracies', in J. F. Clark and D. E. Gardinier (eds) *Political reform in Francophone Africa* (Boulder: Westview Press, 1997) pp. 53–60.

174. Quoted in Bratton, *Democratic experiments,* p. 2.

175. R. J. Mundt, 'Cote d'Ivoire: continuity and change in a semi

democracy', in J. E. Clark and D. E. Gardinier (eds) *Political reform in Francophone Africa* (Boulder: Westview Press, 1997) pp. 191–9.

176.   Seddon, 'Popular protest and class struggle'.
177.   R. Abrahamsen, *Disciplining democracy: development discourse and good governance in Africa*, London: Zed Books, 2000.
178.   Saul and Leys, 'Sub-Saharan Africa', p. 25.
179.   Ibid., p. 26.
180.   For example, Saul, 'Africa: the next'.
181.   Saul and Leys, 'Sub-Saharan Africa', p. 26.
182.   Abrahamsen, *Disciplining democracy*, pp. 135–6.
183.   *Lux* (2003) June–July.
184.   Dibua, 'Students and the struggle', p. 473.

Chapter 2: Contemporary student activism in sub-Saharan Africa

1.   A. Bathily, M. Diouf and M. Mbodj, 'The Senegalese student movement from its inception to 1989', in M. Mamdani and E. Wamba-Dia-Wamba (eds) *African studies in social movements and democracy* (Dakar: CODESRIA, 1995).
2.   E. P. Thompson, *The making of the English working class* (London: Penguin, 1991) p. 8.
3.   N. Akam and R. Ducasse (eds) *Quelle université pour l'Afrique* (Bordeaux: Maison des Sciences de l'Homme D'Aquitaine, 2002).
4.   See Figure 2.1 below.
5.   G. Caffentzis, 'The World Bank and education in Africa', in O. Alidou, G. Caffentzis and S. Federici (eds) *A thousand flowers: social struggles against structural adjustment in African universities* (Trenton, Asmara: Africa World Press, 2000); Y. Lebeau, *Étudiants et campus du Nigéria: recomposition du champ universitaire et sociabilités étudiantes* (Paris: Karthala, 1997).
6.   D. Kerr and J. Mapanje, 'Academic freedom and the University of Malawi', *African Studies Review*, 45 (2) pp. 73–92, 2002, p. 90.
7.   Femi Aborisade, 'Interview', in L. Zeilig (ed.) *Class struggle and resistance in Africa* (Cheltenham: New Clarion Press, 2002).
8.   M. N. Nkongolo, *Le campus martyr* (Paris: L'Harmattan, 2000) pp. 96-8.
9.   P. Konings, 'University students' revolt, ethnic militia, and violence during political liberalization in Cameroon', *African Studies Review*, 45 (2) pp. 179–204, 2002, p. 181.
10.   Ibid.
11.   N. B. Musisi and N. K. Muwanga, *Makerere University in transition: 1993–2000* (Oxford: James Currey, 2003) p. 43.
12.   M. Simui, 'The provision of scholarly information in higher education in Zambia', in P. T. Zeleza and A. Olukoshi (eds) *African universities in the twenty first century*, vol. 2 (Pretoria: CODESRIA/UNISA Press, 2004) pp. 404-5.

13. I. A. Awasom, 'Academic and research libraries in Cameroon: current state and future perspectives', in P. T. Zeleza and A. Olukoshi (eds) *African universities in the twenty first century*, vol. 2 (Pretoria: CODESRIA/UNISA Press, 2004).

14. N. O. Ama and H. O. Ama, 'Students' perceptions of teacher and library quality in tertiary institutions in Namibia: a factor analytic approach', in P. T. Zeleza and A. Olukoshi (eds) *African universities in the twenty first century* (Pretoria: CODESRIA/UNISA Press, 2004) vol. 2, pp. 426–29.

15. M. N. Amutabi, 'Crisis and student protest in universities in Kenya: examining the role of students in national leadership and the democratization process', *African Studies Review*, 45 (2) pp. 157–78, 2002, p. 163.

16. S. Federici, 'The new student movement', in O. Alidou, G. Caffentzis and S. Federici (eds) *A thousand flowers: social struggles against structural adjustment in African universities* (New York: Africa World Press, 2000); Konings, 'University students' revolt'.

17. M. Diouf and M. Mamdani, *Academic freedom in Africa* (Dakar: CODESRIA, 1994); R. Sandbrook, *The politics of Africa's economic recovery* (Cambridge: Cambridge University Press, 1993).

18. World Bank, *Accelerated development in sub-Saharan Africa* (Washington, DC: World Bank, 1981) pp. 81–2.

19. Ibid., p. 82.

20. World Bank, *Education in sub-Saharan Africa: policies for adjustment, revitalization, and expansion* (Washington, DC: World Bank, 1988).

21. Sandbrook *The politics of Africa's economic recovery*, pp. 83–4.

22. Ibid., p. 43.

23. A. Imam and A. Mama, 'The role of academics in limiting and expanding academic freedom', in M. Diouf and M. Mamdani (eds) *Academic freedom in Africa* (Dakar: CODESRIA, 1994) p. 73.

24. Quoted in S. Bako, 'Education and adjustment in Nigeria', in M. Diouf and M. Mamdani (eds) *Academic freedom in Africa* (Dakar: CODESRIA, 1994) p. 152.

25. Caffentzis, 'The World Bank'.

26. P. Marfleet, 'Globalisation and the Third World', *International Socialism Journal*, 2 (81) pp. 91–130, 1998, p. 104.

27. M. Kelly, *Education in a declining economy: the case of Zambia, 1975–1985* (Washington, DC: World Bank, 1991) p. 61.

28. Caffentzis, 'The World Bank', p. 5.

29. Ibid.

30. M. Niang, *M. Wade et l'alternance: le rêve brise du sopi* (Dakar: Harmattan, 2004) p. 67.

31. Caffentzis, 'The World Bank', p. 9.

32. A. Mama, 'Gender studies for Africa's transformation', in T. Mkandawira (ed.) *African intellectuals: rethinking politics, language, gender and development* (London: Zed Books, 2005) p. 98.

33. World Bank, *Higher education in developing countries: peril and promise* (Washington, DC: World Bank, 2000) p. 107.

34. T. Moja, 'Policy responses to global transformation by African higher education systems', in P. T. Zeleza and A. Olukoshi (eds) *African universities in the twenty first century* (Pretoria: CODESRIA/UNISA Press, 2004) vol. 1, p. 26.

35. D. Teferra and P. Altbach (eds) *African higher education: an international reference handbook* (Bloomington: Indiana University Press, 2003).

36. A. Olukoshi and P. T. Zeleza, 'Conclusion', in P. T. Zeleza and A. Olukoshi (eds) *African universities in the twenty first century* (Pretoria: CODESRIA/UNISA Press, 2004) vol. 2, p. 599.

37. World Bank, *Higher education in developing countries*.

38. Ibid., p. 18.

39. Musisi and Muwanga, *Makerere University*.

40. World Bank, *Higher education in developing countries*, pp. 54–5.

41. Ibid., p. 55.

42. Q. O. Obong, 'Academic dilemmas under neo-liberal education reforms: a review of Makerere University, Uganda', in P. T. Zeleza and A. Olukoshi (eds) *African universities in the twenty first century* (Pretoria: CODESRIA/UNISA Press, 2004) vol. 1, p. 118.

43. Ibid.

44. Obong, 'Academic dilemmas', pp. 123, 124.

45. Five countries were nominated as case studies, all apparently showing positive signs of such liberalization. These countries were: Uganda, Ghana, South Africa, Tanzania and Mozambique.

46. Musisi and Muwanga, *Makerere University*, p. xv.

47. How the experience of Makerere University in Uganda demonstrates the benefits of 'democratization' in higher education in a country that has specifically outlawed 'democratization' is never explained.

48. *Étudier au Senegal: guide de l'enseignement superieur et professionnel*, pamphlet (Dakar: Senco 5, 2003) p.4.

49. B. Thaver, 'Private higher education in Africa: six country case studies', in P. T. Zeleza and A. Olukoshi (eds) *African universities in the twenty first century* (Pretoria: CODESRIA/UNISA Press, 2004) vol. 1, p. 71.

50. Ibid., p. 75.

51. For example, A. Verspoor, *A chance to learn: knowledge and finance for education in sub-Saharan Africa* (Washington, DC: World Bank, 2001).

52. P. Bond, *Against global apartheid: South Africa meets the World Bank, IMF and international finance* (Cape Town: University of Cape Town Press, 2002); P. Dwyer and D. Seddon, 'The new wave? A global perspective on popular protest', paper presented at the eighth International Conference on Alternative Futures and Popular Protest, Manchester Metropolitan University, 2–4 April 2002.

53. Caffentzis, 'The World Bank', p. 9.

54. P. Richards, *Fighting for the rain forest: war, youth and resources in Sierra Leone* (London: International African Institute in association with James Currey, 1996); P. Richards, 'Youth, food and peace: a reflection on some African security issues at the millennium', in T. Zack-Williams, D. Frost and A. Thomson (eds) *Africa in Crisis* (London: Pluto Press, 2002).

55. A. Krueger and J. Maleckova, *Education, poverty, political violence, and terrorism: is there a causal connection?* (New York: National Bureau of Economic Research, 2002).

56. Caffentzis, 'The World Bank', p. 11.

57. World Bank, *Higher education in developing countries*, p. 10.

58. D. Bloom, 'Opening address' conference Globalisation and Higher Education: Views from the South Education Policy Unit at the University of the Western Cape, 2001<http://www.tfhe.net/resources/Cape_town.htm>.

59. Ibid.

60. Ibid.

61. Moja, 'Policy responses', p. 23.

62. R. Pithouse (ed.) *University struggles in post-apartheid South Africa* (Trenton, NJ: Africa World Press, 2006) pp. xvi–xvii.

63. D. C. O'Brien, 'A lost generation? Youth identity and state decay in West Africa', in R. P. Werbner and T. O. Ranger (eds) *Post-colonial identities in Africa* (London: Zed Books, 1996).

64. J. D. Barkan, *An African dilemma: university students, development and politics in Ghana, Tanzania and Uganda* (Nairobi: Oxford University Press, 1975) pp. 128–30.

65. O. Alidou, G. Caffentzis and S. Federici, *A thousand flowers: social struggles against structural adjustment in African universities* (Trenton, Asmara: Africa World Press, 2000) p. 103.

66. M. E. Boren, *Student resistance: a history of the unruly subject* (New York: Routledge, 2001).

67. Alidou et al., *A thousand flowers*, p. xiii.

68. For example Committee for Academic Freedom in Africa, University of South Maine, Autumn, 1991 and 1996.

69. Alidou et al., *A thousand flowers*, p. 88.

70. Ibid., p. 93.

71. Konings, 'University students' revolt', pp. 180–1.

72. M. Mamdani, 'The intelligentsia, the state and social movements in Africa', in M. Diouf and M. Mamdani (eds) *Academic freedom in Africa* (Dakar: CODESRIA, 1994) p. 258.

73. Alidou et al., *A thousand flowers*, p. 96. However, it is important to caution against generalizing about the proletarianized status of students. The picture varies across the continent. A survey of students at the national university in Maputo in Mozambique

revealed the over-representation of Maputo students at universities and a correlation between prestigious degree courses and family status (M. Mario and P. Fry, *Higher education in Mozambique: a case study*, Oxford: James Currey, 2003, p. 31). D. Mills ('The "new" African higher education?' *African Affairs*, 103 (413) pp. 667–75, 2004) suggests that the elite status of students in higher education in Mozambique is demonstrated at Eduardo Mondlane University in Maputo where 80 per cent of students speak Portuguese as a first language.

74. Interview with Brian Kagoro, Harare, 23 June 2003.
75. D. Seddon, 'Popular protest and class struggle in Africa: an historical overview', in L. Zeilig (ed.) *Class struggle and resistance in Africa* (Cheltenham: New Clarion Press, 2002); see also D. Seddon and L. Zeilig, 'Class and protest in Africa: new waves', *Review of African Political Economy*, 31 (103) pp. 9–27, 2005.
76. G. Harrison, *Issues in the contemporary politics of sub-Saharan Africa: the dynamics of struggle and resistance* (New York: Palgrave, 2002) p. 114.
77. D. Mwinzi, 'The impact of cost-sharing policies on the living conditions of students in Kenyan public universities: the case of Nairobi and Moi universities', in P. T. Zeleza and A. Olukoshi (eds) *African universities in the twenty first century* (Pretoria: CODESRIA/UNISA Press, 2004) vol. 1, p. 147.
78. Ibid., p. 155.
79. Bathily et al., 'The Senegalese student movement', p. 401.
80. Ibid.
81. Ibid.
82. Ibid., p. 405.
83. O'Brien, 'A lost generation?', p. 65.
84. D. Boyer, 'The African crisis in context: comparative encounters with educational rationalization', *African Studies Review*, 45 (2) pp. 205–18, 2002, p. 210.
85. Konings, 'University students' revolt', p. 180.
86. Federici, 'The new student movement', p. 101.
87. Ibid., p. 103.
88. Boyer, 'The African crisis in context', p. 211.
89. Boren, *Student resistance*, p. 240.
90. Konings, 'University students' revolt' p. 180.
91. 'La démocratie envers et contre tout', *Jeune Afrique*, 27 March–2 April 1991; 'Que veulent les étudiants?' *Jeune Afrique*, 11–16 July 1991.
92. R. Buijtenhuijs and C. Thiriot, *Démocratisation en Afrique au Sud du Sahara 1992–1995* (Talence-Cédex: Centre d'Étude d'Afrique Noire, 1995); Mills, 'The "new" African higher education?', p. 671.
93. A. Mazrui, 'The impact of global changes on academic freedom in Africa: a preliminary assessment', in M. Diouf and M. Mamdani (eds) *Academic freedom in Africa* (Dakar: CODESRIA, 1994) p. 172.

94. A. Alexander and D. Renton, 'Globalisation, imperialism and popular resistance in Egypt, 1880–2000', in L. Zeilig (ed.) *Class struggle and resistance in Africa* (Cheltenham: New Clarion Press, 2002); Marfleet, 'Globalisation'; J. Walton and D. Seddon, *Free markets and food riots: the politics of global adjustment* (Oxford: Blackwell, 1994).

95. Mazrui, 'The impact of global changes', p. 172.

96. J. Saul, *Millennial Africa: capitalism, socialism, democracy* (New Jersey: Africa World Press, 2001).

97. L. Zeilig and D. Seddon, 'Marxism, class and resistance in Africa', in L. Zeilig (ed.) *Class struggle and resistance in Africa* (Cheltenham: New Clarion Press, 2002).

98. Mazrui, 'The impact of global changes', p. 173.

99. 'Le bon mauvais example', *Jeune Afrique*, 29 March–2 April 1991.

100. L. Martins, *Kabila et la révolution congolaise, panafricanisme ou neocolonialisme?* (Anvers: Editions EPO, vol 1, 2002); D. Renton, D. Seddon and L. Zeilig, *The Congo: pillage and resistance* (London: Zed Books, 2006).

101. Nkongolo, *Le campus martyr*, p. 182.

102. T. T. Munikengi and W. Sangol, 'The diploma paradox: University of Kinshasa between crisis and salvation', in T. Trefon (ed.) *Reinventing order in the Congo* (London: Zed Books, 2004) p. 99; G. Nzongola-Ntalaja, *The Congo from Leopold to Kabila: a people's history* (London: Zed Books, 2002) pp. 155–6.

103. Quoted in N. Tengende, *Workers, students and the struggles for democracy: state-civil society relations in Zimbabwe*, Ph.D. dissertation (Roskilde University, Denmark, 1994) pp. 389–92.

104. Quoted in Tengende, *Workers, students*, p. 427.

105. M. Gwisai, *Revolutionaries, resistance and crisis in Zimbabwe: anti-neo-liberal struggles in periphery capitalism* (Harare: ISO pamphlet, 2002).

106. L. Brenner, *Controlling knowledge: religion, power and schooling in a West African Muslim society* (Bloomington: Indiana University Press, 2001) p. 242. See also Buijtenhuijs and Thiriot, *Démocratisation en Afrique*.

107. Brenner, *Controlling knowledge*; Z. K. Smith, 'From demons to democrats: Mali's student movement 1991–1996', *Review of African Political Economy*, 24 (72) pp. 249–63, 1997. The slogan of the AEEM conjures up the atmosphere of the period *Oser lutter, c'est oser vaincre, la lutte continue* (To dare to fight is to dare to overcome, the struggle continues).

108. It is worth noting that Smith ('From demons to democrats', p. 264) interviewed members of the donor community who unanimously maintained that AEEM had a negative impact on the country's democratic governance: 'This negative view was also amply evident in interviews I conducted with members of the World Bank mission in Mali.'

109.   Smith, 'From demons to democrats', p. 249.
110.   Quoted in Smith, 'From demons to democrats', p. 251.
111.   Ibid., p. 263.
112.   Konings, 'University students' revolt'.
113.   Ibid., p. 182.
114.   'Multi-partyism makes progress in Cameroon but the state has broken down'.
115.   Konings, 'University students' revolt'.
116.   P. T. Zeleza, 'Neo-liberalism and academic freedom', in P. T. Zeleza and A. Olukoshi (eds) *African universities in the twenty first century*, vol. 1 (Pretoria: CODESRIA/UNISA Press, 2004) p. 50.
117.   Ibid., p. 59.
118.   Smith, 'From demons to democrats'.
119.   Mamdani, 'The intelligentsia', p. 259.
120.   H. Alavi and T. Shanin, *Introduction to the sociology of developing societies* (New York: Monthly Review Press, 1982); J. Ferguson, *Expectations of modernity: myths and meaning of urban life on the Zambian copperbelt* (Los Angeles: University of California Press, 1999); V. Jamal and J. Weeks, *Africa misunderstood or whatever happened to the rural-urban gap?* (London: Palgrave, 1993).
121.   Harrison, *Issues in the contemporary politics*; Seddon, 'Popular protest and class struggle'; see also Seddon and Zeilig, 'Class and protest'.
122.   Seddon, 'Popular protest and class struggle'.
123.   Harrison, *Issues in the contemporary politics*, p. 119–20.
124.   J. F. Bayart, *The state in Africa: the politics of the belly* (London: Longman, 1993).
125.   Harrison, *Issues in the contemporary politics*, p. 113.
126.   Zeleza, 'Neo-liberalism and academic freedom', p. 52.
127.   Mamdani, 'The intelligentsia', p. 258–9.
128.   Interestingly, while failing to remember that an umbilical cord connects political and economic struggles, the same criticism of 'economism' is made of the trade union movement. This was a point made powerfully by Rosa Luxemburg in her book *The mass strike, the political party, and the trade unions* (Detroit: Marxist Educational Society, 1906).
129.   Bathily et al., 'The Senegalese student movement', p. 401.
130.   See Introdouction, note 15.
131.   Kerr and Mapanje, 'Academic freedom', p. 86.
132.   Ibid., p. 87.

Chapter 3: Reform, revolt and student activism in Zimbabwe

1.   R. Shumba, *Constructing a social identity: the national youth service of Zimbabwe*, MA dissertation (University of Johannesburg, South Africa, 2006).

Notes

2.   'National service: community work or electoral weapon', *Zimbabwe Independent*, 2 February 2002.

3.   'Mugabe takes a stride into tyranny', *Guardian*, 10 January 2002.

4.   *Human development report* (New York: UNDP, 2004) p. 141.

5.   'Financial crisis in Zimbabwe', *Economist*, 15 January 2004.

6.   B. Bomba, 'Creating the tipping point: United Front is the way forward', 2006 <http://www.newzimbabwe.com/pages/opinion185.14626>.

7.   'The plight of students at UZ', *Socialist Worker*, July–August 2001.

8.   *National response brief: Zimbabwe* (Geneva: UNAIDS, 2004) <http://www.unaids.org/nationalresponse/result.asp?action=overall&country=510>.

9.   Zimbabwe's resource colonialism in the DRC: a Briefing Document 2001<http://www.globalwitness.org/projects/zimbabwe/bd_zimbabwe.htm.>

10. A. Astrow, *Zimbabwe: a revolution that lost its way?* (London: Zed Books, 1983).

11. M. Gwisai, 'Revolutionaries, resistance and crisis in Zimbabwe', in L. Zeilig (ed.) *Class struggle and resistance in Africa* (Cheltenham: New Clarion Press, 2002); B. Raftopoulos and L. Sachikonye (eds) *Striking back: the labour movement and the post-colonial state in Zimbabwe, 1980–2000* (Harare: Weaver Press, 2001).

12. ISO activist Luke Kasuwanga, interview, London, 9 July 2001.

13. P. Alexander, 'Zimbabwean workers, the MDC and the 2000 election', *Review of African Political Economy*, 27 (85) pp. 385–406, 2000.

14. N. Kriger, 'ZANU (PF) strategies in the general elections, 1980–2000: discourse and coercion', *African Affairs*, 104 (414) pp. 1–34, 2005, p. 2.

15. Quoted in Alexander, 'Zimbabwean workers', p. 94.

16. Canwell Muchadya, interview, Harare, 18 August 2006.

17. J. Herbst, *State politics in Zimbabwe* (Harare: University of Zimbabwe, 1990) p. 7.

18. P. Bond, *Uneven Zimbabwe: a study of finance, development, and under-development* (Trenton, NJ: Africa World Press, 1998); I. Mandaza, *Zimbabwe: a political economy of transition 1980–86* (Dakar: CODESRIA, 1986); C. van Onselen, *Chibaro: African mine labour in Southern Rhodesia, 1900–1933* (London: Pluto Press, 1976).

19. B. Raftopoulos and I. Phimister, *Keep on knocking: a history of the labour movement in Zimbabwe 1900–1997* (Harare: Baobab Books on behalf of the Zimbabwe Congress of Trade Unions and the Friedrich Ebert Stiftung, 1997).

20. I. Phimister, *Wangi Kolia: coal, capital and labour in colonial Zimbabwe, 1894–1954* (Harare: Boabab Books, 1994) p. 64.

21. Quoted in Raftopoulos and Phimister, *Keep on knocking*, p. 71.

22. Ibid., pp. 69–70.

23. Astrow, *Zimbabwe*; M. Gwisai, *Revolutionaries, resistance and crisis in*

Zimbabwe: anti-neo-liberal struggles in periphery capitalism (Harare: ISO pamphlet, 2002).

24. Astrow, *Zimbabwe*, p. 21; R. Gray, *The two nations: aspects of the development of the development of race relations in the Rhodesias and Nyasaland* (London: Oxford University Press, 1960) pp. 26–7.

25. Astrow, *Zimbabwe*, p. 21.

26. B. Raftopoulos, 'The labour movement in Zimbabwe: 1945–1965', in B. Raftopoulos and I. Phimister (eds) *Keep on knocking: a history of the labour movement in Zimbabwe 1900–1997* (Harare: Baobab Books on behalf of the Zimbabwe Congress of Trade Unions and the Friedrich Ebert Stiftung, 1997).

27. P. Foot, *The politics of Harold Wilson* (London: Penguin, 1968) pp. 259–70.

28. F. Chung, 'Education and the liberation struggle', in N. Bhebe and T. Ranger (eds) *Society in Zimbabwe's liberation war* (Harare: University of Zimbabwe Publications, 1995) vol 2, p. 146.

29. T. Cliff, 'Deflected permanent revolution', *International Socialism*, 1 (12) pp. 15–22, 1963, p. 16.

30. A. Callinicos and J. Rogers, 'Southern Africa after Zimbabwe', *International Socialism Journal*, 2 (9) pp. 1–43, 1980, pp. 9–15.

31. For those fighting against the Rhodesians there was an additional risk – even in the middle of the war Mugabe was murdering his opponents fighting with him in the liberation struggle (Astrow, *Zimbabwe*, pp. 107–8).

32. R. Saunders, *Never the same again: Zimbabwe's growth towards democracy 1980–2000* (Harare: Edwina Spicer, 2000) p. 17.

33. L. Cliffe, 'The politics of land reform in Zimbabwe', in T. A. S. Bowyer-Bower and C. Stoneman (eds) *Land reform in Zimbabwe: constraints and prospects* (Aldershot: Ashgate, 2000) pp. 42–3. The precise figure is still contested. It was subject to the colonial tradition of a gentleman's agreement. See Astrow, *Zimbabwe*, pp. 154–60 for a good examination of the processes taking place during the Lancaster House negiotations.

34. B. H. Kinsey and H. P. Binswanger, *Characteristics and performance of settlement programs: a review* (Washington, DC: Agriculture and Environment Division, Southern Africa Department, World Bank, 1993).

35. P. Bond and M. Manyanya, *Zimbabwe's plunge: exhausted nationalism, neo-liberalism and the search for social justice* (London: Merlin Press, 2002) pp. 114–21.

36. J. Alexander, 'Squatters, veterans and the state in Zimbabwe', in A. Hammer, B. Raftopoulos and S. Jensen (eds) *Zimbabwe's unfinished business: rethinking land, state and nation in the context of crisis* (Harare: Weaver Press, 2003).

37. Ibid. Alexander argues that until February 2000 occupations were often popularly driven, similar to the situation in the early 1980s.

297

38. Quoted in D. Smith, *Mugabe* (London: Sphere, 1981) p. 210.
39. It did not take years for bitterness to build up after independence. There were many who were disillusioned with Mugabe's moderate stand. The incident involving Edgar Tekere, a leading figure in the party and a close confidante of Mugabe, is illustrative. Only a year after independence he was implicated in an attack on a farmhouse and the death of a white farmer. After these events Mugabe, in the words of one commentator at the time, 'spiked the guns of his troublesome left-wing'. Resentment among the left wing and thousands who had waited for victory and liberation was growing (see Smith, *Mugabe*, pp. 209–18).
40. T. Skalnes, *The politics of economic reform in Zimbabwe* (Basingstoke: Macmillan, 1995) p. 5.
41. J. Alexander, J. McGregor and T. Ranger (eds) *Violence and memory: one hundred years in the dark forests of Matabeleland* (Oxford: James Currey, 2000); *Breaking the silence, building true peace: a report on the disturbances in Matabeleland and the Midlands, 1980–1988* (Harare: Legal Resources Foundation, 1997).
42. Saunders, *Never the same again*, p. 18.
43. E. Z. Razemba, *The political economy of Zimbabwe: impact of structural adjustment programme, 1980–1993* (Harare: Aroclar Publishers, 1994) pp. 89–91.
44. Bond, *Uneven Zimbabwe*, p. 150.
45. Razemba, *The political economy of Zimbabwe*, p. 131.
46. Skalnes (*The politics of economic reform*, p. 131) makes this point: 'Chidzero was the one who steered the new economic philosophy through the cabinet.'
47. Gwisai, *Revolutionaries*, p. 4.
48. Ibid., pp. 3–4; see also Alexander et al., *Violence and memory*; and Bond, *Uneven Zimbabwe*.
49. Razemba, *The political economy of Zimbabwe*.
50. P. Jackson, 'The role of the state in business development in Zimbabwe: the case of the textiles and garments sector', 1997 <http://www.idd.bham.ac.uk/research/working_papers/rog_wp.htm>.
51. Bond, *Uneven Zimbabwe*, pp. 92–4.
52. Ibid.
53. Skalnes, *The politics of economic reform*, p. 141.
54. Quoted in Alexander, 'Zimbabwean workers', p. 86.
55. Gwisai, *Revolutionaries*.
56. N. Tengende, *Workers, students and the struggles for democracy: state-civil society relations in Zimbabwe*, Ph.D. dissertation (Roskilde University, Denmark, 1994) p. 426.
57. Luke Kasuwanga, interview, London, 9 July 2001.
58. Gwisai, *Revolutionaries*, pp. 14–15.

59. Tafadzwa Choto, interview, London, 10 July 2001.
60. Quoted in Alexander, 'Zimbabwean workers', p. 89.
61. P. Alexander, 'A worker's voice', *Socialist Review*, 244, 2000.
62. Quoted in L. Zeilig, 'Crisis in Zimbabwe', *International Socialism Journal*, 2 (94) pp. 75–96, 2002, p. 87.
63. P. Bond, *Against global apartheid: South Africa meets the World Bank, IMF and international finance* (Cape Town: University of Cape Town Press, 2002); Raftopoulos and Sachikonye, *Striking back*.
64. Gwisai, *Revolutionaries*.
65. Luke Kasuwanga, interview, London, 9 July 2001.
66. Chenjerai Hunzvi was a qualified doctor who had studied and lived in Eastern Europe. He was fluent in Polish, Romanian and French, and did not return to Zimbabwe until 1990, having left the country on a scholarship in the 1970s. (There was an obituary for him in the *Guardian* in 2001.)
67. J. Ihonvbere, *Economic crisis, civil society and democratization: the case of Zambia* (Trenton, NJ: Africa World Press, 1996); M. Larmer, 'Resisting the state: the trade union movement and working class politics in Zambia, 1964–91', in L. Zeilig (ed.) *Class struggle and resistance in Africa* (Cheltenham: New Clarion Press, 2002).
68. 'Why ZCTU must form a workers party and not a political movement', *Socialist Worker*, May–June 1999.
69. Bond, *Against global apartheid*, pp. 87–106.
70. Quoted in F. Harnon, 'Building a workers party: lessons of the MDC experience for Nigeria', *Workers' Alternative*, October 2000.
71. Ibid.
72. Gwisai, *Revolutionaries*.
73. Saunders, *Never the same again*.
74. In 2002 ZANU-PF stated it intended to seize 8.5 million hectares of land before the presidential elections, which is the majority of land owned by white farmers. It succeeded in doing this by 2003, as the pace of land seizures and occupations came to an end.
75. P. Bond, 'Radical rhetoric and the working class during Zimbabwean nationalism's dying days', *Journal of World-Systems Research*, 7 (1) pp. 52–89, 2001, pp. 66–74.
76. Timothy Chitambure, interview, London, 9 July 2001.
77. Ibid.
78. Alexander, 'Zimbabwean workers'.
79. 'Build the resistance', *Socialist Worker*, March 2001.
80. Bond, *Against global apartheid*; Gwisai, 'Revolutionaries, resistance and crisis in Zimbabwe'; Harnon, 'Building a workers party'.
81. These processes are described in more detail in Chapter 5.
82. Bond, *Against global apartheid*.
83. Luke Kasuwanga, interview, London, 9 July 2001.
84. See Zeilig, 'Crisis in Zimbabwe'.

Notes

85. R. Mugabe, 'Opening speech', in N. T. Chideya, C. E. M. Choikomba, A. J. C. Pgweni and L. C. Tsikirayi (eds) *The role of the university and its future in Zimbabwe* (Harare: Harare Publishing House, 1982) p. 6.

86. Stephen Chisuvi, interview, Harare, 16 May 2003.

87. Hopewell Gumbo, interview, Bulawayo, 28 July 2003.

88. University of Zimbabwe, *Annual report* (Harare: University of Zimbabwe, 1984) p. 3.

89. D. Auret, *A decade of development: Zimbabwe 1980–1990* (Harare: Mambo Press, 1990) p. 30.

90. P. Bianchini, *Ecole et politique en Afrique noire: sociologie des crises et des réformes du système d'enseignement au Sénégal et au Burkina Faso (1960–2000)* (Paris: Karthala, 2004).

91. Ibid., pp. 9–41.

92. Tengende, *Workers, students*, pp. 191–201.

93. S. Nyamfukudza, *The non-believer's journey* (London: Heinemann Educational, 1980) p. 86.

94. One novel, *The Swinging Graduate* (Harare: Juta Zimbabwe, 1995) by Vitalis Nyawaranda, deals specifically with the moral universe of students at UZ. It describes an arrogant and promiscuous graduate at the start of the AIDS pandemic. University life is still presented as aloof and cynical, but now also as a potentially dangerous and uncontrollable space. The enormous status of the university guaranteed its continued expansion after independence.

95. Astrow, *Zimbabwe*, pp. 20–6.

96. M. Gelfand, *A non-racial island of learning: a history of the University College of Rhodesia from its inception to 1966* (Gwelo: Mambo Press, 1978).

97. J. L. Cefkin, 'Rhodesian university students in national politics', in W. J. Hanna and J. L. Hanna (eds) *University students and African politics* (New York: Africana Publishing Company, 1975).

98. Quoted in ibid., p. 135.

99. See Cefkin, 'Rhodesian university students', p. 141; and Chung, 'Education and the liberation struggle', p. 146.

100. Quoted in Cefkin, 'Rhodesian university students', p. 149.

101. Ibid., p. 148.

102. Quoted in ibid.

103. Quoted in Tengende, *Workers, students*, p. 141.

104. Ibid.

105. Knottenbelt quoted in F. Veit-Wild, *Scrapiron blues* (Harare: Baobab Books, 1994) p. 129.

106. Tengende, *Workers, students*, p. 142.

107. Ibid., p. 143.

108. Ibid., p. 144.

109. D. A. Mungazi, *Colonial policy and conflict in Zimbabwe: a study of cultures in collision, 1890–1979* (New York: Taylor & Francis, 1992) p. 85.

110. Arthur Mutambara, interview, Johannesburg, 10 July 2003. The list is indeed long: Zororo Willard Duri (former leading ZANU member), Sobusa Gula-Ndebele (prominent lawyer), Christopher Mutsvangwa (former director general of ZBC), John Majowe (former ambassador to Mozambique), Stan Mudenge (foreign affairs minister), Witness Mangwende (senior ZANU member and government minister), and Kempton Makamure (university lecturer) – a generation that gave up their studies at the university and became the ideological and military leadership of the war.

111. Saunders, *Never the same again*, p. 13.

112. Chung, 'Education and the liberation struggle', p. 141.

113. Ibid.

114. D. B. Moore, 'The ideological foundation of the Zimbabwean ruling class', *Journal of Southern African Studies*, 17 (3) pp. 472–95, 1991.

115. 'Mugabe tells UZ students: shame on you!' *Herald*, 25 April 1996.

116. I. Mandaza, 'Education in Zimbabwe: the colonial framework and the response of the national liberation movement', in *Zimbabwe: towards a new order*, Working Papers, Geneva: United Nations, 341–400, 1980; Moore, 'The ideological foundation'; R. J. Zvobgo, *Colonialism and education in Zimbabwe* (Harare: Sapes Books, 1994).

117. Mandaza, 'Education in Zimbabwe', p. 70.

118. A. Cabral, *Revolution in Guinea: an African people's struggle* (London: Stage 1, 1969) p. 74.

119. Cefkin, 'Rhodesian university students', pp. 157–8.

120. Ibid., p. 158.

121. R. J. Zvobgo, *The post-colonial state and educational reform: Zimbabwe, Zambia and Botswana* (Harare: Zimbabwe Publishing House, 1999) p. 164.

122. 'Riot police clash with stone-throwing UZ Students', *Herald*, 29 June 1995.

123. Talkmore Saurombe, interview, Harare, 5 June 2003.

124. Ibid., emphasis added.

125. Interview with University of Zimbabwe Information Office, 6 March 2005.

126. A document that emerged after independence committing ZANU–PF to a strict anti-corruption code.

127. '478 students held in violent demos', *Herald*, 30 September 1988. The merits of a one-party state were discussed openly (for example by Mandaza and Sachikonye 1991).

128. 'AGO' are Arthur Mutambara's initials. Later generations of student activists describe the importance of the 'AGO' period. Stephen Chisuvi makes his influence clear: 'When I was in my form 1 in Goromonzi High School we used to read about student leaders. I remember that's when I heard the name Arthur Mutambara ... he became a legend because of how the UZ had organized political demonstrations in

which even leading ZCTU leaders had participated ... and how one day such people will form a movement that will destroy the state' (interview with Stephen Chisuvi, Harare, 16 May 2003).

129. Interview with Arthur Mutambara, Johannesburg, 10 July 2003.
130. Brian Kagoro, interview, Harare, 23 June 2003.
131. B. Mutape, 'The dawn of reason: an investigation and anaylsis of the student movements', unpublished manuscript (Harare: University of Zimbabwe, 1999).
132. See Benson Mutape's extraordinary three volume collection ('The dawn of reason') of life at the university. The first volume deals with the first ten years at UZ and focuses on the vibrant social and cultural life at the university. Mutape has been an eyewitness at the university for more than 20 years, first as a student and then librarian. Unfortunately, the collection has not been catalogued at the library and is unpublished. I have been attempting to transfer the volumes to SOAS, currently without success. They resemble an elaborate and detailed scrapbook of life at UZ.
133. Interview with Arthur Mutambara, Johannesburg, 10 July 2003.
134. Ibid.
135. The three most important Marxists at UZ were Shadreck Gutto, Kempton Makamure (both in the law faculty) and Robert McLaren (in the drama department and the initiator of Zambuko Izibuko).
136. See Chapter 2.
137. Zvobgo, *The post-colonial state*, pp. 148–52.
138. Ibid., p. 164.
139. The many referred to are principally an older generation of activists who attempt to valorize their period of activism with the evident degeneration of the student movement today (personal communications with Gwisai and Mutumbara 2003).
140. A number of students supported the University Amendment Act in 1990 in reaction to the indiscipline on campus (see 'Letters to the editor: UZ, a den of hooligans', *Herald*, 27 May 1991), even though it was widely condemned by the student movement.
141. Tengende, *Workers, students*, pp. 236–45.
142. Neither of these terms is used on the campus today.
143. See Chapter 2.
144. See A. Bathily, M. Diouf and M. Mbodj (1995) 'The Senegalese student movement from its inception to 1989', in M. Mamdani and E. Wamba-Dia-Wamba (eds) *African studies in social movements and democracy* (Dakar: CODESRIA, 1995).
145. Gwisai, *Revolutionaries*.
146. Brian Kagoro, interview, Harare, 23 June 2003.
147. Ibid.
148. Ibid.
149. Luke Kasuwanga, interview, London, 9 July 2001.

150.   Saunders, *Never the same again*, p. 71.

151.   Stephen Chisuvi, interview, Harare, 16 May 2003.

152.   Letter to University of Zimbabwe Student Representative Council, Harare, April 1997. It is interesting how the story of students urinating into freezers has entered the national conscience; people will repeat the story today or claim that it happened last year. It is still seen as conclusive proof of the degeneration of student behaviour in much the same way as the indiscipline of students was presented as incontrovertible proof of their degeneration in the 1980s.

153.   This is the alias of Lawrence Chakaredza, a former activist at the university, who believed that he was a descendant of Chief Monomatapa, one of the founders of Great Zimbabwe.

154.   'Former UZ student leaders form body to help in disputes', *The Herald*, 26 April 1996.

155.   Gwisai, *Revolutionaries*, p. 50.

156.   Information Office, University of Zimbabwe, 6 March 2005.

157.   Parliamentary Debates (Harare: Government Printing and Stationery, 1997) p. 2.

158.   Ibid., pp. 12–13.

159.   Zvobgo, *The post-colonial state*, p. 164.

160.   Brian Kagoro, interview, Harare, 23 June 2003.

161.   A. Mutambara, 'National service programs and proposals: Zimbabwe', in D. J. Eberly (ed.) *National youth service: a global perspective*, 1992 <http://www.utas.edu.au/docs/ahugo/NCYS/first/Introduction.html>.

162.   ZANU youth brigades are also not a contemporary phenomenon in Zimbabwe. On the contrary, they were used continually in the 1980s, particularly as the student body broke with the government in the latter part of the decades. The regime increasingly used loyal party youths organized in party structures to defend the ruling party physically. At the ZCTU May Day celebrations in 1990 students who had turned up with critical banners were beaten and chased out of Rufaro stadium by ZANU youths ('Disruption of student participation on May Day', SRC flyer, University of Zimbabwe, 2 May 1990).

163.   Zvobgo, *The post-colonial state*, pp. 157–64.

164.   Brian Kagoro is scathing about the idea that the national union was formed in 1997, arguing that it is simply an attempt by former student leaders to paint themselves in a more favourable light.

165.   C. Fermont, 'Indonesia: the inferno of revolution', *International Socialism Journal*, (2) 80, pp. 3–34, 1998, pp. 18–24.

166.   Nelson Chamisa, interview, Harare, 8 August 2003.

167.   Jethro Mpofu, interview, Bulawayo, 23 May 2003.

168.   Not only was Chamisa only 27 years old (in 2005) but he also proclaimed it regularly, highlighting the MDC's youthfulness in relation to the ruling party's gerontocracy. Often the argument was

advanced to me that the opposition will simply 'out youth' the government.

169. Tinashe Chimedza, interview, Harare, 27 May 2003.
170. Nelson Chamisa rates Hopewell very highly: 'of course Hopewell as the president of the student movement, who had a Marxist understanding of issues, his ideological drive was very important to the student movement.' Hopewell is a leading member of the ISO.
171. Hopewell Gumbo, interview, Bulawayo, 28 July 2003.
172. Ibid.
173. Ibid.
174. Ibid.
175. John Bomba, interview, Bulawayo, 30 July 2003. Hopewell Gumbo says the slogan was generated from grassroots consultations that took place after the WPC in 1999, in fact from an old man attending one of the report back meetings in Masvingo.
176. John Bomba, interview, Harare, 18 January 2005.
177. Job Sikhala, interview, Harare, 31 July 2003.
178. Kriger, 'ZANU (PF) strategies'.
179. Ibid., p. 2.
180. Ibid., p. 1.
181. Shumba, *Constructing a social identity*, p. 1.
182. Zimbabwe Congress of Trade Unions, *Beyond ESAP* (Harare: ZCTU, 1996).
183. SAP was an ISO initiative, although many activists who set up SAP structures in colleges and universities are still unaware of its origin; it rapidly assumed a student identity independent of the ISO (see 'Stop the war on our colleges and universities: build the SAPs', *Socialist Worker*, October–November 2001).
184. Emphasis added.
185. Executive member of ZINASU in 2003.
186. John Bomba, interview, Bulawayo, 22 May 2003.
187. 'UZ likely to delay opening', *Daily Mirror*, 18 August 2004.
188. 'Fee hikes spark student demo', *Herald*, 13 July, 2001.
189. 'Stop the war on our colleges and universities: build the SAPs', *Socialist Worker*, October–November 2001.
190. 'Crisis in education', *Socialist Worker*, March 2002.
191. 'Students continue food demonstration', *Daily News*, 31 May 2001.
192. 'Government's reaction to student protests misguided', *Daily News*, 2 June 2001.
193. 'Riot police police kill student', *Daily News*, 9 April 2001.
194. 'Police, students clash in city', *Star*, 8 June 2001.
195. 'Judge endorses UZ students' suspension', *Daily News*, 27 October 2001. ZINASU student leaders were frequently being picked up and tortured, often from their campus rooms in the night. The information and publicity secretary, Phillip Pasirayi, temporarily disappeared after

being arrested in the middle of the night from UZ, only to appear days later in Avondale police station ('State media now lying full-time to damage MDC', *Daily News*, 23 November 2001), a tactic that was used frequently by the police in Rhodesia (see Cefkin, 'Rhodesian university students', p. 154).

196. See 'Stop the war on our colleges and universities: build the SAPs', *Socialist Worker*, October–November 2001.

197. Bomba was SRC president at NUST.

198. John Bomba, interview, Bulawayo, 30 July 2003.

199. One of the terms in the complex and lyrical linguistic world of student activism in Zimbabwe. It refers to an ethnic group, the Banyamulenge, in the eastern Congo who fought Mobutu in the late 1990s. The UBA prefix refers to the University Bachelors Association, denoting the single (macho) status of male undergraduates.

200. David Matsikidze, interview, 5 June 2003. Matsikidze is a mature student from a farming background. Before he returned to university he worked as a farm manager. When he finishes his degree in agricultural economics he intends to return to farming. In the 2003 SRC election he refused to accept party funding for his campaign and paid for it through a small fruit and vegetable stall he keeps in the student union building. He was widely regarded as independently minded and could be seen arguing fraternally with students. Such fraternal debate was typical of the atmosphere at the university in 2003.

201. David Matsikidze, interview, Harare, 5 June 2003.

202. D. Pankhurst, 'Globalisation and democracy: international donors and civil society in Zimbabwe', in T. Zack-Williams, D. Frost and A. Thomson (eds) *Africa in crisis: new challenges and possibilities* (London: Pluto Press, 2002) pp. 119–22.

203. NYS interviews, Chegutu, Zimbabwe, 10–12 June 2003.

204. A week-long stay away that was meant to turn the tables on the government.

205. NYS interviews, Chegutu, Zimbabwe, 10–12 June 2003.

206. Interview with Tawanda Kanhema, Harare, 5 June 2004.

207. NYS graduates came of age in the week of action. This is not an attempt to excuse them: NYS trainees and graduates have unquestionably been responsible for some of the worst rural violence in the last two years.

208. NYS public meeting at New Ambassador Hotel, Harare, personal recording, 21 August 2003.

209. Pankhurst, 'Globalisation and democracy', pp. 116–17.

210. See N. Ansell, 'Secondary education reform in Lesotho and Zimbabwe and the needs of rural girls: pronouncements, policy and practice', *Comparative Education*, 38 (1) pp. 91–112, 2002; J. Jansen, 'The state and curriculum in the transition to socialism: the Zimbabwean experience', *Comparative Education Review*, 35, pp. 76–91, 1991.

211. Personal communication with M. Gwisai, 2003.
212. See J. Petras, 'NGOs: in the service of imperialism', *Journal of Contemporary Asia*, 29 (4) pp. 429–40, 1999; J. G. Ungpakorn, 'NGOs: enemies or allies?' *International Socialism Journal*, 2 (104) pp. 49–64, 2004.
213. Members of the former ZINASU executive were offered asylum in Norway in 2002 when they were receiving the International Peace Prize on behalf of the national union. Their lives were not at risk in Zimbabwe.
214. John Bomba, interview, Bulawayo, 22 May 2003.
215. Brian Kagoro, interview, Harare, 23 June 2003.
216. Mcdonald Lewanika, interview, Harare, 19 August 2006.
217. John Bomba, interview, Bulawayo, 22 May 2002.
218. Students were the only group to be mobilized during the final push. Malcolm X (1965) commented that students are excellent revolutionaries and easy to mobilize: 'The students didn't think in terms of the odds against them.' They do not consider the impossibility of political change (see Chapter 1).
219. Stephen Chisuvi, interview, Harare, 16 May 2003.
220. Students have called the hall of residence 'Baghdad' since the first Gulf war in 1991. It is for first-year students and has been the scene of particularly violent confrontations (bombardments) with the police. In the aftermath of the demonstration described in the text, Baghdad struck me as a completely appropriate nickname.
221. L. Zeilig, 'Zero, zero, zero pito formation: student activism in Zimbabwe', *Debate* (10) 2004.
222. Philippa (pseudonym), interview, Harare, 14 June 2003.
223. P. Bourdieu, *Bourdieu et le Marxisme* (Paris: Publications L'Etincelle, 1999).
224. Job Sikhala, interview, Harare, 31 July 2003.
225. Ibid.
226. Gwisai, *Revolutionaries*, p. 25.
227. Stephen Chisuvi, interview, Harare, 17 August 2006.
228. John Bomba, interview, Johannesburg, 23 August 2006.
229. Freedom Youth Council, 'Zimbabwe Social Forum youth camp', 2005<http://southafrica.indymedia.org/news/2005/10/ 8946.php.>
230. John Bomba, interview, Johannesburg, 23 August 2006.
231. A. Mutambara, 'The one-party state, socialism and democratic struggles in Zimbabwe: a student perspective', in I. Mandaza and L. Sachikonye (eds) *The one-party state and democracy: the Zimbabwe debate* (Harare: SAPES, 1991) pp. 139–40.
232. Job Sikhala, interview, Harare, 31 July 2003.
233. John Bomba, interview, Harare, 18 January 2005.

Chapter 4: Political change and student resistance in Senegal

1. A. Bathily, *Mai 68 à Dakar ou la revolte universitaire et la democratie* (Paris: Chaka, 1992).
2. L. Zeilig, 'In the age of Wade: political change and the student strike in Dakar 2001', in N. Akam and R. Ducasse (eds) *Quelle université pour l'Afrique* (Bordeaux: Maison des Sciences de l'Homme d'Aquitaine, 2002).
3. B. Fall, *Ajustement structurel et emploi au Sénégal* (Paris: Karthala, 1997).
4. A. Bathily, M. Diouf and M. Mbodj (1995) 'The Senegalese student movement from its inception to 1989', in M. Mamdani and E. Wamba-Dia-Wamba (eds) *African studies in social movements and democracy*, (Dakar: CODESRIA, 1995) p. 401.
5. D. C. O'Brien, 'A lost generation? Youth identity and state decay in West Africa', in R. P. Werbner and T. O. Ranger (eds) *Post-colonial identities in Africa* (London: Zed Books, 1996) p. 65.
6. P. Bianchini, 'Le mouvement étudiant sénégalais: un essai d'interprétation', in M. C. Diop (ed.) *La Société sénéglaise entre le local et le global* (Paris: Karthala, 2002).
7. D. C. O'Brien, 'Charisma comes to town', in D. C. O'Brien and C. Coulon (eds) *Charisma and brotherhood in African Islam* (Oxford: Clarendon Press, 1988) p. 153.
8. M. Diouf, 'Les jeunes Dakarois dans le champs politique', in D. C. O'Brien, M. C. Diop and M. Diouf (eds) *La construction de l'état au Sénégal* (Paris: Karthala, 2000).
9. O'Brien, 'Charisma comes to town', p. 145.
10. M. Mbodj, 'The state of the groundnut economy: a 30 year crisis', in M. C. Diop (ed.) *Senegal essays in statecraft* (Dakar: CODESRIA, 1992) p. 94–8.
11. S. Amin, *L'Afrique de l'ouest bloquée, l'économie politique de la colonisation, 1880–1970* (Paris: Ed. Minuit, 1971) pp. 46–7.
12. Cited in I. Thioub, 'Le mouvement étudiant de Dakar et la vie politique sénégalaise: la marche vers la crise de mai–juin 1968', in H. D'Almeida-Topor, C. Coquery-Vidrovitch, O. Goerg and F. Guitart (eds) *Les jeunes en Afrique: la politique et la ville* (Paris: L'Harmattan, 1992) vol. 2, p. 271.
13. Ibid., p. 276.
14. Ibid., p. 277.
15. M. Lo, *Sénégal: syndicalisme et participation* (Paris: L'Harmattan, 1987) pp. 54–5.
16. Ibid., pp. 9–40.
17. Thioub, 'Le mouvement étudiant', p. 281.
18. Libre association d'individus libres, *Lettre de Dakar* (Paris: Editions Champ Libre, 1978).
19. M. C. Diop, 'Introduction: from "socialism" to "liberalism": the many

phases of state legitimacy' and 'Student unionism: pluralism and pressure politics', in M. C. Diop (ed.) *Senegal essays in statecraft* (Dakar: CODESRIA, 1993).

20. Fall, *Ajustement structurel*, p. xv.
21. M. C. Diop and M. Diouf, *Le Sénégal sous Abdou Diouf: état et société* (Paris: Karthala, 1990).
22. Cited in Correspondance internationale, monthly (Paris, 1987) p. 24.
23. Ibid., p. 25.
24. Ibid., p. 26.
25. K. Sané, *Jeunesse insurgée: la grande insurrection* (Dakar, February 1982).
26. Ibid., p. 46.
27. Diop, 'Introduction', pp. 10–11.
28. M. C. Diop, 'Regards croisés sur le Sénégal: un essai de biographie', in M. C. Diop (ed.) *La societe senegalaise entre le local et le global* (Paris: Karthala, 2002) p. 13.
29. Diop and Diouf, *Le Sénégal*.
30. Fall, *Ajustement structurel*, p. xv.
31. See M. Niang, *M. Wade et l'alternance: le rêve brise du sopi* (Dakar: Harmattan, 2004); A. M. Wane, *Le Sénégal entre deux naufrages? Le Joola et l'alternance* (Paris: L'Harmattan, 2003).
32. W. J. Hanna and J. L. Hanna, *University students and African politics* (New York: Africana Publishing Company, 1975).
33. W. J. Hanna, 'Students, universities and political outcomes', in W. J. Hanna and J. Hanna (eds) *University students and African politics* (London: Africana Publishing Company, 1975) p. 13.
34. A demand, particularly strong at the university, in recent years, is for access to foreign visas, notably for western Europe and the United States (J. Harding, *The uninvited: refugees at the rich man's gate*, London: Profile Books, 2000).
35. Bathily et al., 'The Senegalese student movement'.
36. Established in 1957 as pro-Soviet and campaigning for immediate independence.
37. Established in 1958 under Senghor's leadership.
38. Cited in Thioub, 'Le mouvement étudiant', p. 272.
39. Ibid.
40. Ibid., p. 273.
41. Bianchini, 'Le mouvement étudiant', p. 363.
42. Ibid., p. 63.
43. C. Ly, *Où va l'Afrique?* (Dakar: NIS, n.d.) p. 10.
44. The term is used in a collection of articles from *Vers l'Islam* published between 1953 and 1956 in Ly's *Où va l'Afrique*, a powerful and passionate critique of French colonialism.
45. Quoted in Bathily et al., 'The Senegalese student movement', p. 88.
46. Some branches of the brotherhoods cooperated with AMEAN and joined them at the 1956 congress.

47. Ly, *Où va l'Afrique?*, p. 99.
48. Quoted in Bathily et al., 'The Senegalese student movement', p. 92.
49. Ly, *Où va l'Afrique?*, pp. 100–1.
50. Bathily et al., 'The Senegalese student movement', p. 392.
51. The fusion of religious and political discourse is an important theme in Senegalese politics. Among the left there is no hesitation in incorporating religious language with traditional expressions of the left. *'Inch' Allah'* and *'al hamdulilallah'* are mixed with *'chers camarades'*. More important, perhaps, is the role of Islam on the campus. Few traditional figures of student resistance (like Che Guevara, Malcolm X or even Thomas Sankara) are evident, but famous marabouts – notably Sirigne Salious M'baike – and the ubiquitous image of Cheikh Ahmadu Bamba are present everywhere in bedrooms, cafeterias and restaurants at the university.
52. P. Fougeyrollas, 'L'Africanisation de l'université de Dakar', in J. L. Balans, C. Coulons and A. Richard (eds) *Problèmes et perspectives de l'éducation dans un état du tiers-mondes: le cas Sénégal* (Bordeaux: IEP, 1969) pp. 4–49.
53. F. Gross, 'Dakar's Sorbonne South', *Africa Report*, June 1968, pp. 42–4.
54. Bianchini, 'Le mouvement étudiant', p. 364.
55. Ibid., p. 361.
56. Ibid. Although there may be a number of problems with Bianchini's rather rigid categorization of a social movement, the central question for this study is *understanding* student activism and not locating the movement's definitive date. The activism of students is linked to their social status and is associated with the role they played in the struggle for independence.
57. M. Oquaye, 'Youth, politics and society in Ghana', in F. K. Drah and M. Oquaye (eds) *Civil society in Ghana* (Accra: Friedrich Ebert Foundation, 1996) p. 182.
58. Hanna, 'Students, universities and political outcomes', p. 23.
59. Diop and Diouf, *Le Sénégal*, p. 190.
60. V. Foucher, 'Les "évolués", la migration, l'école: pour une nouvelle interprétation du nationalisme casamançais', in M. C. Diop (ed.) *Le Sénégal contemporain* (Paris: Karthala, 2002).
61. Gross, 'Dakar's Sorbonne'. It was in fact affiliated to the University of Bordeaux.
62. Quoted in Gross, 'Dakar's Sorbonne', p. 43.
63. S. Federici, 'The new student movement', in O. Alidou, G. Caffentzis and S. Federici (eds) *A thousand flowers: social struggles against structural adjustment in African universities* (New York: Africa World Press, 2000) p. 91.
64. At the University of Ibadan, 73 per cent of students were sponsored.
65. Between 1960 and 1981 the Senegalese civil service expanded from 6000 to 67,000 (Foucher, 'Les évolués').

66. Hanna and Hanna, *University students*, p. 4.
67. The expectation of government work, though long since an illusion, was an important theme of the election campaign in 2000, especially among students from the Ecole Normale Supérieure.
68. Hanna and Hanna, *University students*.
69. Hanna, 'Students, universities and political outcomes', p. 266.
70. See O'Brien's strange chapter ('A lost generation?').
71. Hanna, 'Students, universities and political outcomes', p. 21.
72. Diop and Diouf, *Le Sénégal*, p. 190.
73. O'Brien, 'A lost generation?', p. 65.
74. Bathily et al., 'The Senegalese student movement'. An idea that Bianchini criticized.
75. C. Harman, *The fire last time: 1968 and after* (London: Bookmarks, 1988).
76. Bathily, *Mai 68*; P. Bianchini, *Crises et réformes du système d'enseignement sénégalais: contribution à une sociologie politique de l'éducation en Afrique noire*, thèse de troisième cycle études africaines (Bordeaux I: Institut d'études politiques: Centre d'études d'Afrique noire, 1988).
77. 'Le raz de marée de mai 68: quand étudiants et ouvriers font cause commune'; and 'Le regard rétrospectif des acteurs de l'histoire', *Le Soleil*, 28 February 2001.
78. Bathily, *Mai 68*, p. 80.
79. *Le Soleil*, 28 February 2001.
80. Ibid.
81. There was a formation of small left-wing groups: for example (1) the MJML founded immediately after 1968 and affiliated to the Parti Communiste Sénégalais; (2) the Blondinistes (regarded as situationists, a group that attacked the French cultural centre). The name comes from two brothers, one, Omar Blondin Diop played a role in the movement in France in 1968 and was arrested and eventually died under arrest. That led to further student unrest, forcing the government to produce, in 1973, a white paper on Diop's 'suicide'; (3) Xare Bi (a Maoist group including the current leader of AJ, Landing Savane); the leading left organization PAI also underwent an intense period of internal debate over the trauma of 1968, resulting in a split in the organization in 1974 (see P. Bianchini, *Crises de la scolarisation, mouvements sociaux et réformes des systèmes d'enseignement en Afrique noire: le cas du Sénégal et du Burkina Faso*, thèse pour le doctorat de sociologie: Paris VII-Jussieu, 1997, p. 338).
82. Collectif d'Initiative pour la Réorganization du Mouvement Etudiant Sénégalais (CIRMES) composed of members elected by a General Assembly held on 16 November 1978. This in turn led to the creation of Groupe d'Action pour la Reconstruction du Mouvement Etudiant Sénégalais (GARMES). Following the publication of a manifesto, the Union Nationale Patriotique des Etudiants Sénégalais (UNAPES) was founded in March 1979 (Bianchini, *Crises de la scolarisation*, p. 339).

83. The Union Nationale Démocratique des Etudiants du Sénégal (UNDES) emerged after a particularly disruptive political dispute as a rival to And Jeff. UNDES brought together activists from PAI (the Parti de l'Indépendance et du Travail (PIT) from 1981) while the Union Démocratique des Etudiants de Dakar (UDED) grouped militants of the Ligue Démocratique and finally the Collectif formed the RND with several Trotskyists (Bianchini, *Crises de la scolarisation*, pp. 339–41).

84. Bianchini, *Crises de la scolarisation*, p. 40.

85. C. Coulon, *Les Musulmans et le pouvoir en Afrique noire: religion et contre-culture* (Paris: Karthala, 1983).

86. Diouf, 'Les jeunes Dakarois'.

87. 'Le regard rétrospectif des acteurs de l'histoire', *Le Soleil*, 28 February 2001.

88. Ibid. See also Diop and Diouf, *Le Sénégal*.

89. Oumy Ndour, interview, Dakar, 9 March 2001. The traditional solidarity shown by college and *lycée* students to the university is a classic feature of student politics in Senegal. Solidarity between the various institutions is repeated on the occasion of every strike and protest – and this includes the *lycées, collèges* and *écoles primaires*. The division so often made between university politics and other students in the education sector may be questioned (V. Foucher, *Cheated pilgrims: education, migration and the birth of Casamançais nationalism, Senegal*, Ph.D. thesis, University of London, 2002).

90. Assane Dia, interview, Dakar, 4 February 2004.

91. Ibid.

92. Bianchini, 'Le mouvement étudiant', p. 345. The World Bank (*Revitalisation de l'enseignement superieur: les enjeux de la reforme*, Dakar: Départment du Sahel, Bureau régional de la Banque mondiale, p. 31) identified the student movement and its efficient militancy as a hurdle to be overcome.

93. World Bank, *Revitalisation*, p. vii.

94. Ibid., p. 2.

95. From 23,000 students in 1993/4 to 20,000 in 1995/6 (P. Bianchini, 'L'Université de Dakar sous "ajustement": La Banque Mondiale face aux acteurs de l'enseignement supérieur au Sénégal dans les années 90', in Y. Lebeau and M. Ogunsanya, *The dilemma of post-colonial universities*, Ibadan: ABB, 2000, p. 72).

96. Bianchini, 'L'Université de Dakar', p. 72. These criticisms came from students and lecturers.

97. Bianchini, 'Le mouvement étudiant' ; and P. Bianchini, *Ecole et politique en Afrique noire: sociologie des crises et des réformes du système d'enseignement au Sénégal et au Burkina Faso (1960–2000)*, Paris: Karthala, 2004.

98. Bianchini, 'Le mouvement étudiant', p. 372.

99. Bianchini, *Crises de la scolarisation*, p. 352.

100. See Bathily et al., 'The Senegalese student movement'.

101. Bianchini, 'Le mouvement étudiant', p. 386.

102. The erosion of student spending power has led to the proletarianization of the student body. In 1968 the full grant was approximately 22,500 francs (Bathily. *Mai 68*, p. 173) and by 1981 the half-grant, which three-quarters of eligible students received, was only 12,000.

103. At a joint meeting organized by AJ and Ligue Démocratique on 20 March 2004 in Dakar, the AJ spokesperson and minister Mamadou Diop Decroix concluded the meeting by referring to an event in October 1968 when Senghor offered Bathily (then secretary general of UED) overseas scholarships for the student leadership. The 'movement' refused, according to Decroix. He finished the story by commenting (to much hilarity) that today's students could not boast similar principles.

104. D. Abdoulaye, *L'Autre Université*, Dakar: unpublished, 2002.

105. See 'Les tendences d'un raz-de-marée', *Walfadjri*, 2 May 2001. In Tambacouda and Bakel, for example, Wade's party, the PDS, secured 90 seats and the former ruling Parti Socialiste only 10 (*Walfadjri*, 2 May 2001).

106. Diop and Diouf, *Le Sénégal*.

107. 'Les Sénégalais ont repris confiance et se sont mis à travailler et à gagner', *Le Soleil*, 19 March 2004.

108. 'Je ne couvrirai aucun coupable', *Le Matin*, 1 February 2001.

109. Ibid.

110. 'Les leaders en première ligne', *Sud Quotidien*, 12 January 1999.

111. 'Six partis votent me Wade', *Sud Quoditien*, 8 February 1999. However, at the same time political and social change – arguably more profound – was taking place. In an article entitled 'Après 50 années de ménage, la séparation de corps', *Sud Quoditien* reported on 16 January that the largest religious families of leading *marabout*s were prepared to break from the ruling party.

112. 'L'Assemblée de l'université se réunit samedi', *Sud Quotidien*, 25 February 1999.

113. Ibid.

114. 'La candidature unique, gage de l'alternance en l'an 2000', *Sud Quotidien*, 8 March 1999.

115. A system of campaigning that was central to the mobilization of students during the presidential election the following year.

116. 'La candidature unique, gage de l'alternance en l'an 2000', *Sud Quotidien*, 8 March 1999.

117. 'Qui négociera au nom des étudiants?', *Sud Quotidien*, 16 March 1999.

118. 'Des forces dressées pour tuer', *Walfadjri*, 24 March 1999.

119. See letters in *Walfadjri*, of 24 March 1999,

120. 'Etudiants et profs en colère', *Sud Quotidien*, 17 March 1999.

121. 'Une caravane pour l'alternance', *Sud Quotidien*, 19 March 1999.

122. 'Deux universités, cinq lycées et un collège en grève', *Sud Quotidien*, 20 March 1999.

123. Meissa Touré, interview, Dakar, 15 March 2004.

124. Yankhoba Seydi, interview, Dakar, 18 March 2004.

125. 'L'Ugb renoue avec la grève', *Walfadjri*, 20–21 March 1999.

126. 'Le mouvement se généralise', *Sud Quotidien*, 25 March 1999.

127. 'Les étudiants entre déception et espoir' and 'Les Jeunes des partis divisés', *Sud Quotidien*, 1 April 1999.

128. Ibid. The false dichotomy between student politics and national politics is often a problem in understanding student mobilization. Students are divided along party lines, paralysed by these divisions and often corrupted. In these senses they follow national politics.

129. 'Promesse d'une reprise normale', *Sud Quotidien*, 8 April 1999.

130. Mustapha Sourang was the minister of education in 2004.

131. Yankhoba Seydi, interview, Dakar, 18 March 2004.

132. *Sud Quotidien*, 12 August 1999.

133. Sow became the youngest deputy in the legislative elections in 2001 and subsequently the youngest minister (appropriately of youth).

134. Aliou Sow, interview, Dakar, 4 February 2004.

135. Literally 'political migration'.

136. There are several versions of the story of his attack, but the important point in each version is that those who attacked him – sworn political and personal enemies at the time – are now close political friends working in the same government. For example, Déthié Diouf, a long-standing PS militant, who regarded himself as uniquely incorruptible in the student movement, became a technical adviser in the foreign affairs ministry.

137. Without fear of exaggeration, the left (particularly LD–MPT and to a lesser extent AJ–PADS and the PIT) were central in organizing the coalition of parties that supported Wade in the *Coalition de l'Alternance 2000*. In 2004 national coordinator of the Mouvement des Elèves et Etudiants de AJ–PADS, Ibrahima Bâ, explained that the left was aware that 'the only person who could lead the coalition at that moment is Abdoulaye Wade. He was called to return but he was in Paris [1999]'. Bâ described how Wade accepted 'his participation in this coalition. He agreed to front the programme that he had been involved in forming. It was a programme of the left, and he is a liberal' (interview, Dakar, 12 February 2004). Bathily made a similar argument but with a historical slant: 'I do not think Abdoulaye Wade is a liberal. It is important to be reminded of the way the PDS was born in 1974. After having opted for socialism, President Senghor insisted Majmont Diop (Pai) represented the communist current, Boubacar Diop (Mrs) the republican current and Abdoulaye Wade was obliged to become a liberal. I do not think most activists in the PDS know what liberalism is. But Wade is not a liberal; he is more of a socialist. He says it himself

that he is against unfettered liberalism. Never has the state been so visible in the political life of the country' ('Abdoulaye Bathily hausse le ton', *Sud Quotidien*, 6 March 2003). Within a year these arguments had changed as the coalition look set to break apart ('Entretien avec Abdoulaye Bathily', *Walfadjri*, 15 October 2003). None of this, however, should diminish the vital role the left played in bringing the right to power.

138. Idressa Gassama, interview, Dakar, 4 February 2001.
139. See 'Je ne peux plus contrôler les foules', *Walfadjri*, 26–7 February 2000.
140. 'L'opposition prend la rue', *Sud Quotidien*, 3 February 2000.
141. See 'Les étudiants fustigent la semaine de l'emploi', *Sud Quotidien*, 20 January 2000.
142. Ibid.
143. See interview with Abdou Diouf in 'Je changerai au niveau des hommes', *Walfadjri*, 13 March 2000.
144. Seck claimed at the time that his inspiration for the *marche bleue* was partly divine, 'being an assiduous reader of the Book of Saints I became aware that all the prophets who had a mission of liberation have conducted a "walk" and this walk is proof of the maturity of the movement' (in 'La preuve de la bonne santé de Me Wade', *Walfadjri*, 22 February 2000).
145. 'C'est à vous de défendre notre victoire', *Sud Quotidien*, 14 February 2000.
146. 'Les étudiants s'en mêlent', *Sud Quotidien*, 12 January 2000.
147. 'Montée d'adrénaline au campus', *Walfadjri*, 7 March 2000.
148. Diatara was a government adviser and close associate of Idressa Seck. He resigned shortly after Seck's high profile resignation as prime minister in April 2004.
149. Yankhoba Diatara, interview, Dakar, 9 February 2004.
150. Equally, students would often explain (during the interviews in 2004) that they were '*apolitique*' while expounding passionately about the country's political situation. *Apolitique* in this sense meant 'I am not in a political party'.
151. 'Rencontre avec le ministre pour une solution à la crise', *Walfadjri*, 3 March 2000.
152. Yankhoba Diatara, interview, Dakar, 9 February 2004.
153. There were a number of violent confrontations, the worst being on 8 March when students in MEES attacked those organizing the general assembly. According to a report in *Sud Quotidien*, students brandished gas bombs, knives and hatchets, and despite light injuries the strike was renewed for a further 48 hours (10 March). The political motivation for the strike, which had been thinly disguised under the cover of corporatist demands, was expressed openly in the final phase of the election. The result of this – as we have seen – was heightened violence. Violence and the threat of violence escalated from 8 March

when members of the UED received death threats (see 'Grève des étudiants: les dirigeants menacent de mort', *Sud Quotidien*, 13 March 2000).

154. Yankhoba Diatara, interview, Dakar, 9 February 2004.
155. Meissa Touré, interview, Dakar, 15 March 2004.
156. Ibid.
157. 'Dès avril, un nouveau gouvernement', *Walfadjri*, 6 March 2000.
158. 'Les 10 propositions pour un changement avec Diouf', *Sud Quotidien*, 10 March 2000.
159. 'Etudiants et normaliens soutiennent Wade', *Sud Quotidien*, 11 March 2000.
160. 'Les étudiants font monter les enchères', *Sud Quotidien*, 7 March 2000.
161. 'Les jeunes et la présidentielle', *Sud Quotidien*, 27 March 2000.
162. I was introduced to Mor Faye, the secretary general of MEES, by his friend and neighbour Madiop Biteye. They both boasted of playing football together (*Lux*, June–July 2003).
163. Madiop Biteye, interview, Dakar, 5 February 2004.
164. Ibid.
165. Biteye (in an interview on 5 February 2004) explains that the second round of the election coincided with the 'fête de Tabaski'. During the festival each year a huge proportion of the population of Dakar travel to their rural areas to celebrate (it is the only time of the year when it is possible to travel easily around the city). In 2000 Biteye argues that those who had left the city returned the following day to vote in the second round.
166. Ibrahima Bâ, interview, Dakar, 12 February 2004.
167. Coudy Kane, interview, Dakar, 14 February 2004.
168. Meissa Touré, interview, Dakar, 15 March 2004.
169. 'Les partis organisent des voyages gratuits dans le campus', *Sud Quotidien*, 9 March 2000.
170. During the university strike in 2001 the president was already distancing himself from any agreement he had purportedly made with the students: 'Which electoral promises?' he asked in a press conference in January 'Have they told you that? Well they've said nothing to me. Today is the first time I've heard about not honouring electoral promises. ... No student has said that to me. Never' (*Pan-African News Agency* 2001).
171. Nar Ndoye, interview, Dakar, 11 March 2001.
172. For a full breakdown of the results, see 'Rencontre avec le ministre pour une solution à la crise', *Walfadjri*, 3 March 2000.
173. Mbaye Sene, interview, Dakar, 11 February 2004.
174. The theme of 'work' has been important to the Wade campaign. Wade's credo, painted on walls in Dakar, repeated daily by politicians and even put to music is: 'One must work, work a lot, work again, work always.'

175. 'Les jeunes fêtent la victoire de Me Wade', *Sud Quotidien*, 23 March 2000.
176. 'La fin de la traversee du désert', *Walfadjri*, 22 March 2000.
177. Ibid.
178. 'Les étudiants rejoignent les amphithéâtres lundi', *Sud Quotidien*, 24 March 2000.
179. The title of Almamy Mamadou Wane's (2003) study *Le Sénégal entre deux naufrages? Le Joola et l'alternance* ('Senegal between two shipwrecks? The Joola and democratic transition'). The *Joola* was a passenger ferry that sank in 2002.
180. *Sud Quotidien*, 15 January 2001.
181. Alioune Diop, interview, Dakar, 4 March 2001.
182. *Sud Quotidien*, 18 January 2001.
183. Idressa Gassama, interview, Dakar, 4 February 2001.
184. The referendum on the new constitution was held on 7 January, so Biteye is mistaken in this respect.
185. Madiop Biteye, interview, Dakar, 5 February 2004.
186. A virtual civil war inside MEEL had to be mediated by Idressa Seck, the deputy general secretary of the party at the time. See *Le Populaire*, 15 January 2001, for an example of this infighting.
187. Amadou Dieye Wade, interview, Dakar, 3 March 2001.
188. On the demonstration, see 'Justice pour les étudiants'; 'Le PS dénonce un pouvoir dictatorial'; and 'Je ne couvrirai aucun coupable', *Le Matin*, 1 February 2001; and *Sud Quotidien*, 1 February 2001.
189. *Le Matin*, 1 February 2001.
190. See particularly the 1 February 2001 editions of *Sud Quotidien*, *Le Matin*, and even the normally frivolous *Le Populaire*.
191. *Le Matin*, 1 February 2001.
192. See 'Madior Diouf désavoue', 'Les étudiants se radicalisent', and 'Réactions mitigées à l'université', *Le Matin*, 6 February 200.
193. *Le Matin*, 5 February 2001.
194. Ibid.
195. Pan-African News Agency 2001.
196. *Le Matin*, 1 February 2001.
197. 'Le Meel dénonce les exactions' *Le Matin*, 3 February 2001.
198. 'Réactions mitigées à l'université', *Le Matin*, 6 February 2001.
199. *Sud Quotidien*, 2 February 2001.
200. Ibid.
201. '48h renouvelables en attendant la signature du protocole', *Sud Quotidien*, 3 February 2001.
202. Jean-Claude Kongo, interview, Dakar, 3 March 2001.
203. Amadou Dieye Wade, interview, Dakar, 3 March 2001.
204. Idressa Gassama, interview, Dakar, 4 February 2001.
205. Amadou Dieye Wade, interview, Dakar, 3 March 2001.
206. Oumy Ndour, interview, Dakar, 9 March 2001.

207. 'Grève des étudiants: les dirigeants menacent de mort' *Sud Quotidien*, 13 March 2000.

208. *Sud Quotidien*, 2 February 2001.

209. Ibid.

210. Ibid.

211. Natalia Antelava, interview, Dakar, 2 February 2001. Students interviewed in 2004 about the number of people present say there were far fewer than the 100,000 Antelava claimed.

212. According to Deme Abdoulaye (*L'Autre Université*, p. 23) his exact words were 'It is God who had given him to me, and it is he who has taken him back from me. I ask you to calm down and believe in God.'

213. After many years of student mobilization, the Faculté des Lettres has the reputation for being both the most militant and most powerful faculty. This is partly because it has the highest number of students, 13,000 in 2004.

214. Yankhoba Seydi, interview, Dakar, 18 March 2004.

215. Meissa Touré, interview, Dakar, 15 March 2004.

216. Hamidou Bâ, interview, Dakar, 28 January 2004.

217. 'Les Sénégalais ont repris confiance et se sont mis à travailler et à gagner', *Le Soleil*, 19 March 2004.

218. The full extent of the reforms is really rather revealing. They included a reduction in the price of dinner tickets from 165 to 150 CFA francs, breakfast was reduced from 100 to 75 CFA francs, rooms that cost 5000 each term were reduced to 4000, while those at 4000 were now reduced to 3000 CFA francs. There is now a system of grants for all students who have not retaken the year and financial assistance for those without grants.

219. See the official government website: http://www.finances.gouv.sn/sitecso3.html.

220. *Sud Quotidien*, 23 December 2002.

221. 'Les Sénégalais ont repris confiance et se sont mis à travailler et à gagner', *Le Soleil*, 19 March 2004.

222. Deme Abdoulaye, interview, Dakar, 18 March 2004.

223. Madiop Biteye, interview, Dakar, 5 February 2004.

224. Deme Abdoulaye, interview, Dakar, 18 March 2004.

225. Yankhoba Seydi (interview, 18 March 2004) lists the old UED leadership now studying in France: Alionne Diop, Abdou Niang, Khady Ndiaye and Babacar Sarr.

226. Madiop Biteye, interview, Dakar, 18 March 2004.

227. Abdoulaye maintains that during the collection of money for Balla Gaye's family, some student leaders helped themselves, '*quel péché*' (what a sin!) he exclaims.

228. Yankhoba Seydi, interview, Dakar, 18 March 2004.

229. Deme Abdoulaye (2002, p. 26) claims that corruption among the student leadership is ubiquitous: 'How can you understand and accept

that a student asks a minister, after a negotiation session, for lunch money?'

230. Abdoulaye, *L'Autre Université*, p. 25.

231. However, *Walfadjri* was undoubtedly correct to claim that quasi indifference marked the third anniversary (see 'An III de la disparition de Balla Gaye', *Walfadjri*, 31 January 2004).

232. 'Pourquoi l'affaire Balla Gaye est difficile', *Walfadjri*, 8 March 2004.

233. The government even sent for a ballistic expert from France – Jean Rochefort – to investigate the origin of the bullet but his report did nothing to resolve the affair.

234. 'An III de la disparition de Balla Gaye', *Walfadjri*, 31 January 2004.

235. 'Pourquoi l'affaire Balla Gaye est difficile', *Walfadjri*, 8 March 2004.

236. The government uses the term 'assassination', implying an elaborate and complicated plot. This presumably makes it difficult for them to discover who was responsible.

237. Madiop Biteye, interview, Dakar, 18 March 2004.

238. During my interview with him, Sow took me across his palatial office to his desk and, after having presented me with a wad of paper, he announced rather proudly: 'This is my doctorate. I have just returned from a session with my supervisor' (Aliou Sow, interview, 4 February 2004).

239. The principal student leader in the late 1980s and 1990s and minister of the environment under Wade.

240. 'Le toupet d'Aliou Sow récompense', *Walfadjri*, 23 April 2004.

241. Who in sending their children abroad – regarded as faintly contemptuous by students in Senegal – condemn them to political obscurity.

242. Yankhoba Diatara, interview, Dakar, 9 February 2004.

243. Ibrahima Bâ, interview, Dakar, 12 February 2004.

244. Niang, *M. Wade*, pp. 79–119.

245. Yankhoba Seydi, interview, Dakar, 18 March 2004.

246. Ibid.

247. Hamidou Bâ, interview, Dakar, 28 January 2004.

248. Yankhoba Seydi, interview, Dakar, 18 March 2004.

249. By 2004 a senior civil servant in the *Conseil régional de Dakar*.

250. Yankhoba Seydi, interview, Dakar, 18 March 2004.

251. Pape Birahim Ndiaye, interview, Dakar, 18 February 2004.

252. Mor Faye, interview, Dakar, 5 February 2004.

253. Hamidou Bâ, interview, Dakar, 28 January 2004.

254. Pape Birahim Ndiaye, interview, Dakar, 18 February 2004.

255. Ibid. In an interview on 14 February 2004 Coudy Kane, a female doctoral student, draws a distinction between youth and student intellectuals, 'you can be young but be empty headed, but in the realm of ideas you must count on students to advance political change and the future needs such intellectuals and students.' The motto for

Cheikh Anta Diop University – which is emblazoned on their crest – is the Latin expression *Lux Mea Lex* (Light is my Law).

256. Mor Faye, interview, Dakar, 5 February 2004.

257. Ibid.

258. The university is not only a place of foreign enlightenment but also (and presumably equally European in this respect) of debauchery and vice. Deme Abdoulaye's (2002) text *L'Autre Université* can be read as a polemic against these excesses.

259. Cherif Bâ, interview, Dakar, 12 February 2004.

260. Politicians also positively encourage student activism, as part of a prerequisite to good citizenship. Abdoulaye Wade, for example, makes this clear when he explains students' responsibilities today: 'the role of students is to study. The student must demonstrate that they are excellent in these studies. Afterwards, young people must become engaged politically and develop an active involvement in society' (quoted by Aliou Sow in *Lux*, 2003).

261. In important respects student slogans and mobilizations have profoundly changed. This is partly linked to an intelligent under-standing of the limits of university education in Senegal. Almost all university students make yearly applications to study abroad, mostly in France. There is an informal trade in *Coupon de réponse internationale* on campus, which cost 1000 CFA francs and are required by French universities if you want a response to your application. Students also repeatedly raise the slogan of the allocation of 'visas'.

262. *Transhumance politique* is an important phenomenon on campus and at all levels of student activism. Among the leadership it involved Aliou Sow leaving the group of socialist-supporting students organized by Déthié Diouf in 1999, while Déthié Diouf (slower to catch on) abandoned his old political allies to join the PDS in 2001 (after the strike). As Ndiaye recalls: 'He addressed a letter to me when he wanted to join in 2001' (interview, Dakar, 18 February, 2004). However, Aliou Sow holds no grudges: 'Today those who attacked me and beat me up have become my friends and they are indebted to me for lots of things. Simply because I accepted their repentance and proved that we are over the past' (*Lux* 2003).

263. 'Aj/Pads et la Ld/Mpt se démarquent', *Sud Quotidien*, 22 March 2004.

264. I was present at their meeting *L'alternance à mi-parcours, quels defis à relever?* (20 March 2004). They decided to boycott the official PDS celebrations for the fourth anniversary of *alternance*. The criticism of privatization was particularly sharp because of the proposed privatization of the Loterie Nationale Sénégalaise (LONASE).

265. 'Abdoulaye Bathily hausse le ton', *Sud Quotidien*, 6 March 2003.

266. 'Entretien avec Abdoulaye Bathily', *Walfadjri*, 15 October 2003.

267. 'Les Sénégalais ont repris confiance et se sont mis à travailler et à gagner', *Le Soleil*, 19 March 2004.

268. The ambitious new extension of the University in Dakar.
269. 'Les étudiants traînent les pieds', *Sud Quotidien*, 27–28 March 2004.
270. 'Les Sénégalais ont repris confiance et se sont mis à travailler et à gagner', *Le Soleil*, 19 March 2004. Wade's lecture was interesting. It was a serious exposé of the reasons for Africa's underdevelopment. Although his conclusions were typically neo-liberal, arguing that Africa must follow the West and attract private investors, his style was professorial to the extent that his academic justification of NEPAD on a flipchart involved mathematical formulas that were both utterly obscure, and impossible to see, for most of the 1500 people present.
271. D. Harvey, *The condition of postmodernity: an enquiry into the origins of cultural change* (Oxford: Basil Blackwell, 1989).
272. D. Massey, *Space, place and gender* (Cambridge: Polity Press, 1994) p. 150.
273. T. Friedman, *The world is flat: brief history of the globalised world in the 21st century* (London: Allen Lane, 2005).
274. Although Wade's 'liberalism' was certainly not evident in his attitude to university reforms, he resorted to a familiar pattern of 'crisis management' that involved breaking with the advice of the World Bank. The 'liberalism' referred to is the dominant *laissez faire* politics of the Washington consensus that has been accepted more or less unanimously by the political class in Senegal.
275. T. Cliff, 'Deflected permanent revolution', *International Socialism*, 1 (12) pp. 15–22, 1963. See Chapter 1.
276. Cliff, 'Deflected permanent revolution', p. 20.
277. Foucher, 'Les évolués'; E. Gellner, *Nations and nationalism* (Oxford: Blackwell, 1983).
278. Mor Faye, interview, Dakar, 5 February 2004.

Chapter 5. Students of the transition speak: the meaning of student protest

1. A. Callinicos, *The revenge of history* (Cambridge: Polity Press, 1991); and C. Harman, 'The storm breaks', *International Socialism Journal*, 2 (46) pp. 3–93, 1990.
2. A. Bathily, M. Diouf and M. Mbodj (1995) 'The Senegalese student movement from its inception to 1989', in M. Mamdani and E. Wamba-Dia-Wamba (eds) *African studies in social movements and democracy* (Dakar: CODESRIA, 1995).
3. M. Diouf, 'Les jeunes Dakarois dans le champs politique', in D. C. O'Brien, M. C. Diop and M. Diouf (eds) *La construction de l'état au Sénégal* (Paris: Karthala, 2002).
4. P. Bianchini, 'L'Université de Dakar sous "ajustement": la Banque Mondiale face aux acteurs de l'enseignement supérieur au Sénégal dans les années 90', in Y. Lebeau and M. Ogunsanya, *The dilemma of*

post-colonial universities (Ibadan: ABB, 2002); P. Bianchini, *Ecole et politique en Afrique noire: sociologie des crises et des réformes du système d'enseignement au Sénégal et au Burkina Faso (1960–2000)* (Paris: Karthala, 2004).

5. Bianchini, *Ecole et politique*, p. 225.
6. Ibid., pp. 224–8.
7. B. Fall (ed.), *Ajustement structurel et emploi au Sénégal* (Paris: Karthala, 1997) p. xv.
8. G. Nzongola-Ntalaja, *The Congo from Leopold to Kabila: a people's history* (London: Zed Books, 2002) p. 179.
9. T. T. Munikengi and W. Sangol, 'The diploma paradox: University of Kinshasa between crisis and salvation', in T. Trefon (ed.) *Reinventing order in the Congo* (London: Zed Books, 2004) p. 91.
10. See the article entitled '478 students held in violent demos', *The Herald*, 30 September 1988.
11. Catering facilities were taken back into central university control in 2004 after almost six years of privatization (see 'Return of catering services laudable', *The Herald*, 6 September 2004).
12. F. Halliday, 'Students of the world unite', in A. Cockburn and R. Blackburn (eds) *Student power: problems, diagnosis, action* (London: Penguin Books, 1969).
13. See also L. Zeilig, 'Zero, zero, zero pito formation: student activism in Zimbabwe', *Debate* (10) 2004.
14. Halliday, 'Students of the world', p. 23.
15. Bianchini, *Ecole et politique*, pp. 226–7.
16. See Chapter 2.
17. A word of caution needs to be made. One tracer study in Tanzania examined graduate employment of engineers and showed an increase of appointments by the private sector in the 15 years to 1994, but that the state still employed 64 per cent of graduates (D. Mkude, B. Cooksey and L. Levey (2003) *Higher education in Tanzania: a case study*, Oxford: James Currey, 2003).
18. 'Un étudiant se suicide à Pikine', *Le Populaire*, 10 April 2001.
19. Mkude et al., *Higher education*.
20. T. Cliff, 'Deflected permanent revolution', *International Socialism*, 1 (12) pp. 15–22, 1963, p. 17.
21. See T. Dahou and V. Foucher, 'Le Sénégal, entre changement politique et révolution passive', *Politique Africaine*, 96 pp. 5–21, 2004.
22. Cherif Bâ, interview, Dakar, 12 February 2004.
23. J. Manor (ed.) *Rethinking Third World politics* (London: Longman, 1991).
24. Brighton Makunike, interview, Harare, 26 May 2003.
25. Jethro Mpofu, interview, Bulawayo, 23 May 2003.
26. C. Barker, A. Johnson and M. Lavalette (eds) (2001) *Leadership and social movements* (Manchester: Manchester University Press, 2001).
27. C. Barker, 'Robert Michels and the "cruel game"', in C. Barker, A.

Johnson and M. Lavalette (eds) *Leadership and social movements* (Manchester: Manchester University Press, 2001) p. 42.

28. I. Birchall, *Bailing out the system: reformist socialism in Western Europe* (London: Bookmarks, 1986).

29. Quoted in Barker, 'Robert Michels', p. 5.

30. This is, in fact, the subtitle of Michels's famous study *Political parties: a sociological study of the oligarchical tendencies of modern democracy* (New York: Dover, 1959).

31. Barker, 'Robert Michels', p. 5.

32. M. Gwisai, *Revolutionaries, resistance and crisis in Zimbabwe: anti-neoliberal struggles in periphery capitalism* (Harare: ISO pamphlet, 2002) p. 24.

33. M. Lavalette, 'Defending the "Sefton two": contested leadership in a trade union dispute', in C. Barker, A. Johnson and M. Lavalette (eds) *Leadership and social movements* (Manchester: Manchester University Press, 2001) p. 134.

34. Ibid.

35. Gwisai, *Revolutionaries*, p. 27.

36. G. M. Derluguian, 'Che Guevaras in turbans', *New Left Review*, 237, pp. 3–27, 1999, p. 18.

37. N. Harris, *The end of the Third World: newly industrializing countries and the decline of an ideology* (Harmondsworth: Penguin, 1987).

38. Derluguian, 'Che Guevaras', p. 19.

39. Ibid.

40. Hopewell Gumbo, interview, Bulawayo, 28 July 2003.

41. J. L. Cefkin, 'Rhodesian university students in national politics', in W. J. Hanna and J. L. Hanna (eds) *University students and African politics* (New York: Africana Publishing Company, 1975) pp. 157–8.

42. Ibid., p. 158.

43. C. Harman, 'The rise of capitalism', *International Socialism Journal*, 2 (102), pp. 53–86, 2004, p. 80.

44. Ibid.

45. Otherwise we would all presumably *choose* much more favourable circumstances!

46. S. Amin, *Delinking: towards a polycentric world* (London: Zed Books, 1990).

47. This, of course, implies a further importance to struggles in periphery capitalist societies. As relatively weak links in the global hierarchy, it is perhaps in these areas that the chains of capitalist society can be the first to be prised apart (L. Trotsky, *The history of the Russian revolution*, Michigan: University of Michigan Press, 1964).

48. Harman, 'The rise of capitalism', p. 81.

49. Commercie Mucheni, interview, Harare, 9 June 2003.

50. T. Choto, 'Interview', in L. Zeilig (ed.) *Class struggle and resistance in Africa* (Cheltenham: New Clarion Press, 2002) p. 167.

51. O. Oyewumi, *African gender studies* (New York: Palgrave, 2005).
52. P. T. Zeleza, 'Neo-liberalism and academic freedom', in P. T. Zeleza and A. Olukoshi (eds) *African universities in the twenty first century*, (Pretoria: CODESRIA/UNISA Press, 2004) vol. 1, pp. 62–3.
53. Ibid., p. 63.
54. J. Saul, 'Africa: the next liberation struggle', *Review of African Political Economy*, 30 (96) pp. 187–202, 2003.
55. R. Abrahamsen, *Disciplining democracy: development discourse and good governance in Africa* (London: Zed Books, 2000).
56. A. Callinicos, 'Ukraine: is the future orange?' *Socialist Worker*, 11 December 2004.
57. C. Harman, 'Are you being served?', *Socialist Review*, 286, 2004, p. 21.
58. N. Klein, *No logo: no space, no choice, no jobs: taking aim at the brand bullies* (London: Flamingo, 2000).
59. P. Bond, 'Radical rhetoric and the working class during Zimbabwean nationalism's dying days', *Journal of World-Systems Research*, 7 (1) 2001, pp. 201–2.
60. Quoted in Harman, 'Are you being served?', p. 21.
61. J. G. Ungpakorn, 'NGOs: enemies or allies?' *International Socialism Journal*, 2 (104) pp. 49–64, 2004, p. 49.
62. J. Petras, 'NGOs: in the service of imperialism', *Journal of Contemporary Asia*, 29 (4) pp. 429–40, 1999, p. 431.
63. Ungpakorn, 'NGOs: enemies or allies?', p. 58.
64. Ibid.
65. Harman, 'Are you being served?', p. 21.
66. Ibid.
67. John Bomba, interview, Bulawayo, 22 May 2003.
68. K. Marx and F. Engels, *The communist manifesto*, New York: Washington Square Press, 1964, p. 58.
69. Harman, 'The rise of capitalism', p. 82.
70. Or, as Malcolm X (*Malcolm X talks to young people*, New York: Pathfinder, 1992, p. 18) wrote 40 years ago, 'The students didn't think in terms of the odds against them, and they couldn't be bought out.' Malcolm X was one of the sharpest social critics (and activists) of the 1960s; he was also aware of the weaknesses of student activism in the USA. He wrote that American students 'have been noted for involving themselves in panty raids, goldfish swallowing ... not for their revolutionary political ideas or their desire to change unjust conditions. But some students are becoming more like their brothers around the world' (*Malcolm X talks*, pp. 18–19).

Conclusion: the return of the student intelligentsia?

1. See S. Federici, 'The new student movement', in O. Alidou, G. Caffentzis and S. Federici (eds) *A thousand flowers: social struggles*

against structural adjustment in African universities, New York: Africa World Press, 2000; M. Mario and P. Fry, *Higher education in Mozambique: a case study*, Oxford: James Currey, 2003.

2. D. Mills, 'The "new" African higher education?' *African Affairs*, 103 (413) pp. 667–75, 2004, p. 671.

3. J. L. Cefkin, 'Rhodesian university students in national politics', in W. J. Hanna and J. L. Hanna (eds) *University students and African politics* (New York: Africana Publishing Company, 1975) p. 158.

4. V. Foucher, *Cheated pilgrims: education, migration and the birth of Casamançais nationalism, Senegal*, Ph.D. thesis (University of London, 2002); P. Richards, *Fighting for the rain forest: war, youth and resources in Sierra Leone* (London: International African Institute in association with James Currey, 1996).

5. L. Amoore (ed.) *The global resistance reader* (London: Routledge, 2005).

6. M. Mamdani, 'The intelligentsia, the state and social movements in Africa', in M. Diouf and M. Mamdani (eds) *Academic freedom in Africa* (Dakar: CODESRIA, 1994).

7. T. Zack-Williams, D. Frost and A. Thomson (eds) *Africa in crisis: new challenges and possibilities* (London: Pluto Press, 2002).

8. K. Maier, *This house has fallen* (London: Penguin, 2000) pp. 227–49.

9. Richards, *Fighting for the rain forest*.

10. Quoted in P. Richards, 'Youth, food and peace: a reflection on some African security issues at the millennium', in T. Zack-Williams, D. Frost and A. Thomson (eds) *Africa in Crisis* (London: Pluto Press, 2002) p. 36.

11. See R. D. Kaplan, 'The coming anarchy', *The Atlantic Monthly*, 273 (2) pp. 44–76, 1994.

12. See L. Zeilig, 'Blood and diamonds', *Socialist Review*, 277, 2003. For example, 'blood' diamonds were sold by international traders in London and Antwerp.

13. Ezekiel Pajibo, interview, Harare, 28 August 2003.

14. C. Harman, 'The Prophet and the proletariat', *International Socialism Journal*, 2 (64) pp. 3–63, 1994, pp. 9–10.

15. Ibid., pp. 16–17.

16. Ibid., p. 19.

17. 'The men who brought the world to the brink of war', *Observer*, 23 September 2001.

18. Ibid. These conclusions were substantiated in a recent study on rates of education among 'terrorists', which found that 'having a higher standard of living above the poverty line or a secondary-school education or higher is positively associated with participation [in terrorist groups]' (A. Krueger and J. Maleckova, *Education, poverty, political violence, and terrorism: is there a causal connection?* New York: National Bureau of Economic Research, 2002, p. 5).

19. Alhaji Dokubo-Asari was a member of the alienated student intelligentsia in Nigeria, where he led a group trying to wrestle the oil-rich

Niger Delta from multinational oil companies and the government (see Maier, *This house*, pp. 227–49).

20. M. Diouf, 'Les jeunes Dakarois dans le champs politique', in D. C. O'Brien, M. C. Diop and M. Diouf (eds) *La construction de l'état au Sénégal* (Paris: Karthala, 2002) p. 160.

21. See Foucher, *Cheated pilgrims*.

22. The three largest of these associations at the university are the Association des Elèves et Etudiants Musulmans du Sénégal (AEEMS) and the AMEUD. Another was established in September 2001, the Mouvement des Elèves et Etudiants de la Jamaatou Ibadou Rahmane (MEEJIR). This structure is attached to a non-student group, the Jamaatou Ibodou Rahmane, the worshippers of God. The largest and most active of these groups, AEEMS, has almost 1000 members and is well represented at the university and in many schools and colleges in Senegal.

23. The increase in private universities has exploited religious cleavages. A number of 'not-for-profit' universities cater for particular religious groups, there are two examples from Uganda: the Islamic University in Uganda (IUIU) and the Uganda Martyrs University (UMU).

24. Mamdani, 'The intelligentsia', pp. 258–9.

25. See D. Mwinzi, 'The impact of cost-sharing policies on the living conditions of students in Kenyan public universities: the case of Nairobi and Moi universities', in P. T. Zeleza and A. Olukoshi (eds) *African universities in the twenty first century*, vol. 1 (Pretoria: CODESRIA/UNISA Press, 2004).

26. 'Interview with Daniel Bensaid: this movement is directly based on the social question', *Socialist Worker*, 4 April 2006.

27. S. Kouvelakis, 'France: from revolt to the alternative', *International Socialist Tendency Discussion Bulletin*, 8, July 2006.

28. See E. Bircham and J. Charlton, *Anti-capitalism: a guide to the movement* (London: Bookmarks, 2000); A. Callinicos, *An anti-capitalist manifesto* (Cambridge: Polity, 2003).

29. T. Ngwane, 'The new social movements and working class politics in post-apartheid South Africa', Paper presented in Cuba at the Conferencia Internacional La Obra de Carlos Marx y los Desafios del Siglo XXI, 2–8 May 2003.

30. A. Desai and R. Pithouse, 'But we were thousands: dispossession, resistance, repossession and repression in Mandela Park', Centre for Civil Society Research Report, 2003, p. 25< http://www.nu.ac.za/ccs/default.asp?10,24,10,922.

31. Ngwane, 'The new social movements', p. 14.

32. Brian Kagoro, interview, Harare, 23 June 2003.

33. D. Seddon and L. Zeilig, 'Class and protest in Africa: new waves', *Review of African Political Economy*, 31 (103) pp. 9–27, 2005, p. 24.

34. D. Harvey, *A brief history of neo-liberalism* (Oxford: Oxford University Press, 2005) pp. 5–38.
35. M. Larmer and P. Dwyer, 'Four wheel drives and burning tyres: civil society and social movements in southern Africa', Paper presented at the International Sociological Association Congress, Durban, 27 July 2006, pp. 23–4.
36. Stephen Chisuvi, interview, Harare, 16 May 2003.
37. Callinicos, *An anti-capitalist manifesto*, p. 13.
38. Jean-Claude Kongo, interview, Dakar, 3 March 2001.
39. Amadou Dieye Wade, interview, Dakar, 3 March 2001.
40. Jethro Mpofu, interview, Bulawayo, 23 May 2003.
41. E. P. Thompson, *The making of the English working class* (London: Penguin, 1991) p. 12.

Appendix

LIST OF INTERVIEWS

Aborisade, Femi, Lagos, Nigeria, 24 September 2002

Abdoulaye, Deme, Dakar, Senegal, 18 March 2004

Antelava, Natalia, Dakar, Senegal, 2 February 2001

Bâ, Cherif, Dakar, Senegal, 12 February 2004

Bâ, Hamidou, Dakar, Senegal, 28 January 2004

Bâ, Ibrahima, Dakar, Senegal, 12 February 2004

Biteye, Madiop, Dakar, Senegal, 5 February 2004

Bomba, John, Bulawayo, Zimbabwe, 22 May and 30 July 2003; Harare, Zimbabwe, 18 January 2005; and Johannesburg, South Africa, 23 August 2006

Chamisa, Nelson, Harare, Zimbabwe, 8 August 2003

Chimedza, Tinashe, Harare, Zimbabwe, 27 May 2003

Chitambure, Timothy, London, England, 9 July 2001

Chisuvi, Stephen, Harare, Zimbabwe 16 May 2003 and 17 August 2006

Choto, Tafadzwa, London, England, 10 July 2001

Dia, Assane, Dakar, Senegal, 4 February 2004

Diatara, Yankhoba, Dakar, Senegal, 9 February 2004

Diop, Alioune, Dakar, Senegal, 4 March 2001

Faye, Mor, Dakar, Senegal, 5 February 2004

Gassama, Idressa, Dakar, Senegal, 4 February 2001

Gumbo, Hopewell, Bulawayo, Zimbabwe, 28 July 2003

Kagoro, Brian, Harare, Zimbabwe, 23 June 2003

List of interviews

Kane, Coudy, Dakar, Senegal, 14 February 2004
Kanhema, Tawanda, Harare, Zimbabwe, 5 June 2003
Kasuwanga, Luke, London, England, 9 July 2001
Kongo, Jean-Claude, Dakar, Senegal, 3 March 2001
Lewanika, Mcdonald, Harare, Zimbabwe, 19 August 2006
Makunike, Brighton, Harare, Zimbabwe, 26 May 2003
Matsikidze, David, Harare, Zimbabwe, 5 June 2003
Mpofu, Jethro, Bulawayo, Zimbabwe, 23 May 2003
Muchadya, Canwell, Harare, Zimbabwe, 18 August 2006
Mucheni, Commerie, Harare, Zimbabwe, 9 June 2003
Mutambara, Arthur, Johannesburg, South Africa, 10 July 2003
Ndiaye, Pape Birahim, Dakar, Senegal, 18 February 2004
Ndour, Oumy, Dakar, Senegal, 9 March 2001
Ndoye, Nar, Dakar, Senegal, 11 March 2001
NYS interviews, Chegutu, Zimbabwe, 10–12 June 2003
University of Zimbabwe, Information Office, 6 March 2005
Pajibo, Ezekiel, Harare, Zimbabwe, 28 August 2003
Philippa (not her real name), Harare, Zimbabwe, 14 June 2003
Saurombe, Talkmore, Harare, Zimbabwe, 5 June 2003
Sene, Mbaye, Dakar, Senegal, 11 February 2004
Seydi, Yankhoba, Dakar, Senegal, 18 March 2004
Sikhala, Job, Harare, Zimbabwe, 31 July2003
Sougou, Omar, Saint Louis, Senegal, 13 March 2004
Sow, Aliou, Dakar, Senegal, 4 February 2004
Touré, Meissa, Dakar, Senegal, 15 March 2004
Wade, Amadou Dieye, Dakar, Senegal, 3 March 2001

INDEX

Index

Index